BF
683
P78
v.26

Date Due

BRODART, INC.   Cat. No. 23 233   Printed in U.S.A.

THE PSYCHOLOGY
OF LEARNING AND MOTIVATION

Advances in Research and Theory

VOLUME 26

THE PSYCHOLOGY OF LEARNING AND MOTIVATION

Advances in Research and Theory

EDITED BY GORDON H. BOWER
STANFORD UNIVERSITY, STANFORD, CALIFORNIA

Volume 26

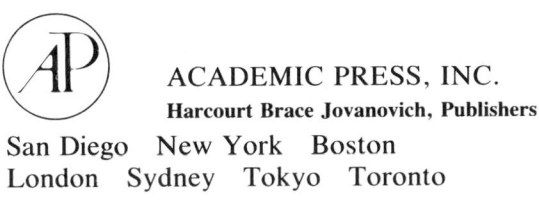

ACADEMIC PRESS, INC.
Harcourt Brace Jovanovich, Publishers
San Diego   New York   Boston
London   Sydney   Tokyo   Toronto

This book is printed on acid-free paper. ∞

Copyright © 1990 by Academic Press, Inc.
All Rights Reserved.
No part of this publication may be reproduced or transmitted in any form or by any means, electronic or mechanical, including photocopy, recording, or any information storage and retrieval system, without permission in writing from the publisher.

Academic Press, Inc.
San Diego, California 92101

United Kingdom Edition published by
Academic Press Limited
24-28 Oval Road, London NW1 7DX

Library of Congress Catalog Card Number: 66-30104

ISBN 0-12-543326-3 (alk. paper)

Printed in the United States of America
90 91 92 93   9 8 7 6 5 4 3 2 1

CONTENTS

Contributors ix

SPATIAL MEMORY IN SEED-CACHING CORVIDS
Alan C. Kamil and Russell P. Balda

I. Introduction	1
II. The Ecological Problem..	2
III. How Do Nutcrackers Find Their Seeds?	4
IV. The Characteristics of Cache Site Memory in Nutcrackers	6
V. Species Differences in Cache Site Memory	12
VI. Noncaching Tests of Spatial Memory...............................	15
VII. Implications and Future Directions...................................	19
VIII. Conclusions...	22
References	23

DETECTING RESPONSE–OUTCOME RELATIONS: TOWARD AN UNDERSTANDING OF THE CAUSAL TEXTURE OF THE ENVIRONMENT
E. A. Wasserman

I. Introduction	27
II. Hume's Theory of Causation...	28
III. Contemporary Animal Learning Theory	32
IV. Causal Perception in Humans	33
V. Research on Response–Outcome Contingency..................	34
VI. Theoretical Analysis of Response–Outcome Relations	74
VII. Concluding Comments	78
References	79

PRIMING OF NONVERBAL INFORMATION AND THE NATURE OF IMPLICIT MEMORY

Daniel L. Schacter, Suzanne M. Delaney, and Elizabeth P. Merikle

I. Introduction	83
II. Review of the Experimental Evidence	85
III. Methodological, Conceptual, and Theoretical Issues	110
References	118

METAMEMORY: A THEORETICAL FRAMEWORK AND NEW FINDINGS

Thomas O. Nelson and Louis Narens

I. Introduction	125
II. A Theoretical Framework for Metamemory	125
III. Methodology and New Findings from Our Research	140
IV. Applications of Our Methodology to Other Areas	168
V. Concluding Remarks	168
References	169

THE NEW MULTIMODAL APPROACH TO MEMORY IMPROVEMENT

Douglas J. Herrmann and Alan Searleman

I. Introduction	175
II. A Review of Current Understanding of Control Processes	177
III. The New Approach to Content Manipulations	180
IV. Current Understanding of Control of Memory Performance through Control of Other Modes	183
V. The New Approach to Control of Memory Performance through Control of Other Modes	183
VI. Discussion	192
References	196

A TRIPHASIC APPROACH TO THE ACQUISITION OF RESPONSE-SELECTION SKILL

Robert W. Proctor, T. Gilmour Reeve, and Daniel J. Weeks

I. Introduction	207
II. Cognitive Phase	210

III.	Associative Phase	225
IV.	Autonomous Phase	229
V.	Conclusions	232
	References	236

THE STRUCTURE AND FORMATION OF NATURAL CATEGORIES

Douglas Fisher and Pat Langley

I.	Introduction	241
II.	Concept Learning	242
III.	Psychological Constraints on Concept Formation	248
IV.	A Model of Concept Retrieval and Learning	258
V.	An Analysis of Memory Phenomena	262
VI.	General Discussion	277
	References	281

Index	285
Contents of Recent Volumes	299

CONTRIBUTORS

Numbers in parentheses indicate the pages on which the authors' contributions begin.

Russell P. Balda, Department of Biological Sciences, Northern Arizona University, Flagstaff, Arizona 86011 (1)

Suzanne M. Delaney, Department of Psychology, University of Arizona, Tucson, Arizona 85721 (83)

Douglas Fisher, Department of Computer Science, Vanderbilt University, Nashville, Tennessee 37235 (241)

Douglas J. Herrmann, Laboratory of Socio-Environmental Studies, National Institute of Mental Health, Bethesda, Maryland 20892 (175)

Alan C. Kamil, Departments of Psychology and Zoology, Neuroscience and Behavior Program, University of Massachusetts, Amherst, Massachusetts 01003 (1)

Pat Langley, Department of Information and Computer Science, University of California, Irvine, California 92717 (241)

Elizabeth P. Merikle, Department of Psychology, University of Arizona, Tucson, Arizona 85721 (83)

Louis Narens, School of Social Science, University of California, Irvine, California 92717 (125)

Thomas O. Nelson, Department of Psychology, University of Washington, Seattle, Washington 98195 (125)

Robert W. Proctor, Department of Psychological Sciences, Purdue University, West Lafayette, Indiana 47907 (207)

T. Gilmour Reeve, Motor Behavior Center, Department of Health and Human Performance, Auburn University, Auburn, Alabama 36849 (207)

Daniel L. Schacter, Department of Psychology, University of Arizona, Tucson, Arizona 85721 (83)

Alan Searleman, Department of Psychology, St. Lawrence University, Canton, New York 13617 (175)

E. A. Wasserman, Department of Psychology, The University of Iowa, Iowa City, Iowa 52242 (27)

Daniel J. Weeks, Motor Behaviour Lab, School of Physical Education, Lakehead University, Thunder Bay, Ontario, Canada P7B 5E1 (207)

SPATIAL MEMORY IN SEED-CACHING CORVIDS

Alan C. Kamil
Russell P. Balda

I. Introduction

Traditionally, the psychological study of animal learning and memory has been conducted in laboratory settings with little reference to the natural history, ecology, or evolution of the species being studied (Kamil, 1988). The emphasis has been on identifying and understanding processes that are general across species and paradigms. There seemed to be an (often unstated) assumption that investigating cognitive processes in natural settings was a poor strategy because of the danger of concentrating on "special" abilities (such as imprinting), limited to specific biological settings. The results of research based in specific ecological questions, from this point of view, would be of little general interest, especially to those primarily concerned with generalizing to human cognitive processing.

In a way, psychologists were encouraged in this approach by the attitude of biologists toward learning and memory. Biologists emphasized genetic contributions to behavior, deemphasizing the general role of learning. Although ethologists were interested in certain forms of learning, particularly imprinting and song learning, they tended to view the types of learning typically studied by psychologists as unimportant.

In the last 20–25 years, however, a variety of phenomena have undermined the assumptions of both psychologists and biologists. In psychology, phenomena such as species-specific defensive reactions (Bolles,

1970), autoshaping (Jenkins & Moore, 1973; Kamil & Mauldin, 1987), and taste-aversion learning (Garcia & Koelling, 1966) have shown that the biology of animals can and does affect the outcome of research using the traditional, arbitrary responses studied in psychological experiments on learning and memory. In biology, phenomena such as optimal foraging (Stephens & Krebs, 1986) and the development of social behavior (Cheney, Seyfarth, & Smuts, 1986) have demonstrated that learning and memory play crucial roles for animals in their natural habitat (see Shettleworth, 1984, for discussion of learning and behavioral ecology). These developments establish that the study of learning and memory must involve both psychological and ecological approaches.

If this conclusion is correct, then psychologists need to broaden the way in which they select problems for study. In biology, as in psychology, one approach is to study general processes. Following this approach, one selects the species for study on the basis of convenience or because it has some desirable characteristic, such as short generation time (as in fruit flies for geneticists). This, of course, is the approach that has dominated animal psychology. But there is an alternative approach in biology, one that looks at organisms and their interactions with their environments. In this approach, one selects species and problems for study based upon natural history and ecology.

Our purpose in this article is to review the results of our studies of the mechanisms underlying cache recovery by members of the crow, jay, and nutcracker family. In this research program, we have combined psychological and ecological approaches to the study of memory, and the results demonstrate the utility of this interdisciplinary strategy. Unlike most psychological research on learning and memory, this research program originated in the study of how a particular species solves a particular ecological problem. It serves as an example of how natural history and ecology can provide the starting point for a research program that produces interesting and surprising data of general importance. We begin by outlining the ecological problem.

II. The Ecological Problem

Many animals must cope with cyclic resource availability. The abundance of food may vary on a daily basis or even on a yearly basis. For example, many nuts and seeds are produced only during a relatively short period of time, usually in the fall in temperate zones. Foragers often contend with this variation in resource availability by harvesting and storing food during periods of abundance, using the cached food during periods of food scarcity (Vander Wall & Smith, 1987). This specialization is shown by many corvids who cache acorns, beech nuts, hazel nuts, pine seeds, etc. Many caching animals create large, centralized food stores, such as the middens of squirrels or the honeycombs of bees. Corvids, however, disperse their cached food in many distinct locations, often buried in the ground (Balda, Bunch, Kamil, Sherry, & Tomback, 1987; Turcek & Kelso, 1968).

A particularly spectacular example of distributed caching is provided by the two members of the *Nucifraga* genus, the Eurasian *(N. cartyocatactes)* and the Clark's *(N. columbiana)* nutcrackers. Our research has focused on the North American species, Clark's nutcracker, which is named for its discoverer, Captain William Clark, who first encountered this bird on the historic Lewis and Clark expedition. The name nutcracker comes from the birds' unusual ability to open the thick hulls of seeds using only the bill. Whereas most birds must hold a seed in the foot and peck at it, nutcrackers commonly remove the shell from seeds with a simple, forceful closing of the bill.

The nutcracker is a bird of the high mountains of western North America, where it is a year-round inhabitant of the coniferous forests. Winters in this habitat are cold, with deep snow, short days, and high winds. This environment is not a very hospitable place to live and breed. Nutcrackers counter these harsh conditions by accumulating a store of food for use during the winter and early spring, when food would otherwise be unavailable.

During August and early September, nutcrackers begin to harvest seeds from the cones of alpine species of pine trees which have just begun to ripen. Green cones are shredded to bits with the long, sharp, sturdy bill, and the extracted seeds are placed in the sublingual pouch located in the floor of the mouth, which can hold up to 95 seeds (Bock, Balda, & Vander Wall, 1973). These seeds may be transported up to 22 km from the harvest site and then buried in thousands of discrete subterranean caches. The seeds in these caches are buried 2–3 cm deep in the soil. The birds usually leave no physical signs of digging on the surface so that these caches are difficult, if not impossible, to detect visually. A single bird can cache up to 33,000 seeds in about 6,600 separate locations during a fall when a bumper cone crop is produced (Vander Wall & Balda, 1977).

These seeds form the bulk of the diet during the winter and the spring breeding season, when other foods are scarce. A single bird needs about 9,900 seeds to survive the winter. About 5 seeds are buried per cache, thus a nutcracker must have access to about 1,980 caches per winter for its own survival. In addition, however, nutcrackers are one of the earliest-breeding birds in North America. Breeding occurs from February to

April when snow covers the ground and nighttime temperatures are below freezing. Young nutcrackers are fed pine seeds removed from caches created during the previous autumn by both parents.

The winter survival and breeding success of the Clark's nutcracker depends upon cached pine seeds. In years when the pine cone crop is poor, the birds usually forego breeding. They leave their breeding area in the mountains, descending to lower altitudes. In such years they do not breed and many of the birds die. The food stored in caches is crucial for these birds, as is the ability to successfully relocate the stored pine seeds (Mewaldt, 1956).

The problem of later utilization of stored food is, of course, an important one for all caching animals. Some animals, such as honeybees or midden-creating squirrels, place all of their stored food in a single larder. For such central-place storers, the major problem is defending the larder against competitors. But animals such as nutcrackers that disperse their food stores face a very different set of problems. First, the caches must be hidden, providing no obvious cues as to their location, so that the stored food is less vulnerable to theft by other animals. Second, the hidden, cached food must be relocated by the original cacher. Many techniques could be used, including direct cues such as odor, systematic cache placement, site preferences, and spatial memory. The first step in any research program investigating cache recovery is to determine how caches are found.

III. How Do Nutcrackers Find Their Seeds?

Field studies of nutcrackers in natural situations clearly show that they can accurately find specific locations of hidden seed caches up to 11 months after making them. For example, Tomback (1980) tabulated the percentage of probe holes that had empty seed hulls next to them, which provides a conservative estimate of success rates (because the birds occasionally fly off with recovered seeds, although they usually husk them at the site). She found that this percentage ranged between 60 and 80%. Vander Wall and Hutchins (1983) observed nutcrackers probing in the ground in the spring, at least 8–9 months after caching, and directly observed hit rates of 44%. Conrads and Balda (1979) have seen nutcrackers probe with 84% accuracy after the birds had made thousands of caches.

These observational data make it clear that cache recovery is a phenomenon worthy of further investigation. Whatever technique the nutcrackers are using, it is highly accurate. Imagine that you are about to dig for a small cache of pine seeds, perhaps 5 cm in diameter, and all you have to dig with is a bill 1–2 cm wide. Even if there were several caches per square meter, hit rates as high as 10% would be impossible to obtain by chance.

Several mechanisms could be employed, but each appears to have a significant problem associated with it:

1. Cues emanating directly from the seeds, such as odor, which direct digging behavior. However, such cues would also be available to competitors and significant amounts of stored food might be lost.
2. Site preferences which direct digging during both caching and recovery. However, such preferences would have to be extremely specific, allowing accuracy on a very fine-grain level.
3. Fixed movement paths which are followed during caching and recovery. Again, these would have to be extremely fine-grained.
4. Memory for specific cache sites. This seems unlikely because of the large number of sites to be remembered and the relatively long duration of memory implied by natural history.

Although the observational field data brought this problem to our attention, it is apparent that controlled experimental testing was necessary to determine the mechanism underlying accurate cache recovery by nutcrackers. The first such study (Balda, 1980) found that a Eurasian nutcracker would cache and accurately recover seeds in a dirt-floor aviary. Most importantly, Balda conducted a control experiment. After the bird had cached, Balda removed the seeds from the caches and reraked the soil. During recovery sessions, the bird returned to the locations where seeds had been buried, demonstrating that cues given off by the cached pine seeds were not necessary for accurate recovery.

Vander Wall (1982) extended these findings with a study of Clark's nutcrackers in an outdoor aviary. He found that when two nutcrackers cached in the same area at different times and then separately recovered caches, each bird only recovered its own caches. This also indicates that direct cues from cached seeds are not responsible for cache recovery. If direct cues were being used, then each bird should have found at least some of the seeds cached by the other bird. In addition, when Vander Wall moved the landmarks in part of the aviary, leaving the cached seeds in place, the birds' digging behavior was displaced away from the seed. The displacement indicated that the birds were using the landmarks to relocate caches.

Kamil and Balda (1985) carried out an additional control. They used a room with 180 holes in the floor. Each hole could either be filled with a tight-fitting, sand-filled cup or be capped with a wooden plug. During caching sessions, most of the holes were plugged, forcing the birds to cache in a widely dispersed, randomly chosen set of holes. During recovery sessions, all holes were open. Even under these conditions, when the experimenters, rather than the birds, chose the cache sites, the birds were able to recover caches accurately. If site preferences were responsible for accurate cache recovery, performance should have deteriorated when the birds were forced to cache in sites chosen by the experimenters. In addition, there was no consistent relationship between cache order and recovery order (see below), eliminating systematic movement patterns as necessary for accurate cache recovery.

These experimental results clearly indicate that the most reasonable explanation for the accurate cache recovery of nutcrackers is spatial memory for cache sites. This, in turn, raises many questions. In the next section, we discuss what is known about the characteristics of the spatial memory system of nutcrackers.

IV. The Characteristics of Cache Site Memory in Nutcrackers

A. The Role of Preferences during Cache Recovery

As described above, only a limited number of holes in the floor are available to the nutcrackers for caching during most of our experiments. In one such experiment (Kamil & Balda, 1985) we directly compared the cache recovery accuracy of four nutcrackers after they were given a large number of holes to select from (90) with accuracy after they were forced to select caches from a very restricted number of holes (8). All four birds recovered their caches at above chance levels during both conditions of this experiment, and the overall level of accuracy was not significantly different between conditions.

One bird in this experiment, however, demonstrated much higher levels of accuracy under the 90-hole condition. This bird had a history of poor performance in other experiments when few holes were present for caching, but performed extremely well after 90 holes were available. It is possible that for this individual, site preferences were important and could only be utilized during the 90-hole condition.

In another experiment (Balda & Kamil, 1989) we compared the cache recovery accuracy of nutcrackers and pinyon jays when each species was given 15 and 90 holes open for caching. Overall, performance was better after the birds had selected cache sites from the 90-hole array. This effect was relatively small for nutcrackers (12%) but was quite large for pinyon jays (33%). This difference is undoubtedly due to the tendency of pinyon jays to place their caches very close together during the 90-hole condition. Then, during recovery, the pinyon jays could simply return to the area where caches where clustered. Pinyon jays may remember the locations of their preferred areas in which they have clumped their caches rather than remembering individual cache sites.

We have performed several other analyses relevant to the question of site preferences. For example, several analyses which divided cache sites into preferred and nonpreferred groups on the basis of visitation during habituation sessions and order of use found no effects (Kamil & Balda, 1985). When different nutcrackers are given the same set of holes as potential cache sites, they show only a slight tendency to avoid certain holes (Kamil & Balda, 1990). In sum, although site preferences exist, they do not appear to have a large effect on cache recovery accuracy in nutcrackers.

B. ORDER EFFECTS

As a nutcracker makes caches, it encounters the cache sites sequentially, in a particular order. We have regularly examined the data from our experiments to determine whether or not there is a consistent relationship between the order of cache creation and any aspect of cache recovery.

In several cases, we have calculated Spearman rank-order correlations between the order of caching and the order of recovery. For each bird, each cache is assigned two numbers, one reflecting its rank in the cache order and the other its rank in the recovery order. The resulting correlation coefficients show a slight overall tendency toward being positive. For example, in one experiment (Kamil & Balda, 1990), Spearman rank-order correlations were calculated for 10 birds. The average correlation was +.01. Three of the individual coefficients were statistically significant (at the $\alpha = .05$ level); one was significantly negative, two positive.

This failure to find a correspondence between caching and recovery orders rules out one simple interpretation of cache recovery. It is clear that the birds do not retrace the path they used during caching sessions while recovering their caches. If they were duplicating the same movement pattern, then the overall correlations would be strongly positive. (Of course, it could be argued that they retrace portions of the caching pattern during recovery. But there are no signs of regular strings of successive recoveries mirroring portions of the caching sequence either.)

Despite the absence of consistent correlations between caching order and recovery order, primacy and/or recency effects could be present. For example, if a nutcracker initially recovers a few of his early caches and a few of his late caches, this would be obscured by an overall correlation analysis. Therefore, we have conducted analyses in which we have divided caches into early, middle, and late groups based on order of creation and calculated mean ranks of recovery for each group. We have never found any differences even approaching significance. In summary, there is no strong relationship between the order in which seeds are cached and the order in which the seeds are recovered during our experiments.

C. DECLINE IN ACCURACY

During virtually all of our experiments, the accuracy of cache recovery declines as recovery proceeds. This decline is much more rapid than the decline in the levels of performance that would be expected by chance (as caches are removed from the room). What could account for this decline in accuracy? One possibility is that the birds remember some sites better than others and recover the better-remembered sites first. If this were true, then forcing the birds to recover their caches in a random order should eliminate the decline in accuracy.

In order to test this prediction, Kamil and Balda (1990) allowed birds to cache throughout the experimental room, so that approximately equal numbers of caches were placed in each quadrant. During the control condition, recovery proceeded as usual, with all holes in the room available during each of the four recovery sessions. During the experimental condition, we controlled recovery order across sessions. During each of the four recovery sessions only one quadrant of the room was available; the holes in the other three quadrants were capped with wooden plugs. Each bird recovered from each of the four quadrants in a different random order across the four recovery sessions.

One factor complicated the analysis. The levels of performance expected by chance declined from session to session only during the control condition because the proportion of holes containing seeds declined as recovery proceeded. Despite this complication, the results clearly supported the hypothesis. Even when recovery accuracy was adjusted to take this difference into account, performance during the control condition declined markedly over sessions, but recovery accuracy was virtually constant during the experimental recovery sessions (Fig. 1). Perhaps the clearest aspect of the results is that during the very first recovery session, when chance levels were identical for the two conditions, recovery accuracy was significantly higher when all holes were available than when only one quadrant was available. It seems clear that the nutcrackers were first recovering the caches that they remembered best.

It is particularly interesting to consider this result in conjunction with the evidence reviewed above that there is no relationship between cach-

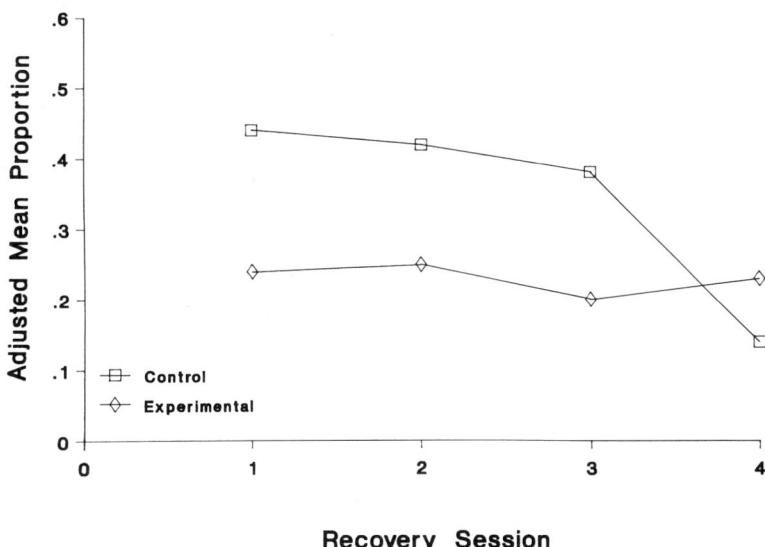

Fig. 1. Performance during cache recovery when all holes were available during each recovery session (control) or when only one quadrant of the room was open during each recovery session (experimental). The modified accuracy score takes into account differences in the levels of performance expected by chance by using the ratio (accuracy − chance)/(1.00 − chance).

ing order and recovery order. It is clear that some sites are remembered better than others and that these sites are recovered first. But caching order has no discernible effect on recovery order. This clearly implies that caching order is unrelated to how well sites are remembered. However, recovery order appears to be a good index of memorability. The best-remembered sites are probably those that are recovered first. We took advantage of this aspect of the cache recovery behavior of nutcrackers to further investigate the causes of differential memory for different cache sites.

The logic of the experiment was simple. Birds were forced to use the same locations as cache sites during two successive cache–recovery cycles. Suppose some sites are better remembered than others because of a physical attribute, such as proximity to a conspicuous landmark. Then if the same sites have caches placed in them twice, they should be recovered in the same order during each cycle.

During the first stage of this experiment, nutcrackers were allowed to make 15–18 caches in 45 holes. After recovering these caches, they were given another caching session with only the previously used holes available for caching. The birds cached in these holes and then they recovered again. During both recovery sessions, the same set of 90 holes was open.

Performance declined significantly as recovery proceeded during both stages, indicating that some sites were, in fact, remembered better than others during each stage. But there was no consistent relationship between the order of recovery during Stage 1 and the order of recovery during Stage 2. Clearly, if the decline in performance is a measure of differential memory, the different recovery orders in response to the same set of cache sites shows that the best-remembered sites were different during the two stages. This presents strong, albeit negative, evidence against any inherent physical characteristic of the sites being responsible for differential memory.

The questions of differential memory for different cache sites and of recovery order need further analysis. If the source of differential memory is not inherent physical differences between sites, perhaps it can be found in different behaviors at different sites during caching. For example, the best-remembered sites may be those at which the caching bird spends the most time or makes the most probes. Detailed analysis of caching behaviors may resolve this issue.

D. What Is the Duration of Cache Site Memory?

The natural history of the nutcracker suggests that cache site memory must have a duration of at least 9–10 months. Nutcrackers have been observed accurately recovering cached seeds in the field in the spring to early summer, at least 9 months after the caches must have been made the previous fall (Vander Wall & Hutchins, 1983). We have begun to explore the duration of cache site memory in the laboratory.

In a pilot study, three nutcrackers were allowed to cache in the fall. Then they were allowed to recover some of their caches 1 week, 3 months, and 6 months later. Performance did decline somewhat from 1 week to 6 months, but some decline is to be expected as recovery proceeds (Kamil & Balda, 1985). The important consideration is that the performance of all three birds was significantly above chance after 6 months.

We are currently conducting a large scale, long-term, between-group experiment. Four groups of six to seven birds each were allowed to cache in the fall. One group was tested after 7 days, another after 3 months, another after 6 months, and another will be tested after 10 months. So far, there are no significant differences, or even a hint of consistent differences, among the 1-week, 3-month, and 6-month groups. Clearly, the limits of nutcracker memory for cache location are greater than 6 months.

E. THE EFFECTS OF PERFORMANCE FACTORS

During cache recovery tasks, nutcrackers perform consistently above chance during laboratory experiments, at levels comparable to those observed in field situations. Accuracy levels of .25 to .70 are not uncommon in field and laboratory. However, it is not clear if the errors that are made under laboratory conditions reflect limits of the spatial abilities of these birds or if some other, performance factors are responsible. Several incidents suggest that some probes we record as errors are not due to failures of memory.

For example, on some occasions we have observed a bird that was previously recovering seeds accurately suddenly begin to frantically search through many adjacent holes. This behavior is characterized by a very rapid probing of holes located next to each other. After some time this behavior ceased and the bird again probed more deliberately with high accuracy. These probes are recorded as errors, but they may represent something other than memory failure. One possibility is that the bird is looking for seeds cached by other birds. This was suggested to us by an episode with one nutcracker during habituation. Through experimenter error, a seed was accidentally left in a hole where it had been placed by another bird during an earlier session. The bird found this seed, perhaps because it was only partially buried. It then proceeded to dig up all empty holes, going rapidly from one to the next. In fact, this bird was ruined as an experimental subject because it would always engage in this behavior thereafter.

On other occasions we have observed birds make numerous errors at the end of a recovery session and not recover their last one or two caches in the room. Upon return to the room at some later time the birds recover these last caches immediately, with no errors. In two cases, we have seen birds recover their last cache and then stop all digging behavior, as if they "knew" there were no more seeds in the room. Taken together these observations offer at least anecdotal evidence that nutcrackers may know more about the location of their caches than their error rates indicate. We have examined the effects of several performance factors on error rates.

Errors may increase near the end of recovery sessions due to satiation. Birds are tested after being deprived of food for 24 hr and then eat the seeds they find. If accuracy is related to hunger levels, then error rates might increase as hunger declines across the session. We tested this possibility (Kamil & Balda, 1985) by testing four nutcrackers under two conditions (with order of testing counterbalanced). Birds were allowed to make up to 12 caches in 27 randomly selected holes. After a 7-day retention intervals birds were allowed to recover their caches. In one condition birds were pre-fed before entering the room for the recovery session, whereas in the other condition birds were deprived of food for 24 hr before testing (our usual procedure). Nutcrackers were consistently above chance under both conditions of the experiment, and there was no significant difference in performance between pre-fed and satiated birds. These results suggest that hunger level is not responsible for the drop-off in performance toward the end of test sessions.

In nature, nutcrackers cache in a variety of substrates, ranging from coarse gravel to fine clays. We have used fine sand as the caching substrate, which is probably easier to dig in than natural substrates. Thus, errors may be relatively inexpensive in our experiments and this may account for some of them. We tested six nutcrackers under two conditions. They cached and recovered from cups that contained fine sand in one condition and from cups filled with a mixture of fine sand and pebbles in the other condition. The pebbles were similar in size to the pine seeds used in the experiment. The birds cached readily during both conditions. The sand/pebble mixture appeared to be more difficult because the pebbles impeded the forceful thrust of the bill normally associated with the creation of a cache. During recovery birds probed more and spent more time at sand/pebble sites. Under the latter condition caches were found with significantly fewer probes than when the cups contained only sand. These results show that recovery accuracy is influenced by the cost of digging and that error rates are not a function of memory alone.

V. Species Differences in Cache Site Memory

Clark's nutcrackers are not the only birds who cope with fluctuation in food availability by storing food for later use in many widely dispersed sites. This adaptation is fairly common among parids (the chickadees and tits; Sherry, 1984) and ubiquitous among corvids (the jays, crows, and nutcrackers; Balda & Kamil, 1989; Goodwin, 1976). Among the corvids, there is considerable variation in the extent to which different species are dependent upon stored food. Three species of the American Southwest, the Clark's nutcracker *(Nucifraga columbiana)*, pinyon jay *(Gymnorhinus cyanocephalus)*, and scrub jay *(Aphelocoma coerulescens)* differ in the extent to which they depend on stored food. They also differ in the extent of their morphological specializations for the harvesting, transport, caching, and recovery of seeds (Vander Wall & Balda, 1981).

Clark's nutcrackers live year-round at high elevations where other foods are not available during winter and spring. They cache between 22,000 and 33,000 seeds in some autumns, and their diet consists of close to 100% stored pine seeds during the unproductive winter months. As noted earlier, nutcrackers have a strong sharp bill, that they use to open tightly closed green pine cones, and a unique sublingual pouch in which they can transport up to 95 whole seeds. In alpine areas these birds breed in March and April and their nestlings can survive on a diet of pine seeds.

Pinyon jays, a highly social species, live at lower elevations, cache thousands of seeds, and eat between 70 and 90% stored pine seeds in winter. These jays can carry up to 45 pine seeds in an expandable esophagus, have a sharp bill (also used to open green pine cones), breed very early in spring, and feed their nestlings some pine seeds.

Scrub jays live year-round in the mild, pinyon-juniper woodland and eat a wide variety of foods. They probably cache no more than 6,000 pine seeds in fall, can transport no more than 4 seeds in mouth and bill, and have a very generalized, blunt bill. These birds breed in early summer.

Thus, these three species vary systematically in the elevations at which they live, the number of seeds they cache, and their morphological specializations for harvesting and storing seeds. Based on these features, the species can be regarded as showing a specialization gradient from nutcracker to scrub jay, with the pinyon jay being intermediate. Are there species differences in the accuracy of cache recovery that reflect this gradient? If so, we expect nutcrackers to perform best, pinyon jays somewhat worse, and scrub jays worst of all.

To answer this question, Balda and Kamil (1989) tested seven birds of each species under two conditions, with order of testing counterbalanced. During one condition, the birds were allowed to select cache sites from 90 opened holes in the room. These holes were spaced evenly throughout the room. Each bird was placed in the room individually and allowed to make 8 caches. The bird was then removed for a 7-day retention interval. During this time we removed all signs of digging activity from the room. The bird was then allowed back in the room with all 90 holes open and seeds present in the holes used by the bird during the caching session. During the second condition, a different set of 90 holes within the caching room was used. During caching, only 15 randomly selected holes (out of the 90) were available to the bird. Again, the bird was allowed to make 8 caches. After another 7-day retention interval birds were allowed into the room to recover their caches with all 90 holes open.

This design was used because different species may employ different mechanisms to locate their seed caches. For example, when birds are given free choice of many cache sites to use, such as during condition 90, they may employ a "caching rule" or demonstrate a preference of some type for certain sets of holes. Then, during recovery sessions only the rule or preference need be remembered. Limiting the number of cache

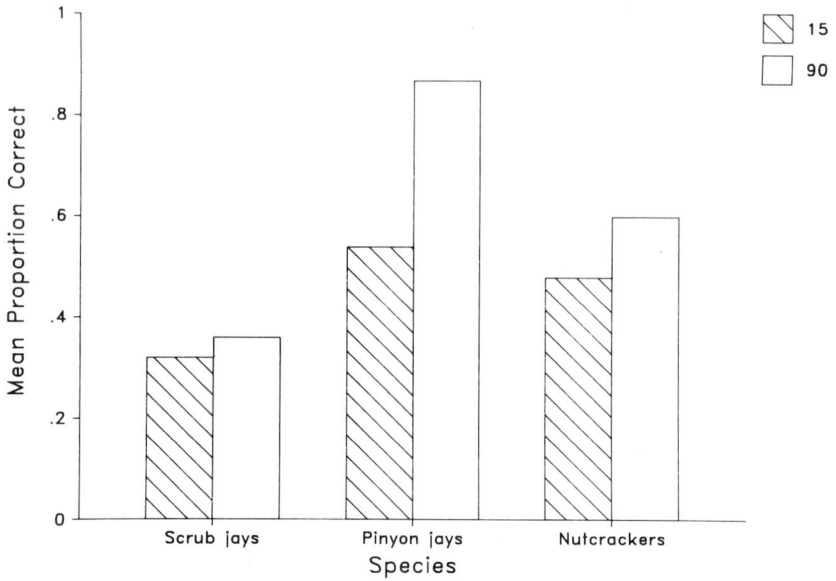

Fig. 2. Mean performance of each species after 90 holes were available for caching (open bars) or after only 15 holes were available (cross-hatched bars). There were always 90 holes available during recovery sessions.

sites, such as during condition 15, would limit these cache placement strategies. In essence, condition 15 forces the bird to place its caches in a set of holes chosen by the experimenters.

All birds readily cached and recovered seeds under both conditions. Accuracy varied as a function of both species and condition (Fig. 2). Scrub jays performed significantly worse than either pinyon jays or nutcrackers, which did not differ from each other. Performance was generally better during the 90-hole condition, especially for the pinyon jays, who performed exceptionally well during condition 90 and showed a marked decline in condition 15. The reason for this marked effect of number of holes available on cache recovery in pinyon jays was the spatial clustering of cache sites described above.

These results support our specialization hypothesis, that the accuracy of cache recovery varies as a function of the ecology and natural history of the species being tested. Nutcrackers and pinyon jays, the two species most dependent on cached seeds in nature, performed significantly better than scrub jays.

VI. Noncaching Tests of Spatial Memory

The comparative experiment demonstrated differences between nutcrackers and scrub jays in cache-recovery accuracy. However, data from seminatural cache-recovery experiments cannot adequately test whether or not these differences are due to species differences in spatial memory. This will require testing the species under conditions that offer more control over parameters such as duration of exposure to the to-be-remembered location. This suggests comparative experiments using more traditional psychological procedures. In order to accomplish this goal, we have begun to test nutcrackers in an analog of the radial maze and with operant procedures.

A. Radial-Arm Maze

During a forced-choice radial-arm maze procedure (e.g., Beatty & Shavalia, 1980), each trial is divided into two parts. During the preretention, information stage, the rat chooses a subset of the arms of the maze. Then, following the retention interval, the animal is given free choice among all of the arms of the maze and rewarded for visiting those arms not earlier visited. This procedure was adapted for nutcrackers by using eight of the holes in our cache-recovery room (Balda & Kamil, 1988). One set of eight holes, arranged in a rough circle, was used throughout the experiment. During each trial, each nutcracker was allowed in the room twice. During the preretention phase only four of the holes were open. These holes were randomly chosen on each trial, and each contained a single pine seed buried below the surface of the sand by the experimenter. After the bird dug up and ate these four seeds, the room lights were flashed as a signal to leave the room. During the retention interval, the bird remained in its cage while the experimenter entered the room, uncapped the four capped holes, buried one seed in each of these previously capped holes, and cleaned up any signs of previous activity. When the retention interval was over, the bird reentered the room for the test phase. During the test phase all eight holes were open, but only holes that had not been visited earlier contained seeds.

During preliminary training, the retention interval was held at 5 min. At first, the birds showed a pattern of visiting all of the available holes in a circular path. However, once we introduced a large set of rocks and logs that made hopping from one hole to the next more difficult, performance improved rapidly, reaching asymptotic levels of over 80%.

After this initial training was complete, we tested the birds with seven

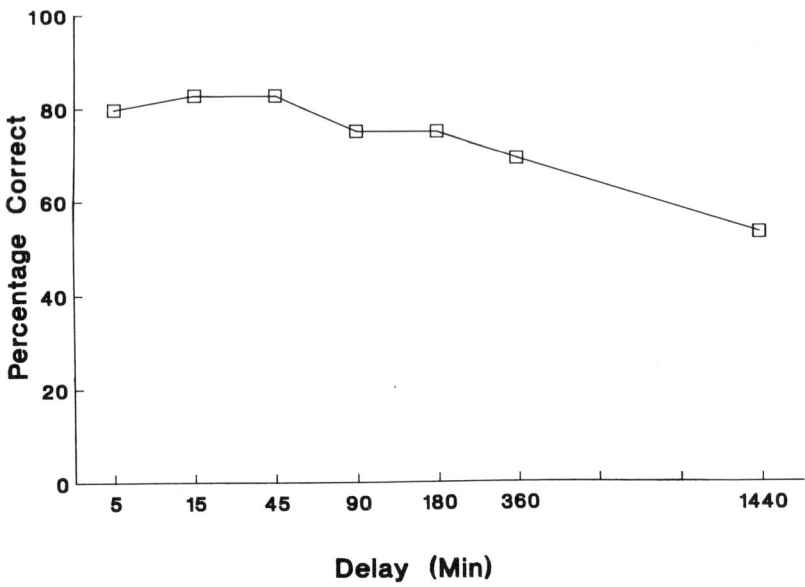

Fig. 3. Mean percentage correct choices during radial-maze analog testing after different duration retention intervals.

different retention intervals ranging between 5 min and 24 hr (Fig. 3). There was no significant decline in performance through 6 hr, but performance after a 24-hr retention interval was close to chance. These results are markedly different from those obtained in similar studies of pigeons and from the cache-recovery results described above.

In comparison to the results of cache-recovery experiments, the performance observed in the radial-maze analog experiment is unimpressive. For example, high accuracy levels after retention intervals of 10–15 days, with 25–30 cache sites to be remembered, have routinely been observed in nutcrackers (Kamil & Balda, 1985). On the surface, this comparison suggests that the nutcrackers may use different memory systems during radial-maze and cache-recovery tests. However, several procedural differences between the tasks may account for the differences.

The most important of these appears to be proactive interference. During radial-maze tests, the set of locations to be remembered changes daily, on each trial. During a cache-recovery experiment the set of locations to be remembered does not change within a single test. Another potentially important factor is the difference in required response strategies. During caching tests of memory, the bird first places a seed in a location, then is required to return to that location. But during radial-maze testing, the bird first removes a seed, then is required to avoid that location. These response differences could also affect performance. We are currently testing the effects of these variables upon cache-recovery and radial-maze analog performances to try to determine if the methodological differences can account for the apparent differences in memory duration.

While the radial-maze results may be unimpressive compared to nutcracker cache-recovery performance, they are quite impressive compared to the performance of pigeons during tests in a radial maze (Roberts & Van Veldhuizen, 1985) as well as open-field tests in radial-maze analogs (Spetch & Edwards, 1986; Spetch & Honig, 1988). For example, Spetch and Honig (1988) obtained the best performance from pigeons in radial-maze-type settings. In their experiment there was very substantial forgetting within 2 hr. The nutcrackers in our radial-maze analog, in contrast, showed no significant forgetting after 6 hr. These differences suggest large species differences among birds in spatial memory ability. Experiments simultaneously testing several species will be required.

In our view, the experiment that would be most useful would be one that compared closely related species that differed in their dependence on cached food. This would directly test the possibility raised by the results of our comparative cache-recovery experiment—that spatial memory varies as a function of this ecological factor. We hope to carry out such an experiment in the near future.

B. Operant Spatial Nonmatching to Sample

Although we have not yet carried out the needed comparative radial-maze study, we have examined the performance of nutcrackers, scrub jays, and pigeons in an operant test of spatial memory. Olson (1989) developed a spatial nonmatching-to-sample procedure during which there were two stages to each trial—a preretention stage and a postretention choice stage. The experiments were conducted in a 1.35-m-long operant chamber, with two pecking keys on the front wall and a single key and a food cup on the rear wall. During the first stage, one of the keys on the front wall, randomly chosen on each trial, was lit. The subject was required to peck this key five times. Then the key was darkened and the retention interval began. During the retention interval, the bird pecked the illuminated key on the back wall. The retention interval ended after the first response following the scheduled retention interval (see below for an explanation of how retention interval was manipulated). At the end of the retention interval, the back key was darkened and both front keys

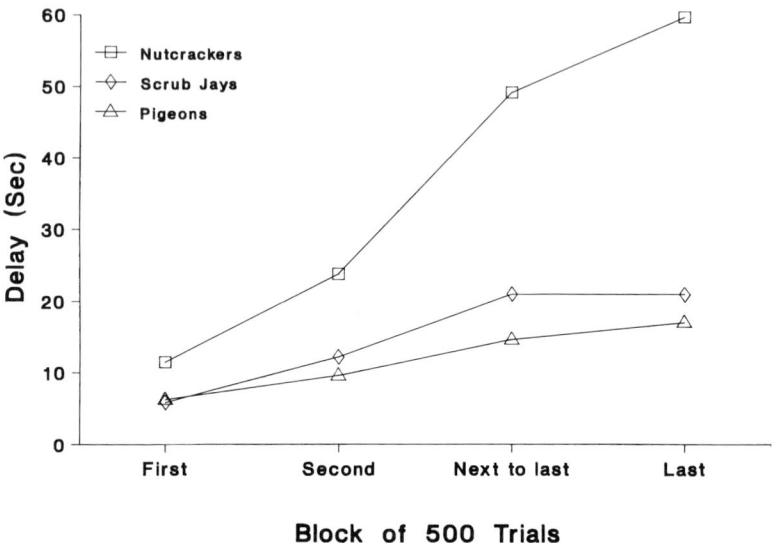

Fig. 4. The mean titrated delay values during blocks of 500 trials of operant spatial nonmatching to sample for each of three species. Because the delay could increase only as long as performance was better than 75% correct, higher values indicate better performance.

lit up. If the bird pecked at the key that was illuminated during the preretention stage of the trial, the trial ended without reinforcement. If the bird chose the front key that was not illuminated during the preretention stage, the trial ended with a reinforcement (a piece of pine seed) delivered in the food cup on the rear wall.

A titration procedure was used to continuously adjust the duration of the retention interval. Whenever a correct choice was made, the interval increased by .1 sec on the next trial; after an incorrect choice, the interval decreased by .3 sec. Thus, the duration of the retention interval kept slowly increasing as long as performance was above 75% correct. The advantage of the titration procedure is that it concentrates data collection at the limits of the abilities of the subjects. In addition, because it is open ended, it is particularly appropriate when the limits of memory for the species being tested are unknown.

Olson has tested three species: nutcrackers, scrub jays, and pigeons. The performance of the nutcrackers was spectacular. They performed well with retention intervals of 70–80 sec and showed no signs of having reached asymptote at the end of the experiment. The pigeons performed very poorly, never consistently achieving retention intervals of 10 sec. The scrub jays performed at levels intermediate to nutcrackers and pigeons, but more like pigeons than nutcrackers (Fig. 4).

Olson (1989) has replicated these effects with nutcrackers and scrub jays, using fixed retention intervals from 0 to 30 sec and varying the memory load. There were four pecking keys on the front wall, and the number of samples presented varied from one to three. During the test phase, there were always two keys illuminated, one of which had been illuminated during the preretention phase. The correct response was to choose the test stimulus that had not been illuminated on that trial. Again, the nutcrackers consistently outperformed the scrub jays.

The results of these two operant experiments demonstrate that the species differences observed during cache recovery also are found during operant tests of spatial memory. They offer strong support for the hypothesis that the differences in cache-recovery accuracy are caused by differences in spatial memory ability. More generally, they suggest a direct relationship between one parameter of natural history, dependence on cached food, and spatial memory.

VII. Implications and Future Directions

Although this research project started from natural history and ecology, the results have many implications of general interest to psychologists. In this section, we discuss three of these implications, with an emphasis on questions that remain for further research.

A. Implications for Comparative Research

Although the psychological literature on animal learning and memory is huge, encompassing thousands of publications, comparative research makes up a relatively small part of this literature. There are many reasons for this relative disinterest in comparative work (for discussion see Beach, 1950; Bitterman, 1960; Kamil, 1988; Staddon, 1989). One of the major reasons, however, has been the absence of a consistent straightforward methodology to circumvent the problems presented by the learning–performance distinction.

The basic problem is simple: The major comparative question of interest to psychologists is that of species differences in cognitive *abilities*. But species differences in any particular situation may be due to factors that affect performance, "contextual variables," rather than species differences (Bitterman, 1960, 1965; Macphail, 1982, 1985). Control by systematic variation is one way to deal with this problem (e.g., Bitterman, 1960; Macphail, 1982). According to this argument, performance factors such as stimulus and response requirements, motivation, and reward should be systematically varied. If a species difference is reliably observed under all variations, it can be concluded that the difference is due to a difference in ability (or process).

The problem with this approach is that it treats the hypothesis of species difference as a null hypothesis which can be disproved only by proving another null hypothesis: that the species difference will appear under all circumstances. This leaves no way, within this framework, to conclusively demonstrate species differences in learning ability. It is always possible that a species difference would disappear under some as yet unspecified and untested set of circumstances (see Kamil, 1988, for a detailed discussion of this issue). In order for comparative research on cognitive abilities to move forward, a way must be found around the very real problems of the learning–performance distinction.

The key to avoiding these problems is to have *a priori* predictions of species differences in cognitive abilities, predictions that can be subjected to multiple independent tests. An approach based on natural history and ecology can provide such predictions based on analyses of the adaptations of species to their natural habitat. Such analyses can provide specific, directional hypotheses about species differences in cognitive processes.

For example, consider the hypothesis that spatial memory abilities will be greater in animals that are most dependent upon scattered cached food stores that are relocated through the use of spatial memory. This hypothesis receives strong support from the differences between nutcrackers and scrub jays, especially in the operant nonmatching experiments. However, a skeptic could always claim that this difference was due to some contextual variable that favored the nutcrackers, no matter how many times it was replicated using control by systematic variation. For example, it could be argued that nutcrackers simply adapt to laboratory environments better than scrub jays.

However, the hypothesis can be tested with other groups of animals. For example, some parids, such as marsh tits and black-capped chickadees, cache seeds while other species of the same genus, such as great tits, do not. Recently, Krebs, Healy, and Shettleworth (in press) compared coal tits and great tits on a "window-shopping" task which required the birds to remember where they had earlier seen seeds. The coal tits, who regularly cache seeds in nature, performed better than the great tits, a noncaching species. If repeated tests of the hypothesis with different groups of animals produce data that support the hypothesis, then the contextual-variable argument becomes untenable. Although performance factors might happen to produce the predicted differences in any one case, they are unlikely to do so in multiple cases.

It should be noted that this strategy uses analysis of the adaptations of animals to the problems encountered in their natural habitat in the selection of both species and paradigms for experiments. The strategy can be used quite generally. For example, Humphrey (1976) has suggested that social functions have been extremely important in the evolution of intellect in animals. Thus, the gauging of social relations among members of the group may be learned, and crucial to biological success (e.g., Bachmann & Kummer, 1980; Goodall, 1986). This hypothesis could be tested by comparative studies of closely related species which vary in their social organization. Most importantly, these tests could be carried out independently in different groups of animals, such as birds and primates.

B. The Generality of Nutcracker Spatial Memory

Why do Clark's nutcrackers perform better than scrub jays during operant spatial nonmatching? This question can be answered at many levels: neural, behavioral, and evolutionary. At the neural level, we do not yet know whether there are systematic differences between nutcrackers and scrub jays. However, research comparing caching and noncaching species (Krebs, Sherry, Healy, Perry, & Vaccarino, in press; Sherry & Vaccarino, in press) has found that there are systematic differences in the relative size of the hippocampus. Caching species have larger hippocampi. At the behavioral level, the best hypothesis is that species differences in spatial memory are responsible, although further tests are needed. And at the evolutionary level, the differences in dependence on cached food leading to neural differences, which in turn produce differences in spatial memory, is the most viable hypothesis. One of the advantages of this approach is that it offers a method of bridging the gap between different levels of explanation of behavioral differences between species.

Each of these tentative explanations has one thing in common: Each implies that the underlying mechanism responsible for accurate cache recovery is the same as that reponsible for performance during the operant task. If this is true, it provides a clear example of natural history influencing behavior in highly artificial and abstract psychological test environments.

The traditional approach to the psychological study of animal learning tended to assume that the behaviors observed during tests in artificial environments (such as operant chambers) were not directly related to the natural behaviors of the animal being studied in any important way (e.g., Skinner, 1959). Biological constraints on learning have challenged that assumption. Phenomena such as species-specific defensive reactions (Bolles, 1970) and autoshaping (Jenkins & Moore, 1973) have demonstrated that there can be a rather direct connection between the natural repertoire of the animal and what it does during a learning experiment.

The logic connecting the performance of nutcrackers during operant spatial tests with their natural history is somewhat different. Spatial relationships are important to most mobile animals (if not all), and spatial memory is widespread. However, in the case of organisms dependent on memory to locate scattered food, memory is particularly important. Therefore, in such cases, natural selection may have acted to improve the spatial memory systems of these animals. Once spatial memory has improved, this improvement will be reflected in any test of spatial memory. This argument suggests that a cognitive ability can be the trait on which selection operates. This, in turn, implies that the research strategies that biologists have used to study the species differences in physical traits can also be adapted to the study of the evolution of cognitive traits. And, of course, cognitive traits are basically physical traits at the level of the structure of the nervous system.

C. Implications for Memory Systems

Sherry and Shacter (1987) have offered a persuasive argument for the evolution of separate memory systems under certain circumstances. If there are two separate natural settings which demand the use of memory, and if the characteristics of the needed memory are functionally incompatible, then separate, specialized memory systems should evolve. This may explain the existence of "habit" or "procedural" memory versus "declarative" or "episodic" memory.

The superior performance of nutcrackers during different types of tasks requiring spatial memory, cache recovery, and operant nonmatching suggests that the spatial memory system that nutcrackers use for cache recovery is not limited to that situation. That is, it appears that the same memory system may be used, although much further work will be needed to be sure of this. However, the hypothesized generality of the nutcracker spatial memory should not be taken as evidence against Sherry and Shacter's (1987) suggestion of separate memory systems in the face of functional incompatibility. The major requirements for a spatial memory system to keep track of cache site location in Clark's nutcrackers appears to be that the system be of large capacity and long duration. These characteristics are not functionally incompatible with other types of functions that spatial memory may serve.

VIII. Conclusions

Our studies of cache recovery and spatial memory began with an issue raised by the natural history and ecology of the nutcracker. We hope that this review of our work has convinced the reader that natural history and ecology can provide a good starting point for research programs that produce data that bear directly on central issues of psychology: the cognitive abilities of animals, the evolution of learning and memory, and the structure of memory, for example. We further hope that readers are encouraged to utilize this strategy in their own research. We are convinced that systematic and widespread use of this strategy will lead to the discovery of many other dramatic and important examples of cognitive processes in animals.

ACKNOWLEDGMENTS

The research reported in this article was supported by NSF grants BNS 82-08286 and BNS 85-19010 and NIH grant MH-44200.

REFERENCES

Bachmann, C., & Kummer, H. (1980). Male assessment of female choice in Hamadryas baboons. *Behavioral Ecology and Sociobiology*, **6**, 315–321.

Balda, R. P. (1980). Are seed-caching systems co-evolved? In R. Nohring (Ed.), *Acta XVI Congressus Internationalis Ornithologici* (pp. 1185–1191). Berlin: Deutsche Ornitologen-Gesellschaft.

Balda, R. P., Bunch, K. G., Kamil, A. C., Sherry, D. F., & Tomback, D. F. (1987). Cache site memory in birds. In A. C. Kamil, J. R. Krebs, & H. R. Pulliam (Eds.), *Foraging behavior* (pp. 645–666), New York: Plenum.

Balda, R. P., & Kamil, A. C. (1988). The spatial memory of Clark's nutcrackers *(Nucifraga columbiana)* in an analog of the radial-arm maze. *Animal Learning and Behavior*, **16**, 116–122.

Balda, R. P., & Kamil, A. C. (1989). A comparative study of cache recovery by three corvid species. *Animal Behaviour*, **38**, 486–495.

Beach, F. A. (1950). The snark was a boojum. *American Psychologist*, **5**, 115–124.

Beatty, W. W., & Shavalia, D. A. (1980). Spatial memory in rats: Time course of working memory and effect of anesthetics. *Behavioral and Neural Biology*, **28**, 454–462.

Bitterman, M. E. (1960). Toward a comparative psychology of learning. *American Psychologist*, **15**, 704–712.

Bitterman, M. E. (1965). Phyletic differences in learning. *American Psychologist*, **20**, 396–410.

Bock, W. J., Balda, R. P., & Vander Wall, S. B. (1973). Morphology of the sublingual pouch and tongue musculature in Clark's nutcracker. *Auk*, **90**, 491–519.

Bolles, R. C. (1970). Species-specific defense reactions and avoidance learning. *Psychological Review*, **77**, 32–48.

Cheney, D., Seyfarth, R., & Smuts, B. (1986). Social relationships and social cognition in nonhuman primates. *Science*, **234**, 1361–1366.

Conrads, K., & Balda, R. P. (1979). Uberwinterungschancen Siberischer Tannenhaher

(*Nucifraga caryocatactes macrorhynchos*) im Invasionsgebeit. *Bericht der Naturwissenschaftlischen Veirens, Bielefeld,* **24,** 115–137.

Garcia, J., & Koelling, R. A. (1966). Relation of cue to consequence in avoidance learning. *Psychonomic Science,* **4,** 123–124.

Goodall, J. (1986). *The chimpanzees of Gombe: Patterns of behavior.* Cambridge, MA: Harvard University Press.

Goodwin, D. (1976). *Crows of the world.* Ithaca, NY: Cornell University Press.

Humphrey, N. K. (1976). The social function of intellect. In P. P. G. Bateson & R. A. Hinde (Eds.), *Growing points in ethology* (pp. 303–318). Cambridge: Cambridge University Press.

Jenkins, H. M., & Moore, B. R. (1973). The form of the autoshaped response with food and water reinforcers. *Journal of the Experimental Analysis of Behavior,* **20,** 163–181.

Kamil, A. C. (1988). A synthetic approach to the study of animal intelligence. In D. W. Leger (Ed.), *Comparative perspectives in modern psychology: Nebraska symposium on motivation* (Vol. 35, pp. 257–308). Lincoln: University of Nebraska Press.

Kamil, A. C., & Balda, R. P. (1985). Cache recovery and spatial memory in Clark's nutcrackers *(Nucifraga columbiana). Journal of Experimental Psychology: Animal Behavior Processes,* **11,** 95–111.

Kamil, A. C., & Balda, R. P. (1990). Differential memory for cache sites in Clark's nutcrackers. *Journal of Experimental Psychology: Animal Behavior Processes,* **16,** 162–168.

Kamil, A. C., & Mauldin, J. E. (1987). A comparative-ecological approach to the study of learning. In: R. C. Bolles & M. D. Beecher (Eds.), *Evolution and learning* (pp. 117–133). Hillsdale, NJ: Erlbaum.

Krebs, J. R., Healy, S. D., & Shettleworth, S. J. (in press). Spatial memory of Paridae: comparison of a storing and a non-storing species. *Animal Behaviour.*

Krebs, J. R., Sherry, D. F., Healy, S. D., Perry, V. H., & Vaccarino, A. L. (1989). Hippocampal specialization of food-storing birds. *Proceedings of the National Academy of Sciences,* **86,** 1388–1392.

Macphail, E. M. (1982). *Brain and intelligence in vertebrates.* London: Oxford University Press (Clarendon).

Macphail, E. M. (1985). Vertebrate intelligence: The null hypothesis. In L. Weiskrantz (Ed.), *Animal intelligence* (pp. 37–50). London: Oxford University Press (Clarendon).

Mewaldt, R. (1956). Nesting behavior of the Clark's nutcracker. *Condor,* **58,** 3–23.

Olson, D. (1989). *Comparative spatial memory in birds.* Unpublished doctoral dissertation, University of Massachusetts, Amherst.

Roberts, W. A., & Van Veldhuizen, N. (1985). Spatial memory in pigeons on the radial maze. *Journal of Experimental Psychology: Animal Behavior Processes,* **11,** 241–260.

Sherry, D. F. (1984). What food-storing birds remember. *Canadian Journal of Psychology,* **38,** 304–321.

Sherry, D. F., & Schacter, D. L. (1987). The evolution of multiple memory systems. *Psychological Review,* **94,** 439–454.

Sherry, D. F., & Vaccarino, A. L. (1989). The hippocampus and memory for food caches in Black-capped chickadees. *Behavioral Neuroscience,* **2,** 308–318.

Shettleworth, S. J. (1984). Learning and behavioral ecology. In J. R. Krebs & N. B. Davies (Eds.), *Behavioral ecology* (2nd ed., pp. 170–196). Sunderland, MA: Sinauer Associates.

Skinner, B. F. (1959). A case history in scientific method. In S. Koch (Ed.), *Psychology: The study of a science* (pp. 359–379). New York: McGraw-Hill.

Spetch, M. L., & Edwards, C. A. (1986). Spatial memory in pigeons *(Columba livia)* in an "open-field" feeding environment. *Journal of Comparative Psychology,* **100,** 279–284.

Spetch, M. L., & Honig, W. K. (1988). Characteristics of pigeons' spatial working memory in an open-field task. *Animal Learning and Behavior, 16,* 123–131.
Staddon, J. R. (1989). Animal psychology: The tyranny of anthropocentrism. In P. P. G. Bateson & P. H. Klopfer (Eds.), *Perspectives in ethology: Whither ethology* (pp. 123–136). New York: Plenum.
Stephens, D. W., & Krebs, J. R. (1986). *Foraging theory.* Princeton, NJ: Princeton University Press.
Tomback, D. (1980). How nutcrackers find their seed stores. *Condor, 82,* 10–19.
Turcek, F., & Kelso, L. (1968). Ecological aspects of food transportation and storage in the Corvidae. *Communications in Behavioral Biology, Part A,* **1,** 277–297.
Vander Wall, S. B. (1982). An experimental analysis of cache recovery in Clark's nutcracker. *Animal Behaviour, 30,* 84–94.
Vander Wall, S. B., & Balda, R. P. (1977). Coadaptations of the Clark's nutcracker and the pinon pine for efficient seed harvest and dispersal. *Ecological Monographs, 47,* 89–111.
Vander Wall, S. B., & Balda, R. P. (1981). Ecology and evolution of food-storage behavior in conifer-seed-caching corvids. *Zeitschrift für Tierpsychologie, 6,* 217–242.
Vander Wall, S. B., & Hutchins, H. E. (1983). Dependence of Clark's nutcracker *(Nucifraga columbiana)* on conifer seeds during the postfledgling period. *Canadian Field Naturalist, 97,* 208–214.
Vander Wall, S. B., & Smith, K. G. (1987). Cache-protecting behavior of food-storing animals. In A. C. Kamil, J. R. Krebs, & H. R. Pulliam (Eds.), *Foraging behavior* (pp. 611–644). New York: Plenum.

DETECTING RESPONSE–OUTCOME RELATIONS: TOWARD AN UNDERSTANDING OF THE CAUSAL TEXTURE OF THE ENVIRONMENT

E. A. Wasserman

I. Introduction

It is a sad truth that experimental psychology is no longer a unified field of scholarship. The most obvious sign of disintegration is the division of the *Journal of Experimental Psychology* into specialized periodicals. Further evidence comes in the form of separate paper sessions at regional, national, and international conventions, separate review panels at extramural funding agencies, and separate training areas in doctoral programs.

Many forces propel this fractionation. First, the explosion of interest in many small spheres of inquiry has made it extremely difficult for an individual to master more than one. Second, the recent popularity of interdisciplinary research has lured many workers away from the central issues of experimental psychology. And, third, there is a growing division between researchers of human and animal behavior; this division has been primarily driven by contemporary cognitive psychologists (e.g., Lachman, Lachman, & Butterfield, 1979), who see little reason to refer to the behavior of animals or to inquire into the generality of behavioral principles.

I raise these points at the outset of this article to help frame later discussion. We will here be considering the study of *causal perception*. This area is certainly at the core of experimental psychology (Boring, 1950).

Yet, pertinent investigations of human behavior have been relatively rare and unsystematic. Rather more numerous and programmatic have been explorations of what some call causal perception in animals (Killeen, 1981; Mackintosh, 1977). Although recent research in animal cognition has taken the tack of bringing human paradigms into the animal laboratory (Roitblat, 1987; Wasserman, 1981), the experimental research that I will describe has adopted the reverse strategy of bringing animal paradigms into the human laboratory. I leave it to the reader to judge whether the behavior of our human subjects differs appreciably from that of other animals.

A further unfortunate fact is that today's experimental psychologists are receiving little or no training in the history and philosophy of psychology. This neglect means that investigations of a problem area are often undertaken without a full understanding of the analytical issues that would help guide empirical inquiry. Certainly, for any comprehension of causal perception, acquaintance with David Hume's ideas is indispensable. Therefore, those ideas will be reviewed briefly before moving on to experimental studies.

II. Hume's Theory of Causation

More than any other thinker, the eighteenth century Scottish philosopher David Hume has shaped our understanding of causality. Hume's insights into causation have directly stimulated the writings of generations of philosophers (Beauchamp & Rosenberg, 1981; Taylor, 1967); less directly, Hume's notions have influenced experimental psychology (Boring, 1950). Although his name is seldom cited by past or present workers in experimental psychology, almost 250 years ago Hume penned a model of causal perception that has profound relevance to modern psychological research and theory (Shanks, 1985). His theory is based on the association of ideas; it is mechanistic rather than ratiocinative; and it is as applicable to nonhuman animals as it is to human beings.

Hume's account of causation entails four major ideas: (1) The notion of necessary connection, which is a key element of our concept of causation, lies not in the objects and events of the world, but in ourselves; necessity is an inner, psychological impression projected onto external events. (2) Certain interevent relations bring about causal impressions. (3) Mechanistic laws govern the strength of association between the ideas of cause and effect. (4) Causal impressions are not unique to humans; nonhuman animals, too, form interevent associations according to the same laws as do human beings. These four notions are next considered in greater detail.

A. Causation as a Psychological Impression

To begin his analysis, Hume argues that, in a sequence of events, there is no sensory experience corresponding to their interconnection. The succession of experiences is given; but, the impression of connection goes beyond the direct sensory evidence.

> All events seem entirely loose and separate. One event follows another; but we never can observe any tie between them. (1777/1951, p. 74)

> When we say therefore, that one object is connected with another, we mean only that they have acquired a connexion in our thought.... (1777/1951, p. 76)

B. Conditions of Causation

Just what information did Hume believe was crucial to forming causal impressions? Here, he listed three primary conditions: (1) spatiotemporal contiguity, (2) priority, and (3) consistent conjunction. These conditions must be met if the strongest impression of causality is to be formed:

1. The cause and effect must be contiguous in space and time.
2. The cause must be prior to the effect.
3. There must be a constant union betwixt the cause and effect. (1739/1964, p. 173)

Hume amplified these three main conditions with three others that would better define and sharpen our causal attributions:

4. The same cause always produces the same effect, and the same effect never arises but from the same cause....
5. [W]here several different objects produce the same effect, it must be by means of some quality, which we discover to be common amongst them....
6. The difference in the effects of two resembling objects must proceed from that particular, in which they differ. (1739/1964, pp. 173–174)

Condition 4 suggests that constant conjunction can be violated in two ways: either a particular cause is not followed by its usual effect or a particular effect is not preceded by its usual cause. Conditions 5 and 6 correspond, respectively, to the methods of *agreement* and *difference*, reified by one of Hume's successors, John Stuart Mill.

C. A Mechanistic Model of Causal Perception

From Hume's "rules by which to judge of causes and effects," one might conclude that causal thinking is decidedly inferential and deliberate. This conclusion would be a serious error. In fact, Hume believes that completely mechanical principles lead us to associate consistently contiguous experiences. One reason Hume arrives at this position is the speed and automaticity of our making causal judgments.

> When we follow only the determination of the mind, we make the transition without any reflection, and interpose not a moment[']s delay betwixt the view of one object and the belief of that, which is often found to attend it. As the custom depends not upon any deliberation, it operates immediately, without allowing any time for reflection.... (1739/1964, p. 133)

A second reason for insisting upon mechanical laws of causal association is the key role that Hume believes the psychological process plays in our adapting to the exigencies of the environment. So central is causal association to survival, Hume refuses to trust it to deliberate, reflective thought. Additionally, he refuses to deny causal association to young infants, whom few would credit with advanced logical capabilities.

> ... as this operation of the mind, by which we infer like effects from like causes, and *vice versa,* is so essential to the subsistence of all human creatures, it is not probable, that it could be trusted to the fallacious deductions of our reason, which is slow in its operations; appears not, in any degree, during the first years of infancy; and at best is, in every age and period of life, extremely liable to error and mistake. (1777/1951, p. 55)

Hume is far more comfortable with placing the process of causal association in the hands of nature, which has evidently endowed us with mental operations as effective as they are automatic.

> It is more conformable to the ordinary wisdom of nature to secure so necessary an act of the mind, by some instinct or mechanical tendency, which may be infallible in its operations, may discover itself at the first appearance of life and thought, and may be independent of all the laboured deductions of the understanding. (1777/1951, p. 55)

What Hume appears to envision is an ability for us to detect the inter-event relations of our environment—the "causal texture" of Tolman and Brunswik (1935)—an ability which does not operate by the systematic application of logic and reason. The real basis of Hume's theory is the association of ideas, with the necessary-and-sufficient species of causal relation occasioning the strongest imaginable association.

Nevertheless, a single pairing of cause and effect is inadequate to forge a firm causal association; repeated pairings strengthen that association.

> The probabilities of causes are . . . all deriv'd from the *association of ideas to a present impression*. As the habit, which produces the association, arises from the frequent conjunction of objects, it must arrive at its perfection by degrees, and must acquire new force from each new instance, that falls under our observation. . . . 'tis by these slow steps, that our judgment arrives at a full assurance. But before it attains this pitch of perfection, it passes thro' several inferior degrees, and in all of them is only to be esteem'd a presumption or probability. (1739/1964, pp. 130–131)

In addition to the number of cause–effect pairings, the consistency of the relation affects the ultimate strength of the causal association.

> When the conjunction of any two objects is frequent, without being entirely constant, the mind is determin'd to pass from one object to the other; but not with so entire a habit, as when the union is uninterrupted, and all the instances we have ever met with are uniform and of a piece. (1739/1964, pp. 132–133)

> [Our causal beliefs] . . . cou'd not produce assurance in any single event . . . unless the fancy melted together all those images that concur, and extracted from them one single idea or image, which is intense and lively in proportion to the number of experiments from which it is deriv'd and their superiority above their antagonists. (1739/1964, p. 140)

D. Comparative Psychology of Causal Association

As we saw earlier, Hume believes that innate, mechanistic laws are involved in causal associations; thus, he can account for the swift and automatic character of our causal impressions as well as their possible presence in young infants. Yet, Hume goes still farther, by asserting the operation of the same associative principles in nonhuman animals. With this extension, he hopes to show not only the breadth of these associative principles, but also their operation in the absence of language or logic.

> . . . any theory, by which we explain the operations of the understanding, or the origin and connexion of the passions in man, will acquire additional authority, if we find, that the same theory is requisite to explain the same phenomena in all other animals. (1777/1951, p. 104)

To begin, Hume argues that animals possess clear intelligence in obtaining pleasure and avoiding pain. No less than humans, animals form associations that promote their survival. Furthermore, as Hume believes is true of humans, animals have no direct sense of interevent connection;

rather, learned associations lead them to expect one event to follow another.

> Beasts certainly never perceive any real connexion among objects. 'Tis therefore by experience they infer one from another. (1739/1964, p. 178)
>
> It is custom alone, which engages animals, from every object, that strikes their senses, to infer its usual attendant, and carries their imagination, from the appearance of the one, to conceive the other, in that particular manner, which we denominate *belief.* (1777/1951, p. 106)

III. Contemporary Animal Learning Theory

It might seem an odd encore to Hume's philosophical speculations, but contemporary theorists of learning in animals have returned to associative accounts of Pavlovian and operant conditioning after becoming dissatisfied with stimulus–response theories. The gist of those associative accounts is very much like Hume's theory of causal perception. Thus, Mackintosh (1977) equates conditioning with the perception of causal relations.

> It is generally accepted that conditioning experiments can be operationally defined as arrangements of correlations or contingencies between events. . . . The most natural interpretation of [Thorndike's and Pavlov's] experiments, therefore, is that animals detect these contingencies: exposed to these particular relationships they learn to associate these correlated events. . . . [Furthermore,] it is easy to show that these associations obey generally accepted associative laws [such as temporal and spatial contiguity and constant conjunction]. (p. 244)
>
> The subjects of a conditioning experiment, by detecting the set of contingencies in effect between various events in their environment, learn what causes those events of significance to them. . . . We are dealing with a primitive form of causal analysis—and one very much easier to study in animal subjects than in humans. . . . (p. 247)

Killeen (1981) adopts a highly similar position. He further relates associative learning to organic evolution.

> Organisms that can predict the future have an enormous evolutionary advantage over those that cannot. . . . Since a good predictor of the near future is the near past, organisms that are sensitive to recent conjunctions are prepared to exploit future conjunctions. If an animal infers from a series of conditioning trials that two stimuli will continue to be paired in the future or that a response will continue to be paired with a reinforcer, we may say that it is making a causal attribution. (p. 91)

Thus, today's researchers of learning in animals are far more prone than their predecessors to use the language of causation in their discussions of conditioning. Just how one conceptualizes the contingencies, conjunctions, and correlations of which Mackintosh and Killeen spoke has been the subject of much discussion (e.g., Gibbon, Berryman, & Thompson, 1974; Granger & Schlimmer, 1986; Hammond & Paynter, 1983; Rescorla, 1967; Seligman, Maier, & Solomon, 1971). So, too, has been the way in which those contingencies have been hypothesized to affect the behavior of organisms (e.g., Bloomfield, 1972; Gibbon & Balsam, 1981; Jenkins, Barnes, & Barrera, 1981; Rescorla & Wagner, 1972). We will turn to these issues later.

IV. Causal Perception in Humans

Given the profundity of Hume's analysis, it is indeed curious that so little experimental attention has been paid to causal perception in humans. Michotte (1963) did conduct some interesting studies of the "launching" effect: the report of one moving object "impelling" motion in another with which it temporally and spatially coincides. Nevertheless, these investigations had rather little impact on later research and theory. Far more influential were the studies of Smedslund (1963) and Jenkins and Ward (1965) into subjects' assessments of interevent consistency or contingency. Unfortunately, the data from these studies cast a dark shadow on humans accomplishing what was becoming a mundane feat for nonhuman animals.

For example, Jenkins and Ward (1965; Experiment I) had subjects press one of two buttons (R_1 or R_2) on each of five different 60-trial problems. The problems differed from one another in the relation that held between pressing R_1 or R_2 and the occurrence of "score" or "no score" outcomes. In three noncontingent problems, the "score" light was equiprobable after R_1 and R_2, although the overall likelihood of the "score" light varied (.133 vs. .133, .500 vs. .500; and .800 vs. .800 for R_1 vs. R_2); in two contingent problems, the probability of the "score" light differed after R_1 and R_2 to varying degrees (.200 vs. .800 and .500 vs. .800 for R_1 vs. R_2).[1] When asked to judge how much control over the trial outcome they could exert by pressing the different buttons—from 0 (no control) to 100 (complete control)—subjects made ratings that were "entirely unrelated to the actual degree of contingency" (p. 1).

Jenkins and Ward found these results to be quite consistent with those of Smedslund (1963) who, using very different methods, had concluded

---

[1] Simply subtracting one probability from the other here allows one to quantify the *strength* of the response–outcome relation from .00 to 1.00.

that "adult subjects with no statistical training apparently have no adequate concept of correlation" (p. 165). Yet, Jenkins and Ward were appropriately careful not to overgeneralize their pessimistic conclusion that "the subjects in the present experiment were without a concept of contingency" (p. 15).

> [This conclusion] is not intended to preclude the possibility that far more valid judgments of the same statistical structures could be made if the events were cast in a different context. An example of such a context might be one in which . . . a momentary input appears against a background of nonoccurrence and is followed, with some probability, by an output event which also appears as the interruption of a resting state. (p. 15)

It just so happens that these possibly more conducive conditions are precisely those of a simple free-operant conditioning arrangement, usually given to animal subjects. Clearly, the highly orderly changes in animal behavior engendered by these operant contingencies (Ferster & Skinner, 1957) suggest that adult humans ought to be no less sensitive to those response–outcome relations. Killeen (1981) had earlier speculated that "the conditions that promote learning [in animals] . . . are often seen to be consistent with . . . situations that elicit a causal inference from naive humans" (p. 89). Thus, we decided to put this proposition to empirical test.

What follows is a brief odyssey through nearly 10 years of research in our Iowa laboratory on humans' detection of response–outcome contingencies.

V. Research on Response–Outcome Contingency

Our original investigations into college students' causal ratings of response–outcome contingencies were based upon a procedure devised by Hammond (1980) to study operant conditioning in rats. The essence of this procedure is to discretize time into brief samples (e.g., 1 sec) and to arrange an outcome *(O)* to occur with one probability if a subject responds *(R)* in a sample and with a different probability if a subject does not respond *(No R)* in a sample. With this method, one can schedule all possible response–outcome relations that are created by independently varying *P(O/R)* and *P(O/No R)*.

Note that the most deterministic causal contingency is one in which *P(O/R)* = 1.00 and *P(O/No R)* = .00. Note also that, with *P(O/R)* = .00 and *P(O/No R)* = 1.00, we can create an equally deterministic preventive contingency. But, such deterministic relations are hardly the only ones possible nor are they likely to be the ones most prevalent in the environment. Thus, *positive contingencies* can vary in strength from .00 to 1.00, so long as $P(O/R) > P(O/No\ R)$; and, *negative contingencies* can vary in strength from .00 to 1.00, so long as $P(O/R) < (P(O/No\ R)$. Finally, *noncontingent relations* are those in which $P(O/R) = P(O/No\ R)$, no matter what overall $P(O)$ is arranged. For simplicity, we will define response–outcome contingency as $P(O/R) - P(O/No\ R)$, recognizing that this so-called "Delta P" measure is one of several ways of expressing both the *sign* and the *strength* of the relation (Allan, 1980).

A. Sensitivity to Response–Outcome Relations

We have conducted several studies of adults' sensitivity to probabilistic response–outcome relations. This section describes both published and unpublished work which discloses that, under proper conditions, humans can be exquisitely sensitive judges of response–outcome contingency.

1. Experiment 1

Our first study (Wasserman, Chatlosh, & Neunaber, 1983, Experiment 1) sought conditions which would support highly sensitive and unbiased judgments of contingency. Following the suggestion of Jenkins and Ward (1965), we used only a single response (contacting a telegraph key) which the subject might or might not perform and a single outcome (the brief illumination of a lamp) which might or might not follow a response. We arranged our contingencies on a free-operant basis because of problems posed by introducing intertrial intervals, during which responses and outcomes are effectively eliminated (see Allan & Jenkins, 1980, 1983; Alloy & Abramson, 1979). And, we contrived our contingencies so as to define responses in either a discrete or a continuous way, in order to emulate different response styles which people use when making causal judgments. Thus, when troubleshooting a malfunctioning radio, an electronics technician might tap a suspicious component; or, when tuning a sputtering engine, an automobile mechanic might change the carburetor setting by turning the adjusting screw to a new location and then hold it there for several seconds.

The response–outcome relations we studied entailed positive, zero, and negative contingencies. Positive contingencies have generally been studied more often than negative contingencies. When both kinds of contingencies were explored, only ratings of relationship strength (not sign) had been taken (Allan & Jenkins, 1983; Alloy & Abramson, 1979).[2] Therefore, we solicited subjects' judgments of both the magnitude and the direction of the contingencies. We also studied several noncontingent relations to ascertain whether judgments were biased by the overall probability of the outcome, as had been reported by others (e.g., Allan & Jenkins, 1980; Alloy & Abramson, 1979).

A total of 72 college students were assigned either to the discrete-response (Tap, $n = 36$) or to the continuous-response (Press, $n = 36$) conditions. They were asked "to find out whether [contacting] a telegraph key has any effect on the occurrence of a white light" by freely responding on the key. They were also told that "in order to make accurate estimates, you must know what happens when you [contact] the key and when you don't [contact] it." Subjects in both conditions were randomly given nine problems to respond to and rate. These problems factorially combined three levels, .125, .500, and .875, of the two conditional probabilities, $P(O/R)$ and $P(O/No\ R)$. The nine problems in turn defined five different response–outcome contingencies, $P(O/R) - P(O/No\ R)$: +.750 (.875 − .125), +.375 (.875 − .500 and .500 − .125), .00 (.875 − .875, .500 − .500 and .125 − .125), −.375 (.500 − .875 and .125 − .500), and −.750 (.125 − .875). Note that the positive and negative contingencies were less than perfect and were symmetrical around zero. Also note that the three noncontingent problems varied according to the overall likelihood of outcome occurrence, $P(O)$, from .125 to .500 to .875.

These probabilities were scheduled slightly differently in the Tap and Press tasks. In the Tap task, 1-sec sampling intervals were defined. If the subject responded on the telegraph key at least once at any time during a sampling interval, $P(O/R)$ was probed at the end of the 1-sec interval; otherwise, $P(O/No\ R)$ was probed. If the probe was positive, a .10-sec illumination of a white outcome light was given, after which another sampling interval began; if the probe was negative, no light was presented and another sampling interval immediately began. Each problem was signaled by illumination of a red problem light and comprised 240 successive sampling intervals. In the Press task, 1-sec sampling intervals were also defined. Here, however, the telegraph key had to be depressed when a 1-sec interval ended in order to probe $P(O/R)$; otherwise, $P(O/No\ R)$ was probed. In all other respects, the Press task was identical to the Tap task.

After each problem, subjects were asked to pick the number from −100 (prevents light from occurring) to 0 (has no effect on light) to +100 (causes light to occur) that best characterized the effect of telegraph-key

---

[2]Shanks and Dickinson (1987) have occasionally used a bidirectional rating scale in their research, published after our initial report.

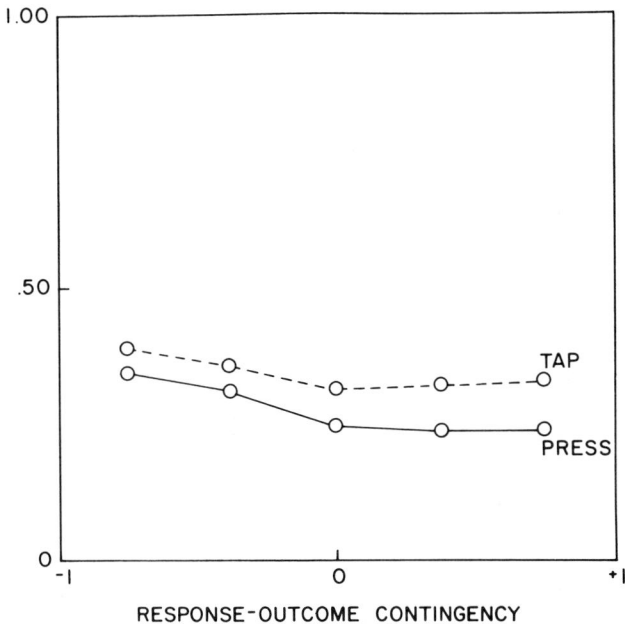

Fig. 1. Mean probability of making a recorded response for Group Tap and Group Press of Experiment 1 at each of the five levels of response–outcome contingency. From Wasserman et al. (1983).

responding. Subjects were also informed that "the problems differ from one another" and that "it is important that you not let your judgment on any given problem affect your judgment on any of the other problems."

Figure 1 shows telegraph-key responding in the Tap and Press conditions at each of the five levels of response–outcome contingency. These 5-point functions were constructed from the nine individual problems, whose data are shown in Table I. Regardless of the contingency, the probability of a recorded response was higher in the Tap task (.34) than in the Press task (.27), possibly because of the way responses were defined in the two tasks. Across both tasks, increases in the contingency led to slight decreases in response probability, especially as the contingency rose from −.750 to .000. This unexpected result might be due to greater difficulty of detecting negative than positive contingencies (Erlick & Mills, 1967), thus requiring more information about the consequences of responding in the negative contingencies. To examine the role of the overall probability of the outcome on response probability, the three noncon-

TABLE I

Mean Probability of Making a Recorded Response in Experiment 1[a]

P(O/R)	P(O/No R)		
	.125	.500	.875
Group Tap			
.875	.33	.33	.31
.500	.32	.34	.34
.125	.30	.38	.39
Group Press			
.875	.24	.22	.23
.500	.25	.25	.30
.125	.26	.33	.34

[a]From Wasserman et al. (1983).

tingent problems were selected from the full problem set.[3] As was true for the full problem set, regardless of the outcome probability, the probability of a response was higher in the Tap task (.31) than in the Press task (.25). However, the probability of the outcome did not systematically affect the probability of telegraph-key responding (see the entries in the positive diagonals of Table I).

Figure 2 shows subjects' scaled ratings (divided by 100 to vary over the same range as the contingencies) in the Tap and Press conditions at each of the five levels of response–outcome contingency. These 5-point functions were constructed from the nine individual problems, whose data are shown in Table II. Across both tasks, ratings rose as a strong function of increases in the contingency. The contingency-rating function from the Tap task was notably steeper than that from the Press task and it more nearly conformed to the positive diagonal in Fig. 2, which represents isomorphism between the subjects' scaled rating scores and the nominal contingencies. To examine the role of the overall probability of the outcome on contingency ratings, the three noncontingent problems were again selected from the full problem set. Here, ratings were not systematically affected by the probability of outcome occurrence (see the entries in the positive diagonals of Table II).

Although the contingency-rating functions in Fig. 2 suggest that the two

---

[3]The response-contingent problems were excluded because there responding affected the probability of an outcome.

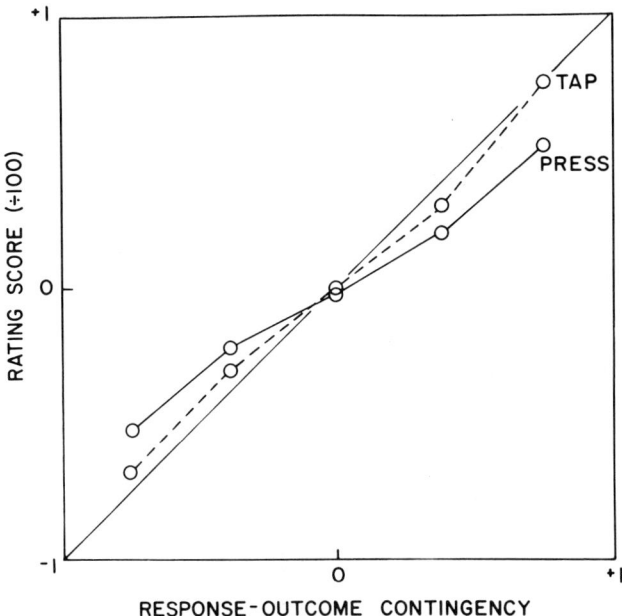

Fig. 2. Mean scaled causal ratings (divided by 100) for Group Tap and Group Press of Experiment 1 at each of the five levels of response–outcome contingency. From Wasserman et al. (1983).

TABLE II

MEAN SCALED RATING SCORES IN EXPERIMENT 1[a]

	P(O/No R)		
P(O/R)	.125	.500	.875
Group Tap			
.875	.75	.24	.01
.500	.36	.02	−.19
.125	−.02	−.41	−.68
Group Press			
.875	.52	.17	−.03
.500	.24	−.04	−.15
.125	.00	−.29	−.52

[a]From Wasserman et al. (1983).

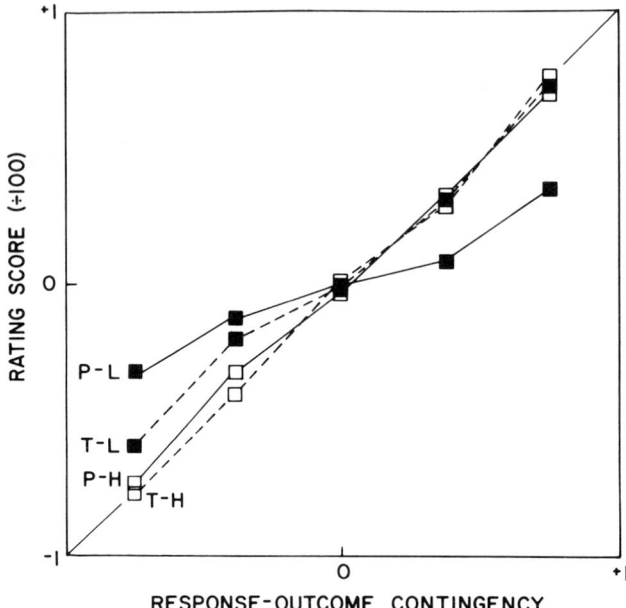

Fig. 3. Mean scaled causal ratings (divided by 100) for Press-Low (P-L), Tap-Low (T-L), Press-High (P-H), and Tap-High (T-H) subgroups in Experiment 1 at each of the five levels of response–outcome contingency. From Wasserman et al. (1983).

tasks directly supported different levels of discriminative performance, the fact that the probability of a recorded response also differed in the two tasks raises another interpretation: Perhaps the shallower contingency-rating function in the Press condition was the result of these subjects' lower likelihood of making a recorded response. Departures in either direction from .50 might compromise the accuracy of subjects' ratings; indeed, with probabilities of a recorded response equal to either .00 or 1.00, ratings would have to reflect guessing.

As one way of exploring the idea that biased sampling of response and nonresponse options contributed to the contingency ratings, subjects in the Tap and Press tasks were first rank ordered according to the overall probability of making a recorded response across all nine problems. Then, each group was split at the median response probability. The four resulting subgroups in order of response probability (in parentheses) were Press-Low (.17), Tap-Low (.23), Press-High (.37), and Tap-High (.44). The contingency-rating functions of these subgroups are depicted in Fig. 3. Consistent with the biased sampling interpretation, increases in the probability of a response toward .50 were associated with progressive steepening of the contingency-rating function, with the Tap-High subgroup's scaled performance virtually isomorphic with the nominal response–outcome contingencies.

Having been inspired by the goal of devising a judgment paradigm that would be highly sensitive to response–outcome contingency, the results of this first experiment were very encouraging. Either of two free-operant tasks could support judgments that were strong functions of contingency; indeed, under certain circumstances, those scaled judgments were almost perfectly associated with an objective measure of contingency, $P(O/R) - P(O/No\ R)$. The strong linearity of the contingency-rating functions and their symmetry about zero indicate that judgments of positive and negative contingencies can be equally accurate. And, failure for the overall likelihood of outcome occurrence, $P(O)$, to influence ratings of noncontingency implies that these free-operant procedures are unbiased by the most commonly reported contaminant of contingency judgments.

2. Experiment 2

Given the unflattering portrait of human causal judgment painted by Jenkins and Ward (1965) and others (Crocker, 1981; Nisbett & Ross, 1980), we were both surprised and delighted by the success of our very first venture into this domain. But what was responsible for this success?

Certainly, the free-operant procedure is a good candidate, with its single response, single outcome, and uninterrupted interaction of responses and outcomes. But, it is unlikely to be entirely responsible for sensitive and unbiased ratings, for Allan and Jenkins (1983) obtained good judgment performance from subjects given a 2-response–2-outcome discrete-trial procedure. Another possible factor was our use of a *bidirectional* rating scale rather than the more common *unidirectional* rating scale.

Experiment 2 (Neunaber & Wasserman, 1986) examined the effect of the different rating methods on subjects' estimates of response–outcome contingency. Two groups were given identical sets of problems. One (as in Experiment 1) was asked to rate both the sign and the strength of the contingencies along a bidirectional -100 to $+100$ scale. The second was asked to rate only the strength of the same contingencies along a unidirectional 0 to 100 scale; these subjects were told to "choose the number between 0 and 100 on the rating scale that best characterizes the degree to which your tapping of the telegraph key controlled the occurrence of the white light, from 'has no control over the light' to 'has complete control over the light.'" If the different rating procedures were without effect, than the *unsigned* scores of the bidirectional group should correspond to the *raw* scores of the unidirectional group. However, if the different rating procedures support different degrees of bias or accuracy, then the scores should differ.

Using the Tap procedure from Experiment 1, 52 college students were assigned to the bidirectional (B, $n = 26$) and unidirectional (U, $n = 26$) rating conditions, and each subject was randomly given 13 150-sample response–outcome contingencies. The problems included four positive and four negative contingencies, $P(O/R) - P(O/No\ R)$: $+.80\ (.90 - .10)$, $+.60\ (.80 - .20)$, $+.40\ (.70 - .30)$, $+.20\ (.60 - .40)$, $-.20\ (.40 - .60)$, $-.40\ (.30 - .70)$, $-.60\ (.20 - .80)$, and $-.80\ (.10 - .90)$. Also included were five noncontingent problems that varied in outcome probability: $P(O/R) - P(O/No\ R) = .00\ (.10 - .10, .30 - .30, .50 - .50, .70 - .70,$ and $.90 - .90)$.

In order to compare performance here with our prior results, the scaled contingency ratings of subjects in the bidirectional condition were first considered separately, retaining the sign of each rating. The upper panel of Fig. 4 shows the resulting mean ratings at each of the nine levels of contingency. Ratings again were a strong direct function of contingency. The lower panel of Fig. 4 shows bidirectional subjects' mean rating scores at each of the five levels of outcome probability in the noncontingent problems. Ratings again were not systematically affected by outcome probability and were very close to zero. These results thus replicate those of Experiment 1 using several different contingencies.

In order to compare ratings on the bidirectional and unidirectional scales, it was necessary to constrain the range of the bidirectional scale to the range of the unidirectional scale. This constraint was accomplished by simply taking the *absolute value* of each rating made on the bidirectional scale. The upper panel of Fig. 5A shows subjects' mean rating scores in both the bidirectional and the unidirectional scale conditions at each of the nine levels of contingency. In both conditions, more extreme positive and negative contingencies occasioned higher ratings; but, in the unidirectional condition, the contingency-rating function was notably shallower, particularly in the region of negative contingencies (also see Allan & Jenkins, 1983, Experiment 2; Alloy & Abramson, 1979, Experiment 4). The lower panel of Fig. 5A shows the mean bidirectional and unidirectional rating scores at each of the five levels of outcome probability in the noncontingent problems. Ratings in neither condition were notably biased by outcome probability, and scores were closest to zero at the highest level of outcome probability. Interestingly, ratings here departed from the programmed value of zero more than the signed bidirectional ratings depicted in the lower panel of Fig. 4. This difference suggests that when both the sign *and* the strength of the contingency are rated (as in

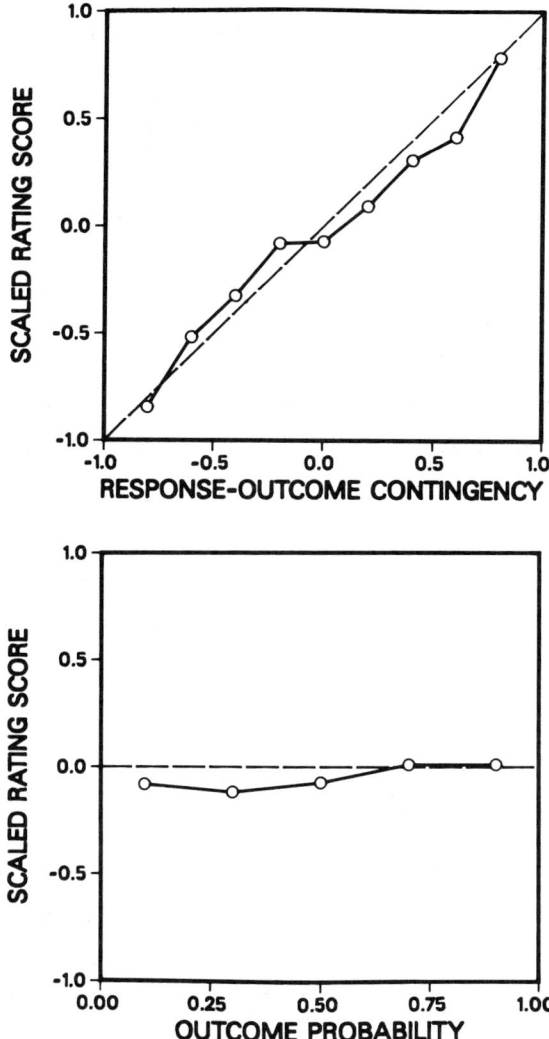

Fig. 4. Mean scaled (divided by 100) *signed* ratings at the nine levels of contingency (upper panel) and the five levels of outcome probability (lower panel) for the bidirectional condition of Experiment 2. From Neunaber and Wasserman (1986).

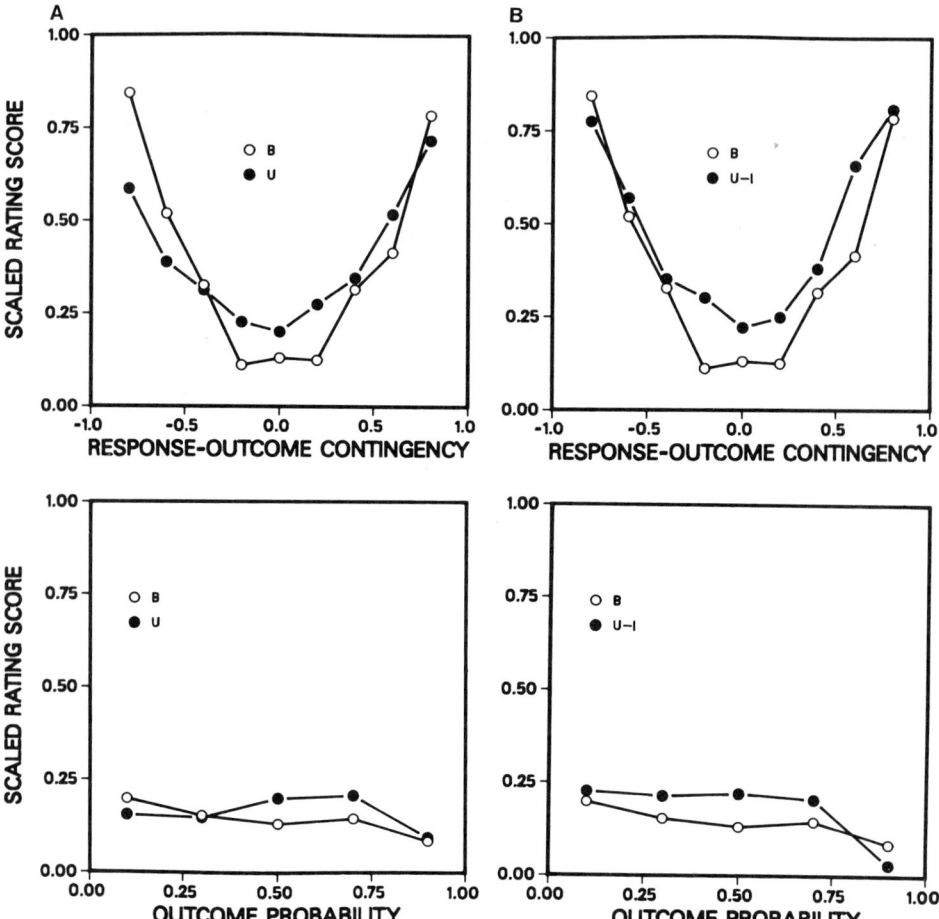

Fig. 5. (A) Mean scaled (divided by 100) *unsigned* ratings at the nine levels of contingency (upper panel) and the five levels of outcome probability (lower panel) for the bidirectional (B) and unidirectional (U) conditions of Experiment 2. From Neunaber and Wasserman (1986). (B) Mean scaled (divided by 100) *unsigned* ratings at the nine levels of contingency (upper panel) and the five levels of outcome probability (lower panel) for the bidirectional (B) and unidirectional-informed (U-I) conditions of Experiment 2. From Neunaber and Wasserman (1986).

the bidirectional condition), subjects' estimates tend to vary around zero in both a positive and a negative direction and to have a mean near zero. However, when only the strength of the relationship is rated—either by taking the absolute value of subjects' scores in the bidirectional condition or by using a unidirectional judgment of control scale—both positive and negative judgments are expressed as positive ratings, thereby producing an upwardly shifted mean.

Just why did ratings differ in the two conditions? Subjects in the unidirectional condition were asked to judge the control their responses exerted over the outcome and they were not told that control referred both to causing and to preventing the outcome. On the other hand, subjects in the bidirectional condition were told of the prevent–cause nature of the contingencies and were asked to make ratings along a bidirectional scale. Thus, the two conditions differed in terms of (1) the nature of the judgment scale and (2) the information given about the prevent–cause nature of control.

To evaluate these two factors, a third condition was studied. In this unidirectional-informed condition (U-I, $n = 26$), subjects were told that "control means that tapping the telegraph key either *causes* the light to occur or *prevents* the light from occurring." Subjects here were given the same 13 contingencies as were subjects in the other two conditions.

The upper panel of Fig. 5B shows subjects' mean rating scores in both the bidirectional and the unidirectional-informed conditions at each of the nine levels of contingency. As in Fig. 5A, more extreme positive and negative contingencies occasioned higher ratings in both conditions; and, although the contingency-rating function of the unidirectional-informed condition was a bit shallower overall, there was no longer any tendency for subjects to underestimate the most extreme negative contingencies. These results suggest that, without specific instructions, subjects using a unidirectional judgment-of-control scale may not spontaneously equate "control" with being able to prevent an outcome, leading them to underestimate negative contingencies. Explicit instructions about causation and prevention eliminated the asymmetry of subjects' judgment of positive and negative contingencies, but the bidirectional scale still supported steeper contingency-judgment functions than the unidirectional scale. The latter result may have been due to a reluctance for subjects given the unidirectional scale to make ratings near the zero end. Because the zero point on the bidirectional scale was in the middle of the range, subjects here may have been less reluctant to make ratings in the zero region. The bottom panel of Fig. 5B shows the mean rating scores in both the bidirectional and the unidirectional-informed conditions at each of the five levels of outcome probability in the noncontingent problems. As in

Fig. 5A, ratings were not upwardly biased as $P(O)$ was increased; ratings were again closest to zero when $P(O)$ was .90.

Subjects' ratings of the noncontingent problems under the different rating-scale conditions deserve special comment, considering rival reports of increasing bias with increasing outcome probability (also see Baker, Berbrier, & Vallee-Tourangeau, 1989; Shanks & Dickinson, 1987). When both the sign and the strength of the contingency were rated, our subjects' estimates had a mean near zero; however, when only the strength of the relationship was assessed, both positive and negative judgments were expressed as positive scores and therefore had an upwardly biased mean. Thus, when only the strength of the response–outcome relationship is rated (as it is in most published reports), it is extremely difficult to discriminate judgments of "causal" control from high judgment variance with a (bidirectional) mean near zero or from an aversion to using the zero end of the scale. We thus urge considerable caution in interpreting the results of studies using a unidirectional rating scale and reporting nonzero mean ratings of noncontingent problems.

All in all, these data persuade us that the bidirectional rating scale we have employed is one key ingredient to our obtaining highly sensitive and generally unbiased estimates of response–outcome contingency.

3. Experiment 3

To this point, the task set for our subjects was purely informational: to find out and report the effect of telegraph-key responding on the white light. Here, we wanted to assess the behavioral effects of making the light a desired outcome; now, each occurrence stood for one "point." By so doing, we could see whether the responding of our humans for points reinforcement, like the behavior of rats for biological reinforcement (Hammond, 1980; Tomie & Loukas, 1983), was directly related to $P(O/R)$ and inversely related to $P(O/No\ R)$. By studying other subjects for whom the light was not an incentive (as in Experiments 1 and 2), we could also see whether judgments of contingency were affected by the nature of the scheduled outcome. A final purpose of this experiment (Chatlosh, Neunaber, & Wasserman, 1985, Experiment 1) was to evaluate the role played by the duration of the sampling interval. Here, it was possible that subjects' sensitivity to response–outcome relations might be decidedly greater when the sampling interval was 1 sec long than when it was 4 sec long, if for no other reason than that shorter response–outcome delays should hold in the former condition (Gruber, Fink, & Damm, 1957; Shanks, Pearson, & Dickinson, 1989).

A total of 108 college students served. Half (points) were told that they would receive one point each time a white light occurred; the other half were instructed as in Experiments 1 and 2 (no points). Within each of these main conditions, subjects were assigned to three subgroups. In the 1-sec (240) condition, each problem consisted of 240 1-sec sampling intervals. In the 4-sec (60) condition, each problem consisted of 60 4-sec sampling intervals, thus equaling the overall duration of each problem in the 1-sec (240) condition. And in the 1-sec (60) condition, each problem consisted of 60 1-sec sampling intervals, thus equaling the total number of sampling intervals in the 4-sec (60) condition. Each of the six resulting subgroups ($n = 18$) was given the same contingencies, instructions, and rating scale as the Tap group in Experiment 1.

The upper panels of Fig. 6 illustrate the mean scaled rating scores of each scheduled contingency, for each subgroup, under both incentive conditions. In all cases, ratings were strong direct functions of the scheduled contingency; there were no notable differences among any of the six depicted functions. The lower panels of Fig. 6 illustrate the mean scaled rating scores in all six conditions as a function of outcome probability in the three noncontingent problems. There was a slight rise in ratings as $P(O)$ rose from .125 to .500 to .875; but, ratings were generally nearest to zero when $P(O)$ was .875. Once again, ratings were not notably different in any of the six depicted functions. Thus, ratings of response–outcome contingency here were made with great sensitivity and little bias despite differences in the incentive value of the outcome, changes in the time sample used for contingency scheduling, and variations in the amount of sampling information. Clearly, the robust judgment data in our probabilistic paradigm are not limited to a specific concatenation of experimental circumstances.

Figure 7 depicts the probability of responding in the points condition, under each of the 5 levels of contingency, in each of the subgroups, over successive blocks of 6 sampling intervals. Certainly within 5 blocks of exposure (30 sampling intervals) all subgroups evidenced contingency-sensitive behavior: responding at high probabilities under positive contingencies (where more responding occasions more points), responding at low probabilities under negative contingencies (where less responding occasions more points), and responding at an intermediate probability under noncontingency (where responding has no effect on points). Over the last half of training, all subgroups showed probabilities of key tapping which were strong direct functions of the scheduled contingency, with the only discernible difference being that response probability varied over a slightly smaller range in the 1-sec (60) condition than in the other two conditions.

The fact that increases in contingency produced *graded* increases in

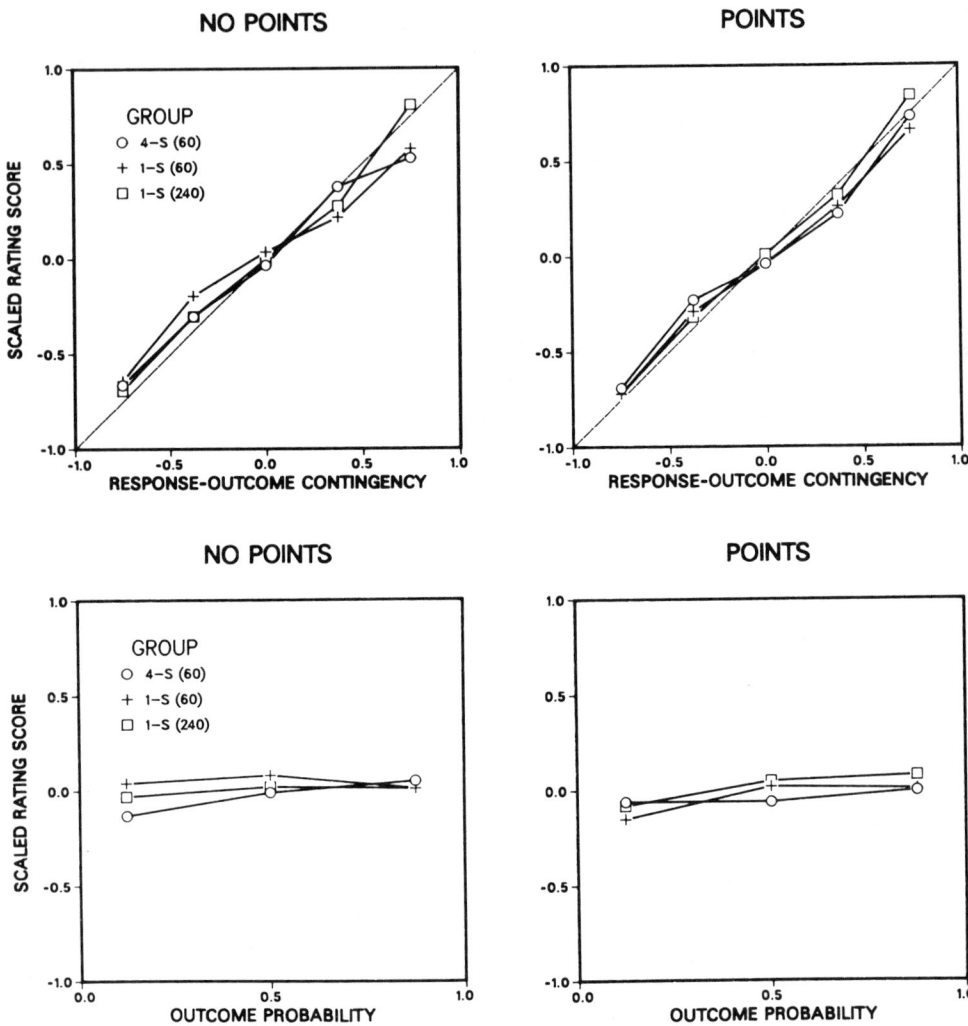

Fig. 6. Mean scaled causal ratings (divided by 100) for the 4-sec (60 samples), 1-sec (60 samples), and 1-sec (240 samples) subgroups in the no-points and points conditions at each of the five levels of response–outcome contingency in Experiment 3 (upper panels). Mean scaled causal ratings (divided by 100) on noncontingent problems for 4-sec (60 samples), 1-sec (60 samples), and 1-sec (240 samples) subgroups in the no-points and points conditions at each of the three levels of outcome probability (lower panels). From Chatlosh et al. (1985).

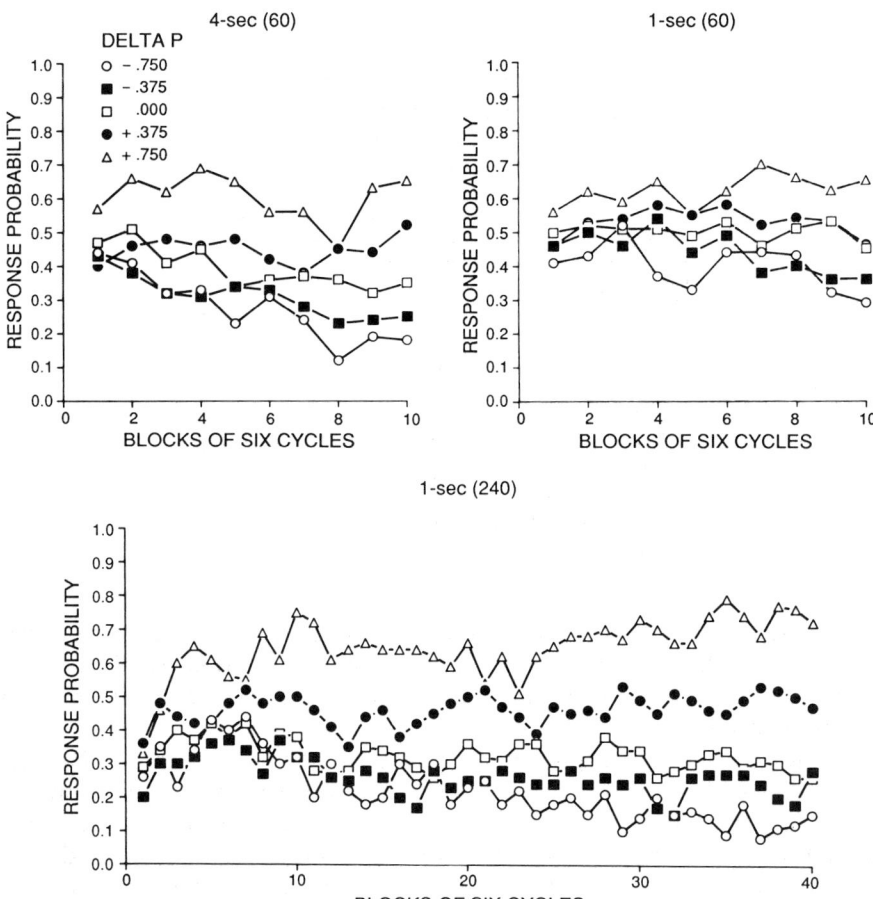

Fig. 7. Mean probability of making a recorded response in blocks of six cycles for each of the five levels of response–outcome contingency in the following groups: 4-sec (60 samples), 1-sec (60 samples), and 1-sec (240 samples) in the points condition of Experiment 3. From Chatlosh et al. (1985).

terminal response probability indicates that subjects were not behaving optimally in terms of maximizing reinforcement. A maximization rule predicts *categorical* responding to contingencies as determined by the *valence* of $P(O/R) - P(O/No\ R)$ [i.e, a step function where $P(R) = 0$ for all negative contingencies and $P(R) = 1$ for all positive contingencies]. Graded differences in response probability as a function of contingency suggest the operation of some other response rule. Conditional matching represents an alternative that might better describe our subjects' response

TABLE III

MATCHING TO CONDITIONAL REINFORCEMENT PROBABILITIES IN EXPERIMENT 3[a]

	P(O/No R)		
P(O/R)	.125	.500	.875
Predicted P(R)			
.875	.875	.636	.500
.500	.800	.500	.364
.125	.500	.200	.125
Obtained P(R)			
.875	.673	.463	.272
.500	.512	.392	.321
.125	.386	.275	.204

[a] Obtained P(R)s are from the last block of training. From Chatlosh et al. (1985).

patterns. It predicts that, for any given reinforcement contingency, response probability should match the relative conditional reinforcement probability in the following manner: $P(R) = P(O/R)/[P(O/R) + P(O/No\ R)]$ (Gibbon et al., 1974).

Table III gives the expected $P(R)$ for each of the problems of Experiment 3, plus the means of the obtained terminal response probabilities (from the last block of six cycles, collapsed across the three subgroups) from the points condition. The expected and obtained probabilities do not closely concur; the range of the obtained means is restricted and response probabilities for zero contingencies are lower than predicted. But, the conditional matching rule does succeed in ranking the means obtained from the nonzero contingencies; and, it correctly orders the obtained response probabilities for equivalent Delta P's that were derived from different pairs of conditional probabilities (i.e., the +.375 and −.375 problems). Observe, finally, that $P(O/R)$ and $P(O/No\ R)$ affected our human subjects' behavior in much the same way as they affect the behavior of nonhuman animals: $P(O/R)$ being directly related and $P(O/No\ R)$ being inversely related to $P(R)$ (Hammond, 1980; Tomie & Loukas, 1983). With only one exception (the .875 − .875 contingency), increases in $P(O/R)$ led to increases in $P(R)$ at all levels of $P(O/No\ R)$; invariably, increases in $P(O/No\ R)$ led to decreases in $P(R)$ at all levels of $P(O/R)$.

Thus, the direct effects of response–outcome contingency on humans' key-tapping behavior were as pronounced as the effects that are less directly measured by subjects' postcontingency reports.

4. Experiment 4

The sensitivity of college students' telegraph-key responding to response–outcome contingencies in Experiment 3 prompted D. K. Franson, D. L. Chatlosh, and me to conduct a further study into this area. Here, contingencies might not only differ from problem to problem, but they might also change *within* the very same problem. No postproblem ratings were taken; instead, telegraph-key tapping was recorded in 5-sec intervals in order to ascertain sensitivity to changes in the prevailing contingency.

A total of 28 college students served. Under the general regime of the points condition in Experiment 3, subjects were told that "this experiment is a game in which you can earn points by getting the white light to come on. Every time the white light comes on, you will earn one point." Subjects were further told that "in some problems it may be to your advantage to tap the key, and in others it may not." Finally, subjects were advised that "to make the task even more challenging, within each problem tapping may have different effects at different times."

Each subject responded to eight schedules; the first was a sample problem that always involved an unchanging contingent relationship. One of the seven remaining randomly scheduled problems also entailed the same unchanging contingent relationship between responses and outcomes. For each of these unchanging schedules, $P(O/R) = .80$ and $P(O/No\ R) = .20$ for all 200 1-sec sampling intervals.[4] Three problems entailed change from a contingent to a noncontingent relationship; in these, the contingency changed from $.80 - .20$ to $.80 - .80$, $.50 - .50$, or $.20 - .20$. The other three problems entailed change from a noncontingent to a contingent relationship; in these, the contingency changed from $.80 - .80$, $.50 - .50$, and $.20 - .20$ to $.80 - .20$. Each problem was signaled by illumination of a green light and comprised 200 1-sec sampling intervals. In schedules that involved an unsignaled contingency change, the change occurred after 100 sampling intervals.

Figure 8 shows preshift (Block -1) and postshift (Blocks 1, 2, 3, 4, 5, 6, 19, and 20) key tapping in the six problems entailing changes in the response–outcome contingency. The top panel illustrates that the shift from noncontingency to contingency occasioned a rapid rise in responding; within a mere 10 sec, key tapping evidenced a notable increase, which either persisted or increased as training continued. Over the course of postshift performance, there was a tendency for key tapping in the $.80 - .80/.80 - .20$ condition to be below that in the $.50 - .50/.80 - .20$ and

---

[4]The data from this schedule are of little interest to us here; but, for the record, responding began near .40 in the first 5-sec block and finished near .70 in the last 5-sec block.

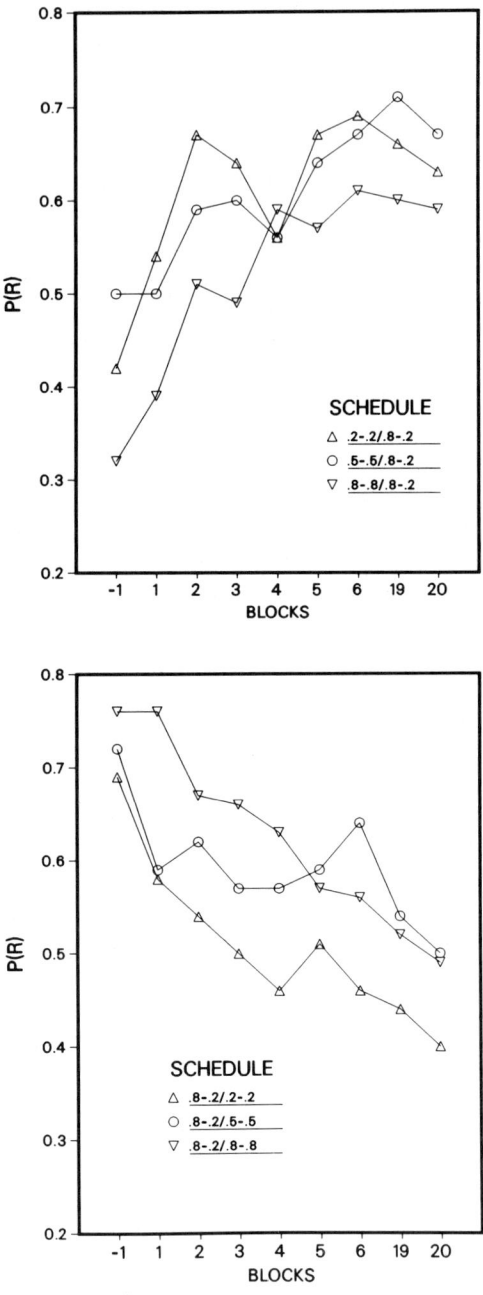

Fig. 8. The probability of key tapping before (Block −1) and after (Blocks 1, 2, 3, 4, 5, 6, 19, 20) a change in the prevailing response–outcome contingency in Experiment 4. The change was either a gain (upper panel) or a loss (lower panel) of control over the point light. Responding is shown as a function of 5-sec blocks of training.

.20 − .20/.80 −.20 conditions. One is tempted to attribute this result to the fact that the .80 − .80/.80 − .20 condition alone did not entail an increase in *P(O/R);* however, over the course of *preshift* performance, responding under the .80 − .80 contingency also fell below that under the .50 − .50 and .20 − .20 contingencies (see Block -1 for representative scores).[5] The bottom panel of Fig. 8 illustrates that the shift from contingency to noncontingency occasioned a fast fall in responding; within just 10 sec, key tapping evidenced a notable decrease, which continued to decline as training continued. Over the course of postshift performance, there was a tendency for key tapping in the .80 −.20/.20 − .20 condition to be below that in the .80 − .20/.50 − .50 and .80 −.20/.80 − .80 conditions. This result may be ascribed to the fact that the .80 −.20/.20 − .20 condition entailed the largest decrease in *P(O/R)*.

In sum, these results clearly document an ability of college students to detect both increases and decreases in the prevailing response–outcome contingency—within only 10 sec. Subsequent unpublished work has obtained similar results with both positive and negative outcomes, in subjects both informed and uninformed of the changing contingencies, and with clinically depressed and nondepressed college students (Neunaber, 1986). The robustness of this result and its dramatic speed relative to that seen in nonhuman animals (cf. Lattal, 1973) is further testimony to the sensitivity of humans to response–outcome contingency.

B. Cognitive Processes of Contingency Judgment

Having demonstrated in the first four experiments that humans can sensitively judge probabilistic response–outcome relations, we now turn to the more difficult question, "Just what cognitive processes participate in judgments of contingency?" This section describes several published and unpublished studies which begin to elucidate the processes of judging response–outcome relations.

1. *Strategy Analysis of Experiment 1*

One approach to understanding the cognitive processes of contingency judgment revolves around the mathematical rules or strategies which subjects may use to compute the prevailing interevent relations.[6] In particu-

---

[5] Here and in prior published work (Chatlosh *et al.*, 1985), we have generally found response probability to be inversely related to outcome probability under conditions of noncontingent points or monetary reinforcement, in clear contrast to expectations based upon Skinner's (1948) analysis of superstitious behavior.

[6] For a review and critique of this area of investigation see Shaklee, 1983.

lar, Allan and Jenkins (1980, 1983) identified five judgment rules that are calculable from the contents of a 2 × 2 contingency table: cell a = R, O; cell b = R, No O; cell c = No R, O; and cell d = No R, No O. The Delta P strategy entails subjects' use of the normatively valid difference in conditional probability metric, $P(O/R) - P(O/No\ R)$, computed from the contingency table as $[a/(a+b)] - [c/(c+d)]$. The somewhat sophisticated, but normatively invalid, Delta D strategy involves subjects' subtraction of the table's diagonal totals $(a + d) - (b + c)$. A third and generally inaccurate rule utilizes only two of the table's four frequency entries—cells a and c. Here, the Delta F comparison is $(a - c)$. Two other invalid rules do not compare the contents of the cells. The Number O strategy entails subjects' use of the total number of outcomes, calculated as $(a + c)$. The Number RO rule involves subjects' use of the number of times that response and outcome coincide—cell a. By correlating each subject's judgments with each of the five strategies, the hope is to pinpoint the cognitive bases of those judgments.

However, as Allan and Jenkins (1983) point out, discrimination among some of the judgment strategies becomes increasingly difficult as $P(R)$ approaches $P(No\ R)$; when $P(R) = P(No\ R)$, three of the rules, Delta P, Delta D, and Delta F, are perfectly correlated with one another. Thus, to get clearer discrimination among the rules, one must examine situations in which $P(R)$ and $P(No\ R)$ are very different from one another.

One such case was reported by Allan and Jenkins (1983, Experiment 3). There, when $P(R) = .70$ and $P(No\ R) = .30$, subjects' contingency ratings were better correlated with the Delta D rule than with the Delta P rule and ratings were relatively inaccurate and strongly biased by $P(O)$; ratings were more accurate, less biased, and better correlated with the Delta P rule when $P(R) = P(No\ R) = .50$. Allan and Jenkins concluded that subjects in *both* conditions were basing their judgments of response–outcome contingency not on the accurate Delta P rule, but on the less accurate Delta D rule. Such rule use could, however, only be seen when $P(R)$ and $P(No\ R)$ were quite different. If subjects in our experiments were also using the Delta D rule rather than the Delta P rule, then the accuracy of the contingency-rating function should have fallen (as it did in Experiment 1) when $P(R)$ decreased from .50 toward .00.

To ascertain rule use in our first experiment, we repeated Allan and Jenkins' strategy analysis on the four subgroups whose data are depicted in Fig. 3. The results of the analysis are given in Table IV. First, the table shows the proportion of subjects in each subgroup having statistically significant positive correlations between contingency ratings and the five different judgment rules. The proportion of subjects whose ratings were reliably correlated with Delta P rose as the mean $P(R)$ of the subgroup

TABLE IV

RESULTS OF THE STRATEGY ANALYSIS OF EXPERIMENT 1: PROPORTION OF SUBJECTS SHOWING SIGNIFICANT CORRELATIONS BETWEEN CONTINGENCY RATINGS AND FIVE DIFFERENT JUDGMENT RULES FOR FOUR DIFFERENT SUBGROUPS[a]

		Strategy					
Subgroup	$P(R)$	Delta P	Delta D	Delta F	Number O	Number RO	None
Press-Low	.17	.50(.50)	.28(.00)	.28(.06)	.00(.00)	.11(.00)	(.44)
Tap-Low	.23	.83(.83)	.61(.00)	.50(.00)	.00(.00)	.50(.06)	(.11)
Press-High	.37	.94(.78)	.89(.16)	.72(.00)	.00(.00)	.28(.00)	(.06)
Tap-High	.44	.94(.44)	.94(.44)	.89(.06)	.00(.00)	.28(.00)	(.06)

[a] Parenthetical scores give the proportion of subjects in each subgroup with a particular rule having the highest significant correlation. If none of the five correlations were significant, the subject was assigned to the "None" category. From Wasserman et al. (1983).

TABLE V

RESULTS OF THE STRATEGY ANALYSIS OF EXPERIMENT 2: PROPORTION OF SUBJECTS SHOWING SIGNIFICANT CORRELATIONS BETWEEN CONTINGENCY RATINGS AND FIVE DIFFERENT JUDGMENT RULES FOR THREE DIFFERENT CONDITIONS[a]

	Strategy					
Condition	Delta P	Delta D	Delta F	Number O	Number RO	None
Bidirectional	.88(.62)	.73(.27)	.31(.00)	.00(.00)	.00(.00)	(.11)
Unidirectional	.58(.42)	.54(.15)	.19(.08)	.04(.00)	.19(.19)	(.15)
Unidirectional with information	.81(.65)	.77(.12)	.23(.08)	.00(.00)	.12(.08)	(.08)

[a] Parenthetical scores give the proportion of subjects in each condition with a particular rule having the highest significant correlation. If none of the five correlations were significant, the subject was assigned to the "None" category. From Neunaber and Wasserman (1986).

rose toward .50. Also, subjects' ratings were usually most highly correlated with the Delta P rule; only in the Tap-High subgroup did the Delta D rule correlate as highly with contingency ratings. In addition, as mean $P(R)$ rose across the subgroups, the proportion of subjects whose ratings were reliably correlated with the Delta D and Delta F rules rose too. Thus, consistent with Allan and Jenkins' analysis, the two frequency comparison rules (Delta D and Delta F) and the probability comparison rule (Delta P) became more difficult to discriminate from one another as $P(R)$ and $P(No\ R)$ became more alike.[7] However, unlike Allan and Jenkins' analysis, the most prevalent strategy type was not Delta D, but Delta P.

The relative prominence of the Delta P strategy can also be seen in other data shown in Table IV. The parenthetical entries in the table give the proportion of subjects in each subgroup with a particular rule having the *highest* significant positive correlation. If none of the five correlations were statistically significant, a subject was assigned to the "None" category.[8] If we first concentrate on the Press-Low and Tap-Low subgroups, where mean $P(R)$ was less than .30, we see that 92% (24 out of 26) of the subjects with identifiable best strategies could be said to have used the Delta P rule; 0% (0 of 26) of the subjects used the Delta D rule. If we next examine the data of the Press-High and Tap-High subgroups, we see that the Delta D rule rises in prominence and that it does so at the expense of the Delta P rule. Thus, we conclude that, of all of the strategy types explored by Allan and Jenkins (1980, 1983), the Delta P rule is the one most likely to have been used by our subjects.

2. *Strategy Analysis of Experiment 2*

We pursued the usefulness of the strategy analysis and the prominence of the Delta P rule in our second experiment, which investigated the judgments of subjects given unidirectional and bidirectional rating scales. The top two rows in Table V show the proportion of subjects in the unidirectional and bidirectional conditions having statistically significant positive correlations between contingency ratings and the five different judgment strategies.[9] The parenthetical table entries give the proportion of subjects in each condition with a particular rule having the *highest* significant posi-

---

[7] No similar trend was seen for the two counting rules, Number O and Number RO, where no more than half of the subjects in any subgroup ever showed a significant correlation between rules and ratings.

[8] For these parenthetical data, the sums of the six strategy categories for each subgroup must equal 1.00.

[9] Only unidirectional and unsigned bidirectional ratings were used in these analyses.

tive correlation. The proportion of subjects in the bidirectional condition whose unsigned ratings were reliably and positively correlated with a particular strategy was highest for Delta P (.88), followed by Delta D (.73) and Delta F (.31). The Number RO and Number O strategies were not used by these subjects. The distribution of significant positive correlations among the five strategies in the unidirectional condition showed a different pattern. Subjects' ratings here were less likely to be significantly correlated with the Delta P (.58), Delta D (.54), and Delta F (.19) strategies, and were more likely to be significantly correlated with strategies that do not entail the comparison of cells in the 2 × 2 contingency table, namely, Number RO (.19) and Number O (.04).

The tendency for subjects in the unidirectional condition to use less sophisticated strategies was generally mirrored in the proportion of subjects in each condition with a particular rule having the *highest* significant positive correlation. Subjects in the unidirectional condition were less likely to use the Delta P (.42 vs. .62) and Delta D strategies (.15 vs. .27) and were more likely to use the less sophisticated Delta F (.08 vs. .00) and Number RO (.19 vs. .00) strategies than were subjects in the bidirectional condition. Subjects in the unidirectional condition were also a bit more likely to have no identifiable judgment strategy (.15 vs. .11).

The results of the analysis for the unidirectional-informed condition are given in the third row of Table V. Informing subjects of the prevent–cause nature of control had a beneficial impact on strategy use. The proportions of subjects having significant positive correlations between contingency ratings and the five different strategies were similar to those obtained for the bidirectional condition. The proportions of subjects in each condition with a particular rule having the *highest* significant positive correlation were also similar for the two conditions.

Thus, under those rating-scale conditions here sustaining the most accurate contingency judgments (bidirectional and unidirectional-informed), individuals' ratings best accorded with the Delta P rule; however, the condition that did not sustain as accurate judgments (unidirectional) did not support as many subjects who were diagnosed to be using the Delta P rule.

3. Experiment 5

The strategy analysis conducted on subjects' contingency judgments in Experiments 1 and 2 is certainly consistent with causal reports being well described by the Delta P rule. Thus, for those subjects making bidirectional ratings who were identified as having statistically significant "best" strategies, some 75% (62 out of 83) could be said to have responded in accord with the Delta P rule. This percentage greatly exceeds that observed in other contingency judgment tasks (see Shaklee, 1983, for a review and Shaklee & Wasserman, 1986, for a specific example) and might be viewed as further testimony to the sensitivity of our contingency judgment procedures.

Yet, it is one thing to say that the Delta P rule describes our subjects' contingency judgments and quite another to say that anything like the complex computations involved in calculating Delta P goes on in our subjects' heads. Thus, Experiment 5 was aimed at further assessing the goodness of fit of Delta P as a *descriptor* of contingency judgments as well as intended as an initial look at Delta P as a plausible *process* of contingency judgment.

To these ends, S. M. Elek, D. L. Chatlosh, and I had 50 college students engage in our customary contingency judgment procedure under the Tap instructions of Experiment 1. Here, however, subjects were given 25 60-sample problems to rate. These problems were generated by the factorial combination of five different levels of $P(O/R)$ and $P(O/No\ R)$: .00, .25, .50, .75, and 1.00. Not only did this mapping of response–outcome contingency greatly exceed the scope and number of contingencies given to subjects in all prior studies, it also afforded us an excellent opportunity to evaluate the nature and extent of the contributions of $P(O/R)$ and $P(O/No\ R)$ to causal judgments, which had not been done earlier due to the rather small number of contingencies heretofore given to subjects.

We were also concerned with the possibility that the same level of contingency constructed from different pairs of conditional probabilities might sustain different causal judgments. Scrutiny of Table II from Experiment 1 in fact discloses that a contingency of $+.375$ was rated *higher* when constructed from .500 and .125 than when constructed from .875 and .500; and, a contingency of $-.375$ was rated *lower* when constructed from .125 and .500 than when constructed from .500 and .875.[10] Because such a result is contrary to Delta P, we could examine this matter with much greater care in the present 5×5 design, where there are many more isocontingency values.

Beyond the usual causal ratings, we also had subjects judge $P(O/R)$ and $P(O/No\ R)$ after each problem ("choose the number between 0 and 100 which best characterizes the likelihood of the light when you tapped the key and when you didn't tap it"). Surely, if individuals subjectively estimate $P(O/R)$ and $P(O/No\ R)$ en route to making a final causal judgment, then they should be able to report these conditional probabilities to us.

---

[10] Also see Table III for related response probability results.

TABLE VI

OBTAINED CAUSAL RATINGS AND ESTIMATES OF $P(O/R)$ AND $P(O/No\ R)$ IN EXPERIMENT 6

	\multicolumn{5}{c}{$P(O/No\ R)$}				
$P(O/R)$	.00	.25	.50	.75	1.00
Obtained causal ratings					
1.00	.85	.52	.37	.13	−.03
.75	.65	.43	.16	.06	−.12
.50	.37	.19	.01	−.19	−.34
.25	.12	−.10	−.14	−.37	−.58
.00	−.08	−.45	−.51	−.66	−.75
Estimated probability: $P'(O/R)$					
1.00	.91	.70	.60	.59	.64
.75	.69	.65	.48	.46	.50
.50	.44	.44	.41	.40	.37
.25	.26	.25	.31	.22	.16
.00	.00	.08	.12	.12	.05
Estimated probability: $P'(O/No\ R)$					
1.00	.05	.30	.56	.73	.86
.75	.09	.38	.56	.64	.83
.50	.17	.43	.58	.71	.77
.25	.09	.39	.57	.73	.84
.00	.04	.49	.61	.75	.91

Those reports could tell us whether equivalent changes in $P(O/R)$ and $P(O/No\ R)$ yielded equivalent changes in subjective estimates as well as whether estimates of one probability were made independently of the other. Finally, we were interested in whether subjects' causal judgments were better fit to their own estimates of $P(O/R)$ and $P(O/No\ R)$ than to the programmed values (Trollier & Hamilton, 1986). This outcome would, of course, require some deviation of causal judgments from Delta P, and it would constitute further confirmation that subjective conditional probability estimates might mediate causal judgments.

The top portion of Table VI shows mean causality judgments under each of the 25 contingencies. Remarkably, at each level of $P(O/No\ R)$ ratings rose as $P(O/R)$ increased, and at each level of $P(O/R)$ ratings fell as $P(O/No\ R)$ increased. Overall, ratings correlated .98 with the scheduled contingencies! This correspondence notwithstanding, there were at least two troubling features of these data, so far as their fit with Delta P is concerned. First, although they were varied over the same range (.00 to .25 to .50 to .75 to 1.00), $P(O/R)$ affected ratings more than did $P(O/No$

R). Across all levels of *P(O/No R)*, *P(O/R)* increased ratings from $-.49$ to $-.21$ to $.01$ to $.24$ to $.37$ (a range of .86); across all levels of *P(O/R)*, *P(O/No R)* decreased ratings from .38 to .12 to $-.02$ to $-.21$ $-.36$ (a range of .74). Second, the same levels of Delta P did not occasion the same causal ratings. With contingencies of $+.75$ and $-.75$, ratings were more extreme when the probabilities from which they were constructed were .00 and .75 than when they were .25 and 1.00. This same trend was apparent when Delta P was $-.25$ and $-.50$.

One possible way out of both of these problems might be to weight differentially the contributions of *P(O/R)* and *P(O/No R)* to causal ratings. Suppose that we adjust Delta P so that only .80 of *P(O/No R)* is subtracted from *P(O/R)*. This move certainly deals with the smaller impact of *P(O/No R)* than *P(O/R)* on causal ratings. However, it erroneously predicts lower causal ratings with smaller pairs of probabilities for *all* contingencies; this error is particularly obvious in the case of noncontingency, where it predicts that ratings will rise from .00 to .05 to .10 to .15 to .20 as *P(O)* rises from .00 to .25 to .50 to .75 to 1.00.

We thus turned to the subjects' *own* reports of *P(O/R)* and *P(O/No R)* for a better fit to their causal ratings. These mean scores are shown in the middle and bottom portions of Table VI. Scrutiny of this table suggests that subjects did give increasing reports of *P(O/R)* and *P(O/No R)* as each probability was raised from .00 to .25 to .50 to .75 to 1.00. Unlike the programmed values, however, equivalent changes in *P(O/R)* and *P(O/No R)* had different effects on behavior. Across all levels of *P(O/No R)*, *P (O/R)* increased ratings from .07 to .24 to .41 to .56 to .69 (a range of .62); across all levels of *P(O/R)*, *P(O/No R)* increased ratings from .09 to .40 to .58 to .71 to .84 (a range of .75). Curiously, this unequal effect of *P(O/R)* and *P(O/No R)* on *probability* ratings is exactly opposite to that found on *causality* ratings. In addition, subjects' judgments of one conditional probability were not independent of changes in the other conditional probability; in each case, but particularly for *P(O/R)*, increases in the other conditional probability reduced the range over which subjects' ratings of the target probability varied.

Although these effects were not heartening to our effort to provide a better fit to the subjects' causal ratings, we did calculate a subjective Delta P' from the estimates of conditional probability shown in the middle and bottom portions of Table VI. It did not fit the ratings at all well. Most erroneous was its predicting ratings far lower than those actually obtained.

This problem can be remedied if we again reduce the effect of *P' (O/No R)* by multiplying it by .80. The resulting predicted and actual obtained causal rating scores are shown in Fig. 9. The fit was quite good. Indeed, compared to all prior metrics, the formula Delta $P' = P'(O/R) - .80[P'(O/No\ R)]$ yielded the smallest point-by-point deviations (both absolute and signed) from subjects' obtained causal judgments. And, of all the metrics, it was best prepared to deal with nonhorizontal isocontingency functions.

At this point in our research, one might conclude that humans not only rate response–outcome relations with extraordinary sensitivity, but that they do so by cognitively computing the relative likelihood of outcome occurrence after they do and do not perform the target response. Whatever error they make in those contingency judgments is due to minor distortions in their estimates of $P(O/R)$ and $P(O/No\ R)$. This account would pledge little allegiance to Hume's more mechanistic and less ratiocinative formulation. Just how likely is it that similar cognitive computations go on in the minds of infants or nonhuman animals, like rats and pigeons? And what are we to make of those numerous cases where humans fail to describe accurately the prevailing contingencies, which stimulated our own investigations?

4. Experiment 6

One clue as to why people may make errors in judging response–outcome contingencies comes from an unpublished study by J. A. Becker, R. S. Bhatt, and me. In this project, 24 undergraduates were asked "to decide which of two buttons, A or B, has an effect on the occurrence of the green light." They were told that "only one button in each problem actually has an effect on the green light, even though the effect may be very slight and you may be quite uncertain as to the accuracy of your choice." Given earlier speculations that subjects performing two active responses may fail to consider the consequences of making *neither* response, subjects were also told that "in order to judge the problems accurately, you should press each button some of the time and also refrain from pressing either button some of the time," an admonition which they did appear to have followed.

The actual problems subjects were given (each comprising 100 1-sec sampling intervals) entailed six different contingencies for responding on the effective button (Re): +.50 (1.00 − .50), +.30 (.80 − .50), +.10 (.60 − .50), −.10 (.40 − .50), −.30 (.20 − .50), and −.50 (.00 − .50). Note that a failure to make Re in a 1-sec sample meant that the green light had a .50 chance of occurring under all six contingencies; making Re in a 1-sec interval had the potential of increasing the probability as high as 1.00

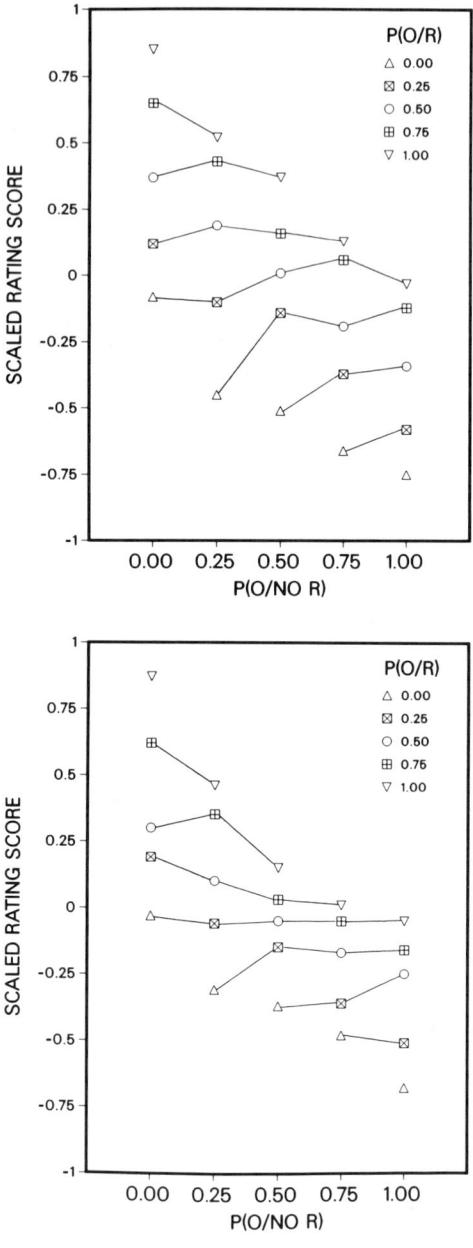

Fig. 9. Mean obtained causal ratings in Experiment 5 as functions of $P(O/R)$ and $P(O/No\ R)$ (upper panel). Expected causal rating scores calculated from $P'(O/R) - .80P'(O/No\ R)$ as functions of $P(O/R)$ and $P(O/No\ R)$ (lower panel). In each case, the interconnected points are from the same level of Delta P $[P(O/R) - P(O/No\ R)]$.

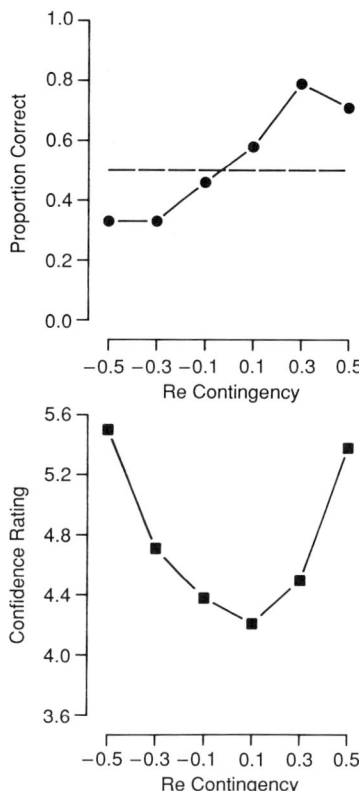

Fig. 10. Proportion of times that subjects correctly identified Re as a function of response–outcome contingency in Experiment 6 (upper panel). Subjects' mean confidence ratings in having correctly chosen Re as a function of response–outcome contingency (lower panel).

or of decreasing it as low as .00 in different problems. At no time did pressing the ineffective button (Ri) have *any* effect on the green light. Appropriate counterbalancing mixed the temporal order of the six contingencies and the spatial location of Re and Ri over the 24 subjects. After each problem, subjects were asked to circle A or B on their response sheet, corresponding to their best guess as to the identity of Re. They were also asked to rate the confidence they had in their choice by circling one digit on a scale from 1 to 9.

The top portion of Fig. 10 shows the proportion of times subjects correctly identified Re as a function of response–outcome contingency. The expected U-shaped function did not emerge. True, accuracy rose as the Re contingency was increased from +.10 to +.30 and +.50; but, it fell as the Re contingency was decreased from − .10 to − .30 and − .50! The decrease in accuracy for negative problems generally mirrored the increase in accuracy for positive problems. The bottom portion of Fig. 10

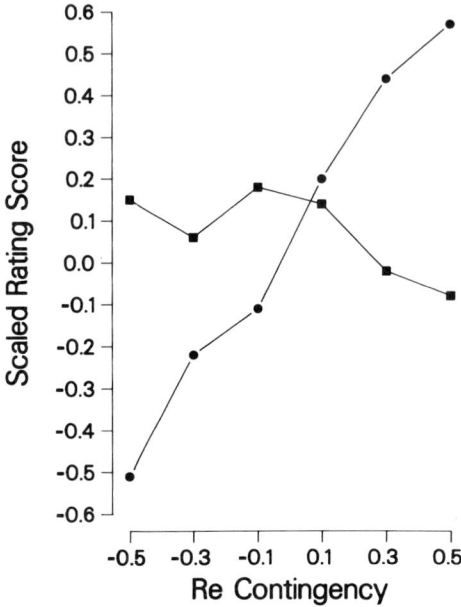

Fig. 11. Mean scaled causal ratings (divided by 100) for Re (●) and Ri (■) as a function of response–outcome contingency in Experiment 6.

shows subjects' mean confidence ratings in having correctly chosen Re as a function of contingency. Here, a clear U-shaped function was obtained. The more the Re contingency varied from zero, the more confident subjects became in their choice; this result was as true for negative as it was for positive contingencies.

What went wrong? Why did subjects mistakenly pick the ineffective over the effective button for negative contingencies? One possibility which we subsequently ruled out was that subjects could not sensitively rate the prevailing contingencies for two or more responses. To examine this notion, we had another 24 students separately rate the causal effectiveness of the same two responses under the same six contingencies. Mean contingency ratings for Re and Ri are shown in Fig. 11. Subjects' ratings of Re appropriately rose as a function of contingency. Subjects' ratings of Ri ranged from − .09 to + .18, with there being some suggestion of a slope opposite that of Re. Thus, subjects were quite able to render rather accurate *concurrent* reports of contingency for two separate responses.

Thus, it would seem that our first group should have had sufficient information about the prevailing contingencies to select correctly the effective button. Interpretive or inferential steps *beyond* the processing of contingency information would appear to be the best candidates for generating erroneous selections here [and in Jenkins and Ward's (1965) original study, where verbal reports but *not* operant responding were uncorrelated with the prevailing contingencies; see particularly their p. 9 for excellent evidence of schedule-controlled behavior]. Such an additional interpretive step might be to label the response with the higher coincidence with the outcome as the more "effective" one, leading subjects correctly to select Re under positive Re contingencies and incorrectly to select Ri under negative Re contingencies. A related interpretive error might be for them to judge that "to exert control over an event" is to cause it to occur but not to prevent it from occurring (see Experiment 2). In either case, further interpretation or inference could override accurate contingency perception. Remember Hume's warning about the fallibility of "higher" cognitive processes?

The possibility that more complex cognitive processes may actually prove detrimental to accurate judgments of contingency provides further justification for the final two experiments to be discussed, which were outgrowths of studies originally aimed at uncovering the behavioral mechanisms of operant conditioning in animals. The methods and analyses of these experiments should prove useful not only to understanding the nature of schedule-controlled behavior, but also to subjects' reports of the prevailing schedules of reinforcement.

5. *Experiment 7*

Within the domain of animal learning, much attention has been paid to the possibility that the critical feature of schedules of reinforcement is the differential likelihood of an environmental event given the occurrence or the nonoccurrence of a response. Such a probabilistic formulation relates directly to the Delta P strategy evaluated with correlational methods in Experiments 1 and 2. It also was the inspiration for Hammond's (1980) probabilistic schedule of reinforcement, which we utilized in the series of six experiments reported above.

Although the successes of the Delta P strategy are noteworthy and the ease of implementing the probabilistic schedule is considerable, several theorists have resisted the temptations to conclude that differential probability is the key to understanding reinforcement schedules and their effects on behavior. Not only does it seem unlikely that rats, pigeons, human infants, and college undergraduates spontaneously compute and compare conditional probabilities, it is also unclear over just what periods of time such computations are or should be calculated.

These issues are particularly salient when one considers a seminal study by Thomas (1981), comprising two experiments concerned with the effects of contiguous appetitive events on rats' lever pressing. In the first, one food delivery was scheduled every 20 sec. Food came at the end of a 20-sec interval if no lever presses were emitted; the first lever press in a 20-sec interval immediately delivered the food. Lever pressing thus advanced the time of food delivery and made it contiguous with lever pressing; but evaluated over each 20-sec interval, there was no differential probabilistic relation between lever pressing and food presentation, because food was given once every 20 sec whether the rat pressed or not. All six rats' lever pressing increased from near 0 responses per minute in the first session to between 22 and 36 responses per minute by the thirtieth session. In the second experiment, the rate-enhancing effect of response–reinforcer contiguity was pitted against the possibly rate-suppressing effect of a negative response–reinforcer relation. The schedule was similar to that in the first experiment: Food delivery came at the end of a 20-sec interval if no lever presses occurred, and food immediately followed the first lever press in a 20-sec interval. However, a response in one 20-sec interval could *cancel* food delivery in the next 20-sec interval. Despite this negative relation, the lever pressing of all six rats increased from 0 responses per minute in the first session to between 6 and 32 responses per minute by the thirtieth session.

These were indeed dramatic demonstrations of the potency of contiguity in associative learning—so dramatic that contiguity appeared to overshadow the contingency between response and reinforcer. But, surely, this result would only hold for animals far less intelligent than human beings!

To explore this comparative issue, we (Wasserman & Neunaber, 1986, Experiment 1) adapted the procedures of Thomas (1981) for use with college students. In our contiguity (C) schedule, each brief flash of a white light signaled the gain of 1 point. Light delivery occurred every t sec without a telegraph-key tap. The first tap in the t-sec interval immediately presented the point light. We also sought to pit contiguity against a negative response–reinforcer relation. Thus, under our C− schedule, a response in interval n immediately presented the point light in that interval but canceled point-light presentation in interval $n + 1$. By monitoring key tapping over the span of 60 t-sec intervals, we could see whether our college students' operant responding was strongly controlled by schedules C and C−. By examining postschedule ratings, we could also see whether subjects were more likely to report that telegraph-key responding caused the light to occur or prevented the light from occurring under the two schedules.

Although our main interest was in the effects of contiguity-promoting schedules, we thought it important to include a noncontingent schedule as a baseline against which to assess the effects of response–reinforcer contiguity.[11] In our I schedule, therefore, the point light was presented every t sec, independently of the subject's key tapping. We expected much less operant responding under this schedule than under the C and C− schedules. We also expected subjects to report that responses had no effect on the point light (see Experiments 1, 2, 3, 5, and 6).

In any experiment with human adults, the instructions they are given can be of great importance to the obtained results. We certainly did not want subjects to respond at high initial rates on the telegraph key because we wished to see response acquisition if at all possible. Therefore, in an attempt to lower subjects' responsivity, we told them that points could be earned either by tapping or by not tapping the key. In addition, we included in the procedures for each individual subject two schedules designed to decrease telegraph-key responding. In the response-contingent omission (O) schedule, the first tap in a t-sec interval omitted presentation of the point light in that interval. In the O− schedule, we included the further negative feature that point-light presentation could be canceled on interval $n + 1$ if the subject tapped the key in interval n. We expected these schedules of reinforcement omission to support even less operant behavior than the I schedule. We also expected subjects to report that on these schedules key tapping prevented the occurrence of the point light.

Finally, we reasoned that the longer the sampling interval, t, the greater the extent to which responding could affect the time of reinforcement. Thus, for different groups of subjects, we set t to 3, 6, or 9 sec to assess whether these different intervals supported different levels of operant responding or different ratings of the five schedules.

The subjects were 24 male and 24 female college students. Subjects were randomly assigned to the 3-, 6-, or 9-sec sampling interval conditions, with the restriction that each group contain an equal number of males and females ($n = 8$). Subjects were instructed as in Experiment 3 concerning the scheduled response–reinforcer relations, their telegraph-key tapping, and their postproblem ratings. The five schedules were presented in a random manner. Each schedule was signaled by illumination of a red light. Each duration of exposure to a given schedule, designated a problem, comprised 60 unsignaled t-sec intervals. Each illumination of the white outcome light lasted 0.10 sec. Responding was scored in terms

---

[11]Thomas (1981) had not included this control for accidental conjunctions of response and reinforcer.

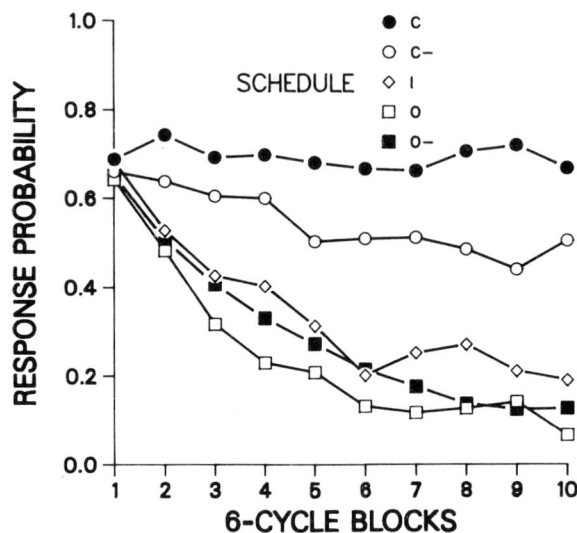

Fig. 12. Mean probability of telegraph-key tapping in successive 6-cycle blocks of training under the five different schedules in Experiment 7. Probability was defined as the proportion of cycles containing at least one key tap. From Wasserman and Neunaber (1986). Copyright by the Society for the Experimental Analysis of Behavior, Inc.

of the number of intervals out of six in which the subject made at least one key tap. This quotient defined the probability of a recorded response and was collected over 10 successive blocks. After every problem, subjects rated the relationship between key tapping and white-light delivery on our usual −100 to +100 scale.

Figure 12 shows the mean probability of key tapping under each of the five schedules in successive, 6-cycle blocks of training across all three time intervals (as this factor proved to be ineffective in modulating responding). In the first training block, all five schedules supported highly similar response probabilities, ranging from .64 to .69. However, as training progressed, responding was differently maintained by the five schedules. Responding stayed high under Schedule C, declined slightly under Schedule C−, and dropped dramatically under Schedules I, O, and O−. In the final block, Schedules C, C−, I, O, and O− supported mean probabilities of responding equal to .67, .51, .19, .07, and .13, respectively.

Figure 13 shows the mean scaled ratings for each of the five schedules across all three time intervals (as this factor again proved to be ineffective in modifying responding). Ratings were moderately positive

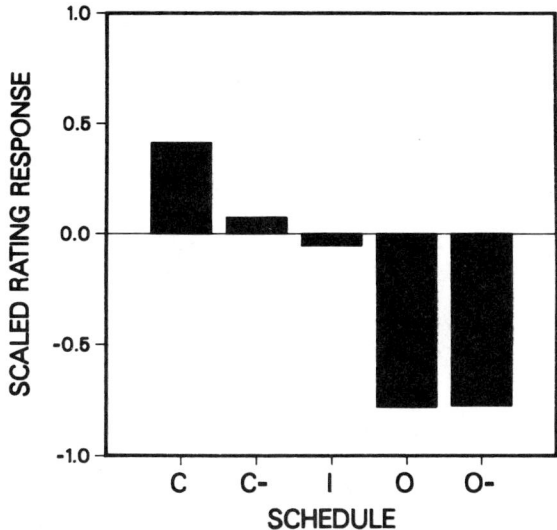

Fig. 13. Mean scaled causal ratings (divided by 100) for the five different schedules in Experiment 7. From Wasserman and Neunaber (1986). Copyright by the Society for the Experimental Analysis of Behavior, Inc.

under Schedule C, slightly positive under Schedule C−, nearest to zero under Schedule I, and similar and highly negative under Schedules O and O−.

Thus, schedules that promoted response–reinforcer contiguity (C and C−) supported more operant behavior and more positive causal ratings than did a schedule of response-independent reinforcement (I). Like rats, humans responded more when the only consequences were to move reinforcers forward in time and to make reinforcers contiguous with the responses that moved them. This response-enhancing effect was also accompanied by positive causal ratings. Unfortunately, a high initial level of responding prevented our obtaining evidence of response acquisition under the contiguity-promoting (C) schedule. Although reduced relative to Schedule C, operant performance and causal ratings were similar under Schedule C−. This reduction could be due to several factors, including fewer response–reinforcer contiguities or the negative response–reinforcer relation of the C− schedule. Schedules of reinforcement omission (O and O−) resulted in more negative causal ratings than did a schedule of response-independent reinforcement, even though key-tap responding under Schedules O and O− did not differ from Schedule I. This pattern of results indicates that a floor effect may have prevented our discerning differences in responding among these three schedules. The most obvious reason for subjects' negative ratings under Schedules O and O− is the negative conditional relation that these schedules entail. Another possibility is that Schedules O and O− involve longer response–reinforcer delays for the designated operant than for other behavior patterns. Later discussion will more thoroughly evaluate this interpretation. Finally, essentially equivalent operant responding and causal ratings were found with the three sampling intervals that we studied. The range of from 3 to 9 sec evidently was not large enough to support measurable differences in behavior.

6. Experiment 8

In point of fact, Hineline (1970) was the first to examine the effects on operant behavior of schedules in which responses could affect *when* but not *whether* an environmental event would occur. He reported that rats' lever pressing was acquired and maintained under procedures that merely delayed inevitable shock presentation (also see Lewis, Gardner, & Hutton, 1976). In addition, Hineline (1977) reported that lever pressing established by shock delay was maintained even when responding *increased* the number of shocks received (also see Gardner & Lewis, 1976). Thus, shock delay may reinforce operant behavior to such a degree that it overshadows a *positive* probabilistic relation between responding and shock delivery.

The present experiment assessed whether human operant behavior is similarly affected by delaying an aversive event. Our adaptation of Hineline's discrete-trial procedure was a free-operant technique, using an outcome-delay (D) schedule that comprised 20 cycles. Each cycle in turn comprised a response time, R_t, followed by an outcome time, O_t. If a subject failed to respond within R_t, the .10-sec red point-loss light was presented at end of R_t. If, however, a subject tapped the telegraph key at least once within R_t, the point-loss light was delayed until the end of O_t, which began right after the end of R_t. Thus, a response within R_t could delay point loss from R_t to $R_t + O_t$. If outcome delay is reinforcing, we expected subjects to respond with high probability and also to report that key tapping prevented the point-loss light from occurring, even though, evaluated over whole cycles, there was no conditional relationship between key tapping and light delivery.

As a control for chance temporal conjunctions between key tapping and point loss, a response-independent (I) schedule was included in which the point-loss light was always presented at the same time (the end of O_t)

every cycle.¹² Here, we expected much less operant responding; we also expected subjects to report that responses had no effect on the loss light.

If delaying an aversive event is reinforcing, is advancing an aversion event punishing? To find out, we included a third schedule—an outcome-advance (A) procedure—in which subjects' key taps during R_t advanced point loss from the end of O_t to the end of R_t. If outcome advance is punishing, we expected least responding in this condition and reports that key tapping caused the point-loss light to occur.

The trio of procedures described so far (Schedules D, I, and A) were illustrated in connection with an aversive event—point loss. This experiment also addressed the symmetry of results obtained with aversive and appetitive consequences. Thus, individual subjects were given second exposures to Schedules D, I, and A, but here the outcome was a .10-sec green light correlated with point gain. Our predictions for operant responding under Schedules D and A with point gain were opposite to those with point loss: Subjects should respond most under Schedule A and least under Schedule D. As was the case for outcomes signifying point loss, we expected Schedule A to support reports of response–outcome causation and Schedule D to support reports of response–outcome prevention. And, as was also true for point-loss outcomes, we expected Schedule I to support intermediate levels of operant responding and reports of no relation between response and outcome.

Finally, we again sought to assess whether the extent of temporal movement of outcomes affected operant responding and causal ratings. For different groups of subjects, we set O_t to 10, 15, or 20 sec. We predicted that the longer the outcome time, the greater the extent of outcome advance and delay, and the greater the behavioral effects of Schedules A and D.

The 36 undergraduate students were randomly assigned to the 10-, 15-, and 20-sec outcome time conditions, with the restriction that each contain an equal number of males and females ($n = 6$). The general regime of this investigation was the same as Experiment 7, except subjects were told that by responding or by refraining from responding they could *gain* points by getting the green light to *come on* and they could *avoid losing* points by getting the red light to *stay off*. Each subject received the outcome-delay (D), response-independent (I), and outcome-advance (A) schedules under both the point-gain and the point-loss conditions. Each problem comprised 20 cycles, and each cycle comprised a response time,

---

¹²Hineline (1970, 1977), had not included this control for accidental conjunctions of response and reinforcer.

R_t, followed by an outcome time, O_t. Depending upon the experimental group, O_t was set to 10, 15, or 20 sec. R_t was set to 5 sec for all experimental groups. The six schedules were presented in a random manner.

Figure 14 shows the mean probability of key tapping under each of the six schedules in successive, 4-cycle blocks of training across the three outcome time conditions (which did not differentially affect responding). The top portion depicts operant performance in the point-gain condition and the bottom portion depicts performance in the point-loss condition. In the first block of training, the probability of responding on the various schedules ranged from .38 to .55; by the final block of training, performance on the different schedules had diverged and ranged from .28 to .60. In general, Schedule A (advance) with point gain and Schedule D (delay) with point loss supported the highest levels of key tapping; responding under these two schedules increased from the first to the last block of training. Schedule D with point gain and Schedule A with point loss generally supported the lowest levels of key tapping; responding under these two schedules tended to decrease as training progressed. And Schedule I with both point gain and point loss generally sustained intermediate levels of key tapping; responding under these two schedules also decreased from the first to the last block of training.

Thus, the movement in time of environmental outcomes can reinforce and punish human operant behavior. Relative to a response-independent schedule, advancing point gain or delaying point loss strengthened responding; relative to a response-independent schedule, delaying point gain or advancing point loss weakened responding. The systematic and symmetrical effects of appetitive and aversive outcomes held even though, considered across cycles, responses had no effect on the probability of point gain or point loss.

Figure 15 shows the mean scaled causal ratings under each of the six schedules for the point-gain and point-loss conditions across the three outcome-time conditions (which again did not differentially affect behavior). Ratings under Schedule A were positive, ratings under Schedule I were near zero, and ratings under Schedule D were negative. Thus, subjects made positive causal ratings of the outcome-advance procedure and negative causal ratings of the outcome-delay procedure. These ratings were made even though, for whole cycles, neither procedure involved a nonzero conditional relationship. Also, subjects did accurately rate their key tapping as having had no effect on outcome presentation under the noncontingent procedure. Response–outcome contiguity therefore played an important role in subjects' response to and rating of temporal schedules of reinforcement.

Although we confirmed the importance of temporal contiguity in the

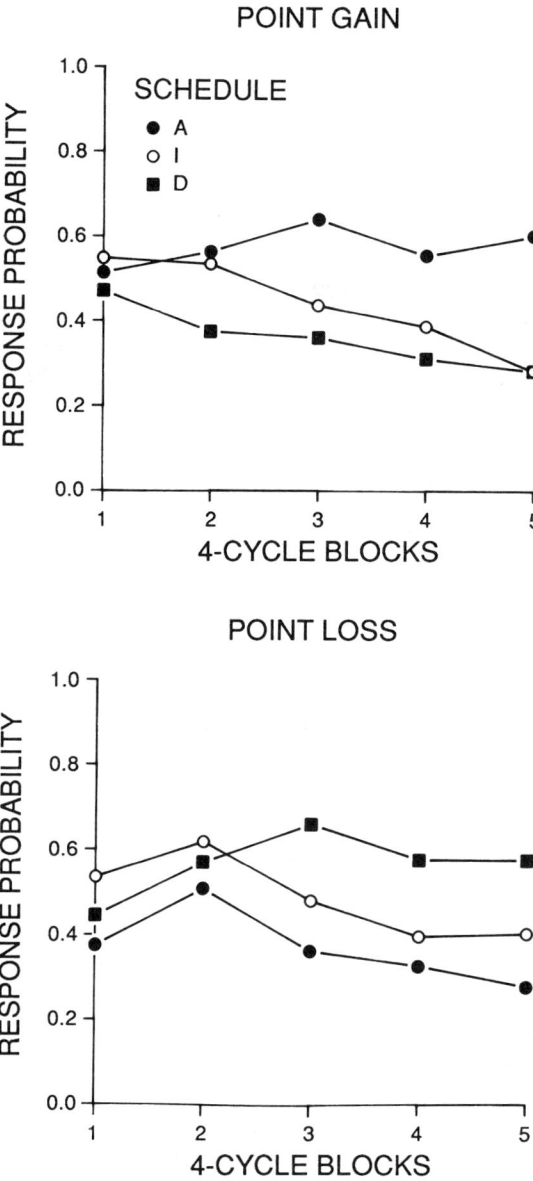

Fig. 14. Mean probability of telegraph-key tapping in successive 4-cycle blocks of training for the point-gain condition under Schedules A, I, and D in Experiment 8 (upper panel). Mean probability of telegraph-key tapping in successive 4-cycle blocks of training for the point-loss condition under Schedules A, I, and D (lower panel). From Wasserman and Neunaber (1986). Copyright by the Society for the Experimental Analysis of Behavior, Inc.

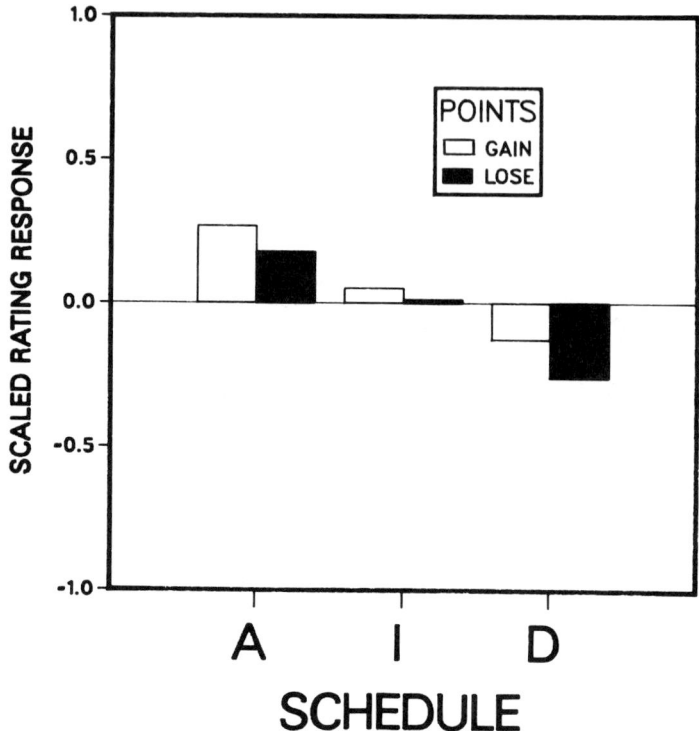

Fig. 15. Mean scaled causal ratings (divided by 100) for Schedules A, I, and D in the point-gain and point-loss conditions in Experiment 8. From Wasserman and Neunaber (1986). Copyright by the Society for the Experimental Analysis of Behavior, Inc.

control of operant behavior and in the report of response–reinforcer relations, we again failed to find a measurable effect of changing a specific temporal parameter of the task. Here, varying O_t from 10 to 20 sec was without effect. In the prior experiment, changing O_t from 3 to 9 sec was without effect. Much greater changes in these independent variables may be necessary before notable effects are observed.

VI. Theoretical Analysis of Response–Outcome Relations

The above review of empirical research on the perception of response–outcome relations and on some of its possible cognitive mechanisms makes it quite clear that human subjects do appreciate that their responses exert control over environmental events. Considering those instances in which reinforcers and punishers were scheduled, Experiments 3 and 4 disclosed that *probabilistic contingencies* lawfully modified college students' operant responding and supported sensitive postschedule ratings of the degree to which responding affected the outcome. In Experiments 7 and 8, *temporal contingencies*—which determine when but not whether to deliver reinforcers or punishers—also robustly changed operant behavior and supported reliable reports of response–outcome causation.

Demonstrating that both temporal and probabilistic schedules of reinforcement influence humans' responding to and rating of contingency relations does not, of course, tell us exactly what feature(s) of those contingencies is (are) influencing their behavior. One possibility is that temporal contiguity and local probabilistic relationship are *independent* contributors to operant conditioning and causal ratings, in much the same way that Hume separately regarded temporal contiguity and consistent conjunction as determinants of causal association. A more parsimonious proposal is that organisms respond to different contingencies with a *single* mechanism. But is that mechanism time based or based on the local conditional relationship between response and reinforcer?

Many theorists (e.g., Seligman *et al.*, 1971) have argued that organisms are principally or exclusively sensitive to the local conditional or probabilistic relationship between response and reinforcer. The concept of conditional relationship is certainly an elegant way of conceptualizing schedules of reinforcement. If we need only calculate *P(O/R)* and *P(O/No R)* and subtract the latter conditional probability from the former, then we can simply and precisely classify schedules of reinforcement and perhaps easily identify the behaviorally relevant feature(s) of those schedules.

In order to make these probabilistic calculations, we must first pick some interval of time during which to decide whether a response did or did not occur. However, choice of that time interval is anything but arbitrary; it critically affects how we classify the schedule (see Thomas, 1983). For instance, consider Schedules A, I, and D of Experiment 8. If we calculate *P(O/R)* and *P(O/No R)* on a cycle-by-cycle basis, then we would conclude that there was no local conditional relation between operant responding and the scheduled outcome because both conditional probabilities equal one and their difference equals zero. However, if we reduce the calculational interval to 5 sec (the value of R_t), then it can be shown that Schedule A would involve a positive conditional relation, Schedule I would involve a zero conditional relation, and Schedule D would involve a negative conditional relation. That there is *some* sampling interval that yields probability-difference scores that jibe with subjects' causal ratings cannot be construed as strong support for this theory;

such correspondence may be purely accidental. Without a priori means of specifying a *particular* sampling interval, the many other virtues of the probabilistic approach are seriously compromised (see also Hammond & Paynter, 1983; Thomas, 1983).

If we reject probabilistic relations as the basis of our subjects' operant behavior and their causal ratings, then we must assess the merits of temporal contiguity as an acceptable analysis. We must, in particular, confront the main problem that theorists have noted for contiguity formulations: Namely, that under probabilistic schedules, operant responding is an inverse function of $P(O/No\ R)$. Certainly, increasing the probability of reinforcement in the absence of operant responding cannot increase the delay between operant responses and reinforcers.

We propose to solve this problem by considering the delays of reinforcement after operant responses *and* after types of behavior other than the specified operant (what can be called nonoperant responses). We thus define *relative contiguity* as the extent to which the delay of reinforcement after occurrences of the specified operant response (d_o) differs from that after nonoperant responses (d_n): specifically, relative contiguity = $d_n - d_o$. If reinforcers are presented independently of behavior, then the delay of reinforcement after any given operant response or any given nonoperant response will be equal and the relative contiguity score of the noncontingent schedule will be zero. If reinforcers follow operant responses with a shorter delay than they follow nonoperant responses, then the relative contiguity score of the schedule will be positive. And if reinforcers follow operant responses with a longer delay than they follow nonoperant responses (as in the case of the O and O− schedules of Experiment 7), then the relative contiguity score of the schedule will be negative.[13]

We expect that subjects' ratings (along our prevent–cause scale) of the relations arranged by various schedules of reinforcement will be a direct function of the relative contiguity scores of those schedules. We further expect that subjects' operant responding will also be a function of the relative contiguity arranged by various schedules. With appetitive outcomes, responding should increase as relative contiguity increases from negative to positive values; with aversive outcomes, responding should decrease as relative contiguity increases from negative to positive values.

Obviously, the notion of relative contiguity will encompass familiar delay-of-reinforcement effects (Renner, 1964; Tarpy & Sawabini, 1974); increases in the delay between operant and reinforcer are ordinarily accomplished without any scheduled decreases in the delay between nonop-

---

[13]For more on computing delays, see Hursh and Fantino (1973) and Moore (1984).

erants and the reinforcer. More noteworthy is the fact that relative contiguity helps us understand why operant responding decreases when $P(O/No\ R)$ is increased in probabilistic schedules of reinforcement. True, there is no increase in d_o when $P(O/No\ R)$ is raised, but there is a decrease in d_n. Thus, operant responding should decrease because of a decrease in relative contiguity, $d_n - d_o$.

Our notion of relative contiguity bears considerable resemblance to Fantino's concept of psychological distance to reward (Fantino, 1977; Hursh & Fantino, 1973) and to Herrnstein's formulation of the matching law (Herrnstein, 1970; see also Shull, Spear, & Bryson, 1981). Whereas their accounts were initially addressed to multioperant concurrent schedules of reinforcement, our analysis centers on the single-operant situation. In the multioperant setting, organisms tend to make responses that hasten the delivery of reinforcers. Even though explicit choices among equally effortful responses are not arranged in the single-operant setting, it is quite reasonable to assume that here, too, organisms make moment-by-moment choices among a wide array of possible classes of behavior. Emitting the response with the shortest delay to reinforcement would then correspond with predictions derived from our notion of relative contiguity.

Our account also aspires to understand subjects' ratings of reinforcement schedules. Some scale of measurement that fixes a response-independent schedule at zero and ranks other schedules above and below that reference level is clearly preferable to alternative mathematical treatments. One way of achieving this result is to divide $d_n - d_o$ by $d_n + d_o$.[14]

Demonstrating the applicability of relative contiguity to the analysis of *probabilistic* schedules of reinforcement would be of limited value if the notion did not help us understand the effects of *temporal* contingencies of reinforcement, such as those in Experiments 7 and 8. Consider Schedule C of Experiment 7. There, operant responses were more likely to be immediately followed by a reinforcer than were nonoperant responses; thus, this schedule involves positive relative contiguity. The same holds true for Schedule C− of Experiment 7, although fewer operant–reinforcer conjunctions per session should tend to make Schedule C− less response enhancing than Schedule C and less likely to support positive

---

[14]This move may also provide a way of understanding why the same contingency constructed from different pairs of conditional probabilities yields different operant and judgment behaviors. Incidentally, because of the inverse interrelation of time and probability, the different behaviors occasioned by the same Delta P values can also be accommodated by dividing $P(O/R) - P(O/No\ R)$ by $P(O/R) + P(O/No\ R)$. The logical interrelation of time and probability will surely give theorists fits; whether our subjects are influenced by one variable or the other is an empirical question, but a difficult one.

causal ratings. What of the advance and delay schedules of Experiment 8? In Schedule A, effective operant responses must precede outcomes by between 0 and R_t sec; no such bias for short delays exists for nonoperant responses. Thus, Schedule A entails positive relative contiguity. In Schedule D, effective operant responses cannot precede outcomes by less than O_t sec; no such bias against short delays exists for nonoperant responses. Thus, Schedule D entails negative relative contiguity.

Relative contiguity therefore does help to explain the behavioral effects of the temporal schedules that we studied. The applicability of this notion to still other schedules of reinforcement would appear to be warranted by these initial positive indications.[15]

VII. Concluding Comments

"There is substantial communality between animal and human associative learning, and . . . the study of human cognitive processes can be informed by the study of animal cognitive processes" (Lovibond, 1988, p. 79). These assertions concerning the evolutionary continuity of mental processes clearly accord with the data and analyses reported in this article. Viewing human and animal behavior from the same comparative perspective is also consistent with Hume's historic formulation of causal association.

Needless to say, many contemporary accounts of causal judgment in humans spring from a more linguistic and ratiocinative vantage point (e.g., Einhorn & Hogarth, 1986; Hilton & Slugoski, 1986). Indeed, such an anthropocentric orientation now dominates the study of human memory and cognition. Nevertheless, we are not alone in believing that a real integration of learning and causal perception in humans and animals is possible (e.g., Alloy & Tabachnik, 1984; Shanks & Dickinson, 1987). Nor are we alone in proposing that important progress toward this integration depends upon elucidating basic associative and perceptual processes, such as those that demonstrably participate in the behavior of nonhuman animals (Gluck & Bower, 1988). We can only hope that another 250 years will not have to pass before experimental inquiry can rule decisively on Hume's original speculations.

Let me finish by underscoring a point originally made by Hume and more recently reiterated by Killeen (1981): namely, that causal inference conveys a biological advantage on an organism. Appreciating the causal

---

[15]The major limitation of relative contiguity is its difficulty contending with historical (or blocking) effects. For more on this problem see Shanks (1989).

texture of the environment does much more than quench one's idle curiosity about what leads to what; it allows one to engage in behaviors which enhance contact with beneficial stimuli and minimize contact with harmful ones. Thus, even though rooted in the introspective inquiries of philosophy, the study of causal perception can be seen as central to empirical research in the behavioral and biological sciences. Fresh insights and approaches may well result from looking at the problem from this different perspective.

ACKNOWLEDGMENTS

The research in this article could not have been conducted and reported without the help of many individuals. Most important were my numerous collaborators; J. Becker, R. Bhatt, D. Chatlosh, S. Elek, D. Franson, and D. Neunaber. Substantial technical support was provided by L. Frei, S. Gilles, R. Hohle, M. O'Hara, J. Paul, A. Schneider, A. Thompson, L. Van Hamme, E. Wetrich, and P. Young. And many constructive suggestions were offered by L. Allan, D. Carlston, I. Levin, M. Losch, J. Moore, and H. Shaklee.

REFERENCES

Allan, L. G. (1980). A note on measurements of contingency between two binary variables in judgment tasks. *Bulletin of the Psychonomic Society,* **15,** 147–149.

Allan, L. G., & Jenkins, H. M. (1980). The judgment of contingency and the nature of the response. *Canadian Journal of Psychology,* **34,** 1–11.

Allan, L. G., & Jenkins, H. M. (1983). The effect of representations of binary variables on judgment of influence. *Learning and Motivation,* **14,** 381–405.

Alloy, L. B., & Abramson, L. Y. (1979). Judgment of contingency in depressed and nondepressed students: Sadder but wiser? *Journal of Experimental Psychology: General,* **108,** 441–485.

Alloy, L. B., & Tabachnik, M. (1984). Assessment of covariation by humans and animals: The joint influence of prior expectations and current situational information. *Psychological Review,* **91,** 112–149.

Baker, A. G., Berbrier, M. W., & Vallee-Tourangeau, F. (1989). Judgements of a 2 × 2 contingency table: Sequential processing and the learning curve. *Quarterly Journal of Experimental Psychology,* **41B,** 65–97.

Beauchamp, T. L., & Rosenberg, A. (1981). *Hume and the problem of causation.* New York: Oxford University Press.

Bloomfield, T. M. (1972). Reinforcement schedules: Contingency or contiguity? In R. M. Gilbert & J. R. Millenson (Eds.), *Reinforcement: Behavioral analysis* (pp. 165–208). New York: Academic Press.

Boring, E. G. (1950). *A history of experimental psychology.* New York: Appleton-Century-Crofts.

Chatlosh, D. L., Neunaber, D. J., & Wasserman, E. A. (1985). Response-outcome contingency: Behavioral and judgmental effects of appetitive and aversive outcomes with college students. *Learning and Motivation,* **16,** 1–34.

Crocker, J. (1981). Judgment of covariation by social perceivers. *Psychological Bulletin,* **90,** 272–292.

Einhorn, H. J., & Hogarth, R. M. (1986). Judging probable cause. *Psychological Review,* **99,** 3–19.

Erlick, D. E., & Mills, R. G. (1967). Perceptual quantification of conditional dependency. *Journal of Experimental Psychology,* **43,** 9–14.

Fantino, E. (1977). Conditioned reinforcement: Choice and information. In W. K. Honig & J. E. R. Staddon (Eds.), *Handbook of operant behavior* (pp. 313–339). Englewood Cliffs, NJ: Prentice-Hall.

Ferster, C. B., & Skinner, B. F. (1957). *Schedules of reinforcement.* New York: Appleton-Century-Crofts.

Gardner, E. T., & Lewis, P. (1976). Negative reinforcement with shock-frequency increase. *Journal of the Experimental Analysis of Behavior,* **25,** 3–14.

Gibbon, J., & Balsam, P. (1981). Spreading association in time. In C. M. Locurto, H. S. Terrace, & J. Gibbon (Eds.), *Autoshaping and conditioning theory* (pp. 219–254). New York: Academic Press.

Gibbon, J., Berryman, R., & Thompson, R. L. (1974). Contingency spaces and measures in classical and instrumental conditioning. *Journal of the Experimental Analysis of Behavior,* **21,** 585–605.

Gluck, M. A., & Bower, G. H. (1988). From conditioning to category learning: An adaptive network model. *Journal of Experimental Psychology: General,* **117,** 227–247.

Granger, R. H., Jr., & Schlimmer, J. C. (1986). The computation of contingency in classical conditioning. In G. H. Bower (Ed.), *The psychology of learning and motivation* (Vol. 20, pp. 137–192). Orlando, FL: Academic Press.

Gruber, H. E., Fink, C. D., & Damm, V. (1957). Effects of experience on perception of causality. *Journal of Experimental Psychology,* **53,** 89–93.

Hammond, L. J. (1980). The effect of contingency upon the appetitive conditioning of free-operant behavior. *Journal of the Experimental Analysis of Behavior,* **34,** 297–304.

Hammond, L. J., & Paynter, W. E., Jr. (1983). Probabilistic contingency theories of animal conditioning: A critical analysis. *Learning and Motivation,* **14,** 527–550.

Herrnstein, R. J. (1970). On the law of effect. *Journal of the Experimental Analysis of Behavior,* **13,** 243–266.

Hilton, D. J., & Slugoski, B. R. (1986). Knowledge-based causal attribution: The abnormal conditions focus model. *Psychological Review,* **93,** 75–88.

Hineline, P. N. (1970). Negative reinforcement without shock reduction. *Journal of the Experimental Analysis of Behavior,* **14,** 259–268.

Hineline, P. N. (1977). Negative reinforcement and avoidance. In W. K. Honig & J. E. R. Staddon (Eds.), *Handbook of operant behavior* (pp. 364–414). Englewood Cliffs, NJ: Prentice-Hall.

Hume, D. (1951). *Enquiries concerning the human understanding and concerning the principles of morals* (2nd ed. edited by L. A. Selby-Bigge). London: Oxford University Press. (Original work published 1777)

Hume, D. (1964). *Treatise of human nature* (edited by L. A. Selby-Bigge). London: Oxford University Press. (Original work published 1739)

Hursh, S. R., & Fantino, E. (1973). Relative delay of reinforcement and choice. *Journal of the Experimental Analysis of Behavior,* **19,** 437–450.

Jenkins, H. M., Barnes, R. A., & Barrera, F. J. (1981). Why autoshaping depends on trial spacing. In C. M. Locurto, H. S. Terrace, & J. Gibbon (Eds.), *Autoshaping and conditioning theory* (pp. 255–284). New York: Academic Press.

Jenkins, H. M., & Ward, W. C. (1965). Judgment of contingency between responses and outcomes. *Psychological Monographs,* **79,** 1–17.

Killeen, P. R. (1981). Learning as causal inference. In M. L. Commons & J. A. Nevin (Eds.), *Quantitative analyses of behavior: Vol. I. Discriminative properties of reinforcement schedules* (pp. 89–112). Cambridge, MA: Ballinger.

Lachman, R., Lachman, J. L., & Butterfield, E. C. (1979). *Cognitive psychology and information processing: An introduction.* Hillsdale, NJ: Erlbaum.

Lattal, K. A. (1973). Response-reinforcer dependence and independence in multiple and mixed schedules. *Journal of the Experimental Analysis of Behavior, 20,* 265–271.

Lewis, P., Gardner, E. T., & Hutton, L. (1976). Integrated delays to shock as negative reinforcement. *Journal of the Experimental Analysis of Behavior, 26,* 379–386.

Lovibond, P. F. (1988). Predictive validity in human causal judgment and Pavlovian conditioning. *Biological Psychology, 27,* 79–93.

Mackintosh, N. J. (1977). Conditioning as the perception of causal relations. In R. E. Butts & J. Hintikka (Eds.), *Foundational problems in the special sciences* (pp. 241–250). Dordrecht, Netherlands: Reidel.

Michotte, A. E. (1963). *The perception of causality* (T. R. Miles & E. Miles, Trans.). London: Methuen.

Moore, J. (1984). Choice and transformed interreinforcement intervals. *Journal of the Experimental Analysis of Behavior, 42,* 321–335.

Neunaber, D. J. (1986). *Behavioral and judgmental sensitivity of depressed and nondepressed individuals to changes in response-outcome contingencies.* Unpublished doctoral dissertation, University of Iowa, Iowa City.

Neunaber, D. J., & Wasserman, E. A. (1986). The effects of unidirectional versus bidirectional rating procedures on college students' judgments of response-outcome contingency. *Learning and Motivation, 17,* 162–179.

Nisbett, R., & Ross, L. (1980). *Human inference: Strategies and shortcomings of social judgment.* Englewood Cliffs, NJ: Prentice-Hall.

Renner, K. E. (1964). Delay of reinforcement: A historical review. *Psychological Bulletin, 61,* 341–361.

Rescorla, R. A. (1967). Pavlovian conditioning and its proper control procedures. *Psychological Review, 74,* 71–80.

Rescorla, R. A., & Wagner, A. R. (1972). A theory of Pavlovian conditioning: Variations in the effectiveness of reinforcement and nonreinforcement. In A. H. Black & W. F. Prokasy (Eds.), *Classical conditioning II* (pp. 64–99). New York: Appleton-Century-Crofts.

Roitblat, H. L. (1987). *Introduction to comparative cognition.* New York: Freeman.

Seligman, M. E. P., Maier, S. F., & Solomon, R. L. (1971). Unpredictable and uncontrollable aversive events. In F. R. Brush (Ed.), *Aversive conditioning and learning* (pp. 347–400). New York: Academic Press.

Shaklee, H. (1983). Human covariation judgment: Accuracy and strategy. *Learning and Motivation, 14,* 433–448.

Shaklee, H., & Wasserman, E. A. (1986). Judging interevent contingencies: Being right for the wrong reasons. *Bulletin of the Psychonomic Society, 24,* 91–94.

Shanks, D. R. (1985). Hume on the perception of causality. *Hume Studies, 11,* 94–108.

Shanks, D. R. (1989). Selectional processes in causality judgment. *Memory & Cognition, 17,* 27–34.

Shanks, D. R., & Dickinson, A. (1987). Associative accounts of causality judgment. In G. H. Bower (Ed.), *The psychology of learning and motivation* (Vol. 21, pp. 229–261). San Diego, CA: Academic Press.

Shanks, D. R., Pearson, S. M., & Dickinson, A. (1989). Temporal contiguity and the judgment of causality by human subjects. *Quarterly Journal of Experimental Psychology, 41B,* 139–159.

Shull, R. L., Spear, D. J., & Bryson, A. E. (1981). Delay or rate of food delivery as determiners of response rate. *Journal of the Experimental Analysis of Behavior,* **35,** 129–143.

Skinner, B. F. (1948). "Superstition" in the pigeon. *Journal of Experimental Psychology,* **38,** 168–172.

Smedslund, J. (1963). The concept of correlation in adults. *Scandinavian Journal of Psychology,* **4,** 165–173.

Tarpy, R. M., & Sawabini, F. L. (1974). Reinforcement delay: A selective review of the last decade. *Psychological Bulletin,* **81,** 984–997.

Taylor, R. (1967). Causation. In P. Edwards (Ed.), *Encyclopedia of philosophy* (Vol. 2, pp. 56–66). New York: Free Press.

Thomas, G. V. (1981). Contiguity, reinforcement rate and the law of effect. *Quarterly Journal of Experimental Psychology,* **33B,** 33–43.

Thomas, G. V. (1983). Contiguity and contingency in instrumental conditioning. *Learning and Motivation,* **14,** 513–526.

Tolman, E. C., & Brunswik, E. (1935). The organism and the causal texture of the environment. *Psychological Review,* **42,** 43–77.

Tomie, A., & Loukas, E. (1983). Correlations between rats' spatial location and intracranial stimulation administration affects rate of acquisition and asymptotic level of time allocation preference in the open field. *Learning and Motivation,* **14,** 449–471.

Trollier, T. K., & Hamilton, D. L. (1986). Variables influencing judgments of correlational relations. *Journal of Personality and Social Psychology,* **50,** 879–888.

Wasserman, E. A. (1981). Comparative psychology returns: A review of Hulse, Fowler, and Honig's *Cognitive processes in animal behavior. Journal of the Experimental Analysis of Behavior,* **35,** 243–257.

Wasserman, E. A., Chatlosh, D. L., & Neunaber, D. J. (1983). Perception of causal relations in humans: Factor affecting judgments of response-outcome contingencies under free-operant procedures. *Learning and Motivation,* **14,** 406–432.

Wasserman, E. A., & Neunaber, D. J. (1986). College students' responding to and rating of contingency relations: The role of temporal contiguity. *Journal of the Experimental Analysis of Behavior,* **46,** 15–35.

PRIMING OF NONVERBAL INFORMATION AND THE NATURE OF IMPLICIT MEMORY

Daniel L. Schacter
Suzanne M. Delaney
Elizabeth P. Merikle

I. Introduction

Implicit memory refers to the unintentional retrieval of information that was acquired during a specific episode on tests that do not require conscious recollection of that episode (Graf & Schacter, 1985; Schacter, 1987). Systematic investigation of implicit memory represents a relatively new research direction in cognitive psychology and neuropsychology. Psychological studies have been traditonally concerned with explicit memory—intentional, conscious recollection of recent events—as expressed on standard recall and recognition tests. During the past several years, however, there has been a virtual explosion of research concerning various kinds of implicit memory, stimulated largely by studies that have shown that implicit memory can be dissociated sharply from explicit remembering. The dissociations have been produced both by a variety of experimental manipulations in normal subjects and by demonstrations that amnesic patients show intact implicit memory despite impaired explicit memory (for review, see Richardson-Klavehn & Bjork, 1988; Schacter, 1987; Shimamura, 1986).

Various forms of learning and retention can be grouped under the general descriptive heading of "implicit memory," including such phenomena as skill learning and conditioning (see Schacter, 1987). Perhaps the most intensively studied type of implicit memory, however, is known as repetition or direct *priming* (e.g., Cofer, 1967; Tulving & Schacter, 1990). Priming refers to a facilitation in performance that is attributable to prior study of a particular set of target items; priming need not and frequently does not involve any conscious recollection of the targets or the study episode in which they were encountered. The target items in priming experiments are typically familiar words, pseudowords, paired associates, and other verbal materials. The heavy emphasis on verbal information in priming studies may be partly attributable to the historical links between research on priming phenomena and concern with issues of lexical representation and access (e.g., Kirsner & Smith, 1974; Morton, 1979; Scarborough, Gerard, & Cortese, 1979; see Schacter, 1987); it may also be partly attributable to the attention devoted to priming recently by "mainstream" memory researchers, who have traditionally used words and word pairs as target items in explicit memory experiments (e.g. Tulving, 1983).

Although priming research has focused on verbal information, it has not done so exclusively: A number of studies have documented and explored priming of nonverbal information. We think that such studies are important for at least four reasons. First, the preoccupation with words and similar verbal items that characterizes a good deal of past and present priming research will likely produce a rather narrow view of the properties and features of implicit memory. Therefore, at this relatively early stage of research it is desirable and perhaps necessary to establish a broad data base in order to delineate critical characteristics of relevant phenomena. A second and related point is that a narrow empirical focus may also be theoretically misleading. Models of priming and implicit memory that are based exclusively on studies of verbal materials could well be led astray by an undue reliance on phenomena that reflect idiosyncratic properties of verbal information. Third, just as research on lexical priming has provided links between studies of memory and language (e.g., Kirsner & Dunn, 1985), research on priming of nonverbal information could help to build bridges between studies of memory and perception (e.g, Schacter, Cooper, & Delaney, 1990). Fourth, it seems clear from an evolutionary perspective that memory did not evolve initially to deal with verbal information; memory for nonverbal information must represent an earlier evolutionary achievement than memory for verbal information (e.g., Rozin, 1976). Since there are good reasons to believe that the evolutionary process of natural selection has shaped the architecture of memory systems (Sherry & Schacter, 1987) and that the memory systems involved in priming are relatively primitive both phylogenetically and ontogenetically (Schacter, 1984; Schacter & Moscovitch, 1984; Squire, 1987; Tulving &

Schacter, 1990), a theoretical and empirical concern with priming of nonverbal information seems particularly appropriate.

In this chapter we review existing evidence on priming of nonverbal information, discuss methodological, conceptual, and theoretical issues that arise from this research, and sketch a preliminary framework for conceptualizing relevant phenomena that integrates implicit memory research with recent neuropsychological studies of perceptual disorders that are produced by brain damage.

II. Review of the Experimental Evidence

We now turn our attention to experimental data on priming of various kinds of nonverbal information. It should be noted from the outset that we focus largely on studies of repetition or direct priming that conform to what we will call the *study–test* paradigm. In a prototypical study–test procedure, a set of items is initially presented to subjects, followed by a delay that is usually measured in minutes, days, or weeks; then a test is given in which subjects perform a task that does not make explicit reference to or require conscious recollection of the previously presented items. Priming is typically revealed by faster or more accurate performance on previously studied items than on nonstudied or baseline items. We will pay relatively little attention to studies in which primes and targets are separated by extremely brief delays on the order of milliseconds. Although several such studies using nonverbal information have been reported (e.g., Bharucha & Stoeckig, 1986, 1987; Henderson, Pollatsek, & Rayner, 1987; Humphreys & Quinlan, 1988), this type of priming involves a rather different set of issues, paradigms, and perhaps mechanisms than those that are of principal concern to us (for review, see Farah, 1989).

Our review is divided into three major sections, corresponding to the three types of materials that have been used most often in studies of nonverbal priming: familiar objects, novel objects and patterns, and familiar and unfamiliar faces. After considering relevant studies, we discuss a number of methodological and conceptual issues that emerge from the review.

A. Priming of Familiar Objects

In studies concerned with priming of familiar objects, subjects are typically exposed first to pictures or line drawings that contain two-dimensional representations of familiar three-dimensional objects—either animate (e.g., a dog or cow) or inanimate (e.g., a table or car). In most experiments, priming is later assessed by requiring subjects to identify some sort of perceptually degraded stimulus: either a *nonverbal* item such as an incomplete, fragmented, or briefly presented drawing of an object, or a *verbal* item such as a fragmented or briefly presented word. We consider first studies of the former type and then discuss studies of the latter type, which focus on issues of transfer between pictures and words.

1. Neuropsychological and Developmental Evidence

Although intensive experimental scrutiny of priming and implicit memory phenomena represents a relatively recent development, a number of relevant studies were reported prior to the recent surge of interest. Perhaps the earliest of them were studies by Heilbronner conducted in the first decade of the twentieth century (cited in Milner, Corkin, & Teuber, 1968; Parkin, 1982). Heilbronner used a picture-fragment completion task in which brain-damaged and normal subjects were initially shown a series of fragmented pictures of common objects and were asked to identify each object; if they were unable to identify an object from a particular fragment, a series of less fragmented pictures was presented until identification was achieved. When subjects again attempted to identify picture fragments after a delay, Heilbronner observed significant savings in identifying previously presented fragments on the second test. This procedure, which came to be known as "Heilbronner's method," was used in a study of three Korsakoff amnesics by Schneider (1912, cited in Parkin, 1982; Kinsbourne, 1989). He found that amnesics exhibited significant savings in identifying previously exposed fragmented pictures across retention intervals ranging from 7 days to 4 months—even though the patients apparently claimed that they had never seen the pictures previously. This observation thus constitutes an early example of what we would now refer to as a dissociation between implicit and explicit memory.

There was apparently little attempt to follow up Schneider's intriguing observations, but a number of similar studies of amnesic patients were reported before the "modern era" of research on implicit memory. Williams (1953) required 31 patients with memory disturbances and 20 control subjects to name a graded series of inkblot silhouettes of familiar animals; each successive silhouette approximated more closely the shape of the target animals. Free recall and "prompted recall," where silhouettes were presented again for identification, were tested after delays of 2 hr and 7 days. Although memory-disordered patients performed at near zero levels on the free recall test, they performed relatively well on the prompted recall test, particularly at the 2-hr delay. Note, however, that on the prompted recall test, subjects were given explicit memory instructions to try to remember which previously shown animal was represented by the silhouette (Williams, 1953, p. 15). In addition, no information was presented concerning the severity of memory disorders in the patient group. Therefore, it is not clear whether Williams' results should be attributed to priming or to explicit memory. Talland (1965) described similar results in his classic monograph on Korsakoff's syndrome. He presented 14 Korsakoff patients with pictures of familiar objects that were fragmented to different degrees and presented briefly on a tachistoscope for varying amounts of time. Talland reported that previously exposed pictures were identified more readily on a subsequent test than were a novel set of similar fragmented pictures. However, Talland made no mention of any dissociation between this priming effect and patients' inability to recollect their prior experiences. Instead, he simply noted that "Amnesic patients are evidently able to form and retain for a while memory images, in the sense that other persons do" (p. 170).

Probably the best-known study on priming of familiar objects in amnesic patients was reported by Warrington and Weiskrantz (1968), who used the graded series of fragmented pictures developed by Gollin (1960) together with a procedure similar to the one used by Heilbronner and by Schneider. Each of six amnesic patients was presented on an initial trial with the most incomplete version of an object, followed by increasingly less fragmented instances until identification was achieved. The identical procedure was then repeated on four subsequent trials within the same day; five further trials were given on a second and a third day of testing, respectively. Warrington and Weiskrantz (1968) found that all of the amnesic patients exhibited considerable savings—that is, priming—across trials and days. They argued that their findings show long-term retention of specific objects by amnesic patients, and not some sort of nonspecific practice effect, because no improvements in identification performance were observed when fragments of different objects were presented on successive trials. Significantly, however, the learning or priming exhibited by the amnesic patients, though substantial, was not normal; control subjects showed consistently higher levels of identification performance than did amnesics. Although Warrington and Weiskrantz did not distinguish explicitly between the form of memory tapped by the identification task and the form of memory involved in standard recall and recognition tests, they did point out that ". . . in addition to the rapidity and uniformity in learning this task, patients find it a much less exacting test of memory than more conventional ones. They treat it more as a 'guessing game' than a formal test of memory" (1968, p. 974).

Milner *et al.* (1968) used the Gollin figures and a procedure similar to the one described by Warrington and Weiskrantz in a study of the densely amnesic patient H.M. (Scoville & Milner, 1957). In their experiment, a 1-hr delay intervened between initial presentation of the fragmented pictures and the second presentation or test. Milner *et al.* reported a 48% reduction in H.M's identification errors from initial presentation to test. This facilitation or priming effect was observed even though H.M. ". . . did not remember having taken the test before" (1968, p. 230). Consistent with the data of Warrington and Weiskrantz, however, the priming effect observed in H.M. was not normal; a group of 10 matched control subjects showed a 77% reduction in error rate under identical experimental conditions. Milner *et al.* argued that normal subjects showed a larger facilitation because they made use of "verbal [explicit] memory" (1968, p. 231) abilities not available to H.M. in order to retrieve object names and thereby supplement identification performance.

Priming of familiar objects has been observed in amnesic patients with a number of procedures other than the fragmented-pictures task. Warrington and Weiskrantz (1978) reported a study using the McGill Anomalies Test, in which a picture of an otherwise common scene contains a familiar object in an inappropriate place. Warrington and Weiskrantz (1978) recorded the time it took for amnesic patients to detect the anomalous object and found that they did so more quickly on their second attempt than on their first (see also Baddeley, 1982). Meudell and Mayes (1981) reported a similar finding with a task that involved finding a hidden object in a cartoon. They further found that amnesic patients did not discriminate between previously presented and new cartoon pictures when tested with an explicit recognition test. Crovitz, Harvey, and McClanahan (1981) presented eight amnesic patients of mixed etiologies with two pictures containing hidden figures (e.g., a cow) that are typically not perceived immediately on initial viewing (Carmichael, 1951; Dallenbach, 1951) and noted the time required to perceive the figures. Twenty-four hr later, two old and two new hidden figures were presented and patients again attempted to spot them. Crovitz *et al.* found that patients perceived the old figures much more quickly on the second presentation than on the first, and more quickly than new figures, even though several patients expressed no explicit recollection for the initial presentation of the figures. These results thus demonstrate a relatively long lasting item-specific priming effect. However, Crovitz *et al.* did not include a control group in their study, so it is difficult to know whether amnesic patients exhibited normal priming on this task.

Perhaps the most important finding from these neuropsychological studies is that priming of familiar objects can be observed even when recall and recognition are reduced or absent, thereby indicating that such priming cannot be based solely on explicit memory processes. On the other hand, in most of the published studies, priming effects in amnesic patients are smaller than those observed in control subjects; we shall return to this point later.

Relevant evidence has also been provided by studies in which priming of familiar objects has been observed in young children and older adults whose performance on explicit memory tests is impaired. The first developmental study concerning what we would now call priming of familiar objects was reported by Gollin (1960) in an article that described the fragmented pictures that have come to be known as the Gollin figures. Gollin exposed a series of increasingly complete fragments of familiar objects to 4- to 5-yr-old children and adults and noted how much information was required to achieve identification of the object. He then re-presented old fragments together with new picture fragments than had not been presented previously. Gollin found that both children and adults required less information to identify old than new fragments, the magnitude of this savings or priming effect appeared to increase as a function of the similarity between study and test fragments, and there was even savings in identifying new or nonpresented fragments. These results suggest that children acquired general skill at the fragment completion task as well as specific information about individual objects. However, no explicit memory tests were used, so it is difficult to know whether the observed item-specific effects were attributable to priming or explicit remembering (see also Gollin, 1961, 1962, 1965, 1966).

Parkin and Streete (1988) used the fragmented-pictures paradigm to investigate priming and explicit memory in 3-, 5-, and 7-yr-old children as well as adults. Pictures were initially presented in their most incomplete form, followed by presentation of progressively more complete fragments until identification was achieved. Old and new picture fragments were then presented after retention intervals of 1 hr and 2 weeks. Results indicated that younger children initially required more trials to achieve identification than did older children and adults. To avoid potential confoundings attributable to this baseline difference, Parkin and Streete evaluated priming by expressing savings in identification performance on the second presentation of a fragment as a proportion of identification performance on the first presentation. This proportional analysis revealed significant priming in all subject groups and, most importantly, no effect of age on the magnitude of priming. Results also indicated that the priming effect was attributable to the acquisition of item-specific information and not to the acquisition of general skill: Exposure to fragmented pictures did not facilitate subsequent identification of new pictures. In contrast to the priming results, there was a large effect of age on a yes/no recognition test, with levels of explicit memory increasing steadily from the 3-yr-olds to the adults. The magnitude of priming declined between the 1 hr-to-2 week retention interval in all subject groups (though not as much as recognition), but each age group still showed considerable priming even at the long delay.

Carroll, Byrne, and Kirsner (1985) investigated priming in 5-, 7-, and 10-yr-old children with a paradigm in which subjects studied common objects in various conditions and then named pictures of old and new objects. Priming on this task is indicated by faster naming of old than new objects. Although older children were somewhat faster overall than were younger children to name both old and new pictures, all age groups showed a priming effect of comparable magnitude. In contrast, recognition accuracy increased systematically as a function of increasing age. These data are thus consistent with Parkin and Streete's results insofar as they show a developmental dissociation between implicit and explicit memory. Note, however, that Carroll *et al.* (1985) assessed priming with a *latency* measure and explicit memory with an *accuracy* measure. It is possible that priming would have shown a developmental trend comparable to that observed on the recognition task if it, too, had been assessed with an accuracy measure.

A dissociation between priming and explicit memory for familiar objects has also been observed in research on elderly adults. Mitchell (1989) examined the performance of old and young subjects on a picture-naming task in which old and new items were intermixed in a single long list. Target pictures were named on an initial presentation and then were named again after lags consisting of 5, 25, or 50 intervening items. Mitchell observed a robust facilitation of naming latency in young and old subjects at all lags, although there was some decrease in facilitation as lag increased. Most importantly, the magnitude of this priming effect was equivalent in the young and old subjects, even though older subjects were impaired significantly on explicit tests of memory. The elderly recalled fewer picture names than did the young and also performed less accurately on a yes/no recognition test for the prior occurrence of the pictures. As in the Carroll *et al.* (1985) study, however, the apparent implicit/explicit dissociation could also be interpreted as a dissociation between accuracy and latency measures.

Despite some interpretive problems, the foregoing studies of young children and elderly adults extend the neuropsychological evidence by showing robust priming of nonverbal information in subject groups characterized by impaired performance on explicit memory tests. This pattern of dissociation is, in turn, generally consistent with the larger literature on priming of words and other familiar verbal items in amnesic and elderly subjects who show deficits on explicit tests (see Schacter, 1987; Shimamura, 1986).

2. Evidence from Normal Young Adults

The studies discussed in the preceding section were concerned mainly with priming in memory-impaired populations. Nevertheless, they also demonstrated priming of familiar objects in normal adults who acted as control subjects. An early study that can be interpreted as demonstrating object priming in normal subjects was reported by Leeper (1935), who found that exposure to fragmented pictures of objects facilitated subsequent perception of the objects even after a retention interval of approximately 3 weeks. More recently, several studies have provided evidence on the separability of priming and explicit memory that complements the evidence discussed in the previous section by showing that object priming and explicit memory can be dissociated experimentally in normal young adults.

Carroll et al. (1985, Experiment 1) examined the effects of two types of study processing on subsequent picture-naming latency and recognition performance in college students: a deep or elaborative encoding task in which subjects judged whether target objects are animate or inanimate, and a shallow encoding task in which they attempted to find a small inked-in cross that had been drawn on the contour of some of the objects. As expected, recognition memory was more accurate following deep than shallow encoding. Despite this difference in explicit remembering, however, picture-naming latencies were facilitated equally following the two encoding tasks. As noted earlier, however, interpretation of results from this study is not entirely straightforward, because recognition was assessed with an accuracy measure and priming was assessed with a latency measure. It is conceivable that if priming had been assessed with an accuracy measure, the levels-of-processing manipulation would have influenced the magnitude of priming, just as it influenced recognition accuracy; alternatively, if recognition had been assessed with a latency measure, it might have been insensitive to the levels-of-processing manipulation, as was observed for priming. Moreover, in other experiments with children Carroll et al. (1985, Experiments 3 & 4) observed a levels-of-processing effect on naming latency; however, the effect was not observed when baseline differences among experimental conditions were removed. This inconsistent pattern of results highlights the need to treat Carroll et al.'s data with interpretive caution.

Mitchell and Brown (1988) also compared picture-naming latencies and recognition accuracy in an experiment with college students. Subjects named pictures of familiar objects in an initial session; the pictures were then re-presented for naming (intermixed with new pictures) after retention intervals ranging from 1 to 6 weeks. Explicit memory was assessed with a standard yes/no recognition test. Mitchell and Brown observed that initial naming of a picture facilitated subsequent naming performance by about 70 msec at all retention intervals. Recognition memory, by contrast, declined significantly across delays. Mitchell and Brown also observed that the magnitude of the priming effect was independent of whether or not subjects made accurate recognition judgments. This finding thus extends previous reports of stochastic independence between word priming and explicit memory (e.g., Hayman & Tulving, 1989; Jacoby & Witherspoon, 1982; Tulving, Schacter, & Stark, 1982). However, this study is also characterized by the questionable comparison of accuracy and latency measures discussed earlier.

A recent experiment in our laboratory has provided evidence of dissociation between implicit and explicit memory for familiar objects under conditions in which similar measures were used to assess both types of memory (Schacter & Merikle, in preparation). This study, like the experiments by Carroll *et al.* (1985), examined the effects of a levels-of-processing manipulation on priming and explicit memory. Subjects were exposed to line drawings of familiar objects and performed either a *semantic* orienting task, in which they generated functions for the depicted object, or a *structural* orienting task, in which they counted the number of vertices in each object. Priming was assessed by presenting perceptual fragments of studied and nonstudied objects. Fragments were selected that preserved minima of curvature in the object contour, thereby providing useful perceptual information about each object [the fragments and corresponding drawings were selected from various sources by Merikle & Peterson (in preparation)].

In previous studies using fragmented pictures of objects, including those discussed earlier, priming has been assessed by requiring subjects to try to identify each object (e.g., Hirshman, Snodgrass, Mindes, & Feenan, in press; Snodgrass, 1989; Warrington & Weiskrantz, 1968; Weldon & Roediger, 1987). Unfortunately, when subjects are required to identify a fragmented object, they may well attempt to make use of any kind of information that can aid identification, including episodic information that is retrieved through intentional or explicit strategies. Because most studies using fragmented pictures employ procedures akin to the ascending method of limits, where subjects are given exposure to several fragments and are allowed a considerable amount of time to try to identify them, it seems quite likely that standard picture-fragment paradigms encourage the use of explicit memory strategies. The fact that amnesic patients do not show entirely normal priming in the picture-fragment completion task is consistent with the idea that this task typically involves an explicit memory component.

We attempted to overcome these problems and reduce the contribution of explicit memory to fragment completion performance by altering fragment completion instructions so that subjects were told to respond quickly to each perceptual fragment with *the first object that comes to mind* (see also Heindel, Salmon, & Butters, in press) and were also told that there was no correct/incorrect response on the task. A separate group of subjects was given the same perceptual fragments together with explicit memory instructions to try to remember the correct object from the study list. Results revealed that the magnitude of priming was virtually identical following the semantic and structural orienting tasks. By contrast, explicit memory performance was significantly higher following the semantic task than following the structural task. Because the same cues (i.e., perceptual fragments) were used on the implicit and explicit tasks, and performance on both tasks was assessed with the same accuracy measure, we can be confident that this pattern of results reflects a dissociation between priming and explicit memory.

An experiment by Jacoby, Baker, and Brooks (1989) provides evidence for a somewhat different type of dissociation. Subjects were exposed to pictures of common objects in two different ways: (1) pictures were fully exposed on a computer monitor for 7 sec and subjects were required to name them; (2) pictures were "clarified" by a procedure in which random noise dots were gradually replaced by dots from a target picture until subjects could name the depicted object, at which point the fully clarified picture remained on the screen for 7 sec. Memory for the pictured objects was tested explicitly with a free recall test in which subjects were instructed to remember the names of presented objects. Priming was assessed with an identification test that incorporated the clarification procedure; old and new pictures were clarified until subjects could name them, and the amount of clarification required for identification was measured. Jacoby *et al.* reasoned that the extra processing of visual detail in the clarification study condition would benefit identification performance but not free recall of the object name. Moreover, since the additional processing time in the clarification condition yielded a longer retention interval than in the full-exposure condition, there was reason to predict lower free recall performance in the former condition than in the latter. Results were consistent with these expectations: Free recall performance was higher in the full-exposure study condition than in the clarification study condition, whereas the opposite pattern of results was observed on the clarification test—there was more priming in the clarification study condition than in the full-exposure study condition.

The dissociations observed in the foregoing experiments, together with the neuropsychological and developmental evidence, suggest that different mechanisms are involved in priming and explicit memory for familiar objects. A number of studies have provided information about the properties of the representations and processes that support priming. Lachman and Lachman (1980), for example, examined the extent to which priming on a picture-naming task is based on encoding the *visual* properties of objects, as opposed to encoding or activating the lexical information represented by the object's name. To investigate the issue, they examined performance on a yes/no recognition test that included previously studied objects as well as new objects. The actual purpose of the recognition test was to induce subjects to encode the visual properties of objects without requiring overt production of object names; that is, Lachman and Lachman assumed that making a yes/no judgment about the prior occurrence of an object would not entail overt naming of the object. The critical items in the experiment were thus the new or lure objects that had not been presented previously. These lure objects were subsequently presented with a set of entirely new objects on a picture-naming task. Lachman and Lachman found that subjects named the objects that had appeared previously as lures on the recognition test faster than the entirely new objects, thus suggesting that object priming can occur even when subjects do not name the objects at the time of encoding. Unfortunately, no systematic evidence was presented to show that subjects did not in some manner activate the object's name during the recognition test. Nevertheless, these data do show that priming of picture naming need not involve prior *overt* naming of objects during an encoding task. On the other hand, Lachman and Lachman also found that the magnitude of the priming effect on naming latency depended on properties of the object name: Objects that elicited the same name from virtually all subjects appeared to produce less priming than objects that elicited several different names. In addition, some priming of picture naming was observed following processing of the picture name alone, but not nearly as much as was observed following presentation of the picture itself.

A related series of experiments has investigated questions concerning the *specificity* of priming effects with familiar objects: Is the phenomenon based on the activation of some sort of generic or abstract code that represents an object's prototypical features, or does priming reflect specific characteristics of the particular object encoded by the subject on a study trial? Two types of evidence are relevant to this question. First, as noted earlier, in a developmental study Gollin (1960) found that initial "training" on a fragmented version of a picture produced greater subsequent savings (priming) in identifying that fragment than did initial training by exposure to the entire picture. More recently, Snodgrass and Feenan (1989) have replicated and extended these findings with adults and have also shown that priming is greater when the same picture fragment is presented for identification at study and test than when different fragments are used, although there was still significant priming in the different-fragment condition. These kinds of results suggest that priming is based at least in part on a representation of the specific features of objects presented for study, and not solely on an abstract or generic object code. However, explicit memory processes may have played some role in the observed specificity effects. As noted earlier, when training procedures like those in the Gollin and the Snodgrass and Feenan studies are used, explicit memory likely contributes to savings on the identification test (Snodgrass, 1989; Snodgrass & Feenan, 1989). The results of Jacoby *et al.* (1989) with the clarification procedure at least partly address this issue, because they observed specificity effects on an identification test—maximal priming when objects were identified via the clarification technique at both study and test—even though free recall was lower when pictures were studied by "clarification" than with full exposure. Accordingly, it seems unlikely that those explicit memory processes that underlie *free recall of an object's name* contributed to the specificity effect on priming. However, this study provides only partial and equivocal evidence that the specificity effect is attributable to priming and not to explicit memory. It is quite possible that if Jacoby *et al.* had assessed explicit remembering with a recognition test in which subjects were given the same nominal cues as on the identification test, together with intentional retrieval instructions, specificity effects might well have been observed.

A somewhat different type of specificity effect was reported in an early study by Bartram (1974) in which subjects named photographs of familiar objects across blocks of trials. Following the initial naming of an object, there were four critical experimental conditions: (1) the same object was presented again in the same view as on initial presentation; (2) the same object was presented again, but photographed from a different view than on initial presentation; (3) a physically different object with the same name as the target was presented (e.g., photographs of two different cups were named at study and test); and (4) a photograph of a physically different object with a different name was presented. Relative to the baseline level of performance in Condition 4, naming latencies were significantly faster in each of the first three conditions, thereby indicating the presence of priming. Most importantly, however, the largest priming effect was observed for identical objects, less priming occurred for the same object from a different view, and the least amount of priming was found for different objects with the same name (see also Bartram, 1976).

Warren and Morton (1982) reported a similar pattern of results in a study in which subjects initially named either pictures of objects or their verbal labels (e.g., a picture of a clown or the word *clown*). Subjects were then given brief tachistoscopic exposures to pictures and were required to identify them. Some pictures were identical to those named initially, some depicted different objects with the same name (e.g., a picture of a different clown than had been studied), and some had not been previously studied. In their first experiment, Warren and Morton observed significant priming of identical pictures together with a nonsignificant trend for priming of same-name pictures. They argued that the failure to observe significant priming of same-name objects was attributable to the use of explicit memory strategies. According to Warren and Morton (1982, p. 122), if some subjects used an explicit retrieval strategy of attempting to "match" the test picture with a previously studied picture, they would be less likely to find an acceptable match when same-name (but different-object) pictures were exposed. In a second experiment, they attempted to reduce the contribution of explicit memory to picture-identification performance by increasing the length of the study list and testing only a small proportion of the study list items. The obtained pattern of results was quite similar to those observed in the first experiment, except that now the priming effect in the same-name condition was statistically significant. In addition, there was greater priming in the identical condition than in the same-name condition, thus providing some evidence for specificity. Finally, Warren and Morton also observed in both experiments that naming a picture's verbal label at the time of study produced *no* priming on subsequent identification performance, a finding that we shall elaborate on in the next section of the article. Consistent with the results of Warren and Morton, Jacoby *et al.* (1989) found evidence for priming in both identical and same-name conditions with their picture-clarification procedure but also reported more priming in the former condition than in the latter.

The foregoing studies thus suggest that at least some of the priming effect observed on identification and naming tasks is attributable to an encoded representation of the specific object presented at the time of study (more priming in identical than in same-name condition); however, these studies also suggest that priming may be based in part on the activation of a more abstract object representation (significant priming in the same-name condition). Nevertheless, interpretation of these results is not entirely straightforward, because the contribution of explicit memory processes has not been sufficiently scrutinized. It is possible that the observed specificity effects are attributable to explicit memory processes, perhaps because priming in a same-name condition is reduced by subjects' use of intentional retrieval strategies, as suggested by Warren and Morton.

A recent study in our laboratory addresses this issue directly (Schacter & Bowers, in preparation). Subjects were shown pictures of familiar objects and performed either a semantic orienting task (function generation) or a structural orienting task (vertex counting), as in the previously described study by Schacter and Merikle (in preparation). After a delay of several minutes, subjects in both groups were given a priming task in which pictures of objects were exposed for 50 msec (preceded and followed by a pattern mask) and subjects attempted to identify them. The tested objects were (1) *identical* to a previously studied object, (2) different exemplars of the object that had the *same name,* or (3) *new* objects that had not been previously studied. After the identification test, subjects were shown the same pictures and were asked to make yes/no recognition judgments about whether they had seen an object of the kind depicted by the picture on the initial study list (i.e., "yes" responses were correct for both identical and same-name objects).

The experiment yielded three important results. First, recognition memory performance for both identical and same-name objects was significantly higher in the semantic encoding condition than in the structural encoding condition. Second, the magnitude of priming for identical objects did not differ in the semantic and structural conditions: Identification accuracy increased from about 70% for new objects to about 85% for identical objects in both encoding conditions. Thus, the levels-of-processing manipulation produced an implicit/explicit dissociation on the object-identification task, just as it did on the object-completion task used by Schacter and Merikle (in preparation). Third, and perhaps most important, there was *no* priming of same-name objects in the structural condition, together with a marginally significant trend for priming of same-name objects in the semantic condition. The failure to observe any priming of same-name objects following structural encoding is particularly important: If, as suggested by Warren and Morton (1982), explicit memory somehow inhibits priming in a same-name condition, then more priming of same-name objects should have been observed following structural encoding than following semantic encoding, because explicit memory was lower in the former than in the latter condition. However, an opposite pattern of results was observed. Contrary to Warren and Morton, then, our data suggest that facilitation of identification performance for same-name objects may be *attributable to*—rather than *inhibited by*—explicit memory processes and that "genuine" structurally based priming is restricted to identical objects. Of course, it will be necessary to replicate these findings before firm theoretical conclusions can be drawn.

Suggestive evidence concerning the specific type of structural information involved in object priming is provided by Biederman and Cooper (1989b). In an initial experiment, subjects named contour-deleted objects from brief presentations during the first block of trials. On the second block, three types of objects were named: some were *identical* to those named on the first trial (i.e., same object, same contour deletion), some were *complements* of the object named on the first trial (i.e., same object, composed of edges and vertices that were deleted on the initial trial), and some were different objects with the *same name*. Biederman and Cooper observed some priming (faster and more accurate naming) for same-name objects, which they attributed to nonvisual factors (e.g., name or concept priming). More importantly, they observed significantly greater priming for identical and complementary objects, with no difference between these two conditions. The latter finding indicates that priming is not based on some sort of "literal" representation of object features, because objects in the identical and complementary conditions were composed of entirely different contours yet showed equivalent priming. By contrast, in a second experiment Biederman and Cooper constructed complementary objects by deleting alternate convex components or geons (Biederman, 1987) and found significantly less priming in the complementary condition than in the identical condition. Indeed, there was no more priming in the complementary condition than in the same-name condition.

Biederman and Cooper's results suggest that object priming may depend critically on the encoding of structural components of objects. However, two points about their study should be noted. First, they did not include an explicit memory test in either experiment, so we do not know whether and to what extent explicit memory processes contributed to the observed pattern of results. Second, they presented no evidence to support their assumption that priming in the same-name condition is based exclusively on nonvisual information. As noted earlier, Warren and Morton have argued that priming in this condition reflects priming of an abstract, but visual, representation of an object. However, the Schacter and Bowers finding discussed earlier that there is no priming in a same-name condition following a structural encoding task does provide some support for Biederman and Cooper's claim.

In a related study, Biederman and Cooper (1989a) found that priming in their paradigm was unaffected by changes in retinal location (i.e., hemifield of presentation) and left/right orientation of an object between first and second naming trials, even though subjects possessed relatively good explicit memory for location and orientation information. Although these results suggest that object priming is based on an orientation-free representation, Jolicouer (1985) has reported effects of orientation change on priming of naming latencies. In an initial experiment, Jolicouer showed that the time to name drawings of familiar objects increases linearly as the objects are rotated increasingly further from upright. More importantly for the present purposes, Jolicouer showed in two additional experiments that this effect of orientation decreases with practice at naming rotated objects. The effect of practice was item specific, in the sense that repeated naming of rotated objects did not reduce the effect of orientation on novel objects; the effect was observed only for rotated objects that were previously named.

Jolicouer and Milliken (1989) have extended these results to show that initial naming of objects in various rotations reduces subsequent effects of orientation on naming times of previously presented objects relative to a condition in which objects are initially only in upright form. To the extent that the "practice" effects observed by Jolicouer can be taken as expressions of priming, these data suggest that information about the orientation of familiar objects plays a role in priming of naming latencies. Although this conclusion may appear inconsistent with Biederman and Cooper's (1989a) findings, these investigators examined effects of left/right orientation changes, whereas Jolicouer has focused on changes from upright orientation. It should also be noted that information about orientation appears to play an important role in explicit memory performance (Rock & DiVita, 1987; Rock, DiVita, & Barbeito, 1981), so detailed comparisons of the effects of orientation change on priming and explicit memory are clearly necessary in order to understand more fully the role of orientation information in implicit and explicit memory for familiar objects.

3. Picture/Word Transfer

A number of studies concerned with priming of nonverbal information have examined transfer of priming between pictures of familiar objects and the corresponding object names. Perhaps the earliest such study was reported by Winnick and Daniel (1970). In their experiment, subjects were exposed to pictures of familiar objects or to words corresponding to the pictured objects. Priming was assessed with a word-identification test and explicit memory was assessed with a free recall test. Winnick and Daniel observed a striking dissociation between these two memory tests: Free recall was higher following study of a picture than study of the corresponding word, but priming effects on the word-identification test were greater following study of the word than study of the picture. Indeed, there was only a slight priming effect in the pictorial study condition.

Although Winnick and Daniel's findings were largely overlooked in subsequent years (see Roediger & Weldon, 1987; Schacter, 1987), they were confirmed and extended by two studies that appeared nearly a decade later. Scarborough et al. (1979) required subjects to name concrete words or corresponding pictures and then examined performance on a lexical decision test in which words from the two study conditions (as well as new words and nonwords) were presented, and subjects decided as quickly as possible whether each letter string constituted a word or a nonword. Prior study of a word produced significant facilitation of lexical decision latency, but prior study of pictures produced no priming. In contrast, a subsequent experiment showed that recognition memory was higher for previously studied pictures than words, thus providing a dissociation similar to that observed by Winnick and Daniel. Consistent with the results of Scarborough et al., Durso and Johnson (1979) found that initial naming of a picture produced no priming of naming latency when subjects subsequently named the corresponding word, although considerable priming was observed when the same picture was named again. However, Durso and Johnson also reported an asymmetry in priming: Initial naming of a word facilitated subsequent naming of the pictorial equivalent, although priming was not as robust as in a word–word condition. Durso and Johnson found a similar pattern of results with a task that involved repeated categorization of words and pictures. Consistent with these results, it was noted earlier that Lachman and Lachman (1980) found that study of words produced significant, albeit reduced, priming on a subsequent picture-naming task relative to study of their pictorial equivalents. Warren and Morton (1982), however, found that studying words produced no priming on a subsequent test of picture identification from brief tachistoscopic exposures.

The foregoing experiments suggest that there is little if any priming from pictures to words on a variety of tests. Some picture–word priming has been documented, however, in subsequent studies. Kroll and Potter (1984) required subjects to make "reality" decisions concerning whether letter strings represented real words or nonwords and whether line drawings represented real objects or nonobjects. Large repetition priming effects on decision latencies were observed in word–word and picture–picture conditions. Significant, albeit substantially reduced, priming was found from pictures to words. In contrast to previous studies, however, no priming was found from words to pictures. Kirsner, Milech, and Stumpfel (1986) examined priming on a tachistoscopic word-identification test following a study task in which subjects classified words on their pictorial equivalents as living or man-made. Significant priming was found in both the word–word and the picture–word conditions, although the former condition yielded more priming than did the latter. When a study task was used that required subjects to judge the real-world size of words or pictorial equivalents, similar amounts of priming were found on a subsequent word-identification test. However, Kirsner *et al.* also showed that the "intramodal" component of priming (i.e., word–word transfer) could be dissociated from the "intermodal" component (i.e., picture–word transfer), inasmuch as a word frequency manipulation affected the intermodal but not intramodal type of priming. Kirsner *et al.* also showed that studying pictures yielded higher levels of explicit memory on a yes/no word-recognition test than did studying words, in contrast to the priming data.

Weldon and Roediger (1987) examined the effects of studying words or their pictorial equivalents on two subsequent tests: word-fragment completion and free recall. They observed a striking crossover interaction between the two tests similar to the pattern first reported by Winnick and Daniel; free recall performance was higher for pictures than for words, whereas there was greater priming on the fragment completion test for words than for pictures. Weldon and Roediger found that studying pictures produced some priming on the fragment completion test, but the effects were quite small. Conversely, additional experiments showed that studying pictures of objects produced large priming effects on a picture-fragment completion test.

Hirshman *et al.* (in press) reported several experiments that used a study task in which subjects studied target words by generating a sentence that contained each word. Priming was assessed with a picture-fragment completion task using the ascending method of limits procedure described earlier (e.g., Gollin, 1960; Snodgrass, 1989). Hirshman *et al.* observed significant word–picture priming in this experiment and two similar ones, and on the basis of these results argued for a conceptual component to priming. Several features of this study, however, limit the force of this conclusion. First, Hirshman *et al.* did not use a picture–picture condition, so we do not know whether the word–picture priming effects that they observed were smaller than picture–picture priming effects, as has been observed previously. Second, and perhaps more importantly, it was noted earlier that when priming on a picture-fragment completion task is assessed with the ascending method of limits, as was done in the Hirshman *et al.* study, explicit retrieval processes likely play a major role in task performance. Thus, the word–picture transfer reported by these investigators may be entirely or largely attributable to explicit retrieval. Hirshman *et al.* attempted to deal with this possibility by comparing performance on the picture-fragment completion task and a free recall task (in which subjects recalled target words). They found little correlation between free recall and picture completion performance and thus argued that word–picture priming is not attributable to explicit memory. Unfortunately, this line of reasoning is not compelling, because the same outcome might have been observed even if subjects had in fact treated the picture completion test as an explicit cued recall test; that is, free recall of words and explicit cued recall of pictures may not be strongly correlated. As discussed elsewhere in this article, to evaluate the possible contribution of explicit memory to a priming effect on an allegedly implicit task, it is necessary to use the same nominal cues on the two tasks and vary only task instructions (see discussion on pp. 110–112). Comparisons of the kind made in the Hirshman *et al.* study do not speak directly to the role of explicit memory processes, so their data must be treated with interpretive caution.

Despite the variability and occasional inconsistencies among the foregoing studies, it seems safe to conclude that there is generally a good deal less priming from pictures to words and words to pictures than from words to words or pictures to pictures. Whether or not *no* intermodal priming is found, or *reduced* levels of intermodal priming are observed compared to an intramodal condition, varies across experiments and likely depends on tasks and materials in ways that are not yet well understood. Nevertheless, the generally reliable finding that priming is reduced in intermodal conditions indicates that the physical form of a stimulus plays a large role in priming. Moreover, the finding that studying familiar pictures enhances recall and recognition of corresponding words, while producing little or no priming on word identification, fragment completion, and lexical decision tests, indicates that form-based information plays a different role in priming than in explicit memory. Note, however, that the crucial importance of form information is observed only for *repetition* or *direct* priming; studies of *semantic* or *associative* priming have consistently provided evidence of extensive and even complete transfer between pictures and words (e.g., Vanderwart, 1984). We shall return to this point later when considering theoretical interpretations of nonverbal priming.

B. Priming of Novel Objects and Patterns

Although the studies considered in previous sections include a wide variety of tasks, experimental procedures, and subject populations, in all experiments either the study or the test materials consisted of photographs, pictures, or line drawings of common objects. These materials are thus familiar to subjects before the initial study presentation in the sense that the objects that they depict are represented in long-term memory prior to the experiment. The fact that most studies on priming of nonverbal information have used familiar materials with preexisting memory representations has a number of theoretical implications that will be discussed shortly. Nevertheless, there have been some, albeit relatively few, studies that have examined priming of novel or unfamiliar nonverbal information.

One set of relevant findings is provided by studies of the "mere exposure" effect (Zajonc, 1980) on preference judgments. In an experiment by Kunst-Wilson and Zajonc (1980), subjects were exposed for 1 msec to line drawings of novel shapes (irregularly shaped octagons). They were then given two types of forced-choice tests: (1) a recognition test in which an old and a new octagon were presented and subjects indicated which shape had been presented previously; and (2) a preference test in which an old and a new octagon were presented and subjects indicated which shape they liked better. Since the latter task does not require conscious recollection of the study exposure, it can be viewed as an implicit memory test that may be influenced by priming. Although subjects did not perform significantly higher than chance on the recognition test, they showed a reliable preference for the previously exposed octagon. Seamon, Brody, and Kauff (1983) reported that exposure effects on preference judgments were larger when target shapes were initially exposed in the right than in the left visual field, whereas a left-visual-field advantage was observed for recognition. Johnson, Kim, and Risse (1985) found normal exposure effects on preferences for novel melodies in amnesic patients who were impaired on a recognition test, thereby providing further evidence for a dissociation between preference judgments and explicit memory.

Mandler, Nakamura, and Van Zandt (1987) questioned whether the effects observed in the foregoing studies reflect a fundamental difference between cognition (indexed by recognition memory) and affect (indexed by preference judgments), as had been argued by Zajonc (1980). As in the Kunst-Wilson and Zajonc and Seamon *et al.* studies, Mandler *et al.* gave subjects brief (2 msec) exposures to unfamiliar shapes and then tested recognition and preference judgments for old and new shapes in two different subject groups. In addition, however, Mandler *et al.* also required two other subject groups to judge which of two test stimuli (one old and one new) seemed *brighter* or which of the two seemed *darker*. Consistent with previous results, they observed a reliable preference for old shapes under conditions in which recognition memory did not differ from chance. More importantly, Mandler *et al.* also found that subjects showed a similar tendency to judge previously exposed shapes as either brighter or darker than new shapes in the appropriate conditions. These results suggest that the dissociation between preference and recognition judgments observed in previous studies is not based on a fundamental split between cognition and affect, but rather reflects a nonspecific priming effect that can be expressed in a variety of judgments independently of explicit memory.

A number of studies have examined priming of novel nonverbal information using implicit tests that are in some respects similar to the identification, completion, and lexical decision tasks that have been used extensively in the verbal domain. Two recent experiments have focused on priming of dot patterns. In a neuropsychological study of the severely amnesic patient H. M. (Gabrieli, Milberg, Keane, & Corkin, in press), the target materials were spatial arrangements of five dots from a 3×3 matrix that were connected by four lines to form a specific pattern. After exposing a series of such patterns to H.M. and a group of control subjects, priming was assessed with a "dot-completion" test in which unconnected five-dot arrangements were presented and subjects were asked to draw any figure that connected the dots with straight lines. There were a number of possible completions for each figure, and the question of principal interest was whether subjects would tend to connect the dots to form previously studied figures. Results indicated robust and similar levels of priming in H.M. and control subjects; dot patterns on the completion test were connected to form previously studied figures at significantly higher than baseline levels. Moreover, a dissociation between priming and explicit memory was observed: H.M. showed intact pattern priming despite his severe impairment on a recognition test in which subjects were asked to remember explicitly which patterns had been presented previously.

Musen and Treisman (1990) also examined priming of novel dot patterns with a different implicit test. In their study, college students were shown 50 dot patterns similar to those used by Gabrieli *et al.*, consisting of five dots from a 3×3 matrix that were connected by four lines. Priming was assessed after delays of 1 hr, 3 hr, or 7 days with a perceptual identification test in which old and new dot patterns were presented briefly, and subjects tried to copy the correct pattern on an empty 3×3 grid. Exposure time on the identification test was calibrated so that baseline accuracy in copying patterns without any study exposure was about 40–45% correct. Musen and Treisman observed significant priming effects in their experiment—subjects copied significantly more old than new patterns—and the magnitude of priming was largely unaffected by length of retention interval. Explicit recognition of the patterns, by contrast, declined across the delay. In addition, recognition and priming exhibited stochastic independence (e.g., Tulving *et al.*, 1982); the probability of recognizing a particular pattern was uncorrelated with the probability of producing that pattern from a brief exposure.

Several other recent studies have examined priming of novel two-dimensional and three-dimensional shapes and objects. As noted earlier, Kroll and Potter (1984) examined priming with an object decision task in which subjects decided whether drawings of either familiar, real-world objects or constructed nonobjects did or did not exist in the world. Both objects and nonobjects were repeated after lags of three or ten intervening items in a continuous sequence during which subjects made object decisions. Kroll and Potter found that subjects were faster to make such decisions about nonobjects on the second presentation of a drawing than on the first; similar effects were observed for familiar objects. Thus, priming was observed in this experiment for both novel items with no preexisting memory representations and familiar items that have preexisting representations.

A rather different type of object decision task was used in a series of experiments by Schacter *et al.* (1990). The materials in these experiments were two-dimensional drawings of novel, unfamiliar three-dimensional objects. Although none of the target objects actually exist in the real world, half of the drawings depict structurally *possible* objects whose surfaces and edges are connected in such a way that they could exist in three-dimensional form. The other half of the drawings, in contrast, represent *impossible* objects that contain surface, edge, or contour violations that would make it impossible for them to exist in three-dimensional form (e.g., Penrose & Penrose, 1958). To assess priming of these objects, Schacter *et al.* devised an object decision test in which subjects were given brief (100 msec) exposures to possible and impossible objects and were required to decide whether each object was structurally possible or impossible; half of the test objects had been studied several minutes earlier and half were new. The main question was whether priming of novel objects would be observed—that is, whether study of possible and impossible objects increased the accuracy of subsequent object decisions. Explicit memory was assessed with a standard yes/no recognition test.

In an initial experiment, priming on the object decision task was found following a study task that was intended to induce subjects to encode information about the global three-dimensional structure of the objects (indicating whether each object faced primarily to the left or right). By contrast, no priming was observed following a study task that required encoding the local features of target objects (indicating whether each object had more horizontal or vertical lines). The magnitude of priming in the left/right condition was about the same whether or not the object decision task was preceded by a recognition task on which all critical objects were exposed; that is, mere exposure to an object on the recognition task did not produce priming on the object decision task. Priming also showed stochastic independence from recognition memory. Significantly, priming was found only for the structurally possible objects; no priming of structurally impossible objects was observed in this study or in subsequent experiments. However, recognition memory for impossible objects was only slightly less accurate than was recognition of possible objects.

The results of this experiment were interpreted as suggesting that priming on the object decision test depends on prior encoding of a global three-dimensional *structural description* (Marr, 1982; Marr & Nishihara, 1978) of target objects. By this view, the failure to find priming of impossible objects indicates that it is difficult to form a global structural description of such objects. In a subsequent experiment, the left/right encoding task was compared to an *elaborative* encoding task in which subjects had to think of a familiar object from the real world that each target object reminded them of most. As expected, this encoding task yielded higher levels of explicit memory performance on the recognition test than did left/right encoding; the elaborative task required subjects to relate target objects to preexisting semantic knowledge of objects, thus producing a distinctive and hence highly memorable episodic memory representation (e.g., Jacoby & Craik, 1979). The striking result, however, was that *no* priming was observed following the elaborative task, whereas the left/right task again produced substantial priming. One potential reason for the failure to observe priming following elaborative encoding was that subjects often produced two-dimensional elaborations of the objects and did not encode them as three-dimensional structures. In a third experiment, an attempt was made to induce subjects to achieve three-dimensional elaborations by requiring them to indicate whether each object reminded them most of a type of furniture, a household object, or part of a building. Significant priming was observed following this task; however, these priming effects were no greater than those observed following the left/right task, even though the three-dimensional elaboration task produced higher recognition performance than did the left/right task.

As noted above, the fact that priming was observed for possible but not impossible objects suggests that subjects are unable to form global structural descriptions of impossible objects. Schacter *et al.* noted, however, that a number of alternative interpretations of this finding could not be excluded. For example, the target objects for these experiments were selected initially on the basis of a pilot study in which subjects were given unlimited time to classify them as possible or impossible; only those objects that yielded high levels of intersubject agreement were included in the target set. However, whereas there was 97% agreement about the possible objects, there was less agreement (87%) concerning the impossible objects. It is thus possible that priming of impossible objects could be observed if a set of objects were used that yielded close to 100% agreement with unlimited viewing time. In more recent studies (Schacter, Cooper, Delaney, Peterson, & Tharan, in preparation), a new set of impossible objects that conformed to this criterion was used, and a number of other procedural changes were made to increase the likelihood of observing priming for structurally impossible objects. Nevertheless, these experiments, like the earlier studies, have yielded no evidence for priming of impossible objects—even after four repetitions of the left/right encoding task. Interestingly, four vs. one study list repetitions had no effect on priming of possible objects—similar amounts of priming were observed in both study conditions—even though explicit memory for possible and impossible objects was significantly higher following four than following one study list repetition. Thus, the overall pattern of data suggests that subjects can encode local features and parts of impossible objects that are sufficent to support reasonably high levels of recognition memory, but do not and perhaps cannot form global descriptions of impossible objects that are needed to support priming on the object decision test.

A recent study by Kersteen-Tucker (1989) has yielded a pattern of results that in some respects parallels the one observed in the foregoing experiments. Kersteen-Tucker examined priming of novel, unfamiliar polygons in a continuous-response procedure in which subjects decided whether each of a series of polygons was symmetrical or nonsymmetrical; half of the targets were symmetrical and half were not. Target polygons were repeated after lags of zero, one, four, or eight intervening items. The dependent measure was latency to make the symmetry judgment, and priming was indicated by faster response latencies to repeated than to nonrepeated polygons. Kersteen-Tucker observed a significant priming effect at all lags for symmetrical polygons, although the magnitude of the effect declined across lags. By contrast, no priming was observed for nonsymmetrical polygons, even at the zero lag. Thus, just as possible but not impossible objects showed priming on the object decision task, symmetrical but not nonsymmetrical shapes showed priming on the symmetry judgment task. However, explicit memory for the shapes was not investigated in Kersteen-Tucker's experiment.

C. Priming of Familiar and Unfamiliar Faces

There have been only a few studies concerned with priming of faces, but they have yielded several suggestive experimental facts. Bruce and Valentine (1985) reported two experiments that were motivated by Warren and Morton's work on priming of familiar objects. In their first experiment, subjects were initially presented with either pictures of familiar faces (e.g., politicians, entertainers) or the corresponding printed names. In the former condition, subjects were required to name the face; in the latter they read aloud the printed name. Priming was assessed after a 20-min filled delay with a task in which subjects were given brief exposures to faces and attempted to name them. The duration of presentation was manipulated using the ascending method of limits: Presentation of a particular face began at 10 msec and was increased by 10 msec/exposure until subjects identified the face twice in succession. Priming was assessed by comparing subjects' naming thresholds in four different conditions defined by the prior history of the faces: (1) neither the face nor name of the face had been presented in the naming phase of the experiment *(baseline)*; (2) the name but not the face had been presented *(name)*; (3) the same face had been presented *(same)*; and (4) a different view of the face had been presented during naming *(different)*. Bruce and Valentine found that, relative to baseline, comparable levels of priming were observed in the name and different conditions, while significantly greater priming was found in the same condition. These results were thus similar to the analogous picture priming data of Warren and Morton (1982), except that no priming was found in the name condition of the Warren and Morton study. Bruce and Valentine noted, however, that they might have observed priming in the name condition because a naming response was required on their test. To investigate this issue, they performed a second experiment in which priming was assessed with a familiarity test that did not require naming: Subjects had to indicate as quickly as possible whether the face was familiar to them, and the dependent variable was latency to make the familiarity judgment. Using the same four study conditions as in the first experiment, Bruce and Valentine reported significant priming in the different condition, even greater priming in the same condition, and, most importantly, no priming in the name condition. These results suggest that the priming observed in the name condition in Experiment 1 was likely attributable to a facilitation of name production.

Similar results were reported in subsequent study by Young, McWeeny, Hay, and Ellis (1986, Experiment 4). Subjects in their experiment were initially exposed to either the faces or the names of politicians and unfamiliar people. When exposed to faces, subjects made either a *familiarity decision* (i.e., Is this face familiar?) or a *semantic decision* (i.e., Is this face a politician?). When exposed to names, they made a *name-familiarity decision* (i.e., Is this name familiar?). Priming was assessed with the semantic decision task; latency to make the semantic decision was the dependent variable. Young *et al.* found significant and comparable amounts of priming for familiar faces following both the familiarity and the semantic decision tasks; no priming of unfamiliar faces was observed following either task. In addition, no priming for either familiar or unfamiliar faces was observed following the name-familiarity judgment. Thus, as in the Bruce and Valentine study, when a face-judgment test does not require a naming response, prior exposure to a name does not produce priming.

The Young *et al.* study also suggests that unfamiliar faces, unlike unfamiliar objects, may not be susceptible to priming. This notion receives some additional support from an investigation by Bentin and Moscovitch (1988). They assessed priming with a *face-decision* task in which the critical stimuli were either pictures of normal but unfamiliar faces or faces with scrambled features ("nonfaces"). Subjects decided whether each configuration formed a normal human face or a nonface on two successive presentations of critical targets that were separated by lags of 0, 4, or 15 intervening items. Priming was observed for both faces and nonfaces only in the zero lag condition. In contrast, on an analogous lexical decision task, familiar words showed priming at all lags whereas nonwords showed priming only at lag zero. In subsequent experiments, Bentin and Moscovitch attempted to increase the "strength" of the memory representation for unfamiliar faces by varying study task and number of repetitions. Nevertheless, they found no priming of unfamiliar faces beyond lag zero on the face-decision task. However, when subjects were given an explicit recognition task, memory for the unfamiliar faces was observed even at the longest lag, thus suggesting that some sort of representation of these faces had been formed.

Both the Young *et al.* and Bentin and Moscovitch studies, then, failed to find priming of unfamiliar faces on two different types of implicit tests (semantic decision and face decision). Some unpublished data suggestive of priming for unfamiliar faces, however, was alluded to briefly in an article by Tulving (1985). In the cited experiment, subjects were initially presented with "shadow drawings" of unfamiliar faces. Priming was then assessed by presenting old and new shadow drawings and asking subjects to indicate whether or not they could "see" a face in the drawing (some drawings did not represent faces); explicit memory was assessed with a yes/no recognition test. Tulving reported that subjects correctly identified more old than new shadow faces and that this priming effect exhibited stochastic independence from recognition memory.

III. Methodological, Conceptual, and Theoretical Issues

The studies that we have reviewed indicate that priming of nonverbal information can be observed across a wide range of tasks and materials. Priming has been observed on fragment completion, picture-identification, picture-naming, object decision, preference, face-naming, semantic decision, and pattern identification/completion tasks; and priming has been demonstrated both for familiar objects and shapes as well as for novel objects and patterns that have no preexisting memory representations. We now turn to some of the major methodological and conceptual issues that arise from this literature. We consider first the possible contributions of explicit memory and naming processes, respectively, to performance in priming paradigms. We then consider alternative accounts of the phenomena that we have reviewed and conclude by outlining a preliminary theoretical framework for conceptualizing priming of nonverbal information.

A. CONTRIBUTIONS OF EXPLICIT MEMORY

The studies that have been considered in this chapter all share one critical feature: They have assessed the influence of information acquired during an episode on subsequent performance with implicit memory tests that do not make explicit reference to, or require conscious recollection of, the prior study episode. It is precisely because such tests have been used that we refer to the phenomena of interest as expressions of *priming* and not *remembering*. However, as indicated earlier in the article the fact that a test does not require explicit remembering of a prior episode does not preclude the possibility that subjects will make use of explicit memory processes. For example, we have noted several times that the standard picture-fragment completion task, which has been used in numerous studies of priming, is readily influenced by explicit memory processes (e.g., Snodgrass, 1989).

The possibility that explicit memory processes influence performance on nominally implicit tests raises some tricky interpretive issues. Consider, for example, the finding that amnesic patients show significant, but not normal, priming on the picture-fragment completion task (e.g., Milner et al., 1968; Warrington & Weiskrantz, 1968). The fact that amnesics show *some* priming despite near chance levels of recognition performance indicates that the observed priming cannot be attributed to explicit memory. However, the additional fact that amnesic patients show lower levels of completion performance than do control subjects can be interpreted in two different ways. First, the processes that support object priming in amnesics may be impaired. Second, priming may be intact in amnesics, but normal subjects supplement completion test performance by engaging in explicit retrieval strategies (e.g., Milner et al., 1968). The same sort of interpretive problem arises when an experimental variable has parallel effects on explicit and implicit tests. The parallel pattern of results may on the one hand reflect an important similarity between implicit and explicit memory; on the other hand, it may be attributable to the use of explicit retrieval strategies on a nominally implicit test.

In a general discussion of the issue, Schacter, Bowers, and Booker (1989) put forward a method for dealing with this problem, alluded to earlier in the article, called the *retrieval intentionality criterion*. This criterion consists of three key components: (1) the same nominal cues should be presented to subjects on implicit and explicit tests; (2) only the implicit/explicit nature of test instructions should be varied; and (3) an experimental or subject variable should be identified that produces dissociations between implicit and explicit task performance. Schacter et al. argued that when an implicit/explicit dissociation is observed under these conditions, the possibility that subjects use explicit strategies on the implicit test can be ruled out. Adherence to this criterion provides a noncircular means for interpreting parallel effects on implicit and explicit tasks. If parallel effects of experimental variables A and B are observed within the same paradigm that also produces a dissociation between variables C and D, then we can be confident that the observed parallel effects are not attributable to explicit memory processes (see Schacter et al., 1989, for more extensive discussion).

Applying this logic to the research that we have reviewed, only a few studies have produced dissociations in strict conformity with the retrieval intentionality criterion (Gabrielli et al., in press; Kunst-Wilson & Zajonc, 1980; Mandler et al., 1987; Mitchell, 1989; Musen & Treisman, 1990; Parkin & Streete, 1988; Schacter et al., 1990; Schacter & Bowers, in preparation; Schacter & Merikle, in preparation). Several studies have documented similar dissociations under conditions in which the nominal cues differed on implicit and explicit tests (e.g., Hirshman et al., in press; Jacoby et al., 1989; Weldon & Roediger, 1987; Winnick & Daniel, 1970);

as discussed previously, this sort of comparison is not entirely satisfactory. Other investigations have attempted to examine the contribution of explicit memory processes to priming through different types of analyses (e.g., Snodgrass & Feenan, 1989; Warren & Morton, 1982). Unfortunately, however, a large number of studies on priming of nonverbal information have not included explicit memory tests. Therefore, we must remain uncertain about the possible role of explicit remembering in many of the phenomena reviewed earlier. Until appropriate dissociations are produced, interpretive caution should be exercised when attempting to draw theoretical inferences from priming studies about the processes and systems involved in implicit and explicit memory.

B. FACILITATION OF NAMING VERSUS PRIMING OF NONVERBAL INFORMATION

A second issue with important interpretive implications that has been acknowledged in the literature concerns the role of object naming in priming effects. The question is whether we can safely attribute observed performance facilitations to priming of *nonverbal* information—representations of objects, patterns, faces, and the like—or whether these effects are attributable to overt or covert naming processes. As discussed by several investigators (e.g., Bruce & Valentine, 1985; Lachman & Lachman, 1980), subjects may generate names of familiar objects at the time of study, and facilitated access to object names may produce priming on subsequent tests. And even when unfamiliar objects or patterns are used, it is always possible that subjects code them verbally during study and that priming is attributable to retrieval of verbal codes at test.

One reason why this issue must be considered seriously is that most of the implicit tests that have been used to assess priming of nonverbal information involve a naming response; identification of fragmented or briefly presented pictures and picture naming are the most prominent examples. One type of evidence relevant to this issue is that studying words yields little if any priming on picture completion and identification tests (Warren & Morton, 1982; Weldon & Roediger, 1987) and reduced (relative to pictures) though significant priming on picture-naming tests (Durso & Johnson, 1979; Lachman & Lachman, 1980). These results suggest that simple generation of a verbal label is not a major source of priming on nonverbal tests. On the other hand, naming a word during the study phase has produced some priming in several studies, thereby suggesting that name generation may play some role in priming on picture identification and naming tests. Moreover, even if naming a *word* at the time of study produced no priming, it is still logically possible that priming depends crucially on generating a name for a studied *picture*. Lachman and Lachman (1980) attempted to exclude this possibility by demonstrating that presentation of lure pictures on a yes/no recognition test produced significant facilitation on a subsequent picture-naming test. However, the theoretical significance of this finding depends critically on the validity of the rather uncertain assumption that subjects do not generate an object name when making a recognition decision about a lure item. Bruce and Valentine (1985) found that naming a face produced priming on a subsequent face-naming task but not on a semantic decision task, thereby suggesting that naming processes may play a role on some though not all implicit tests.

Several additional findings call into question the importance of object naming during the study phase for subsequent priming. First, priming is higher when the *same* object is presented at study and test than when a *different* object with the same name is presented (Bartram, 1974; Biederman & Cooper, 1989b; Jacoby et al., 1989; Schacter & Bowers, in preparation; Warren & Morton, 1982). Second, the specific *orientation* of an object at study and test appears to influence priming, at least under some conditions (Bartram, 1974; Jolicouer, 1985; Jolicoeur & Milliken, 1989). These findings suggest that priming depends on specific visual attributes of encoded objects and cannot be explained as a simple consequence of generating an object name at the time of study. However, with the exception of the Schacter and Bowers study, these experiments have not produced implicit/explicit dissociations in conformity with the retrieval intentionality criterion discussed in the preceding section. Until appropriate dissociations are produced in these paradigms, it could be argued that the observed specificity effects reflect the use of explicit memory processes and thus may not speak directly to the role of naming processes in priming.

A third kind of evidence is provided by the finding of robust priming for novel objects and patterns that do not have any names, under conditions in which observed implicit/explicit dissociations rule out the possibility that priming is attributable to explicit memory (Gabrielli et al., in press; Kunst-Wilson & Zajonc, 1980; Mandler et al., 1987; Musen & Treisman, 1990; Schacter et al., 1990). Of course, it could be argued that even though novel objects and patterns do not have agreed-upon names, subjects may attempt to code them verbally anyway and that it is this verbal coding that supports priming. Existing evidence, however, casts doubt on this possibility: Priming of novel shapes has been observed under conditions of brief exposure at which subjects do not reliably detect the presence of the shapes (Kunst-Wilson & Zajonc, 1980), and when subjects were *required* to generate verbal labels for unfamiliar objects in the study by Schacter *et al.* (1990, Experiment 2), no priming was observed on a subsequent object decision test. A fourth and related source of evidence is provided by the finding of robust priming on fragment completion (Schacter & Merikle, in preparation) and object identification (Schacter & Bowers, in preparation) tasks following a vertex-counting encoding task in which subjects did not overtly name target objects.

In summary, although the role of naming and verbal labeling in priming of allegedly nonverbal information clearly requires more extensive study, at least two tentative conclusions can be advanced. First, when implicit tests are used that require a naming response, prior naming may contribute to priming. Second, there are good reasons to believe that priming of nonverbal information on implicit tests that do not require a naming response (e.g., object decision, semantic decision, preference, dot-pattern identification, and completion) is independent of prior naming. Accordingly, we suggest that progress in understanding priming of nonverbal information will be facilitated by development of implicit tests that do not require naming responses.

C. Theoretical Accounts

The literature that we have reviewed encompasses a number of theoretical issues and problems that reflect the concerns of the various contributors to it: Some investigators have been concerned primarily with the nature of semantic memory processes; others have attempted to use priming as a tool to investigate the structure of object representations; and still others have focused on the nature of the processes and systems that underlie implicit and explicit memory. Thus, for example, one of the key issues that has motivated a number of studies of picture–word transfer concerns whether pictures and words share a common, amodal representation or whether there are separate, form-based representations for the two types of materials (e.g., Durso & Johnson, 1979; Kirsner *et al.*, 1986; Kroll & Potter, 1984; Lachman & Lachman, 1980). The fact that modest and sometimes negligible amounts of priming are observed between pictures and words supports the idea that separate form-based representations exist. As noted earlier, however, high levels of picture–word transfer in *semantic* priming paradigms suggest the existence of an amodal level of semantic representation that is distinct from modality-specific form-based representations (for discussion, see Kirsner *et al.*, 1986; Riddoch & Humphreys, 1987; Snodgrass, 1984; Vanderwart, 1984). Thus, any attempt to explain repetition priming of nonverbal information in terms of semantic processes is unlikely to succeed.

An early theoretical account of picture priming was offered by Warren and Morton (1982), who argued that priming of familiar objects reflects the temporary activation of a preexisting representation of the object that they called a *pictogen*. A pictogen was held to be an abstract representation of all objects with the same name (e.g., all clocks). Thus, the pictogen is a sort of nonverbal equivalent of the *logogen,* a term coined by Morton (1979) to refer to abstract lexical representations that are presumed to underlie word priming effects. The data that we have reviewed, however, present several problems for the pictogen view: Priming of nonverbal information can last for days and weeks whereas activation of a pictogen was held to decay extremely rapidly; priming has been demonstrated for novel objects and patterns that have no preexisting pictogens; and some priming effects appear to be more specific than would be expected if they were based on activation of an abstract pictogen.Thus, just as logogen theory has serious problems handling the data from verbal priming experiments (e.g., Jacoby, 1983; Richardson-Klavehn & Bjork, 1988; Roediger & Blaxton, 1987; Schacter, 1987, in press), the pictogen view cannot account for all of the data on nonverbal priming.

In contrast to the pictogen view, Weldon and Roediger (1987) and Jacoby *et al.* (1989) have proposed an episodic account of priming that they have applied to nonverbal materials. By their view, implicit memory can be understood by applying principles that have proven useful in understanding explicit memory, such as transfer-appropriate processing and encoding specificity. More specifically, they have argued that performance on such tests as picture identification and completion is primarily *data driven*—that is, guided by physical features of test cues. Consistent with the principle of transfer-appropriate processing (e.g., Roediger & Blaxton, 1987), it is thus argued that priming on these tasks depends on access to episodic representations of specific physical features of target materials. Performance on standard explicit tests of recall and recognition, in contrast, typically depends on subject-initiated, *conceptually driven* processing. This view can thus accommodate the general finding of a large form-based component in object priming, is consistent with observed specificity effects, handles a number of implicit/explicit dissociations, and is not embarrassed by instances of long-lasting priming. One serious problem with this view, however, is that it does not provide an account of preserved priming of either words or nonverbal materials in amnesic patients (for discussion, see Hayman & Tulving, 1989; Schacter, in press).

D. Priming and Perceptual Representation Systems

An alternative approach that incorporates some of the foregoing ideas and extends them into a multiple memory systems framework has been described in detail in several recent papers (Schacter, in press; Schacter et al., 1990; Tulving & Schacter, 1990). The basic idea is that priming on data-driven implicit tests depends on a class of presemantic *perceptual representation systems* that are dedicated to the representation and retrieval of information about the form and structure, but not the meaning, of words and objects. This general notion is motivated by two independent lines of evidence. The first is provided by priming experiments. Several studies of object priming reviewed in this article (e.g., Carroll et al., 1985; Schacter et al., in press; Schacter & Bowers, in preparation; Schacter & Merikle, in preparation), as well as various studies of verbal priming (e.g., Graf & Mandler, 1984; Jacoby & Dallas, 1981; Schacter & McGlynn, 1989), have shown that priming effects are robust following structural encoding tasks and do not require any semantic study processing. In addition, a number of studies have shown that priming is sensitive to changes in structural or surface feature information (e.g., Bartram, 1974; Jacoby et al., 1989; Schacter & Bowers, in preparation; Weldon & Roediger, 1987). Thus, experimental evidence from implicit memory studies indicates that priming on data-driven tests such as completion and identification is a structurally based, presemantic phenomenon.

Second, neuropsychological research on patients with selective deficits of reading and object processing has provided evidence for presemantic perceptual systems. The crucial observations take the form of striking dissociations between impaired access to semantic knowledge of words or objects on the one hand together with relatively intact access to structural knowledge on the other (e.g., Ellis & Young, 1988). In the verbal domain, for example, several studies have demonstrated intact access to visual and orthographic knowledge of words despite impaired acccess to word meaning (e.g., Funnell, 1983; Schwartz, Marin, & Saffran, 1979). These studies, together with converging evidence from neuroimaging research using the technique of positron emission tomography (Petersen, Fox, Posner, Mintum, & Raichle, 1988), point to the existence of a presemantic *visual word-form system* (Warrington Shallice, 1980) that appears to be involved in various verbal priming effects (Schacter, in press).

More directly relevant to the present concerns, other neuropsychological research suggests the existence of a presemantic system that is dedicated to handling information about the form and structure of visual objects. The key evidence comes from studies of patients with various forms of object agnosia, who are typically unable to recognize common objects. A number of studies have shown that such patients perform relatively well on tests that tap *structural* knowledge of objects despite severe impairments on tests that tap *associative* or *functional* knowledge of the same objects (cf. Riddoch & Humphreys, 1987; Sartori & Job, 1988; Warrington, 1982; Warrington & Taylor, 1978). Following Riddoch and Humphreys (1987), we refer to this system as the *structural description system* (Schacter et al., 1990).

In view of the aforementioned evidence that various nonverbal priming effects are observed independently of semantic study processing and are affected by study–test changes in the physical form and structure of target materials, we suggest that the structural description system plays an important role in priming of nonverbal information. Because this system is hypothesized to operate exclusively on the form and structure of objects and does not handle associative, functional, or contextual information about them, we think that it plays a limited role in explicit memory for a previous encounter with an object. Explicit remembering appears to require the involvement of an episodic memory system (Tulving, 1983) that represents various kinds of information about the content of an event and relates them to a spatiotemporal context.

The idea that a presemantic structural description system plays an important role in implicit memory for nonverbal information represents a beginning hypothesis that requires a good deal of further development. For example, the extent to which this system is involved in priming will likely depend on the exact nature of the implicit memory test that is used. Though we think that the structural description system is involved in nonverbal priming when data-driven implicit tests are used, different processes will likely be tapped when conceptually driven tests are used (see Schacter, in press; Tulving & Schacter, 1990). Similarly, more detailed hypotheses are required concerning exactly what types of information the system handles and how they are expressed on implicit memory tests. Despite these and other gaps in the framework, this idea has the virtue of specifying a candidate system that is involved in nonverbal priming and suggesting an underlying structural basis for transfer-appropriate processing models. At the same time, it also provides an explicit link between implicit memory research and neuropsychological studies of reading and object-processing deficits that can help to guide future studies concerned with priming of nonverbal information and the nature of implicit memory.

Acknowledgments

Preparation of this article was supported by National Institute on Aging Grant 1 RO1 AGO8441-01 and by a grant from the Air Force Office of Scientific Research to D. L. Schacter.

REFERENCES

Baddeley, A. D. (1982). Amnesia: A minimal model and an interpretation. In L. S. Cermak (Ed.), *Human memory and amnesia*. Hillsdale, NJ: Erlbaum.
Bartram, D. J. (1974). The role of visual and semantic codes in object naming. *Cognitive Psychology*, **6**, 325–356.
Bartram, D. J. (1976). Levels of coding in picture-picture comparison tasks. *Memory & Cognition*, **4**, 593–602.
Bentin, S., & Moscovitch, M. (1988). The time course of repetition effects for words and unfamiliar faces. *Journal of Experimental Psychology: General*, **117**, 148–160.
Bharucha, J. J., & Stoecking, K. (1986). Reaction time and musical expectancy: Priming of chords. *Journal of Experimental Psychology: Human Perception and Performance*, **4**, 403–410.
Bharucha, J. J., & Stoecking, K. (1987). Priming of chords: Spreading activation or overlapping frequency spectra? *Perception & Psychophysics*, **41**, 519–524.
Biederman, I. (1987). Recognition-by-components: A theory of human image understanding. *Psychological Review*, **94**, 115–147.
Biederman, I., & Cooper, E. E. (1989a). *Evidence for complete translational and reflectional invariance in visual object recognition*. Unpublished manuscript.
Biederman, I., & Cooper, E. E. (1989b). *Priming contour-deleted images: Evidence for intermediate representations in visual object recognition*. Unpublished manuscript.
Bruce, V., & Valentine, T. (1985). Identity priming in the recognition of familiar faces. *British Journal of Psychology*, **76**, 373–383.
Carmichael, L. (1951). Another hidden-figure picture. *American Journal of Psychology*, **64**, 137–138.
Carroll, M., Byrne, B., & Kirsner, K. (1985). Autobiographical memory and perceptual learning: A developmental study using picture recognition, naming latency, and perceptual identification. *Memory & Cognition*, **13**, 273–279.
Cofer, C. N. (1967). Conditions for the use of verbal associations. *Psychological Bulletin*, **68**, 1–12.
Crovitz, H. F., Harvey, M. T., & McClanahan, S. (1981). Hidden memory: A rapid method for the study of amnesia using perceptual learning. *Cortex*, **17**, 273–278.
Dallenbach, K. M. (1951). A picture puzzle with a new principle of concealment. *American Journal of Psychology*, **64**, 431–433.
Durso, F. T., & Johnson, M. K. (1979). Facilitation in naming and categorising repeated pictures and words. *Journal of Experimental Psychology: Human Learning and Memory*, **5**, 449–459.
Ellis, A., & Young, A. (1988). *Human cognitive neuropsychology*. London: Erlbaum.
Farah, M. (1989). Semantic and perceptual priming: How similar are the underlying mechanisms? *Journal of Experimental Psychology: Human Perception and Performance*, **15**, 188–194.
Funnell, E. (1983). Phonological processes in reading: New evidence from acquired dyslexia. *British Journal of Psychology*, **74**, 159–180.
Gabrieli, J. D. E., Milberg, W., Keane, M. M., & Corkin, S. (in press). Intact priming of patterns despite impaired memory. *Neuropsychologia*.
Gollin, E. S. (1960). Developmental studies of visual recognition of incomplete objects. *Perceptual and Motor Skills*, **11**, 289–298.
Gollin, E. S. (1961). Further studies of visual recognition of incomplete objects. *Perceptual and Motor Skills*, **13**, 307–314.

Gollin, E. S. (1962). Factors affecting the visual recognition of incomplete objects: A comparative investigation of children and adults. *Perceptual and Motor Skills,* **15,** 583–590.
Gollin, E. S. (1965). Perceptual learning of incomplete pictures. *Perceptual and Motor Skills,* **21,** 439–445.
Gollin, E. S. (1966). Serial learning and perceptual recognition in children: Training, delay, and order effects. *Perceptual and Motor Skills,* **23,** 751–758.
Graf, P., & Mandler, G. (1984). Activation makes words more accessible, but not necessarily more retrievable. *Journal of Verbal Learning and Verbal Behavior,* **25,** 553–568.
Graf, P., & Schacter, D. L. (1985). Implicit and explicit memory for new associations in normal and amnesic patients. *Journal of Experimental Psychology: Learning, Memory, and Cognition,* **11,** 501–518.
Hayman, C. A. G., & Tulving, E. (1989). Contingent dissociation between recognition and fragment completion: The method of triangulation. *Journal of Experimental Psychology: Learning, Memory, and Cognition,* **15,** 222–240.
Heindel, W. C., Salmon, D. P., & Butters, N. (in press). Pictorial priming and cued recall in Alzheimer's disease. *Brain and Cognition.*
Henderson, J. M., Pollatsek, A., & Rayner, K. (1987). Effects of foveal priming and extrafoveal preview on object identification. *Journal of Experimental Psychology: Human Perception and Performance,* **13,** 449–463.
Hirshman, E., Snodgrass, J. G., Mindes, J., & Feenan, K. (in press). Conceptual priming in fragment completion. *Journal of Experimental Psychology: Learning, Memory, and Cognition.*
Humphreys, G. W., & Quinlan, P. T. (1988). Priming effects between two-dimensional shapes. *Journal of Experimental Psychology: Human Perception and Performance,* **14,** 203–220.
Jacoby, L. L. (1983). Perceptual enhancement: Persistent effects of an experience. *Memory & Cognition,* **9,** 21–38.
Jacoby, L. L., Baker, J. G., & Brooks, L. R. (1989). Episodic effects on picture identification: Implications for theories of concept learning and theories of memory. *Journal of Experimental Psychology: Learning, Memory and Cognition,* **15,** 275–281.
Jacoby, L. L., & Craik, F. I. M. (1979). Effects of elaboration of processing at encoding and retrieval: Trace distinctiveness and recovery of initial context. In L. S. Cermak & F. I. M. Craik (Eds.), *Levels of processing and human memory* (pp. 1–21). Hillsdale, NJ: Erlbaum.
Jacoby, L. L., & Dallas, M. (1981). On the relationship between autobiographical memory and perceptual learning. *Journal of Experimental Psychology: General,* **110,** 306–340.
Jacoby, L. L., & Witherspoon, D. (1982). Remembering without awareness. *Canadian Journal of Psychology,* **36,** 300–324.
Jolicoeur, P. (1985). The time to name disoriented natural objects: *Memory & Cognition,* **13,** 289–303.
Jolicoeur, P., & Milliken, B. (1989). Identification of disoriented objects: Effects of context of prior presentation. *Journal of Experimental Psychology: Learning, Memory, and Cognition,* **15,** 200–210.
Johnson, M. K., Kim, J. K., & Risse, G. (1985). Do alcoholic Korsakoff's syndrome patients acquire affective reactions? *Journal of Experimental Psychology: Learning, Memory, and Cognition,* **11,** 27–36.
Kersteen-Tucker, Z. (1989). *Long term repetition priming with symmetrical polygons and words.* Manuscript submitted for publication.
Kinsbourne, M. (1989). The boundaries of episodic remembering: Comments on the second

section. In H. L. Roediger, III & F. I. M. Craik (Eds.), *Varieties of memory and consciousness: Essays in honour of Endel Tulving* (pp. 179–191). Hillsdale, NJ: Erlbaum.

Kirsner, K., & Dunn, J. (1985). The perceptual record: A common factor in repetition priming and attribute retention. In M. I. Posner & O. S. M. Marin (Eds.), *Mechanisms of attention: Attention and performance XI* (pp. 547–565). Hillsdale, NJ: Erlbaum.

Kirsner, K., Milech, D., & Stumpfel, V. (1986). Word and picture identification: Is representational parsimony possible? *Memory & Cognition, 14,* 398–408.

Kirsner, K., & Smith, M. C. (1974). Modality effects in word identification. *Memory & Cognition, 2,* 637–640.

Kroll, J. F., & Potter, M. C. (1984). Recognizing words, pictures, and concepts: A comparison of lexical, object, and reality decisions. *Journal of Verbal Learning and Verbal Behavior, 23,* 39–66.

Kunst-Wilson, W. R., & Zajonc, R. B. (1980). Affective discrimination of stimuli that cannot be recognized. *Science, 120,* 557–558.

Lachman, J. L., & Lachman, R. (1980). Age and the actualization of world knowledge. In L. W. Poon, J. L. Fozard, L. S. Cermak, D. Arenberg, & L. W. Thompson (Eds.), *New directions in memory and aging* (pp. 285–311). Hillsdale, NJ: Erlbaum.

Leeper, R., (1935). A study of a neglected portion of the field of learning—The development of sensory organization. *Journal of Genetic Psychology, 46,* 41–75.

Mandler, G., Nakamura, Y., & Van Zandt, B. J. S. (1987). Nonspecific effects of exposure on stimuli that cannot be recognized. *Journal of Experimental Psychology: Learning, Memory, and Cognition, 13,* 646–649.

Marr, D. (1982). *Vision.* San Francisco, CA: Freeman.

Marr, D., & Nishihara, H. K. (1978). Representation and recognition of the spatial organization of three-dimensional shapes. *Proceedings of the Royal Society of London, Series B 200,* 269–294.

Meudell, P. R., & Mayes, A. R. (1981). The Claparede phenomenon: A further example in amnesics, a demonstration of a similar effect in normal people with attenuated memory, and a reinterpretation. *Current Psychological Research, 1,* 75–88.

Milner, B., Corkin, S., & Teuber, H. L. (1968). Further analysis of the hippocampal amnesic syndrome: 14 year follow up study of H.M. *Neuropsychologia, 6,* 215–234.

Mitchell, D. B. (1989). How many memory systems? Evidence from aging. *Journal of Experimental Psychology: Learning, Memory, and Cognition, 15,* 41–49.

Mitchell, D. B., & Brown, A. S. (1988). Persistent repetition priming in picture naming and its dissociation from recognition memory. *Journal of Experimental Psychology: Learning, Memory, and Cognition, 14,* 213–222.

Morton, J. (1979). Facilitation in word recognition: Experiments causing change in the logogen model. In P. A. Kolers, M. E. Wrolstad, & H. Bouma (Eds.), *Processing models of visible language* (pp. 259–268). New York: Plenum.

Musen, G., & Treisman, A. (1990). Implicit and explicit memory for visual patterns. *Journal of Experimental Psychology: Learning, Memory, and Cognition, 16,* 127–137.

Parkin, A. J. (1982). Residual learning capability in organic amnesia. *Cortex, 18,* 417–440.

Parkin, A. J., & Streete, S. (1988). Implicit and explicit memory in young children and adults. *British Journal of Psychology, 79,* 361–369.

Penrose, L. S., & Penrose, R. (1958). Impossible objects: A special type of visual illusion. *British Journal of Psychology, 49,* 31–33.

Petersen, S. E., Fox, P. T., Posner, M. I., Mintum, M., & Raichle, M. E. (1988). Positron emission tomographic studies of the cortical anatomy of single-word processing. *Nature (London) 331,* 585–589.

Richardson-Klavehn, A., & Bjork, R. A. (1988). Measures of memory. *Annual Review of Psychology,* **36,** 475–543.

Riddoch, M. J., & Humphreys, G. W. (1987). Visual object processing in optic aphasia: A case of semantic access agnosia. *Cognitive Neuropsychology,* **4,** 131–186.

Rock, I., & Divita, J. (1987). A case of viewer-centered perception. *Cognitive Psychology,* **19,** 280–293.

Rock, I., DiVita, J., & Barbeito, R. (1981). The effect on form perception of change of orientation in the third dimension. *Journal of Experimental Psychology: Human Perception and Performance,* **7,** 719–732.

Roediger, H. L., III, & Blaxton, T. A. (1987). Retrieval modes produce dissociations in memory for surface information. In D. S. Gorfein & R. R. Hoffman (Eds.), *Memory and cognitive processes: The Ebbinghaus centennial conference* (pp. 349–379). Hillsdale, NJ: Erlbaum.

Roediger, H. L., III, & Weldon, M. S. (1987). Reversing the picture superiority effect. In M. A. McDaniel & M. Pressley (Eds.), *Imagery and related mnemonic processes; theories, individual differences, and applications* (pp. 151–174). New York: Springer-Verlag.

Rozin, P. (1976). The psychobiological approach to human memory. In M. R. Rosenzweig & E. L. Bennett (Eds.), *Neural mechanisms of learning and memory.* Cambridge, MA: MIT Press.

Sartori, G., & Job, R. (1988). The oyster with four legs: A neuropsychological study on the interaction of visual and semantic information. *Cognitive Neuropsychology,* **5,** 105–132.

Scarborough, D. L., Gerard, L., & Cortese, C., (1979). Accessing lexical memory: The transfer of word repetition effects across task and modality. *Memory & Cognition,* **7,** 3–12.

Schacter, D. L. (1984). Toward the multidisciplinary study of memory: Ontogeny, phylogeny, and pathology of memory systems. In L. R. Squire & N. Butters (Eds.), *The neuropsychology of memory.* New York: Guilford.

Schacter, D. L. (1987). Implicit memory: History and current status. *Journal of Experimental Psychology: Learning, Memory, and Cognition,* **13,** 501–518.

Schacter, D. L. (in press). Perceptual representation systems and implicit memory: Toward a resolution of the multiple memory systems debate. *Annals of the New York Academy of Sciences.*

Schacter, D. L., & Bowers, J. Manuscript in preparation.

Schacter, D. L., & Merikle, E. P. Manuscript in preparation.

Schacter, D. L., Bowers, J., & Booker, J. (1989). Intention, awareness, and implicit memory: The retrieval intentionality criterion. In S. Lewandowsky, J. C. Dunn, & K. Kirsner (Eds.), *Implicit memory: Theoretical issues.* Hillsdale, NJ: Erlbaum.

Schacter, D. L., Cooper, L. A., & Delaney, S. M. (1990). Implicit memory for unfamiliar objects depends on access to structural descriptions. *Journal of Experimental Psychology: General,* **119,** 5–24.

Schacter, D. L., Cooper, L. A., Delaney, S. M., Peterson, M. A., & Tharan, M. Manuscript in preparation.

Schacter, D. L., & McGlynn, S. M. (1989). Implicit memory: Effects of elaboration depend on unitization. *American Journal of Psychology,* **102,** 151–181.

Schacter, D. L., & Moscovitch, M. (1984). Infants, amnesics, and dissociable memory systems. In M. Moscovitch (Ed.), *Infant memory* (pp. 173–216). New York: Plenum.

Schneider, K. (1912). Uber einige klinisch-pathologische Untersuchungsmethoden und ihre Ergebnisse. Zugleich ein Beitrag zur Psycholopathologie der Korsakowschen Psy-

chose. [On certain clinical-pathological methods of research and their results. Together with a contribution to the psychopathology of Korsakoff's psychosos]. *Zeitschrift fuer Neurologie und Psychiatrie,* **8,** 553–616.
Schwartz, M. F., Marin, O. S. M., & Saffran, E. M. (1979). Dissociations of language function in dementia: A case study. *Brain and Language,* **7,** 277–306.
Scoville, W. B., & Milner, B. (1957). Loss of recent memory after bilateral hippocampal lesions. *Journal of Neurology, Neurosurgery and Psychiatry,* **20,** 11–21.
Seamon, J. G., Brody, N., & Kauff, D. M. (1983). Affective discrimination of stimuli that are not recognized: II. Effect of delay between study and test. *Bulletin of the Psychonomic Society,* **21,** 187–189.
Sherry, D. F., & Schacter, D. L. (1987). The evolution of multiple memory systems. *Psychological Review,* **94,** 439–454.
Shimamura, A. P. (1986). Priming effects in amnesia: Evidence for a dissociable memory function. *Quarterly Journal of Experimental Psychology,* **38A,** 619–644.
Snodgrass, J. G. (1984). Concepts and their surface representations. *Journal of Verbal Learning and Verbal Behavior,* **23,** 3–22.
Snodgrass, J. G. (1989). Sources of learning in the picture fragment completion task. In S. Lewandowsky, J. C. Dunn, & K. Kirsner (Eds.), *Implicit memory: Theoretical issues.* Hillsdale, NJ: Erlbaum.
Snodgrass, J. G., & Feenan, K. (1989). *Priming effects in picture fragment completion: Support for the perceptual closure hypothesis.* Manuscript submitted for publication.
Squire, L. R. (1987). *Memory and brain.* New York: Oxford University Press.
Talland, G. A. (1965). *Deranged memory.* New York: Academic Press.
Tulving, E. (1983). *Elements of episodic memory.* London: Oxford University Press (Clarendon).
Tulving, E. (1985). How many memory systems are there? *American Psychologist,* **40,** 385–398.
Tulving, E., & Schacter, D. L. (1990). Priming and human memory systems. *Science,* **247,** 301–306.
Tulving, E., Schacter, D. L., & Stark, H. A. (1982). Priming effects in word-fragment completion are independent of recognition memory. *Journal of Experimental Psychology: Learning, Memory, and Cognition,* **8,** 336–342.
Vanderwart, M. (1984). Priming by pictures in lexical decision. *Journal of Verbal Learning and Verbal Behavior,* **23,** 67–83.
Warren, C., & Morton, J. (1982). The effects of priming on picture recognition. *British Journal of Psychology,* **73,** 117–129.
Warrington, E. K. (1982). Neuropsychological studies of object recognition. *Philosophical Transactions of the Royal Society of London, Series B* **298,** 15–33.
Warrington, E. K., & Shallice, T. (1980). Word-form dyslexia. *Brain,* **103,** 99–112.
Warrington, E. K., & Taylor, A. M. (1978). Two categorical stages of object recognition. *Perception,* **7,** 695–705.
Warrington, E. K., & Weiskrantz, L. (1968). New method of testing long-term retention with special reference to amnesic patients. *Nature (London)* **217,** 972–974.
Warrington, E. K., & Weiskrantz, L. (1978). Further analysis of the prior learning effect in amnesic patients. *Neuropsychologia,* **16,** 169–177.
Weldon, M. S., & Roediger, H. L., III (1987). Altering retrieval demands reverses the picture superiority effect. *Memory & Cognition,* **15,** 269–280.
Williams, M. (1953). Investigation of amnesic defects by progressive prompting. *Journal of Neurology, Neurosurgery and Psychiatry,* **16,** 14–18.
Winnick, W. A., & Daniel, S. A. (1970). Two kinds of response priming in tachistoscopic recognition. *Journal of Experimental Psychology,* **84,** 74–81.

Young, A. W., McWeeny, K. H., Hay, D. C., & Ellis, A. W. (1986). Access to identity-specific semantic codes from familiar faces. *Quarterly Journal of Experimental Psychology,* **38A,** 271–295.

Zajonc, R. B. (1980). Feeling and thinking: Preferences need no inferences. *American Psychologist,* **35,** 151–175.

METAMEMORY: A THEORETICAL FRAMEWORK AND NEW FINDINGS

Thomas O. Nelson
Louis Narens

I. Introduction

Although there has been excellent research by many investigators on the topic of metamemory, here we will focus on our own research program. This article will begin with a description of a theoretical framework that has evolved out of metamemory research, followed by a few remarks about our methodology, and will end with a review of our previously unpublished findings. (Our published findings will not be systematically reviewed here; instead, they will be mentioned only when necessary for continuity.)

II. A Theoretical Framework for Metamemory

A. THREE ABSTRACT PRINCIPLES OF METACOGNITION

Our analysis of metacognition is based on three abstract principles that have been individually used in isolation by other authors:

Principle 1: The cognitive processes are split into two or more specifically interrelated levels. Figure 1 shows the basic structure, which contains two interrelated levels that we call the *meta-level* and the *object-level*, following the usage of those terms by the mathematician Hilbert

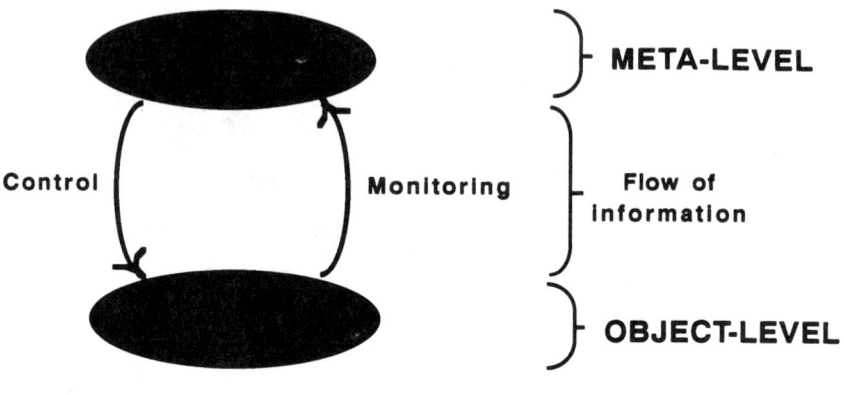

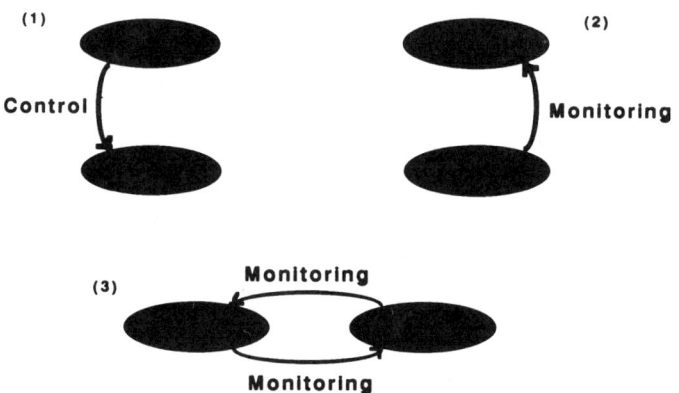

Fig. 1. Upper panel shows a theoretical mechanism consisting of two structures (meta-level and object-level) and two relations in terms of the direction of the flow of information between the two levels (notice the asymmetric aspect of each relation). Lower panel shows (1) a nonhomeostatic mechanism without any feedback, (2) a spylike mechanism that has information about the system but no control (e.g., a time traveller who isn't allowed to affect history), and (3) a mechanism with a symmetric relation, such that neither component is meta-level with regard to the other (e.g., two department chairmen discussing their respective departments).

(1927; i.e., "metamathematics") and by the philosopher Carnap (1934; i.e., "metalanguage"). Generalizations to more than two levels can be developed, but we have no need to do so for this article.

Principle 2: The meta-level contains a dynamic model (e.g., a mental simulation) of the object-level. Conant and Ashby (1970) gave a demonstration for the necessity of such an assumption if the system is to control a dynamic process so as to change from a given state to some other goal state.

Principle 3: There are two dominance relations, called *"control"* and *"monitoring,"* which are defined in terms of the direction of the flow of information between the meta-level and the object-level. This distinction in the direction of flow of information is analogous to that in a telephone handset, as discussed next.

1. Control

The basic notion underlying control—analogous to speaking into a telephone handset—is that the meta-level *modifies* the object-level. In particular, the information flowing from the meta-level to the object-level either changes the state of the object-level process or changes the object-level process itself. This produces some kind of action at the object-level, which could be (1) to initiate an action, (2) to continue an action (not necessarily the same as what had been occurring because time has passed and the total progress has changed, e.g., a game player missing an easy shot as the pressure increases after a long series of successful shots), or (3) to terminate an action. However, because control per se does not yield any information from the object-level, a monitoring component is needed that is logically (even if not always psychologically) independent of the control component.

2. Monitoring

The basic notion underlying monitoring—analogous to listening to the telephone handset—is that the meta-level is *informed* by the object-level. This changes the state of the meta-level's model of the situation, including "no change in state" (except perhaps for a notation of the time of entry, because the rate of progress may be expected to change as time passes, e.g., positively accelerated or negatively accelerated returns). However, the opposite does not occur, i.e., the object-level has no model of the meta-level. The main methodological tool for generating data about metacognitive monitoring consists of the person's subjective reports about his or her introspections.

3. Role of Subjective Reports about Introspection for Inferences about Monitoring

During the past decade or so, subjective reports about introspection have been resurrected in a form that circumvents the serious flaws in the older version used by turn-of-the-century psychologists. Methodological rigor is increased when people are construed as imperfect measuring devices of their own internal processes and when the assumption that introspection yields a veridical picture of the person's internal processes is not made. This distinction in our use of subjective reports is critical and can be highlighted by noticing an analogy between the use of introspection and the use of a telescope. One use of a telescope (e.g., by early astronomers and analogous to the early use of introspection) is to assume that it yields a perfectly valid view of whatever is being observed. However, another use (e.g., by someone in the field of optics who studies telescopes) is to examine a telescope in an attempt to characterize both its valid output and its distortions. Analogously, introspection can be examined as a type of behavior so as to characterize both its correlations with some objective behavior (e.g., likelihood of being correct on a subsequent test) and its distortions.

Thus we try to recognize and avoid the potential shortcomings of introspection (e.g., Nisbett & Wilson, 1977) while capitalizing on its strengths (e.g., Ericsson & Simon, 1980, 1984). We view introspective reports as data to be explained, in contrast to the Structuralists' view of introspective reports as descriptions of internal processes; i.e., we regard introspection not as a conduit to the mind but rather as a source of data to be accounted for by postulated internal processes.

Although previous writers such as Nisbett and Wilson (1977) have underscored the possibility of distortions in introspective monitoring, they have not emphasized its potential role—even with its distortions—of affecting control processes. *A system that monitors itself (even imperfectly) may use its own introspections as input to alter the system's behavior.* One of our primary assumptions is that in spite of its imperfect validity and in spite of its being regarded by some researchers as only an isolated topic of curiosity, introspection is a critical component in the total memory system. In attempting to understand that system, we examine the person's introspections so as to have some idea about the input that the person is using.

The person's reported monitoring may, on the one hand, miss some aspects of the input and may, on the other hand, add other aspects that are not actually present. Indeed, one of our goals is to characterize both the accuracy and the distortions that are present in people's introspections. This is analogous to one traditional view of perception, where what is perceived is different from what is sensed (i.e., perception conceptualized as sensation plus inference), except that what is analogous to the objects being sensed is here the object-level memory processes.

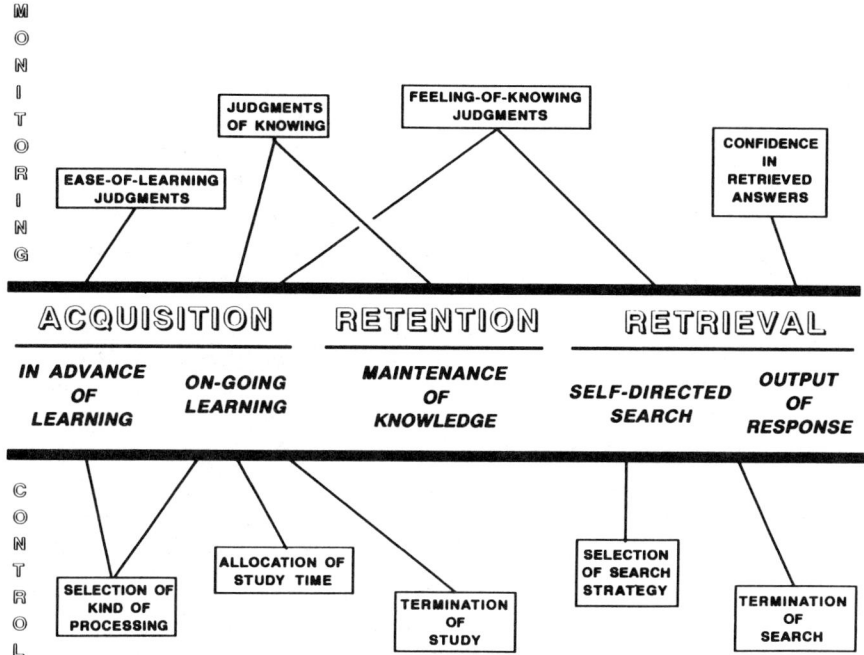

Fig. 2. Main stages in the theoretical memory framework (listed inside the horizontal bars) and some examples of monitoring components (shown above the horizontal bars) and control components (shown below the horizontal bars).

B. THE MONITORING AND CONTROL OF HUMAN MEMORY

An overview of our theoretical framework is shown in Fig. 2. The monitoring and control processes are grouped in terms of the overall stages of the system, as discussed next, and the reader is invited to consider them in the context of a college student studying for an upcoming examination.

1. Acquisition Stage: In Advance of Learning

Two components that occur in advance of learning consist of the person's goal and the person's plan to achieve that goal.

a. Determining One's Goal: The Person's Norm of Study. When the person becomes aware of the to-be-remembered items and the anticipated type of test, he or she makes a judgment about the level of mastery that will be needed for a given item at the time of the anticipated test. When a delay is expected to occur between acquisition and the retention test, then the person's *theory of retention* (Maki & Berry, 1984) is used to modulate how well each item would have to be mastered now, in order for it to still be remembered on the retention test. The product—of the desired ease of retrieval during the retention test, modulated upward by however much extra learning the person believes will be needed to breach the retention interval—is the overall degree of mastery the person believes should be attained during acquisition, which is referred to as the person's *norm of study* (Le Ny, Denhiere, & Le Taillanter, 1972).

   b. *Formulating a Plan to Attain the Norm of Study.* After the norm of study has been determined, the person makes a decision about how to attain that goal, i.e., formulates a plan. This has several parts, involving several kinds of monitoring judgments that need to be distinguished.

First, a distinction should be drawn between retrospective monitoring (e.g., a confidence judgment about a *previous* recall response) vs. prospective monitoring (e.g., a judgment about *subsequent* responding). The latter are subdivided further into three categories in terms of the state of the to-be-monitored items:

1. Ease-of-learning (EOL) judgments occur in advance of acquisition, are largely inferential, and pertain to items that have not yet been learned. These judgments are predictions about what will be easy/difficult to learn, either in terms of which items will be easiest or in terms of which strategies will make learning easiest.
2. Judgments of learning (JOL) occur during or after acquisition and are predictions about future test performance on currently recallable items.
3. Feeling-of-knowing (FOK) judgments occur during or after acquisition (e.g., during a retention session) and are judgments about whether a given currently nonrecallable item is known and/or will be remembered on a subsequent retention test.

Perhaps surprisingly, EOL, JOL, and FOK are not themselves highly correlated (Leonesio & Nelson, 1990). Therefore, these three kinds of judgments may be monitoring somewhat different aspects of memory, and whatever structure underlies these monitoring judgments is likely to be multidimensional (speculations about some possible dimensions occur in R. Krinsky & Nelson, 1985, and Nelson, Gerler, & Narens, 1984, esp. pp. 295–299).

   c. *Ease-of-Learning Judgments.* Initially, the person makes and EOL judgment about the degree of difficulty for each item (or set of items) in terms of acquiring that item to the degree of mastery set by the norm of study. Underwood (1966) showed that EOL is an accurate predictor of the rate of learning during experimenter-paced study trials, and we showed that EOL is related to how much study time is allocated to each item during self-paced study trials (Nelson & Leonesio, 1988, discussed below).

d. A Priori Choice-of-Processing Judgments. After making EOL judgments, the person decides which of the various kinds of processing to use on the to-be-retrieved items, and this decision can affect the rate of learning.

e. Initial Plan for the Allocation of Study Time. When planning the allocation of study time, the person may first determine the total time to allocate (e.g., 4 hr of study for an upcoming exam). The kind of retention test that is anticipated may affect both the planned allocation of self-paced study time and how that self-paced study time is apportioned among the items (Butterfield, Belmont, & Peltzman, 1971), including massed vs. distributed self-controlled rehearsals (Modigliani & Hedges, 1987).

We investigated the relation between EOL and the allocation of self-paced study time, with the major finding being that people study longer on the items they believe in advance will be harder (Nelson & Leonesio, 1988). The specific model explored in that research is reproduced here in Fig. 3, both to illustrate how hypothetical causal relations between monitoring and control processes can be explored and to show how the theoretical constructs of the framework can be operationalized, with monitoring constructs typically being operationalized via an introspective report (e.g., EOL judgment) and control constructs being operationalized by some other empirical outcome (e.g., elapsed time during self-paced study).

2. Acquisition Stage: The Ongoing Learner

The focus here is on the changes in both the learner's plan and the learner's performance. Figure 4 shows a model of some hypothetical causal relations between several metacognitive components during the ongoing aspects of acquisition. This model may be useful both as a guide to the components discussed here and as an example of one way that stronger models can be developed within our framework. The metacognitive components contained in the model are shown in the upper portion of Fig. 4; the lower portion includes a basic memory model (cf. Atkinson & Shiffrin, 1968; Ericsson & Simon, 1980), containing a working memory (cf. short-term memory, STM) that is separate from long-term memory (LTM).

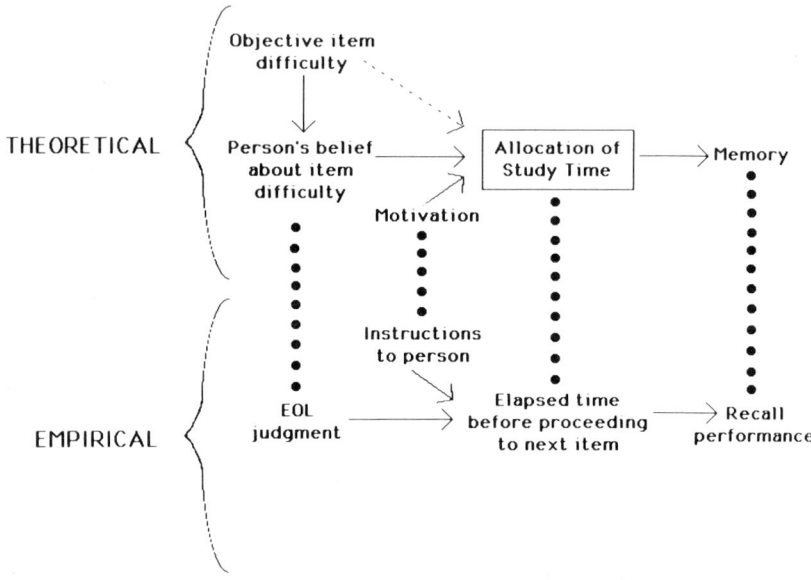

Fig. 3. A model of the allocation of self-paced study time, with arrows indicating hypothesized causal connections and dotted lines indicating the way in which each theoretical construct is operationalized (after Nelson & Leonesio, 1988).

The upper left corner of Fig. 4 shows three metacognitive components discussed earlier that give rise to the person's norm of study. Following attempts to learn a given item, a judgment is made about the current state of mastery for that item (namely, an FOK judgment if the item is not currently recallable, or a JOL if the item is currently recallable). When the current state of mastery reaches the norm of study, the person terminates study of that item (i.e., exits from the sequence). However, when the current state of mastery has not reached the norm of study, the person allocates more study time to the item, chooses a strategy from his metacognitive library of strategies (which may reside in a portion of permanent memory—not shown in Fig. 4; cf. the concept of "metacognitive knowledge" in Flavell, 1979), and implements the strategy in an attempt to attain the desired degree of mastery for that item. Then the cycle recurs. Each of these hypothesized aspects of the ongoing cycle is elaborated below.

a. Feeling of Knowing for Currently Nonrecallable Items. Nelson and Leonesio (1988, Experiment 3) found that FOK judgments made after failed attempts at recall of general-information items were positively cor-

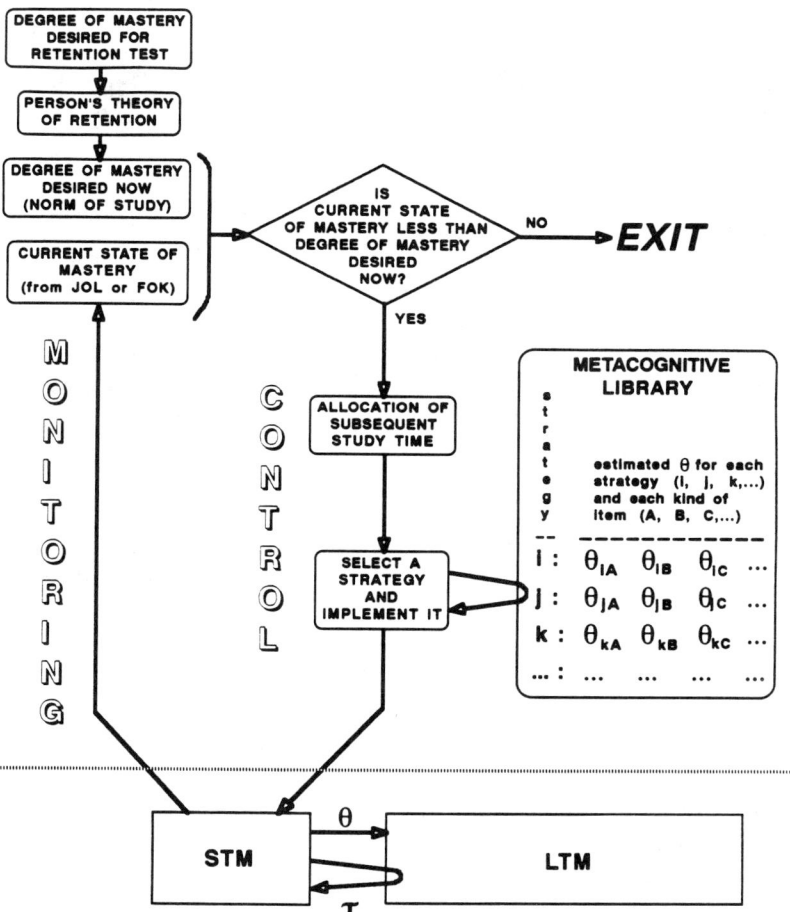

Fig. 4. Example of some metamemory components (shown above the dotted line) during acquisition. Curved-return arrow indicates that a given component obtains information from another component. Information is acquired into LTM at a rate θ and is retrieved from LTM with probability τ (Atkinson & Shiffrin, 1968; other views of storage and retrieval, including the substitution of working memory for STM, could easily be substituted instead). The metacognitive library tells for each available strategy (i, j, k, ...) the estimated rate of acquisition it will yield for various kinds of items (A, B, C, ...).

related with the subsequent allocation of self-paced study time on those items (cf. Figs. 3 and 4 above). However, as in the case of EOL, the magnitude of that correlation was far from unity, indicating that additional mechanisms underlie the person's allocation of study time (discussed below).

b. Judgments of Learning for Currently Recallable Items. According to Ericsson and Simon (1980), the monitoring per se occurs in STM. This does not, however, imply that information in LTM cannot be monitored—e.g., people are aware that they know their own names. Information that is in LTM may be monitored by first copying it into a working memory, also referred to as STM (cf. lower portion of Fig. 4), such that the person can functionally monitor both STM and LTM (latencies of that monitoring are reported in Wescourt & Atkinson, 1973). Unfortunately, however, people may mistakenly assess their JOL by monitoring information that is only in STM, not in LTM. When that occurs, the JOL predictions are likely to be accurate for predicting subsequent short-term recall of that information but may be inaccurate for predicting subsequent long-term recall (e.g., on a later examination). Would it be possible to produce more accurate JOL predictions for subsequent long-term recall if people made their JOL after a brief delay from when a given item was studied, so as to minimize recall of the to-be-judged information from STM and instead require recall from LTM? We have begun research on this topic, and preliminary results (J. Dunlosky & T. O. Nelson, unpublished) indicate that the answer to this question is affirmative.

c. Updating the Allocation of Study Time during a Particular Study Trial of an Item. In contrast to Fig. 3 but as indicated in Fig. 4, there may be an ongoing allocation of study time to an individual item in the list, such that the person continues studying until his or her JOL for the item reaches the norm of study. The circumstances under which people sharpen their differential study time (i.e., devote much more study time to harder items and much less study time to easier items) have not yet been established (but see Nelson & Leonesio, 1988; Mazzoni, Cornoldi, & Marchitelli, 1990).

Related to this, we found that college students terminate self-paced study on a given item long before it has been mastered well enough for subsequent recall (Nelson & Leonesio, 1988). For instance, in our Experiment 1, people who were specifically instructed to continue the self-paced study of each item until they were sure that they would be 100% correct on an upcoming recall test ended up having only 49% correct recall when tested after the study phase. That research examined only one self-paced study trial per item. Future research should determine whether the same or different results occur during multitrial acquisition, because people routinely learn information to mastery, and this needs to be reconciled with the Nelson and Leonesio findings. The role of motivation in allocating study time should also be explored more fully.

d. Termination of Acquisition. How does a learner decide when to terminate acquisition? Figure 4 can be regarded as one answer to this question, with termination occurring when the JOL reaches the norm of study, as discussed above.

3. Retention Stage

The major metacognitive activity during this stage is the maintenance of previously acquired knowledge (see Bahrick & Hall, 1990). Several factors may underlie the person's decision about how and when to review. For instance, the person may have a theory of forgetting that includes the hypothesis (empirically confirmed by Leonesio & Nelson, 1982) that the hardest item to learn will be the hardest item to retain.

People potentially could capitalize on their metacognitive monitoring of items to decide how much subsequent study to devote to various items that cannot be recalled on a given maintenance test. Perhaps the mechanism would be similar to that for acquisition, where additional processing of a given to-be-retrieved item depends upon the discrepancy between the desired degree of mastery for the item vs. the assessed degree of mastery (cf. Fig. 4). For nonrecallable items, the person's FOK may help to direct whatever maintenance—more aptly, "relearning" for nonrecallable items—is allocated (Nelson *et al.*, 1984, Experiment 1; Nelson & Leonesio, 1988, Experiment 3).

4. Retrieval Stage: Termination

Nickerson (1980) distinguished between memory retrieval that is versus is not self-directed. Although knowledge about both kinds of retrieval is important for memory theory, our framework focuses on self-directed retrieval. The self-direction occurs not in the searching itself (which we assume to be automatic once it is initiated—see Fig. 5), but rather in setting up the particular cues to initiate the search (e.g., by consciously thinking of the last episode in which the item was retrieved or by consciously going through the alphabet as cues for the first letter of the sought-after answer).

Some components we suppose are involved in the termination of the retrieval stage are shown in Fig. 5, which shows mechanisms for continuing vs. terminating the stage of memory retrieval.

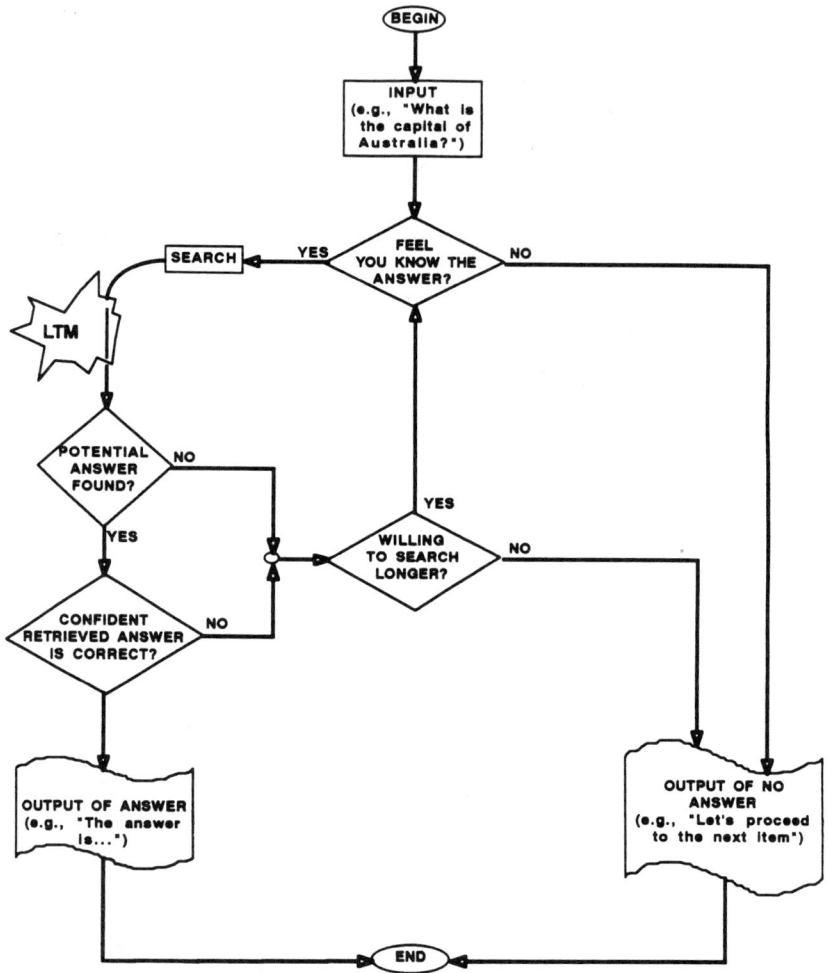

Fig. 5. Some metamemory components in the retrieval stage in human memory.

a. Quick Initiation/Termination of Retrieval. The metacognitive decision to initiate a search appears to be based on a very rapid, preliminary FOK judgment (Reder, 1987, 1988). This may be similar to the decision that people make in television game shows such as "Jeopardy" that require the player to signal rapidly that he or she can answer a given question. Upon presentation of a general-information question, people can make fairly accurate FOK judgments (about whether or not they could recall the answer) with a latency that is shorter than the latency of actually recalling the answer. Accordingly, in Fig. 5 this preliminary FOK judgment precedes recall (see Schreiber, Nelson, and Narens' research discussed in Section III, B, 7, a).

This mechanism may be similar to the one postulated in Juola *et al.*'s (1971) model for a "fast yes" or "fast no" response in yes/no recognition. The "fast no" may be based on the person's belief of never having encountered the requested information, as in Kolers and Palef's (1976) "knowing not" (also see Nelson *et al.*, 1984, p. 297, for the role of memory for prior encounters as a basis for FOK.)

b. Placement of Retrieval-Termination Threshold for Nonretrieved Items. As indicated in Fig. 5, when a potential answer is not found on a given search through memory, people presumably make a decision about whether they are willing to expend more time searching for the answer (i.e., using some kind of costs/rewards rules). If they are, and if the FOK is still positive, the search continues. However, the FOK may no longer be positive enough to continue. That is, there may be an evaluation of progress that is dynamic for a given item (e.g., an evaluation in terms of whether there has been sufficient progress to continue). When someone either is no longer willing to continue searching for the item or has a reduced FOK that no longer exceeds the FOK threshold for claiming to know the answer, the process is terminated with an omission error (indicated in the right-hand side of Fig. 5). The relationship between FOK and how long the retrieval stage continues prior to an omission error has been established empirically: Greater FOK is correlated with a longer latency of an omission error (Nelson *et al.*, 1984, Fig. 3).

The aforementioned mechanisms for terminating searching should be distinguished sharply from the ones in the left-hand side of Fig. 5, where a potential answer is retrieved and output. Then when the outputed answer is incorrect—i.e., a commission error—the relationship between FOK and the latency of that error is nil (Nelson *et al.*, 1984, Fig. 3). Commission-error latencies probably involve a complicated mix of confidence judgments and other factors (discussed below). Moreover, people's FOK is not completely accurate and is sometimes mistaken because they retrieve the wrong referent (e.g., retrieving Sydney in response to the question, "What is the capital of Australia?"; R. Krinsky & Nelson, 1985; also see Schacter & Worling, 1985).

Omission versus commission errors have also yielded different effects on other aspects of metacognition. For instance, college students typically have a greater FOK for commission-error items than for omission-error items, even though there is no difference in subsequent recognition memory on the two kinds of items (R. Krinsky & Nelson, 1985).

The person's expected reward for correct retrieval can affect the decision to continue or terminate searching (i.e., the threshold for "willingness to search longer" in Fig. 5). Although incentive can affect how long the person will continue before terminating the retrieval stage (Loftus & Wickens, 1970), there is no empirical evidence about whether greater incentive can produce a greater probability of retrieving during a given amount of retrieval time.

5. *Retrieval Stage: Output of Response*

Several potential psychological mechanisms may underlie the decision to output a single retrieved answer. Some versions of generation-recognition models of recall (e.g., Bahrick, 1970) propose that a "recognition stage" occurs in which the person makes a yes/no recognition judgment and on that basis decides whether to output the answer that he or she retrieved (i.e., "generated"). If the person retrieves only one response that seems plausible, then presumably that response is evaluated against a confidence threshold like the one indicated in Fig. 5 (confidence judgments per se are discussed in the next section). Perhaps this process is mediated by some kind of conscious recollection.

A variant of the aforementioned mechanism is what might be labeled the test-until-deemed-successful strategy: If the amount of confidence for the first answer that the person retrieves is below the confidence threshold, and if the person continues to search but does not retrieve any other potential answers for that item, then the confidence threshold might be lowered (i.e., a dynamic process). Accordingly, the initially retrieved answer might be output even though it was not associated with enough confidence to be output earlier.

Another strategy can occur in which people output an answer even when they are not convinced that it is correct, but rather only that it has a good likelihood of being correct. This satisficing strategy consists of "aiming at the good when the best is incalculable . . . some stop rule must be imposed to terminate problem-solving activity. The satisficing criterion provides that stop rule: retrieval ends when a good-enough alternative is found" (Simon, 1979, p. 3).

Any of the aforementioned strategies may also be modulated by external factors. For instance, the person's threshold for outputting a retrieved answer might be affected by the costs vs. rewards associated with commission vs. correct responses and/or might also be affected by drugs. The likelihood of commission errors during recall is known to increase after the ingestion of marijuana (Hooker & Jones, 1987; Pfefferbaum, Darley, Tinklenberg, Roth, & Kopell, 1977) or lithium (Weingartner, Rudorfer, & Linnoila, 1985) but is unaffected by alcohol (Nelson, McSpadden,

Fromme, & Marlatt, 1986). Although marijuana affects the threshold for outputing retrieved answers, it has no effect on the probability of correct recall (or on the FOK threshold for saying that correct recognition would occur). Nelson *et al.* (1990) found a related outcome at Mount Everest: High altitude decreased the likelihood of commission errors without affecting the probability of correct recall.

6. Retrieval Stage: Confidence Judgments after Recall

The confidence judgments that occur after the recall that the confidence pertains to are interesting, but their interpretation is difficult because they are validated retrospectively (in contrast to monitoring judgments such as EOL, JOL, and FOK, all of which are validated prospectively).

The usual finding is that people are overconfident—in terms of absolute scales—about their preceding memory performance (for a review, see Lichtenstein, Fischhoff, & Phillips, 1982), and this finding occurs across a wide variety of conditions (e.g., the degree of overconfidence about recall is approximately the same for normal and alcohol-intoxicated people; Nelson, McSpadden *et al.*, 1986). However, sometimes near-perfect calibration does occur (e.g., Nelson *et al.*, 1990).

Moreover, the reported confidence about the likelihood of an outputed answer being correct is not necessarily a direct measure of the person's internal confidence. For instance, when the person has retrieved two plausible answers for an item—each of which is associated with high internal confidence—but the experimenter allows only one to be output, the reported confidence may be low (because of the person's awareness that the other answer may be the correct one). However, if subsequently the person receives feedback that the outputed answer was wrong, then he or she may give a high FOK judgment—in contrast to the aforementioned low confidence judgment—because of the belief that the remaining answer must be correct. Accordingly, the probability of reminiscence (i.e., correct recall on a subsequent test after incorrect recall of the answer on a previous test, without any intervening study of the answer) is greater for commission-error items ($p = .29$) than for omission-error items ($p = .05$), perhaps because during the original test the person may sometimes think of two possible answers (one of which is correct and the other of which is incorrect), output the incorrect one, and then output the other one on a subsequent test of that item (Nelson *et al.*, 1984).

C. REFINING THE COMPONENTS OF THE THEORETICAL FRAMEWORK

Earlier we mentioned that Fig. 2 showed only a skeleton of our framework. Fleshing out that skeleton can be accomplished by what is referred to in set-theory terminology (e.g., Shafer, 1976) and computer-assisted-design (CAD) terminology (e.g., Snow, 1987) as "coarsening" and "refining."

Within our framework, a coarsened node is a node that is elaborated at a greater level of specificity (i.e., containing more detail) somewhere else in the framework, and this elaboration at a greater level of specificity is the refinement. The key idea is that larger or smaller degrees of specificity can occur for any component of interest in the framework. To illustrate how refinement can occur, Fig. 6 shows the relation between the coarsened nodes of "Termination of Study" and "Termination of Search" that appeared in Fig. 2 and their refinement that appeared in Figs. 4 and 5, respectively.

Notice an important characteristic of this approach to theorizing: There is no need to preestablish any primitives at a "lowest level of specificity" or even to speculate about what the lowest level of specificity might be like. Also, a particular refinement may for convenience be represented as a coarsened node when it appears in the refinement of still other nodes.

III. Methodology and New Findings from Our Research

At the outset of our research on metamemory (circa 1975), we were aware of two findings about metamemory that seemed paradoxical in terms of the then-prevailing theories of memory. The first finding (Hart, 1965) was that individuals who failed to recall answers to general-information questions can nevertheless evaluate whether or not they know the answer, and such evaluations are positively correlated with their performance on a subsequent recognition test of the previously nonrecalled items. How could subjects consciously and validly monitor such nonrecallable answers?

The second finding (Juola, Fischler, Wood, & Atkinson, 1971; Kolers & Palef, 1976) was that subjects are able to give very fast and valid "No" answers to questions about whether they could recall specific items, and these "No" answers occur more quickly than a search of memory (i.e., a search of memory would take more time than the latency of the "No" response; for direct evidence that the latencies of FOK judgments are shorter than the latencies to search memory, both for "No" responses and for "Yes" responses, see Reder, 1987, 1988). How could a subject know about the presence/absence of an item in memory without first completing the memory search for it?

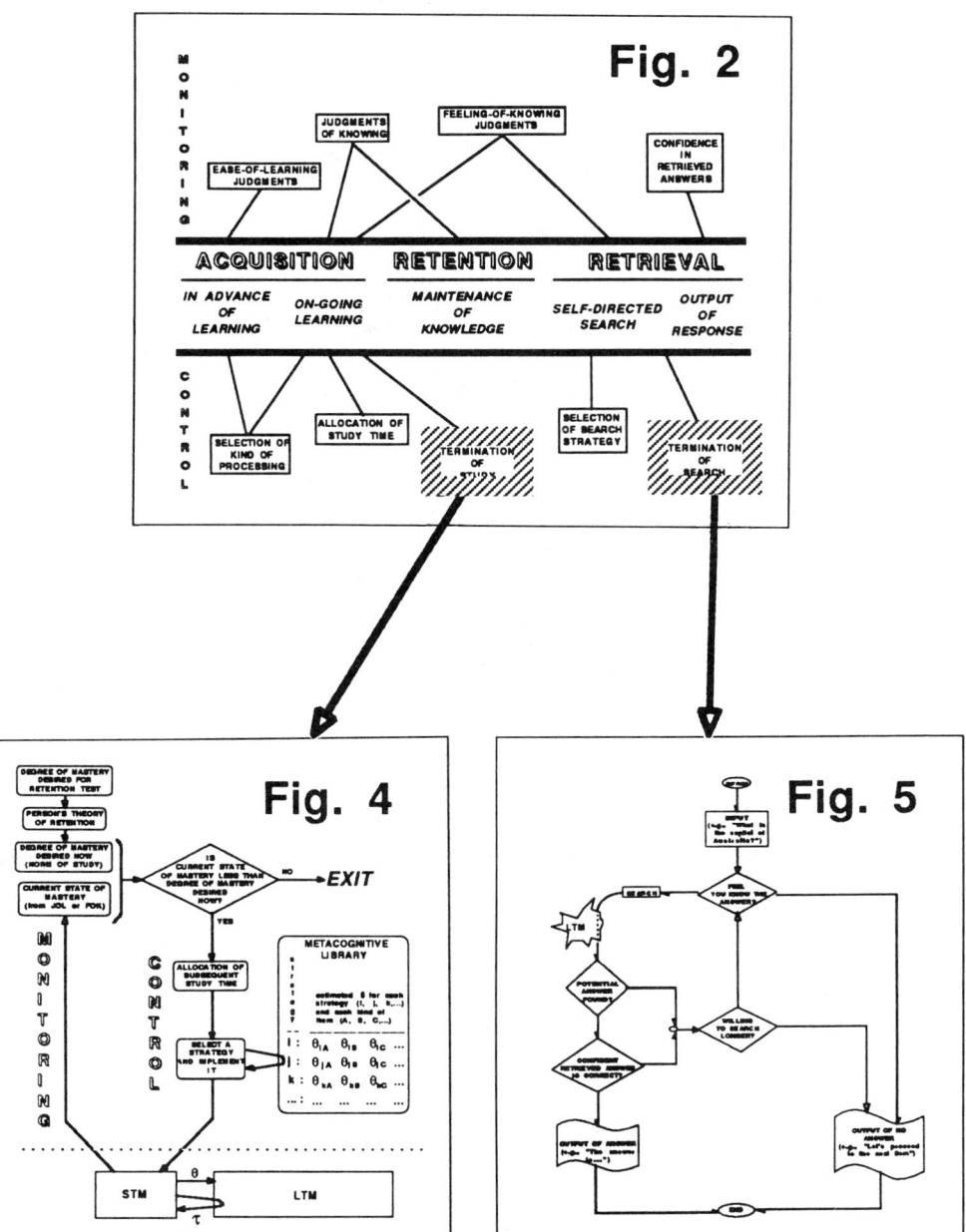

Fig. 6. Current status of refinement of coarsened nodes in the theoretical framework (see text for explanation of coarsening/refining).

A. Remarks about Our Methodology

We were intrigued by these paradoxes and decided to develop a research program to investigate metamemory experimentally. Analogous to the traditional psychophysical/measurement techniques in which people are construed as measuring devices of external stimuli, our approach to metamemory research was to construe people as measuring devices of their own *internal* stimuli. We hoped that this would allow us to determine how people monitored their own object-level cognitions (when we compared their judgments with our own assessments of their object-level cognitions, so as to see distortions) and also might give us information about their object-level cognitions that our assessments did not show. Accordingly, we based our methodology on obtaining, scaling, and comparing introspective judgments similar to those from psychophysical paradigms. However, the paradigm had to be modified both because of theoretical considerations and because of various practicalities (e.g., in metamemory experiments, the experimenter collects relatively few observations—with respect to the usual psychophysical case—from relatively many people—again with respect to the usual psychophysical case). We also had a major problem to deal with (as do the researchers in psychophysics and in recognition memory; see Shepard, 1967), namely, to avoid confounding two aspects of the person's judgments: (1) accuracy of the judgment (e.g., as had been assessed by d' in psychophysics) vs. (2) placement of the decision threshold for making the judgment (e.g., as had been assessed by β in signal-detection theory); for our investigations of metamemory, we sought both an a priori solution via new data-collection techniques and an a posteriori solution via new data-analysis techniques that led us to consider alternatives to d'.

1. Remarks about Data Analysis for Metacognitive Judgments

Although the signal-detection measure of sensitivity d' had been a useful statistic to compare performance across individuals and conditions in psychophysics, for various reasons (elaborated in Nelson, 1984, 1987; Nelson, McSpadden *et al.*, 1986) we chose to use Goodman and Kruskal's gamma, G, as the measure of metacognitive accuracy. In contrast to d', no distributional assumptions need to be made for G (such assumptions are critical for the use of d' and are untestable in most metamemory situations; for relevant discussions, see Lockhart & Murdock, 1970; Nelson, McSpadden *et al.*, 1986). In contrast to other correlations such as Pearson r or Spearman rho, G is unaffected by ties, which are unavoidable in metamemory research and are otherwise problematic. Also, the expected value of G is constant across changes in the person's threshold for being confident. Finally, G has a very general interpretation in terms of telling the probability of accurate detection (see Nelson, 1984, Eq. 7; 1987, p. 305; Nelson, McSpadden *et al.*, 1986, Eq. 1), which yields a quantitative metric for the degree of FOK accuracy that is both intuitive and superior to any comparisons of difference scores (e.g., as in Hart, 1965, 1967; see Nelson, 1984, for reasons).

After evaluating all of the available measures, we concluded that G is the best measure of detection accuracy for research on metacognition (for more recommendations regarding the use of G, see Nelson, 1984, 1986).

2. Remarks about Data Collection for Metacognitive Judgments

a. Ratings vs. Rankings. One way to obtain people's metacognitive confidence judgments is to collect confidence ratings on an M-place Likert scale about the person's subjective impressions on each item (where $M \geq 2$). Then the validity of those judgments can be determined either (1) by plotting a calibration curve to determine the accuracy of absolute confidence (i.e., confidence for a given item relative to the person's threshold for being confident; Lichtenstein *et al.*, 1982) or (2) by computing G to determine the accuracy of relative confidence (i.e., confidence for one item relative to another).[1]

Our application to psychophysical techniques stressed the relative aspects of metacognitive judgments via a paired-comparison ranking methodology (Nelson & Narens, 1980a; other advantages and disadvantages of rankings vs. ratings are discussed by Coombs, 1964). However, we now also use Likert rating scales, with our focus being on the relative aspects of those ratings (by analyzing the rating data via G, as described in Nelson, 1984) as well as on the absolute aspects (via calibration curves), and we do retests on the ratings to assess the stability of the person's threshold; e.g., Nelson et al. (1990; Nelson, McSpadden *et al.*, 1986). Nevertheless, when an investigator is not interested in the absolute aspects of FOK ratings and has the extra time that the ranking procedure usually requires for each subject, the dividend will be, as shown in a large experiment by Lam (1987), that the standard deviation in FOK accuracy across subjects is somewhat smaller for the ranking procedure (SD = .36)

---

[1]The two kinds of accuracy may yield different conclusions when computed on the same set of data. For instance, confidence may be 100% accurate in the relative sense (i.e., $G = +1.0$) but inaccurate in the absolute sense (e.g., overconfidence, as shown by a calibration curve); this kind of pattern occurred in Nelson, McSpadden *et al.* (1986). In the terminology of Lichtenstein and Fischhoff (1977), relative confidence is reflecting resolution whereas absolute confidence is reflecting calibration, and resolution (in comparison to calibration) "is a more fundamental aspect of probabilistic functioning" (p. 181).

than for the rating procedure (SD = .41), probably because there is a greater tendency for changes in people's thresholds to be neutralized by the ranking procedure. Lam (1987) also showed that the reliability of FOK judgments is greater for rankings than for ratings and that the correlation between FOK rankings and ratings ranges from + .71 to + .87 (the larger correlation is for ratings on a 6-place Likert scale whereas the smaller correlation is for ratings on a 2-place Likert scale). Also, a compromise ranking/rating procedure for use in FOK research has been developed by Shimamura and Squire (1986).

b. Laboratory Paired Associates vs. General-Information Questions. In research where we are interested in the effects of acquisition variables on metamemory, the items are laboratory paired associates such as number—word pairs, whereas in research where we are interested only in the effects of retrieval variables, the items are general-information questions (Nelson & Narens, 1980b; see next paragraph). The former allow for control over the process of acquisition, whereas the latter are fundamentally a version of paired-associate items (e.g., stimulus = "What is the capital of Finland?" and response = "Helsinki"), with the advantages of eliminating the stage of having to teach the items to the person and also having greater stability of recall than does newly learned information.

3. *FACTRETRIEVAL Computer Program for Metamemory Research*

First, we constructed 300 general-information questions and collected normative data on them (Nelson & Narens, 1980b). Next, we put 240 of those questions into a computer program called FACTRETRIEVAL that tests recall, collects FOK judgments, and tests recognition (Shimamura, Landwehr, & Nelson, 1981). Finally, we enlarged that program into a more sophisticated version called FACTRETRIEVAL2 (Wilkinson & Nelson, 1984) that collects confidence judgments about previous recall, in addition to containing both ranking and rating versions of FOK judgments about upcoming recognition, and that offers many other advantages (e.g., control over the difficulty levels of the items presented to the person, more recognition alternatives per item, assessment of retest reliability of the FOK judgments, and more thorough analysis of the data, including an analysis of response latencies).

B. Some New Findings from Our Research

It is not possible here to summarize all of our metamemory findings from the past 15 years. Instead, we will emphasize those findings that have not yet appeared in print and will only briefly mention a portion of those already published.

The findings below are organized around several themes, as indicated by the side headings. (All differences mentioned as significant had $p < .05$.)

1. Amount of Information Deposited in Long-Term Memory Is Important for Metacognitive Monitoring

a. Our Early Experiments. Our first experiment on metamemory was conducted in 1976 at the University of California, Irvine, and used a paired-comparison ranking methodology on number–word pairs immediately after they had been presented to each subject once during study (a protocol for one subject appears in Nelson & Narens, 1980a). We found that people were very consistent in their FOK judgments, both in terms of transitive FOK paired comparisons (i.e., if Item A is chosen over Item B, and Item B is chosen over Item C, then Item A will have a high probability of being chosen over Item C) and in terms of retest reliability (for near-perfect retest reliability, see Nelson, Leonesio, Landwehr, & Narens, 1986, Fig. 2), but those judgments had nearly no validity for predicting upcoming recognition! This difference between reliability and validity, which we replicated[2] in other unpublished experiments during 1977–1979, was so extreme that for awhile we used a fun-house mirror analogy to describe our subjects' metamemories, wherein what people see when looking in such a mirror is a reliable but nonvalid image of themselves.

After exploring several blind alleys, including the eventually rejected possibilities that (1) people are inherently poor at monitoring their memories, and/or (2) the structure of the underlying items is compromised of both forward and backward traces (in which the person monitored the strength of the forward trace, whereas recognition tapped the strength of the backward trace), we eventually concluded that the lack of FOK validity we had observed was due to the items never having been registered well enough in LTM to be monitored by the metacognitive system. Here is how we came to that conclusion.

b. Effect of Degree of Learning and Retention Interval on FOK Accuracy. In 1979, we conducted an experiment (T. O. Nelson & L. Narens, unpublished) in which three groups ($n = 27$ or 28 subjects/group) differed

---

[2]Researchers other than us have also discovered situations in which people have no validity at monitoring their ongoing learning until the items first become recallable after a filled retention interval that exceeds the limits of STM (e.g., Vesonder & Voss, 1985).

in terms of the degree of learning and the delay of the retention test. The retention test consisted of recall, followed by paired-comparison FOK judgments about the person's subjective likelihood of recognizing answers that he or she did not recall, and ended with 4-alternative-forced-choice (4-AFC) recognition test on every nonrecalled item so as to assess the accuracy of the FOK judgments. The results for each group were: (1) the first group, who had an immediate test after one study trial per item, yielded 35% correct recall, and 63% of the subjects had a positive (vs. negative) G for FOK accuracy at predicting the recognition of nonrecalled items (not significant); (2) the second group, who had a delayed test 1 week after acquisition via one correct recall per item, yielded 45% correct recall, and 71% of the subjects had a positive (vs. negative) G (marginally significant); (3) the third group, who had a delayed test 3 weeks after acquisition via one correct recall per item, yielded 25% correct recall, and 86% of the subjects had a positive (vs. negative) G (significant FOK accuracy, $p < .001$). Thus, the level of recall did not determine FOK accuracy (i.e., the first group's level of recall was bracketed by the second and third groups) and the people in all three groups attended to every item during presentation (i.e., all items entered STM), but what mattered was to ensure that the items could be recalled from LTM during acquisition (i.e., only the last two groups showed indications of FOK accuracy). However, from this experiment we could not tell whether the critical factor for FOK accuracy was the degree of learning or the length of the retention interval. Therefore, another experiment was needed to separate the effects of those two factors.

In 1980, we conducted a paired-associate experiment (L. Narens & T. O. Nelson, unpublished) on three more groups: (1) the first group, who had a delayed test 1 week after acquisition via one correct recall per item, yielded 29% correct recall and had little FOK accuracy (mean $G = +.15$); (2) the second group, who had a delayed test 4 weeks after acquisition via one correct recall per item, yielded 15% correct recall and also had little FOK accuracy (mean $G = +.14$); however, (3) the third group, who had a delayed test 4 weeks after acquisition via four correct recalls per item, yielded 38% recall and had significant FOK accuracy (mean $G = +.36$). Thus, not the length of the retention interval but rather the degree of learning is critical for FOK accuracy.

c. Our First Published Experiment on Metamemory. The aforementioned findings led to an experiment in 1981 to establish the importance of the degree of learning on FOK accuracy, which was our first published experiment on metamemory (Nelson, Leonesio, Shimamura, Landwehr, & Narens, 1982). We found that 4 weeks after acquisition, FOK accuracy was nil for items that had originally been learned to a criterion of only one correct recall (median $G = .00$), but FOK accuracy was substantial for items that had originally been overlearned to a criterion of four correct recalls per item (median $G = +.41$). But by what mechanism does the degree of learning affect the accuracy of metacognitive judgments?

d. Mechanism for the Overlearning Effect on Metacognitive Accuracy. The two-part psychological mechanism that seems to underlie this effect is the following:

1. Metacognitive judgments attempt to discriminate between different items and therefore will increase in accuracy as the difference between the to-be-judged items increases, and
2. overlearning may enhance the stability of retention and apparently also increases the differences between items.

For instance, Leonesio and Nelson (1982) found that the degree of learning during acquisition would strongly modulate the gamma correlation between item difficulty (i.e., the number of trials required for the first correct recall during acquisition) and subsequent recall retention: For items that were learned to a criterion of one correct recall during acquisition, this correlation was $+.02$; for items learned to a criterion of two correct recalls during acquisition, the correlation was $-.15$; and for items learned to a criterion of four correct recalls during acquisition, the correlation was $-.25$ (i.e., items that required more trials before the first correct recall were less likely to be remembered during the subsequent retention test).

e. Empirical Support for the Item-Discrimination Mechanism. In accord with the above, Leonesio (1985) found that for overlearned items the correlation between FOK and recognition (namely, $G = +.28$) dropped to nonsignificance when item difficulty was partialled out (namely, $G = +.01$), suggesting that item difficulty—in particular, the differences in difficulty between items—is a factor that modulates the degree of FOK accuracy. Also in accord with Statement (1) above, Nelson, Leonesio et al. (1986) found that FOK accuracy on general-information questions ranged from $G = .00$ for items that are adjacent in the person's FOK rank ordering to $G = +.77$ for discriminating between the top and bottom items in the person's rank ordering. Thus, like a pan balance, people are reasonably fine as measuring devices, but they have limits in terms of the objects between which they can validly discriminate (cf. signal/noise ratio). In this case, the relevant difference is in terms of underlying memorability (analogous to a difference in mass for the pan-balance case), such that the more different the items, the more likely the metacognitive discriminations are to be valid. This point is important not only for theoretical formulations of metamemory, but also for conclusions about methodology; for instance, a low value of G does not necessarily imply that the task is insensitive or that the person cannot monitor accurately, but rather the obtained value of G reflects a combination of the task, the person's ability to monitor, and the degree of differences among the to-be-monitored items. Using more or less discriminable items will produce greater or lesser degrees of accurate metacognitive discriminations between the to-be-monitored items.

f. Overlearning and the Relation between EOL Judgments, JOL, and FOK Judgments. Because EOL judgments occur prior to acquisition (i.e., before overlearning begins), they cannot tap overlearning but rather can only tap item difficulty.[3] However, in contrast to EOL judgments, JOL can tap both item difficulty and the degree of learning (because JOL occur after acquisition). Not surprisingly, therefore, subsequent recall retention is predicted significantly better by JOL ($G = +.31$) than by EOL ($G = +.12$), as shown by Leonesio and Nelson (1990). Also during the retention session, the recognition of nonrecalled items is predicted as well by JOL (which had been made 4 weeks earlier) as by FOK judgments (which had been made immediately prior to the recognition test), and those two kinds of judgments are not themselves highly correlated with each other and therefore may tap different aspects of memory (see Leonesio & Nelson, 1990).

2. *FOK May Be Perfectly Valid at Tapping a Large Number of Aspects of LTM but the Accuracy of FOK for Predicting Criterion Performance May Nevertheless Be Imperfect*

There are at least two possible reasons, in addition to the methodological one mentioned above (i.e., items not different enough for the person to be able to discriminate between them), that the observed FOK accuracy may underestimate the actual FOK accuracy at monitoring information in LTM.

---

[3]Moreover, Leonesio and Nelson (1990) showed that those EOL judgments have far-from-perfect accuracy at monitoring item difficulty (e.g., the mean correlation between EOL judgments and the number of trials required to learn the various items in a constant-study-time situation is only $G = -.22$), and the relatively low magnitude of this correlation is not due to inadequate range in the number of trials required to learn the various items (e.g., the mean correlation between the number of learning trials and subsequent recall 4 weeks later was $G = -.48$).

1. No single criterion task may tap the full set of information tapped by the FOK. As just one example of this possibility, consider the typical criterion task—namely, recognition—that is used to validate the accuracy of FOK. We know that recognition does not completely tap the information in memory (e.g., savings occurs for nonrecognized items, Nelson, 1978), so some of the information in memory that is tapped by FOK may be overlooked by recognition (and perhaps vice versa, of course). Given the view that memory is multidimensional rather than unidimensional (e.g., Bower, 1967), it is even possible that the FOK may be tapping more aspects of memory than any single criterion task. That is, different criterion tasks tap different aspects of memory, and the current view is that no particular task is strictly more sensitive (in the technical sense; Nelson, 1978) than all other criterion tasks (for a review of the rapidly growing literature that shows how different tasks are dissociated from one another and tap different aspects of memory, see Richard-Klavehn & Bjork, 1988).

2. FOK does not detect small amounts of new information coming into memory that may affect criterion performance. We recently discovered a situation in which the FOK can be less sensitive than recall for detecting information in memory (Jameson, Narens, Goldfarb, & Nelson, 1990). In that research, a nonrecalled general-information answer was very briefly flashed while the person was attending to the corresponding general-information question. The very brief flash contained either the correct answer or a nonsensical answer. Following the flash, the person either (1) immediately attempted to recall the answer to the question and then immediately gave an FOK judgment about whether he or she knew the answer (Experiment 1), or (2) immediately gave an FOK judgment without any intervening attempt at recall (Experiment 2, which was run as a control in case the effects of the flash dissipated during the immediate-recall phase in Experiment 1, before the FOK judgment occurred).

The results, summarized in Table I, show that the new information added to memory by the very brief flash affected recall without affecting FOK. This is in accord with the aforementioned findings that the FOK can tap only those aspects of information that previously had been well-established in LTM and does not detect new incoming information. Consistent with such a conclusion, the FOK can validly discriminate between nonrecalled items that will soon have the correct answer flashed tachistoscopically (Nelson *et al.*, 1984, Exp. 1). Taken together, these results from our 1984 and 1990 research suggest that the residual information in LTM that is tapped by the FOK can be augmented by incoming flashed information that the FOK does not detect. Whether this incoming flashed

TABLE I

EFFECT OF A PERCEPTUAL FLASH (OF THE CORRECT ANSWER VS. NONSENSE) ON THE SUBSEQUENT PROBABILITY OF RECALL AND THE FEELING OF KNOWING (FOK)[a]

	Answer that was flashed	
Dependent variable	Correct answer	Nonsense
Experiment 1: p(recall)	.28	.10
Experiment 1: FOK rating	5.4	5.2
Experiment 2: FOK rating	6.1	6.1

[a] The entry for p(recall) is the mean (across subjects) of each individual subject's p(recall). The entry for FOK rating is the mean (across subjects) of each individual subject's median FOK rating (higher values indicate a stronger feeling of knowing). Although flashing the correct answer (vs. nonsense) yielded a significant improvement in recall beyond the reminiscence that occurred in the nonsense condition, no significant effect occurred on the feeling of knowing. Data are from Jameson et al. (1990).

information should be conceptualized as residing in STM or in unconscious memory (cf. Marcel, 1983) is an open question, whose answer may have ramifications for conceptions about the limits of metacognitive monitoring.

Thus, the FOK can tap LTM information that by itself is insufficient to trigger correct recall, whereas recall can be based on the conglomerate of both the preflash information in LTM and a boost from flashed information that the FOK does not tap. From this research, we now know that at least some information in the overall memory system is not tapped by FOK, and therefore the question arises concerning the degree to which people do have direct (or privileged) access to their own idiosyncratic memories.

3. Privileged Access

Do people have privileged access to idiosyncratic information in their memories about the to-be-retrieved items? We examined this question in two ways.

a. Judge/Observer Experiments. We (T. Jameson, T. O. Nelson, R. J. Leonesio, & L. Narens, unpublished) modified our standard FACTRETRIEVAL paradigm as follows. One person (designated the Target subject—the standard subject in FACTRETRIEVAL) went through recall until missing the answers to 15 questions. Then he or she made FOK rankings of those 15 items. Meanwhile—and here's the new twist—while the Target was going through recall, another person (designated the Observer) observed the Target's performance during recall (i.e., the Observer saw the Target's face, saw how long the Target paused to think about the answer to each question, saw how well the Target did on related questions, and saw what the Target typed as a recall response to a given question). Then the Observer went to another computer room and independently ranked those same 15 items in terms of how likely the Target would be to recognize the correct answer to each missed item. Finally, yet another person (designated the Judge), who never saw the Target or the Target's answers during recall, also ranked those same 15 items in terms of how likely the Target would be to recognize the correct answer to each missed item. Subsequently the Target went through a 4-AFC recognition test on each item, so as to provide the criterion performance that allowed us to assess the predictive accuracy of the Target's, Observer's, and Judge's predictions about the Target.

The hypothesis we tested was the following. The Judge would have some above-chance accuracy at predicting the Target's recognition performance, based on the Judge's knowledge of the general difficulty of each of the various items. The Observer would have the same knowledge about general item difficulty that the Judge had, but also by virtue of having watched the Target during attempted recall of each item would have some specific extra knowledge about what the Target might know (e.g., if the Target paused to think awhile before answering or made a close guess at the answer), and therefore the Observer would be more accurate than the Judge at predicting the Target's subsequent recognition. The Target would have all of the above information, plus "privileged" information about his own idiosyncratic memory (e.g., remembering that he or she had learned a particular item in high school) and therefore should be the best possible predictor of his or her subsequent recognition performance.

The results, shown in the left side of Fig. 7, generally confirmed the aforementioned hypothesis about the relative predictive accuracy of the Target, Observer, and Judge for predicting the Target's subsequent recognition performance. All three sets of predictions had above-chance accuracy, and the Target's predictive accuracy was significantly greater than the Judge's, with the Observer's predictive accuracy being intermediate between them (but not significantly different from either the Target or the Judge).

Because the overall predictive accuracy in that experiment was somewhat low, we ran another experiment containing a few methodological

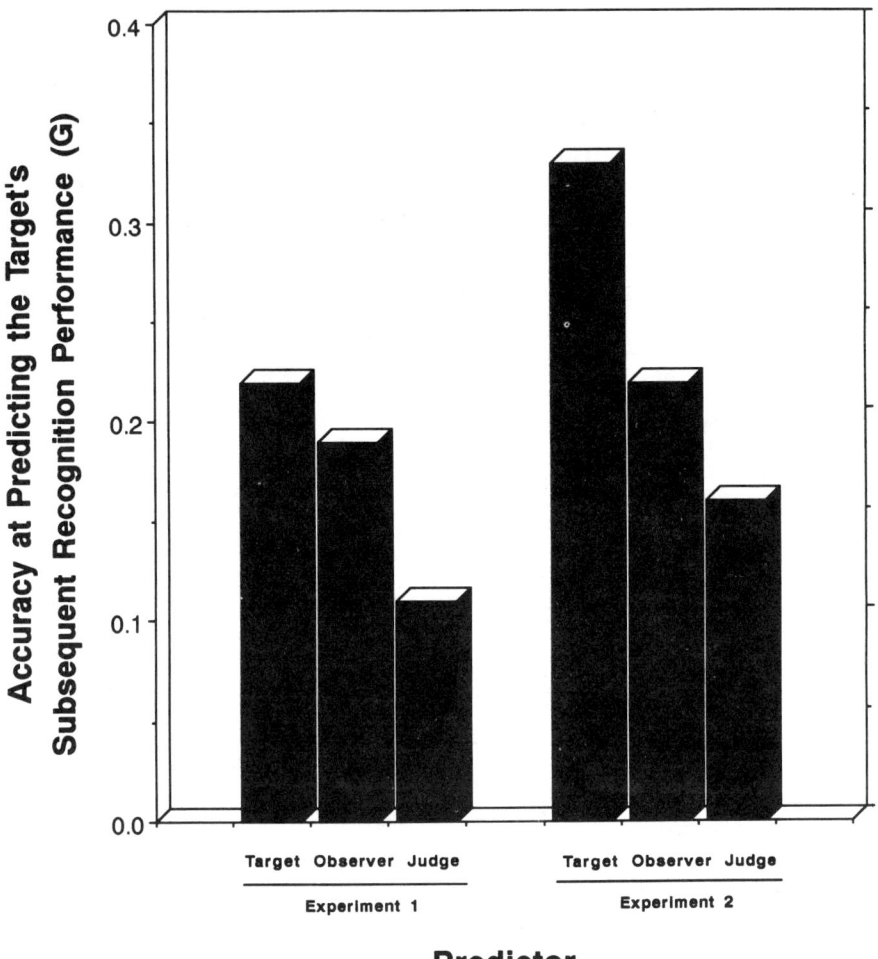

Fig. 7. Accuracy at predicting the target's subsequent recognition performance on non-recalled items (in terms of mean G) for three predictors (the Target, the Observer, and the Judge) in two experiments.

changes. In particular, during recall the items were not randomly sampled but instead were sampled more systematically to utilize the full range of general-information questions in FACTRETRIEVAL, and the recognition test was made less noisy by using 8-AFC instead of 4-AFC (both of these changes yield greater overall predictive accuracy; see above). Also, instead of being in the same room with the Target, the Observer watched the Target through a one-way mirror from an adjacent room during the recall phase.

The results, reported in the right side of Fig. 7, showed greater predictive accuracy overall than in the previous experiment. Most important, the general pattern and the qualitative conclusions from the statistical tests were the same as in the previous experiment. Thus people apparently do have idiosyncratic information at their disposal during retrieval, and this idiosyncratic information can benefit predictions about their subsequent memory performance. But does this idiosyncratic information about their own memories yield the best possible predictive accuracy about their subsequent performance, or is there a way to improve predictive accuracy even more?

b. Normative Predictions vs. the Individual's Own FOK Predictions. It is worth mentioning that Nelson, Leonesio *et al.* (1986) found that for predicting an individual's subsequent memory performance on currently nonrecalled items, the individual's own FOK predictions were significantly better (mean $G = +.28$) than normative FOK predictions (means $G = +.12$) derived from the average of his or her peers' predictions about their own memory performance, but the individual's FOK predictions were significantly worse than predictions derived from the normative probability of correct recall (mean $G = +.38$). We made several attempts to induce individuals to utilize (while making FOK judgments) their estimates of normative recall, in hopes that this might yield an improvement in FOK accuracy. Unfortunately all of our attempts failed to improve people's FOK accuracy, perhaps because people are poor at trying to intuit the normative probability of recall on items that they themselves cannot recall (Nickerson, Baddeley, & Freeman, 1987). However, M. Calogero (unpublished research conducted in our laboratory) found that people who are given the normative probability of recall as they make FOK judgments for each item do have significantly greater FOK accuracy ($G = +.58$) than other people who are not given those normative probabilities ($G = +.40$), indicating that people will utilize normative information when it is available (in his experiment, the accuracy from predictions derived solely from the normative probability of recall was $G = +.55$). Next, we turn to the question of what the information is that does underlie people's FOK judgments.

4. *Some Factors Underlying People's FOK Judgments (versus FOK Accuracy)*

To inquire about whether a given factor "affects FOK accuracy" is to ask whether the factor affects the relationship between the FOK judgments and the criterion task (e.g., in the above-mentioned research this was the relationship—as assessed by G—between FOK judgments and subsequent recognition performance). By contrast, to inquire about whether a given factor "affects FOK judgments" is to ask whether the factor affects the magnitude of FOK, as assessed by the median FOK rank or the median FOK rating. These two possible meanings of "an effect on FOK" are mathematically independent of each other. The former kind of effect was examined above. The latter kind is examined next.

a. Overlearning Affects Not Only FOK Accuracy but also Affects the Magnitude of FOK. Nelson et al. (1982) reported that the median FOK rank varied across items that differed in the degree of original learning: Items originally learned to a criterion of one recall per item had a median FOK rank of 5.8; items with one additional overlearning trial had a median FOK rank of 6.8; and items with three additional overlearning trials had a median FOK rank of 8.4.

This effect of overlearning on the magnitude of metacognitive judgments was extended recently by Leonesio and Nelson (1990). They investigated a situation in which people (1) made JOL at the end of acquisition, and (2) subsequently made FOK judgments 4 weeks later on items incorrectly recalled during the retention test (using a retention-session procedure similar to the one from Nelson et al., 1982). A major finding, shown in Fig. 8, was that overlearning has a greater effect on JOL than on subsequent FOK judgments.

In all of the aforementioned experiments, the overlearning trials were a combination of study-test trials (e.g., "three additional overlearning trials" meant three additional overlearning study trials and three additional overlearning test trials). But which portion—overlearning study or overlearning test—were the FOK judgments being affected by?

b. Overlearning Study Trials vs. Overlearning Test Trials. An experiment by T. O. Nelson, T. Rideout, and R. J. Leonesio (unpublished) had people learn a paired-associate list in which one-third of the items were learned to a criterion of one correct recall per item, another one-third had six overlearning study trials after the item was correctly recalled, and the remaining one-third had six overlearning test trials after the item was first correctly recalled. Four weeks later, the median FOK rank for items not recalled on the retention test was 6 for the items that had originally been learned to a criterion of one correct recall, 8 for the items that had received six overlearning study trials, and 8 for the items that had received six overlearning test trials (each of the latter two sets of items differed significantly from the first but did not differ from each other). Thus, both the overlearning study trials and the overlearning test

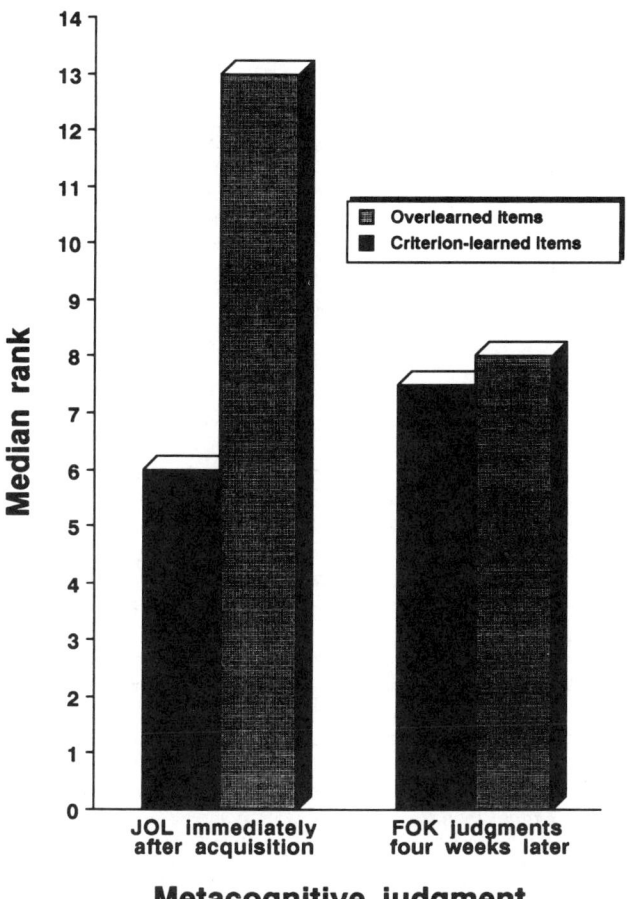

Fig. 8. Median JOL rank and FOK rank (1 = low) for items that were acquired to a criterion of one correct recall (leftmost in each pair of bars) vs. four correct recalls. The effect of overlearning is greater on JOL than on FOK.

trials affect the magnitude of subsequent FOK, and to approximately the same degree.

c. Actual Overlearning vs. Claimed Overlearning. Although overlearning has an effect on FOK, we wondered if that effect was a direct one or instead was mediated by whether the person was aware that the item had been overlearned. An experiment by T. O. Nelson and S. Gilispie (unpublished) attempted to tease those two factors apart.

The college-student subjects each received study-test trials on a paired-

TABLE II

EFFECT OF ACTUAL FREQUENCY OF PREVIOUS RECALLS VS. CLAIMED FREQUENCY OF PREVIOUS RECALLS ON SUBSEQUENT FOK JUDGMENTS[a]

Claimed frequency of previous recalls	Actual frequency of previous recalls		
	1	5	Overall
1	10	**10**	10
5	**16**	18	17
Overall	12	14	

[a] The entry is the median (across subjects) of each individual subject's median FOK rank for the items in that cell (higher values indicate a stronger feeling of knowing). Although both the actual and the claimed frequency of previous recalls had an overall significant effect, notice that the feeling of knowing is affected more by the person's claimed frequency than by the actual frequency of previous recalls. This can be seen in two ways: by comparing the effect manifest in the row marginals with the effect manifest in the column marginals, or, perhaps even better, by comparing the two internal-cell values shown in boldface (i.e, the person's feeling of knowing was stronger for items that had actually been recalled once but which he or she believed to have been recalled five times than for items that were believed to have been recalled once but that had actually been recalled five times).

associate list, wherein 16 items were learned to a criterion of one correct recall per item while the remaining 16 were overlearned (five correct recalls per item). A retention session occurred 3–7 weeks later (this difference in retention interval had no effect on recall or on FOK judgments and therefore will not be discussed further), consisting of three stages: (1) recall of every item, followed by (2) several judgments on every nonrecalled item, the two most pertinent for present purposes being the students' forced-choice frequency judgments of whether a given item had originally been learned to a criterion of one or five correct recalls and the students' FOK judgments (which occurred either before or after—counterbalanced—the other judgments had been made), followed by (3) 8-AFC recognition.

Table II shows that the person's FOK was related more to his or her

TABLE III

EFFECT OF ACTUAL FREQUENCY OF PREVIOUS RECALLS VS. CLAIMED FREQUENCY OF PREVIOUS RECALLS ON THE SUBSEQUENT RECOGNITION THAT THE FOK IS ATTEMPTING TO PREDICT[a]

Claimed frequency of previous recalls	Actual frequency of previous recalls		
	1	5	Overall
1	34	42	38
5	41	53	47
Overall	38	47	

[a] The entry is the mean (across subjects) of each individual subject's percentage correct recognition for the items in that cell. Both the actual and the claimed frequency of previous recalls have an overall significant effect (and to the same degree).

claimed frequency of previous recalls than to his or her actual frequency of previous recalls. Although this can be seen by comparing the two pairs of marginals, it is perhaps most evident by noticing that the FOK was greater for items that the person believed he or she had previously recalled five times but actually had been recalled only once (median FOK = 16) than for items believed to have been previously recalled only once but that had actually been recalled five times (median FOK = 10). Put another way, most of the effect of overlearning on FOK judgments is mediated by the person's beliefs about whether the items had been overlearned; i.e., the person's memory of prior overlearning (presumably taken together with rules of inference) mediates the effect of prior overlearning on FOK judgments. This is quite different from a direct or "automatic" effect of overlearning, in which the effect on a particular dependent variable occurs regardless of whether or not the person remembers that one item had occurred more frequently than another item during study.

However, this pattern of FOK judgments is not entirely reflecting the recognition that the person was attempting to predict, as shown in Table III. In particular, the percentage correct recognition was affected approximately equally by both the claimed frequency (probably due to other differences in the items—the row headings are labels for the subjects' aggregations, not for an independent variable) and the actual frequency.

This greater effect on the FOK by the claimed frequency than by the actual frequency can also be seen in another way. We correlated (across items for each subject) the FOK with three other variables: (1) claimed frequency of previous recalls, (2) actual frequency of previous recalls, and (3) recognition performance. The mean correlations were, respectively, + .40, + .23, and + .16. Although all three correlations are significantly greater than zero, FOK is more related to the claimed frequency of previous recall than to the actual frequency of previous recall; moreover, FOK is more related to the claimed frequency of previous recall than to the recognition that the FOK is attempting to predict.

These results suggest a new hypothesis—which we dub the No-Magic Hypothesis—for how FOK judgments should be conceptualized, namely, the person (1) considers particular recallable properties of the to-be-retrieved item (e.g., "I recalled it few/many times on previous occasions"), in conjunction with (2) rules about how those properties are related to the subsequent criterion performance that the person is trying to predict (e.g., "subsequent recognition is more likely for an item that I previously recalled many times than for an item that I previously recalled few times"). Notice that this way of making FOK judgments would utilize only suprathreshold information about remembered attributes of the item (including incorrectly remembered suprathreshold information!), along with rules for how to utilize that information in the FOK judgments. Thus, according to the No-Magic Hypothesis, the FOK does not reflect any monitoring of unconscious information at all. Put another way, the FOK does not directly monitor a given unrecalled item in memory, but rather the FOK monitors recallable aspects related to that item, such as the item's acquisition history or partial/related recalled components.

5. *Learning-to-Learn Effects for FOK Judgments*

Can FOK accuracy be improved by sheer practice? This question was explored in two experiments by T. O. Nelson, R. J. Leonesio, and L. Narens (unpublished) that were modifications of the standard FACTRETRIEVAL computer program. In Experiment 1, each subject attempted to recall answers to general-information questions until 45 questions had been missed. Then the subject went through three blocks of 15 nonrecalled items per block. For the first block, the subject made FOK judgments and then received a 7-AFC recognition test on each of the 15 items, followed by the same sequence for the second block and then for the third block. After each block, 58 subjects received feedback (seeing a table of their FOK judgments and their recognition performance on every item), and another 58 subjects received no feedback.

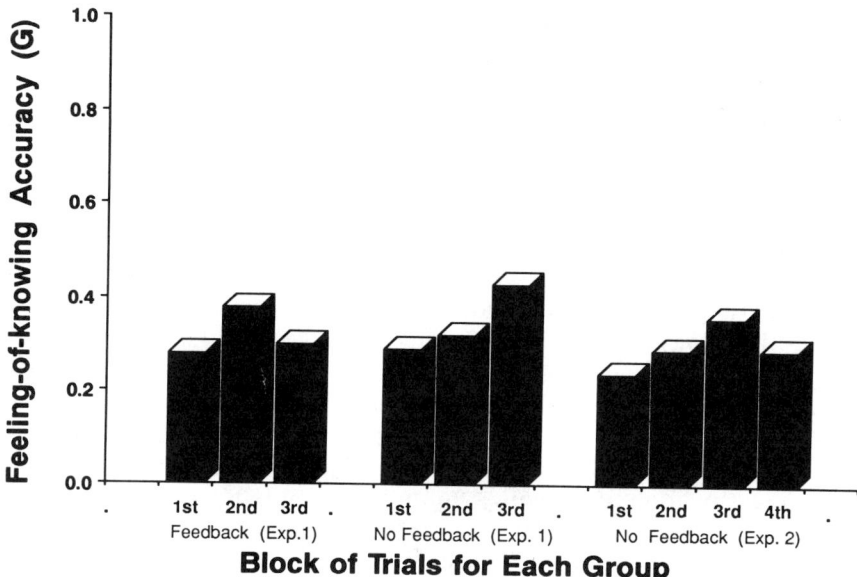

Fig. 9. Feeling-of-knowing accuracy (in terms of mean G) on each block of trials for each group (Feedback or No Feedback) in two experiments.

The resulting FOK accuracy is shown in the left and middle portions of Fig. 9. There was no significant change in the feedback group and there was not even a trend of uniformly increasing FOK accuracy (left side of Fig. 9). However, in the no-feedback group a small but significant increase in FOK accuracy occurred from Block 1 to Block 3, $t(57) = 2.69$ (middle portion of Fig. 9).

In an attempt to replicate and extend this finding that by sheer practice without feedback, people can learn to make FOK judgments more accurately, data were examined in Experiment 2, where only the no-feedback condition was run. Following recall on general-information questions so as to isolate 40 nonrecalled items, each of 36 subjects went through four blocks of 10 items per block. During each block, the subject made FOK judgments, followed by a 4-AFC recognition test on each item, and no feedback was given between blocks.

The resulting FOK accuracy, shown in the right side of Fig. 9, was not significantly different across the four blocks and the pattern was not even in accord with the hypothesis of uniformly increasing FOK accuracy across blocks. Thus we conclude that there is no systematic change in FOK accuracy across blocks of items, and the effect of learning to learn by sheer practice on FOK judgments is small if it occurs at all (i.e., negligible).

Looked at differently, the FOK accuracy of sizeable groups of people appears to be fairly stable across blocks of FOK judgments and does not change in any systematic way. This stability of a group's FOK accuracy can be a methodological advantage because it allows the use of within-subject designs to assess the effect of a given independent variable on FOK accuracy. At the same time, however, researchers should be aware that an individual subject's scores of FOK accuracy vary widely for all known FOK procedures and items (Nelson, 1988), such that (by present-day methodology) individual differences in FOK accuracy are unstable. An important challenge for future research is to discover ways of achieving stable individual scores of FOK accuracy, for use both in theoretical-memory research (e.g., so that such scores can be correlated meaningfully with other individual differences) and in applied settings (e.g., diagnostic classification of a newly admitted hospital patient or a poorly performing student). For instance, perhaps a standardized set of items can be found that yields stable performance (as in an optometrist's eye test) or perhaps a very large number of items would have to be examined for each individual (as in traditional psychophysics experiments). Whether or not these conclusions about stable FOK accuracy for groups of subjects, in conjunction with unstable individual differences in FOK accuracy, extend to other kinds of metamemory judgments (e.g., JOL) is an open question.

6. *Relation between Metacognitive Monitoring and Metacognitive Control during Acquisition: The Allocation of Self-Paced Study Time*

In the theoretical framework above, Fig. 4 shows some interactions during acquisition between metacognitive monitoring processes and metacognitive control processes. We have conducted several experiments pertaining to that topic.

Nelson and Leonesio (1988) found that the allocation of study time is not simply a direct effect of item difficulty but rather is mediated by the person's EOL and FOK judgments about item difficulty (similar to the person's memory of overlearning being a mediator between the actual amount of overlearning and subsequent FOK, as described earlier). Thus the person's metacognitive monitoring may mediate much of the effect of a given independent variable on the person's control of cognitive processing. This illustrates one way in which we can sometimes improve our predictions about how people will control their own cognitive processing if we obtain metacognitive monitoring judgments (which comprise part of the input people use when they adjust the parameters of their control processes). However, we also want to know the conditions under which people's metacognitive monitoring is to some degree irrelevant to their control processes during acquisition. A few specific examples will help to illustrate.

In Nelson and Leonesio's Experiment 1, the mean correlation between EOL and study time was $-.3$ (i.e., items believed to be harder were allocated more self-paced study time). However, there was incomplete compensation for differences in item difficulty during self-paced study. That is, the mean correlation between EOL and recall after self-paced study was not zero (which would have indicated that the extra study time allocated to the items believed to be harder had completely compensated for the differences in item difficulty), but rather was a hefty $G = +.48$. Thus, items perceived as easier were more likely (than items perceived as harder) to be recalled, even after self-paced study in which some extra study time had been allocated to the items perceived as harder. In Experiments 2 and 3, Nelson and Leonesio (1988) found that this incomplete compensation also occurs for FOK judgments and the subsequent self-paced allocation of study time, and the absolute magnitude of the correlation between FOK and self-paced study time was not very large.

Therefore, in a follow-up study (T. O. Nelson & R. J. Leonesio, unpublished), we decided that the computer rather than the person would control the study time per item (cf. Groen & Atkinson, 1966), but the computer would base the distribution of study times on the person's FOK judgments. Four different ways of allocating various study times were examined. All four groups ($n = 52$ Ss/group) made FOK judgments on nonrecalled general-information items (as in Nelson & Leonesio, 1988, Experiment 3), after which the groups received different distributions of study time per nonrecalled item (but the same total study time for the entire set of nonrecalled items): (1) The constant-time group had 4.3 sec of study on every item; (2) the random-assignment-of-different-times group had a random assignment of 8 vs. .5 sec per item, regardless of FOK[4]; (3) the More-Time-To-Low-FOK group had 8 sec per item on the 50% of the items with the lowest FOK and .5 sec per item on the 50% with the highest FOK; and (4) the more-to-high-FOK group had 8 sec per item on the 50% with the highest FOK and .5 sec per item on the 50%

---

[4] A prerequisite for interpreting the results was that the difference in study time was substantial enough to produce differences in subsequent recall, and this prerequisite was confirmed when the mean correlation between the amount of study time and subsequent recall in the random-assignment-of-study-time group was significantly greater than zero ($G = +.39$).

with the lowest FOK. Subsequently, the mean percentage correct recall for each of the four groups was 63.9, 64.5, 64.4, and 56.7, respectively. The more-time-to-high-FOK group did significantly worse than the other three groups, which did not differ significantly. These results demonstrate that allocating extra study time to items that people believe they already know (but currently cannot recall) is an inefficient allocation of extra study time, but the surprising finding is that allocating extra study time to items which people believe they don't already know was no better than allocating the same amount of time to all items and wasn't even better than allocating different amounts of study time randomly! Perhaps with a wider range in the allocation of study time per item (e.g., as would be shown by a higher value—ideally, near +1.0—of the correlation in footnote 4) there would be a greater effect of allocating extra study time to items which are believed to be more difficult. Or perhaps the correlation between EOL/FOK and actual item difficulty is too low (i.e., perhaps inaccurate monitoring of item difficulty is giving misleading information for the control of the allocation of study time).

7. *Relation between Metacognitive Monitoring and Metacognitive Control during Retrieval: Termination of Memory Searching*

In the theoretical framework, interactions between metacognitive monitoring processes and metacognitive control processes also occur during retrieval, and we have recently begun several lines of research on this topic.

a. Role of "Preliminary FOK Judgments" Prior to Searching for an Answer. The first construct in the hypothesized retrieval process (see Fig. 5) is a Preliminary FOK Judgment in which the person decides whether to terminate the retrieval stage or to proceed with a search of memory for the to-be-retrieved item. Empirical confirmation of this hypothetical construct requires that the latency of such FOK judgments be shorter than the latency of correct recall for the requested item. Previous research by Reder (1987, 1988) had confirmed this speculation by asking people either to make binary (i.e., do/don't know) FOK judgments or to retrieve the sought-after answer, and she found that the FOK latencies were indeed shorter than the latencies for retrieving the correct answer.

We utilized Reder's finding to explore a related question, namely, should we conceptualize the Preliminary FOK as consisting of a single FOK component that taps only the presence of information in memory (which we refer to as the *single-counter FOK hypothesis*) or should the conceptualization be in terms of two FOK components, one of which taps the presence of information in memory and the other of which taps the absence of such information (which we refer to as the *dual-counter FOK hypothesis*)? That is, for the single-counter FOK hypothesis, imagine that there is one counter which is incremented as information comes into the metacognitive system to indicate the presence of the item in memory (e.g., memories of having recalled the item during a recent acquisition session, etc.), and assume that when the amount of accumulating information exceeds a threshold, the FOK response of "will recognize" occurs. Then the only way that a "won't recognize" FOK judgment would occur is by default (i.e., time passes without enough information accumulating to indicate that the item is present in memory and eventually the person responds with "won't recognize").

By contrast, for the dual-counter FOK hypothesis, imagine that one counter—the Affirmative-FOK counter—keeps track of accumulating affirmative information that the item is stored in memory, while another counter—the Negative-FOK counter—keeps track of accumulating negative information that the item is not stored in memory. Thus the "won't recognize" judgment does not occur by default but rather occurs by an accumulation of information directly supporting that judgment. Although the threshold mechanism for the dual-counter FOK hypothesis is unspecified, one possibility is that a difference threshold must be exceeded (i.e., the absolute magnitude of the difference between the value of the Affirmative-FOK counter minus the value of the Negative-FOK counter must exceed a threshold; then if the difference is positive, the "will recognize" response occurs, whereas if the difference is negative, the "won't recognize" response occurs, and if the value does not yet exceed the threshold, then the search for more positive/negative information continues).

We (T. Schreiber, T. O. Nelson, & L. Narens, unpublished) tested the single-counter vs. dual-counter hypotheses by having each person ($n = 10$) say aloud as quickly as possible an FOK judgment from a 6-place Likert scale (1 = "completely certain I would not even recognize the correct answer") upon presentation of each of 239 general-information questions from the FACTRETRIEVAL program. The single-counter hypothesis predicts that the latencies of making FOK judgments should be an inverse monotonic function of the FOK judgment; e.g., a judgment of FOK = 6 should have the shortest latency, and a judgment of FOK = 1 (the default judgment if no threshold for accumulating affirmative information is eventually exceeded) should have the longest latency. By contrast, the dual-counter hypothesis predicts that the latencies of making FOK judgments should be a nonmonotonic function of the FOK judgments; i.e., judgments of FOK = 6 and FOK = 1 should have the shortest latencies, with the FOK judgments nearer the center of the FOK rating scale having the longest latencies.

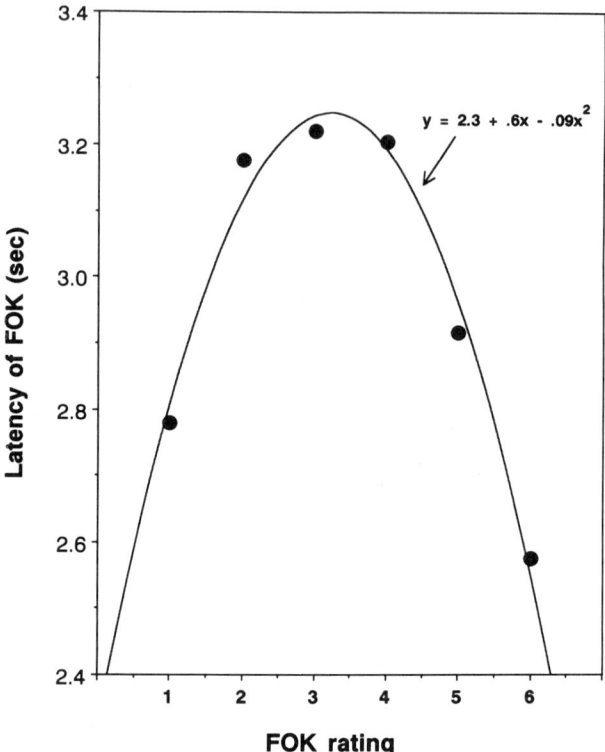

Fig. 10. Median of individual-subjects' median latency of FOK ratings is shown for each FOK rating.

Figure 10 shows the results, in terms of medians of individual-subject median latencies for each FOK rating category.[5] A nonmonotonic pattern is obvious in Fig. 10, which confirms the dual-counter hypothesis that there is both an Affirmative FOK to tap the presence of information in memory and a Negative FOK (cf. "knowing not" in Kolers & Palef, 1976) to tap the absence of information in memory and to allow for quick termination of retrieval when an answer is not known (as in the right branch of Fig. 5).

[5]After a given subject finished making a Preliminary FOK judgment on the 239th item, a recall test occurred on every item to assess the recall latencies. At every FOK rating, the latency of correct recall was longer than the corresponding latency of FOK judgment (the median of individual-subject median latencies of correct recall ranged from a low of 2.9 sec for FOK = 6 to a high of 5.6 sec for FOK = 1), replicating and extending the findings from Reder (1987).

This section focused on how a rapid Preliminary FOK judgment can affect the latency of the termination of retrieval. Next we consider how the ongoing FOK (see the center of Fig. 5) might affect the latency of retrieval termination for longer-latency omission errors[6] (right branch of Fig. 5).

   b. Relation between Ongoing FOK and the Latency of Recall Errors. Our previous research had shown that the correlation between FOK and the latency of omission errors is substantial (Nelson *et al.*, 1984) and this was replicated by Nelson *et al.* (1990), where that correlation was $G = +.60$. This is in accord with the center and right branches of Fig. 5, in which the person's FOK affects whether the overall retrieval stage will be continued or terminated, namely, people terminate the retrieval stage more quickly on items for which they have a low FOK. Given this substantial correlation, if FOK accuracy could somehow be improved, so might efficiency improve for terminating retrieval (i.e., people might be more likely to continue to search for items that are known and be more likely to terminate the retrieval stage for items that are not known). In accord with this idea, neuropsychological patients such as Korsakoffs have poor FOK accuracy (Shimamura & Squire, 1986) and they also tend to terminate prematurely when searching memory and therefore have poor recall performance (Hirst, 1982, p. 454).

   Contrary to the aforementioned substantial correlation between FOK and the latency of omission errors, the correlation between FOK and the latency of commission errors is nil for general-information items (Nelson *et al.*, 1984; also replicated by Nelson *et al.*, 1990, where that correlation was $+.03$) or even slightly negative for laboratory paired associates (Nelson *et al.*, 1982). Thus only a negligible correlation occurs between FOK judgments and the amount of time that the person searches before outputing a commission error. Such a conclusion is not in conflict with the conclusion about the relation between FOK and omission errors because the mechanisms are presumably different for omission errors (right branch of Fig. 5) vs. commission errors (left branch of Fig. 5). The latter involves other metacognitive judgments besides FOK, and we consider those other metacognitive judgments next.

   c. Relation between Metacognitive Confidence Judgments and the Latency of Recall. Nelson *et al.* (1990) asked people to make retrospec-

---

[6]For most retrieval situations, the latency of omission errors is substantially longer than the latency of correct responses (e.g., in Nelson, *et al.*, 1984, the average correct-response latencies ranged from 9.8 to 15.2 sec across three groups of subjects, whereas the average omission-error latencies ranged from 20.5 to 25.1 sec. In Nelson *et al.*, 1990, where the responses were spoken rather than typed into a computer, the average correct-response latency was 2.9 sec, whereas the average omission-error latency was 9.9 sec.).

tive confidence judgments about the accuracy of their previous recall response immediately after outputting that response. In contrast to the aforementioned nil relation between FOK and the latency of commission errors ($G = +.03$), the correlation between retrospective confidence judgments and the latency of commission errors was substantial ($G = -.40$). The direction of this correlation indicates that people have greater confidence for items that they retrieve quickly. This different pattern for FOK vs. confidence judgments (when computed on the identical set of commission-error latencies) confirms the idea that different metacognitive judgments tap different aspects of memory (additional evidence is reported in Leonesio & Nelson, 1990) and is in accord with the left branch of Fig. 5, where the final component that affects the output of commission-error responses is the person's confidence. Also in accord with that idea, the correlation between retrospective confidence judgments and the latency of correct recall is substantial ($G = -.55$) (Nelson et al., 1990). Thus people have greater confidence for answers that they retrieve quickly, regardless of whether those answers are wrong (i.e., commission errors) or correct.

Given the aforementioned facts that (1) confidence judgments are correlated with the latency of recall, regardless of whether that recall is correct or a commission error (Nelson et al., 1990), and (2) latencies tend to be longer for commission errors than for correct recall (Nelson et al., 1984; replicated in Reder, 1987, and in Nelson et al., 1990) the following question arises: Is anything other than the latency of recall responsible for retrospective confidence being greater for correctly recalled items than for commission errors? That is, perhaps the only reason that confidence is greater for correctly recalled answers than for commission errors is because the former are recalled faster than the latter, with confidence being based entirely on recall latency.

A test of this Confidence-Determined-Entirely-by-Latency Hypothesis occurred in an experiment by T. O. Nelson and M. Calogero (unpublished) in which people went through the recall phase of FACTRETRIEVAL2 on 106 general-information questions and made retrospective confidence judgments immediately after outputting each answer. For data analysis, the items were categorized into correct recalls and commission errors (omission errors are irrelevant because retrospective confidence judgments did not occur after omission errors). For each subject, the items in each of those two categories were Vincentized into six blocks (i.e., the first block consisted of the one-sixth of the items that had the shortest recall latencies, and so on to the sixth block, consisting of the one-sixth of the items for which that subject had the longest recall latencies), and the median response latency of the items within each block was

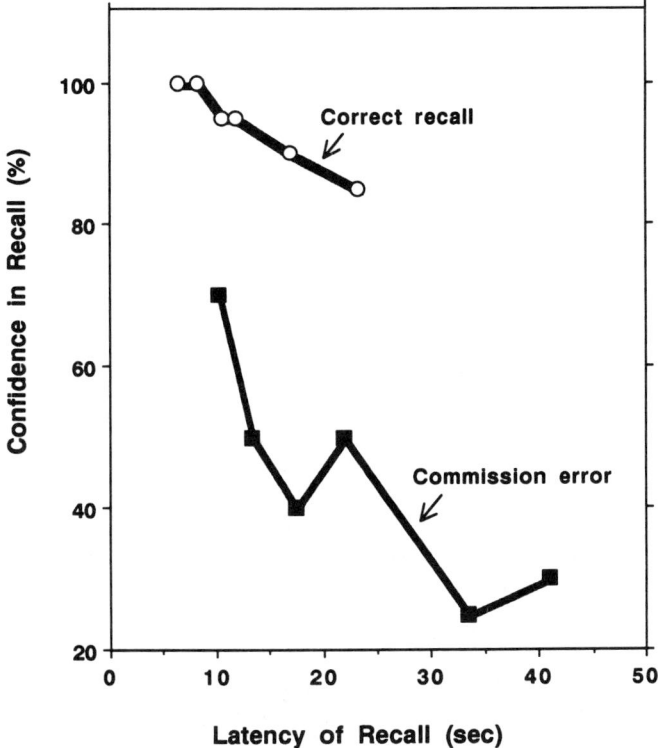

Fig. 11. Confidence in recall for each category of recalled answer (correct recall or commission error) at each Vincentized block of one-sixth of the items ordered in terms of the latency of recall. The value on the abscissa corresponds to the mean of the individual subjects' median latencies, and the value on the ordinate corresponds to the mean of the individual subjects' median confidence for that sixth of the items.

determined. Then the median confidence judgment was determined for the items in each of those six blocks. Finally, the means (across subjects) of those individual-subject median latencies and median confidence judgments were plotted in bivariate form, separately for the categories of correct recall vs. commission error (see Fig. 11).

Several conclusions can be drawn from Fig. 11. First, as expected from the correlations mentioned earlier, retrospective confidence tends to decrease as the latency of recall increases, both for correct recalls and for commission errors. Second and alternatively, the greater the confidence, the shorter the recall latency tends to be (cf. left branch of Fig. 5). Third and most important for the Confidence-Determined-Entirely-by-Latency Hypothesis, the two curves clearly do not lie one atop the other (especially notice the portions of the curves for latencies in the range from 10 to 22 sec), whereas one curve atop the other should have occurred if the latency of recall had been the sole determiner of confidence. Thus, something in addition to the latency of recall is affecting the person's confidence and is producing greater confidence for correct recall than for commission errors. We do not yet know what that something is, but future research should attempt to isolate and identify it.

IV. Applications of Our Methodology to Other Areas

Our methodology, including versions of the FACTRETRIEVAL paradigm, has been used in many other laboratories to investigate both the domain of traditional memory research and related areas. We and our past and present co-workers have also applied this methodology to the following areas. Developmental psychology: Butterfield, Nelson, and Peck (1988) examined changes in metamemory across the life span from 6 to 70 years old. Neuropsychology: Shimamura and Squire (1986, 1988) examined metamemory in neuropsychological populations such as Korsakoff patients and chronic alcoholics, and Janowsky, Shimamura, and Squire (1989) examined metamemory in frontal-lobe patients. Special education: S. Krinsky (1988) examined metamemory in the deaf. Problem solving: Metcalfe (1986) examined metacognitions for solving problems, and Metcalfe and Wiebe (1987) discovered dynamic changes in metacognitions during problem solving. Psychopharmacology: Nelson, McSpadden *et al.* (1986) examined the effects of acute alcohol intoxication on metamemory. Naturalistic settings: Nelson *et al.* (1990) examined the way that metamemory is affected by extreme altitude at Mount Everest.[7]

V. Concluding Remarks

As mentioned earlier, our research in metamemory was initiated by the "paradoxical" findings that people can accurately predict their subsequent likelihood of recognizing nonrecallable items and that they can quickly and accurately decide—on the basis of no more than a cursory search through memory—that they will not retrieve particular sought-

---

[7]The pattern of results obtained at extreme altitude was in several ways the opposite of the pattern obtained from the alcohol-intoxicated people described in Nelson, McSpadden *et al.* (1986).

after items. Those findings led us to develop a methodology based on psychophysical methods that we used to empirically investigate people's "feeling of knowing." The results of our experiments convinced us that we were dealing with only a part of a complex metacognitive system and that to account adequately for feeling-of-knowing phenomena, a larger perspective was needed. This eventuated in the present theoretical framework that emphasizes the role of control and monitoring processes.

The embedding of the feeling of knowing in a richer framework helped to dissipate the paradoxical nature of the feeling of knowing. Moreover, in terms of our theoretical framework, an immediate goal of metamemory research is to explain the accuracy of metacognitive judgments in terms of remembered information, that is, to give a "No-Magic" explanation, like the one described above.

When we began 15 years ago, there were relatively few metamemory researchers and a paucity of solid empirical results about metamemory. We are pleased that today there are many capable, active investigators and a wealth of solid empirical findings. For our own work, we see the next big challenge to be the development of specific theories that will explicate the role of control and monitoring processes in human memory.

ACKNOWLEDGMENTS

Without the continuous support of NIMH during the past 10 years, the research reported here would not have occurred. Preparation of this article was supported by NIMH grant MH32205. We thank Harry Bahrick for helpful comments on an earlier draft.

REFERENCES

Atkinson, R. C., & Shiffrin, R. M. (1968). Human memory: A proposed system and its control processes. In K. W. Spence & J. T. Spence (Eds.), *The psychology of learning and motivation* (Vol. 2). New York: Academic Press.

Bahrick, H. P. (1970). Two-phase model for prompted recall. *Psychological Review*, 77, 215–222.

Bahrick, H. P., & Hall, L. K. (in press). Preventive and corrective maintenance of access to knowledge. *Applied Cognitive Psychology*.

Bower, G. H. (1967). A multicomponent theory of memory trace. In K. W. Spence (Ed.), *The Psychology of Learning*. New York: Academic Press.

Butterfield, E. C., & Belmont, J. M. (1971). Relations of storage and retrieval strategies as short-term memory processes. *Journal of Experimental Psychology*, 89, 319–328.

Butterfield, E. C., Belmont, J. M., & Peltzman, D. J. (1971). Effects of recall requirement on acquisition strategy. *Journal of Experimental Psychology*, 90, 347–348.

Butterfield, E. C., Nelson, T. O., & Peck, G. (1988). Developmental aspects of the feeling of knowing. *Developmental Psychology*, **24**, 654–663.

Carnap, R. (1934). *Logische syntax der sprache*. Vienna: Springer.

Conant, R. C., & Ashby, W. R. (1970). Every good regulator of a system must be a model of that system. *International Journal of Systems Science*, **1**, 89–97.

Coombs, C. (1964). *A theory of data*. New York: Wiley.

Ericsson, K. A., & Simon, H. A. (1980). Verbal reports as data. *Psychological Review*, **87**, 215–251.

Ericsson, K. A., & Simon, H. A. (1984). *Protocol analysis: Verbal reports as data*. Cambridge, MA: MIT Press.

Flavell, J. H. (1979). Metacognition and cognitive monitoring: A new area of cognitive-developmental inquiry. *American Psychologist*, **34**, 906–911.

Groen, G., & Atkinson, R. C. (1966). Models for optimizing the learning process. *Psychological Bulletin*, **66**, 309–320.

Hart, J. T. (1965). Memory and the feeling-of-knowing experience. *Journal of Educational Psychology*, **56**, 208–216.

Hart, J. T. (1967). Memory and the memory-monitoring process. *Journal of Verbal Learning and Verbal Behavior*, **6**, 685–691.

Hilbert, D. (1927). Uber das Unendliche. *Jahresbericht der Deutschen Mathematiker-Vereinigung*, **36** 201–215.

Hirst, W. (1982). The amnesic syndrome: Descriptions and explanations. *Psychological Bulletin*, **91**, 435–460.

Hooker, W., & Jones, R. (1987). Increased susceptibility to memory intrusions and the Stroop interference effect during acute marijuana intoxication. *Psychopharmacology*, **91**, 20–24.

Jameson, K. A., Narens, L., Goldfarb, K., & Nelson, T. O. (1990). The influence of subthreshold priming on metamemory and recall. *Acta Psychologica*, **73**, 55–68.

Janowsky, J. S., Shimamura, A. P., & Squire, L. R. (1989). Memory and metamemory: Comparisons between patients with frontal lobe lesions and amnesic patients. *Psychobiology*, **17**, 3–11.

Juola, J. F., Fischler, I., Wood, C. T., & Atkinson, R. C. (1971). Recognition time for information stored in long-term memory. *Perception & Psychophysics*, **10**, 8–14.

Kolers, P. A., & Palef, S. R. (1976). Knowing not. *Memory & Cognition*, **4**, 553–558.

Krinsky, R., & Nelson, T. O. (1985). The feeling of knowing for different types of retrieval failure. *Acta Psychologica*, **58**, 141–158.

Krinsky, S. (1988). *The feeling of knowing in deaf adolescents: A metamemorial study*. Doctoral dissertation, University of Washington, Seattle.

Lam, T. (1987). *An empirical investigation of extraneous factors and data collection procedures in the measurement of the feeling-of-knowing*. Doctoral dissertation, University of Washington, Seattle.

Le Ny, J. F., Denhiere, G., & Le Taillanter, D. (1972). Regulation of study-time and interstimulus similarity in self-paced learning conditions. *Acta Psychologica*, **36**, 280–289.

Leonesio, R. J. (1985). *Three measures of metamemory: Before you know, after you know, and after you don't know but feel you do*. Master's thesis, University of Washington, Seattle.

Leonesio, R. J., & Nelson, T. O. (1982). Postcriterion overlearning reduces the effectiveness of the method of adjusted learning. *Behavior Research Methods and Instrumentation*, **14**, 320–322.

Leonesio, R. J., & Nelson, T. O. (1990). Do different metamemory judgments tap the same

underlying aspects of memory? *Journal of Experimental Psychology: Learning, Memory, and Cognition.*
Lichtenstein, S., & Fischhoff, B. (1977). Do those who know more also know more about how much they know? *Organizational Behavior and Human Performance,* **20,** 159–183.
Lichtenstein, S., Fischhoff, B., & Phillips, L. D. (1982). Calibration of probabilities: The state of the art to 1980. In D. Kahneman, P. Slovic, & A. Tversky (Eds.), *Judgment under uncertainty: Heuristics and biases* (pp. 306–334). New York: Cambridge University Press.
Lockhart, R. S., & Murdock, B. B. (1970). Memory and the theory of signal detection. *Psychological Bulletin,* **74,** 100–109.
Loftus, G. R., & Wickens, T. D. (1970). Effect of incentive on storage and retrieval processes. *Journal of Experimental Psychology,* **85,** 141–147.
Maki, R. H., & Berry, S. L. (1984). Metacomprehension of text material. *Journal of Experimental Psychology: Learning, Memory, and cognition,* **10,** 663–679.
Marcel, A. (1983). Conscious and unconscious perception: Experiments on visual masking and word recognition. *Cognitive Psychology,* **15,** 197–237.
Mazzoni, G., Cornoldi, C., & Marchitelli, G. (1990). Do memorability ratings affect study-time allocation? *Memory and cognition,* **18,** 196–204.
Metcalfe, J. (1986). Feeling of knowing in memory and problem solving. *Journal of Experimental Psychology: Learning , Memory, and Cognition,* **12,** 288–294.
Metcalfe, J., & Wiebe, D. (1987). Intuition in insight and noninsight problem solving. *Memory & Cognition,* **15,** 238–246.
Modigliani, V., & Hedges, D. G. (1987). Distributed rehearsals and the primacy effect in single-trial free recall. *Journal of Experimental Psychology: Learning, Memory, and Cognition,* **13,** 426–436.
Nelson, T. O. (1978). Detecting small amounts of information in memory: Savings for nonrecognized items. *Journal of Experimental Psychology: Human Learning and Memory,* **4,** 453–468.
Nelson, T. O. (1984). A comparison of current measures of the accuracy of feeling-of-knowing predictions. *Psychological Bulletin,* **95,** 109–133.
Nelson, T. O. (1986). BASIC programs for computation of Goodman-Kruskal gamma coefficient. *Bulletin of the Psychonomic Society,* **24,** 281–283.
Nelson, T. O. (1987). The Goodman-Kruskal gamma coefficient as an alternative to signal-detection theory's measures of absolute-judgment accuracy. In E. Roskam & R. Suck (Eds.), *Progress in mathematical psychology,* Vol. 1, pp. 299–306 Amsterdam: Elsevier/North-Holland.
Nelson, T. O. (1988). Predictive accuracy of the feeling of knowing across different criterion tasks and across different subject populations and individuals. In M. M. Gruneberg, P. Morris, & R. N. Sykes (Eds.), *Practical aspects of memory* (Vol. 2). New York: Wiley.
Nelson, T. O., Dunlosky, J., White, D. M., Steinberg, J., Townes, B. D., & Anderson, D. (1990). *Cognition and metacognition at extreme altitude on Mount Everest.* Manuscript under review.
Nelson, T. O., Gerler, D., & Narens, L. (1984). Accuracy of feeling-of-knowing judgments for predicting perceptual identification and relearning. *Journal of Experimental Psychology: General,* **113,** 282–300.
Nelson, T. O., & Leonesio, R. J. (1988). Allocation of self-paced study time and the 'labor-in-vain effect.' *Journal of Experimental Psychology: Learning, Memory, and Cognition,* **14,** 476–486.
Nelson, T. O., Leonesio, R. J., Landwehr, R. S., & Narens, L. (1986). A comparison of

three predictors of an individual's memory performance: The individual's feeling of knowing versus the normative feeling of knowing versus base-rate item difficulty. *Journal of Experimental Psychology: Learning, Memory, and Cognition,* **12,** 279–287.
Nelson, T. O., Leonesio, R. J., Shimamura, A. P., Landwehr, R. F., & Narens, L. (1982). Overlearning and the feeling of knowing. *Journal of Experimental Psychology: Learning, Memory, and Cognition,* **8,** 279–288.
Nelson, T. O., McSpadden, M., Fromme, K., & Marlatt, G. A. (1986). Effects of alcohol intoxication on metamemory and on retrieval from long-term memory. *Journal of Experimental Psychology: General,* **115,** 247–254.
Nelson, T. O., & Narens, L. (1980a). A new technique for investigating the feeling of knowing. *Acta Psychologica,* **46,** 69–80.
Nelson, T. O., & Narens, L. (1980b). Norms of 300 general-information questions: Accuracy of recall, latency of recall, and feeling-of-knowing ratings. *Journal of Verbal Learning and Verbal Behavior,* **19,** 338–368.
Nickerson, R. S. (1980). Motivated retrieval from archival memory. In *Nebraska Symposium on Motivation* (pp. 73–119).
Nickerson, R. S., Baddeley, A., & Freeman, B. (1987). Are people's estimates of what other people know influenced by what they themselves know? *Acta Psychologica,* **64,** 245–259.
Nisbett, R. E., & Wilson, T. D. (1977). Telling more than we can know: Verbal reports on mental processes. *Psychological Review,* **84,** 231–259.
Pfefferbaum, A., Darley, C., Tinklenberg, J., Roth, W., & Kopell, B. (1977). Marijuana and memory intrusions. *Journal of Nervous and Mental Disease,* **165,** 381–386.
Reder, L. M. (1987). Strategy selection in question answering. *Cognitive Psychology,* **19,** 90–138.
Reder, L. M. (1988). Strategic control of retrieval strategies. In G. Bower (Ed.), *The psychology of learning and motivation* (Vol. 22). San Diego, CA: Academic Press.
Richardson-Klavehn, A., & Bjork, R. A. (1988). Measures of memory. *Annual Review of Psychology,* **39,** 475–543.
Schacter, D. L., & Worling, J. R. (1985). Attribute information and the feeling-of-knowing. *Canadian Journal of Psychology,* **39,** 467–475.
Shafer, G. (1976). *A mathematical theory of evidence.* Princeton, NJ: Princeton University Press.
Shepard, R. N. (1967). Recognition memory for words, sentences, and pictures. *Journal of Verbal Learning and Verbal Behavior,* **6,** 156–163.
Shimamura, A. P., Landwehr, R. F., & Nelson, T. O. (1981). FACTRETRIEVAL: A program for assessing someone's recall of general-information facts, feeling-of-knowing judgments for nonrecalled facts, and recognition of nonrecalled facts. *Behavior Research Methods and Instrumentation,* **13,** 691–692.
Shimamura, A. P., & Squire, L. R. (1986). Memory and metamemory: A study of the feeling-of-knowing phenomenon in amnesic patients. *Journal of Experimental Psychology: Learning, Memory, and Cognition,* **12,** 452–460.
Shimamura, A. P., & Squire, L. R. (1988). Long-term memory in amnesia: Cued recall, recognition memory, and confidence ratings. *Journal of Experimental Psychology: Learning, Memory, and Cognition,* **14,** 763–771.
Simon, H. A. (1979). *Models of thought.* New Haven, CT: Yale University Press.
Snow, J. (1987). *Design.* Cambridge, MA: Meta Software.
Underwood, B. J. (1966). Individual and group predictions of item difficulty for free learning. *Journal of Experimental Psychology,* **71,** 673–679.
Vesonder, G. T., & Voss, J. F. (1985). On the ability to predict one's own responses while learning. *Journal of Memory and Language,* **24,** 363–376.

Weingartner, H., Rudorfer, M. V., & Linnoila, M. (1985). Cognitive effects of lithium treatment in normal volunteers. *Psychopharmacology*, **86**, 472–474.
Wescourt, K. T., & Atkinson, R. C. (1973). Scanning for information in long- and short-term memory. *Journal of Experimental Psychology*, **98**, 95–101.
Wilkinson, T. S., & Nelson, T. O. (1984). FACTRETRIEVAL2: A Pascal program for assessing someone's recall of general-information facts, confidence about recall correctness, feeling-of-knowing judgments for nonrecalled facts, and recognition of nonrecalled facts. *Behavior Research Methods, Instruments and Computers*, **16**, 486–488.

THE NEW MULTIMODAL APPROACH TO MEMORY IMPROVEMENT

Douglas J. Herrmann
Alan Searleman

I. Introduction

Memory improvement is one of the world's oldest professions. For more than 2000 years, various people have claimed to be experts capable of changing a person's memory performance for the better. It has been known that learning can be facilitated by rehearsal since at least the sixth century B.C. Development of better ways to rehearse began soon thereafter when, in 477 B.C., the poet Simonides noted that he was able to remember who attended a banquet by imagining the people in their places at the banquet table. Many who followed Simonides (such as Cicero) reasoned that if memory for who attended a banquet could be augmented by imagining the people in a spatial array at a banquet table, then memory for the contents of any kind of information (such as points in a speech) could also be facilitated by imagining the ideas in different spatial locations (loci).

The method of loci and other procedures of mental control derived from the loci method (such as the peg method) have been passed down over the centuries (Yates, 1966). Today, as in ancient Greece, these loci-based methods are what commercial memory-improvement ventures (books, courses) recommend (Bellezza, 1982; Higbee, 1988; West, 1985; Young & Gibson, 1962). In psychology, research into the effectiveness of the classical methods of memory improvement methods began in the

1970s. Generally, these methods have been shown to increase the learning of lists substantially, and sometimes dramatically (as much as 100 to 300% more than a control group, e.g., Bower, 1970; McDaniel & Pressley, 1987).

Nevertheless, psychologists and a variety of other specialists (psychiatrists, physicians, speech pathologists, and others) have been developing new methods of memory improvement because the classical methods (loci, peg, and others) have not always yielded an adequate improvement in memory performance. The classical methods have been found to be inadequate for two reasons. First, it has generally been believed that these methods could be applied to almost any memory task. However, research has repeatedly shown that these methods are not useful for all tasks. For example, they are less readily applied to more complex material (such as learning a poem, a document, or a story) than to simpler material (such as learning a shopping list). They are not applicable at all to some situations (such as trying to mentally register someone's face). In addition, the classical methods are taxing for most people to use, so taxing that people trained in their use rarely continue to use them much beyond the period of memory training (Bellezza, 1983; Higbee, in press; Lapp, 1983). Even psychologists who specialize in remedying memory problems rarely use these methods themselves, despite being especially familiar with their use (Parks, Cavanaugh, & Smith, 1986).

This is not to say that the classical methods should not be part of a program of memory improvement. These methods do have a place in such programs, but they must be imparted to the kind of person who is inclined to their use. Additionally, instruction in the classical methods should prepare a person to use the methods for those situations for which the methods are most effective.

Because the classical methods were found inadequate, many researchers and practitioners concluded it was necessary to develop new methods for memory improvement (Bachman, in press; Druckman & Swets, 1988; Herrmann, Rea, & Andrzejewski, 1988; Khan, 1986; Labouvie-Vief & Gonda, 1976; McEvoy & Moon, 1988; Poon, 1980; Pressley, Borkowski, & Schneider, 1987; Pressley, Forrest-Pressley, Elliott-Faust, & Miller, 1985; Wilson & Moffat, 1984; Yesavage, 1985; Yesavage, Sheikh, & Lapp, 1990). The development of new memory-improvement methods was approached in two ways. First, new methods were developed to mentally manipulate information that supplemented or supplanted the classical methods. Second, new methods were developed to alter memory processing by manipulating the processing of other psychological modes (defined as one of the other major psychological subsystems). To provide a common basis for discussion of these nonmemory modes, we will arbitrarily designate them as physiological condition, emotional state, attitudes, social behaviors, sensory and motoric use of the environment, and thought (see Royce, 1973).

The purpose of this article is to review recent findings of the new approach to memory improvement and to demonstrate the relevance of this research to memory theory. The article will begin by examining current understanding of control processing of mental content. Findings that have led to a new understanding of the control of mental content will be discussed and, then, the new methods of such content control will be reviewed. The article will then briefly examine the understanding of the control of memory performance attained through control of other processing modes. Examples will demonstrate that control is possible in modes other than by manipulation of mental content; attempts to improve memory by altering control in these modes will be examined. Finally, the theoretical implications of this new approach will be considered.

II. A Review of Current Understanding of Control Processes

Prior to the advent of the new approach to memory improvement, control processes were understood as they were defined by Atkinson and Shiffrin (1968), i.e., as active manipulations of stimulus and task information. Control processes were conceived to influence which information is operated on by basic memory processes (registration, retention, and retrieval). Because the term *control* begs the question of who or what is doing the controlling, some researchers have preferred to use other terms for the kind of processing that Atkinson and Shiffrin labeled as involving "control" (for example, Flavell, 1977, used "acquired" processes instead of control processes). Despite terminological disputes, the term *control process* has prevailed (Baddeley, 1986). Since control processes are often taken to be conscious and deliberate, other researchers have contrasted control processes with those that have become automatic with practice (Hasher & Zacks, 1979; Shiffrin & Schneider, 1977; cf. Cheng, 1985). Regardless of degree of automaticity, control processes have usually been thought of as similar to software—with practice refining the program so that the processes are executed automatically. Some have also proposed that large amounts of experience with memory tasks may alter basic hardware, i.e., normally permanent physiological mechanisms (see Baltes & Kliegel, 1986; Rosenzweig, 1984), but such proposals have yet to be integrated into memory models.

Initial research into the effects of control processes focused on the quantitative variations in such processes across information being learned

(Rundus, 1971). The quantitative approach was extremely useful. For example, this approach showed that the primacy effect in free recall was due to people rehearsing the early items on a list more than subsequent items. Moreover, memory deficiencies were found to be compensated in some cases by directions to rehearse (Belmont & Butterfield, 1971). Soon, it was pointed out by Craik and Lockhart (1973) that, besides quantity, the quality of processing had effects as well. Subsequently, it was shown that effective memory performance required that retrieval processes be compatible with the kinds of attributes that were encoded during learning (C. D. Morris, Bransford, & Franks, 1977). These developments led to innovations in memory skill training in a variety of situations (Brown, Bransford, Ferrara, & Campione, 1983).

Qualitatively, there are essentially two kinds of control processes that manipulate informational content, to be learned or retrieved, in a *memory task*. One kind of control process operates on specific aspects of the mental representation of the content, while the other kind of control process operates on the representation of content in general by regulating the timing of the deployment of content manipulations. Their nature and effectiveness are briefly reviewed below.

A. Content-Specific Manipulations

These manipulations focus attention on some, or all, of the attributes of the content, sensory or informational, presented in a memory task. By directing attention to specific attributes of task content, basic processes register a representation of these attributes in memory and stimulate previously established memories so that they lead a memory to be "retrieved."

Some content-specific manipulations are known to people who are naive to memory training. Naive manipulations of specific aspects of content include, for example, repetition, forming images, and rhyming. Normal people do not need formal instruction in the use of such processes. These types of processes are acquired in the course of development in ways that are not yet fully understood. Table I illustrates the frequency of usage of some naive manipulations in each of two different learning tasks.

Other such manipulations require that people first study certain technical information necessary to the proper use of the manipulation (Bellezza, 1982; Yates, 1986). Technical manipulations include, for example, the classical methods and other ad hoc mnemonics passed on from generation to generation. These manipulations are called "technical" in that they cannot be used until a person has memorized certain information. Typi-

TABLE I

Proportion of Subjects Reporting the Use of Naive Mnemonics in Two Verbal Learning Paradigms[a]

Kind of mnemonic used	Free recall	Paired associates
Simple repetition	6	14
First-letter mnemonic	38	16
Clustering	31	9
Descriptive story	22	8
Personal experience	6	7
Verbal mediation	0	8
Imagery mediation	0	15
Phonetic clustering	0	14
Other	0	9

[a] Free-recall data were drawn from Blick and Waite (1971) and paired-associate data from Boltwood and Blick (1970).

cally, a person must memorize an encoding scheme that later may be used to transform to-be-learned information into another representational format. For example, the method of loci requires a person to first commit to memory a physical expanse (a chair, a church, a stadium) with distinct locations. This physical expanse then serves as an encoding scheme that a person can use to store information in memory.

There are two reasons that technical manipulations like the method of loci work. First, the transformed information provides an alternate record to that initially encoded. The alternate record (called a retrieval structure by Chase and Ericsson, 1982) may later aid recall in case the initial record is not readily recalled (Atkinson, 1975; Bellezza, 1981, 1986; Ericsson, 1985; Ericsson & Oliver, 1989). Second, the process of transforming information into an alternate form requires the learner to pay greater attention to the original stimulus, thus causing the untransformed memory representation to be more detailed than it would be otherwise.

B. Content-General Manipulations

These manipulations allocate the amount of content-specific manipulations over the information to be processed (R. E. Johnson, 1980). For example, a content-general manipulation may distribute processing time evenly over task content (e.g., during learning) or it may allocate processing more to one portion of the content than to another portion. Like content-specific manipulations, content-general manipulations may be naive or technical in that technical content-general manipulations require some instruction before they are used. For example, naive rehearsal requires that content be manipulated at equal intervals, whereas one technical form of rehearsal, which is very effective, dictates an exponential increase in intervals between rehearsals (Landauer & Bjork, 1978; Landauer & Ross, 1977).

We take pains to distinguish content-general manipulations from content-specific manipulations since the distinction is relevant to any theory of control processing and to new approaches to improve memory processing.

III. The New Approach to Content Manipulations

A. EFFECTIVENESS OF CONTROL-PROCESS PRACTICE

The proficiency of processing is well known to increase with practice (Anderson, 1982; Shiffrin & Schneider, 1977; Schneider & Shiffrin, 1977). However, memory-improvement research has shown that the increased proficiency resulting from practice transfers little or not at all to other memory tasks (Perkins, 1985). For example, a subject increased his digit span nearly 10-fold after months of practice but afterward possessed just a normal letter span (Chase & Ericsson, 1982). Similarly, subjects given extensive practice at recalling examples of specific categories demonstrate a minimally increased recall level for other categories (Herrmann, Buschke, & Gall, 1987). Such research has led to the conclusion that memory skills function like production systems, which become more specific as practice increases. Truly superior memory production systems may require several months (Chase & Ericsson, 1982) or even years to develop (Hunt & Love, 1972).

B. REPRESENTATIONAL TENDENCY OF CONTENT MANIPULATIONS

Research in basic memory processes, as noted above, has revealed that content manipulations have a representational tendency, i.e., that there are certain stimuli or kinds of content with which a control process is most effective. For example, processes at retrieval must address the same kinds of attributes as were processed during acquisition or else retrieval will not be as effective. Thus, a list of words learned by rhyming the words with each other or with associates will be elicited more effectively by a rhyme cue than by a cue which is similar in meaning to list words. Conversely, a list of words learned by relating the meanings of the words with each other or with associates will be elicited more effectively by a semantically similar cue than by a cue which rhymes with list words (McDaniel & Kearny, 1984; C. D. Morris *et al.*, 1977). New methods of retrieval have been developed by making retrieval processes appropriate to the kind of memory to be retrieved. For example, recall of an autobiographical experience can be increased substantially by "guiding" a person's recall through the potential attributes for such experiences (time, location, people present) (Geiselman, Fisher, MacKinnon, & Holland, 1986). Also autobiographical recall can be enhanced by other procedures such as recalling landmark events surrounding the experience in question (National Center for Health Statistics, 1989).

Recent research in everyday memory indicates that the specificity of content in memory tasks is often greater than previously envisioned (Cohen, 1989; Day, 1988). Similarly, research in memory improvement indicates that the specificity of content-specific manipulations is greater as well. For example, naive manipulations vary in effectiveness across tasks in ways that suggest that the representational bias of these manipulations pertains to just a few memory tasks (Intons-Peterson & Fournier, 1986). For example, the first-letter mnemonic is obviously designed for learning a word list but not for learning prose, and certainly not to register someone's face in memory. Classical manipulations have also been found to favor certain tasks, e.g., the method of loci is best suited for serial learning, whereas interactive imagery is well suited for paired-associate learning (Herrmann, 1987).

Memory-improvement researchers have taken the issue of specificity of content manipulations farther than the laboratory. They have shown also that memory skills are task specific and that they become more specific as practice increases. The likelihood of continued usage of a content manipulation (i.e., manipulation maintenance) appears to be linked to the specificity of a manipulation (Intons-Peterson & Fournier, 1986). As noted earlier, in the introduction, the classical methods of memory improvement are rarely maintained by either the students or the teachers of these methods (Bellezza, 1983; Higbee, 1988; Lapp, 1983; Parks *et al.*, 1986). Apparently, decreases in specificity of manipulations lead to increased demand for attentional capacity and processing, making manipulations more and more taxing to use.

It has also been shown that besides some content manipulations being more effective than others, some manipulations can actually lessen memory performance. For example, processing facial features some time after initial encoding of a face can impair subsequent recognition of a face (J. W. Schooler & Engstler-Schooler, in press). Also, various kinds of absent-mindedness have revealed that control processes often go awry or

TABLE II

Task/Content-Specific Manipulations for Three Memory Tasks

Appointments	Remembering what you were just doing	Remembering to put the gas cap back
Imagine what you will be doing just before the appointment	Repeat the name of the action to yourself	Put the cap in an obvious place
Imagine the face of your watch set to the appointment time next to the person to be met	Make notes of your actions as the day progresses	Put a clothespin on your dash
Use an alarm	Carry an object in your hand that reminds you of the intended action	Have a wire connect your gas cap to your car

steps of such processes are omitted (Norman, 1981; Reason & MyCielska, 1983). Such findings indicate that memory skill involves not only the acquisition of effective control processes but also the elimination of habitual processes that impair memory performance (Herrmann, 1989).

In order to impact more durable memory processes, researches working within the new approach have chosen to teach content manipulations that are even more specific than the ones investigated in the laboratory (Jacoby & Dallas, 1981). Probably the best example of such an approach is the face–name imagery technique. This method involves teaching people to transform a person's name into an imaginable object and then mentally to locate the image on the person's face. This method has been found to increase name recall to faces substantially (Malpass, 1981; P. E. Morris, Jones, & Hampsen, 1977) with usage of the method maintained over time (Herrmann, Rea, Andrzejewski, & Moore, 1989).

The number of task-specific manipulations is great. Surveys given to adults of all ages indicate that over 100 memory tasks in everyday life sometimes create difficulties for people and that task-specific manipulations exist or are easily developed for each task (Herrmann, 1989). Table II illustrates content manipulations appropriate for three everyday (prospective) memory tasks.

Methods such as these are advanced in publications intended for the elderly: for example, by the National Council for Aging (Garfunkel & Landau, 1981); Turner Geriatric Services, University of Michigan Medical Center (Stern & Fogler, 1989). These methods have been used as part of memory-improvement courses at Hamilton College and the University of South Florida (McEvoy & Moon, 1988), described in greater detail later in this article. This new approach to memory improvement recognizes the task specificity of content manipulations and has highlighted the distinction between content-specific and content-general manipulations. The importance of content-general manipulations has been shown especially in research in study skills (Weinstein, Goertz, & Alexander, 1988; see also McDaniel & Pressley, 1987) but also in everyday memory performance. However, much more research is needed to develop a systematic understanding of the differences among content-general manipulations.

IV. Current Understanding of Control of Memory Performance through Control of Other Modes

Memory research has traditionally attributed memory performance to variables that influence the functioning of the memory system (P. E. Morris, 1977; West, 1990). For some researchers the relevant variables have been physiological (facilitating substances; anatomical structures). For other researchers, the relevant variable has been informational (stimulus or cue attributes). As has just been discussed, the control process has largely been conceived of as involving control of informational content (Herrmann & Searleman, 1989). Virtually every memory text in print interprets control processes in this manner. However, the inadequacies of the classical methods (as well as increased demand in the 1970s for more methods of memory improvement, i.e., to augment education, to support the elderly, to assist the neurologically impaired) pressured researchers to look beyond content control processing for means of memory improvement.

V. The New Approach to Control of Memory Performance through Control of Other Modes

Somewhat independently, but seemingly collectively, many researchers and clinicians have recently sought to improve memory by controlling processing in other modes (Bachman, in press; Druckman & Swets, 1988; Herrmann *et al.*, 1988; Khan, 1986; McEvoy & Moon, 1988; Poon, 1980; Pressley *et al.*, 1987; Pressley, Levin, & Ghatala, 1984; Wilson & Moffat, 1984; Yesavage, 1985; Yesavage *et al.*, in press). The variables of the other process modes are divided into two broad categories—*content-process* modes and *condition-process* modes.

TABLE III
Process Modes That Affect Memory Performance

Content-Process Modes
  Content manipulation: Directs attention to information to affect registration and retrieval
  Physical environmental manipulation: Directs attention to objects and events to facilitate memory
  Social environmental manipulation: Alters social interactions to direct attention to information that facilitates memory

Condition-Process Modes
  Physical condition: Actions that enhance general attention by improving physiological states
  Emotional state: Actions that enhance general attention by improving emotional and motivational states
  Attitude toward the task: Actions that enhance general attention by fostering a postive and realistic view of memory tasks

The content modes directly alter the way that stimulus content is encoded and/or retrieved. These modes include the well-known content manipulations, specific and general, and two other modes, i.e., manipulations of the physical environment and manipulations of social interactions. The condition-process modes involve a deliberate attempt to alter modes of processing that influence memory indirectly. These modes include manipulations of physical condition, emotional state, and attitudes. Because the influence of condition modes is indirect, control of these modes must occur before a memory task, or in its early stages, so there is sufficient time for the mode to affect memory performance. Thus, control of these modes usually must accrue over time, considerably prior to the task. It may be seen that the condition-process modes operate on "hardware," whereas the content-process modes operate, like "software," on contents of memory system. Below we briefly review evidence that people can control these various modes at least temporarily and also evidence that people can be trained to use these process modes to improve their memory performance. These modes, along with content manipulations, are listed in Table III, according to the two broad categories.

A. Content-Process Modes

1. Physical Environment

a. Control. Considerable research in the past decade has demonstrated that awareness of environmental context is important to memory-performance (Bjork & Richardson-Klavehn, 1989). In addition, everyday-memory research has shown that people may control physical stimuli (e.g., position or mark objects, write notes), either for acquisition or for retrieval, akin to the way experimenters manipulate such conditions. In so doing, the individual controls such stimuli, like experimenters do, to facilitate memory performance. There are many ways that people appear to influence memory performance by manipulating physical characteristics of stimuli (Miyata & Norman, 1986). For instance, virtually every normal adult assists his or her memory in nontechnical ways, such as in making notes or in placing objects in conspicuous places as reminders (Cavanaugh, Grady, & Perlmutter, 1983; Harris, 1984; Intons-Peterson & Fournier, 1986; Jackson, Boyers, & Kerstholt, 1988; Parks et al., 1986; Winograd & Soloway, 1985). Additionally, many people make use of one or more commercial memory aids (such as a credit-card wallet that signals an alarm when a credit card is not replaced; a car finder—a radio remote control that activates the horn in your car when you cannot recall where it was parked; or a plant alarm to remind you that a plant is thirsty) (Herrmann & Petro, in press). Graphs and tables remind people of research findings and hypothetical functional relationships (Kosslyn, 1989; Larkin & Simon, 1987). Graphic images (on television, microprocessors, and in the media) can facilitate learning (Caplan & Schooler, 1990) or may facilitate the remembering of a face (Davies, 1982). Files and piles of papers on one's desk may serve to cue oneself (Hertel, 1988).

b. Improved Control. While not all known external aids have been used in memory-improvement programs, many have been . The use of external memory aids has become a popular prescription for memory problems among the elderly. As mentioned earlier, the National Council on Aging distributes a booklet advocating a mixture of content and external-aid manipulations for memory training with the elderly (Garfunkel & Landau, 1981) as does the Turner Geriatric Center at the University of Michigan Medical Center (Stern & Fogler, 1989). Similarly, Harris (1980) recommended in *Concord* (the journal of the British Association for Service to the Elderly) a variety of external aids to help the elderly with memory problems.

Several sources have proposed the use of commercial devices, with caveats about the difficulties of doing so, for patients with severe memory problems (e.g.,, Naugle, Prevey, Naugle, & Delaney; 1988; Wilson, 1987; Wilson & Moffat, 1984). Some research has assessed the relative effectiveness of different aids with self-report measures (Herrmann & Petro, in press; Intons-Peterson & Fournier, 1986), although no research has assessed the effects of instructions to use these aids on objective memory performance.

Finally, microprocessors have been used as teaching machines (Skillbeck, 1984). One such use has been to facilitate the reacquisition of memory skills. Another has been to teach an amnesic person necessary knowledge to hold a job (Schachter & Glisky, 1986). Also, a variety of software is sold now that provides a person with exercises to improve memory (e.g., Ryan, 1986).

2. Social Environment

a. Control. Much, possibly the majority, of memory processing is carried out in response to others. Casual conversation or serious discussion often requires a person to pick up information needed in the future or to recall information acquired in the past. Much of this information pertains to social situations and many social interactions depend on memory for this information (Wegner, Giuliano, & Hertel, 1985). Failure to remember properly in social contexts can be embarrassing (Goffman, 1961).

Accordingly, people attempt to facilitate the performance of memory tasks in social context by controlling the rate of information exchange or by directing the conversation to a new topic. For example, people can sometimes inadvertently recall something which they had recalled moments before: A person may recall a fact in a conversation in a manner that reveals a lack of awareness of the preceding recall (Koriat, Ben-Zur, & Sheffer, 1988). Such repetition is embarrassing when pointed out because it suggests lack of control of "one's faculties." People can avoid inadvertent repeated recalls by conversational skills. One such skill involves reiterating what oneself and others have just said. Such a strategy aids encoding who said what and delays the input of new information. It is also possible to buy time for retrieval of hard-to-remember information through the use of conversational ploys that slow a conversation or restrict it to just one or two topics. Time needed for retrieval can be secured by asking questions of a questioner or by referring questions to another person (Rabbitt, 1981). In some cases, a person can ask someone else to perform a memory task, either to commit something to memory or to recall something forgotten (Intons-Peterson & Fournier, 1986). Finally, successful performance of a memory task also involves the appropriate choice of words for which recall may be expressed. Over- or understatement of what one can or did learn will create certain undeserved impressions of one's memory ability (Gentry & Herrmann, 1990).

b. Improved Control. Outside of memory-improvement research, conversational skills have been taught primarily for social purposes, i.e., to enhance self-presentation. The only memory-improvement training that has addressed conversational control is work done by the first author at Hamilton College (discussed later in the article) which indicated that this training is helpful to memory performance. It is also relevant that remedial work with head-injured patients often includes teaching the relatives of these patients forms of conversational control that may facilitate the memory performance of the patients (Gervasio, 1988). Similarly, the development of memory skills is now conceived as dependent on the nature of social interactions which impart a skill to a child (Belmont, 1989).

B. Condition-Process Modes

1. Physical Condition

a. Control. A person's memory performance is affected by aspects of his or her physical condition, aspects which may be under a person's control. Such control typically involves eliminating an impaired state, although it may be argued that in some cases facilitation occurs by improving a condition above what is normal for an individual. First, people can strive for better memory performance by good eating habits (Logue, 1986; Wurtman, 1981, 1982) and by not eating too much (Smith, 1988). Second, people can improve their memory performance through exercise (Stamford, Hambacher, & Fallica, 1974). Third, to the extent that it is possible, maintenance of good health serves to optimize memory performance (Miller, 1976; cf. Cutler & Grams, 1988; Willis, Yeo, Thomas, & Garry, 1988). Fourth, a good memory can be ensured by avoiding the use of various common substances that may impair memory such as alcohol (Birnbaum & Parker, 1977; Hashtroudi & Parker, 1986) and tobacco (Peeke & Peeke, 1984; Spilich, 1986; cf. Wittenborn, 1988). Various psychotropic substances also impair memory such as marijuana (Block & Wittenborn, 1984; Darley, Tinklenberg, Hollister, & Atkinson, 1973; Lister & Weingartner, 1987), coffee under certain conditions (Bowyer, Humphrey, & Revelle, 1983; Erikson *et al.*, 1985; Eysenck & Folkard, 1980; Petros, Beckwith, Erikson, Arnold, & Sternhagen, 1987; Revelle, Humphreys, Simon, & Gilliland, 1980; cf. Loke, 1988), some tranquilizers (valium) (Meerwaldt, 1986), and sedating antidepressants (Curran, Sakulsriprong, & Lader, 1988). Fifth, a better memory performance can be achieved if memory work is done at optimum times of the day. For example, people perform better if they do so at a time other than right after waking (Tilley & Statham, 1989) and possibly in the afternoon (Folkard & Monk, 1980), as well as by avoiding disruptions of their sleep cycle (although, see Idzikowski, 1984; Wilkinson, 1961, 1963) and by avoiding performing memory tasks late at night (Folkard & Monk, 1980).

b. Improved Control. Another way to have an immediate effect on memory is through the use of memory drugs (Idzikowski, 1988). Various prescription drugs enhance memory performance in neurologically impaired people and in some cases in normals as well (Curran *et al.*, 1988; Lawlor, Sunderland, Martinez, Molchan, & Weingartner, in press). However, such drugs are not readily obtained by people with normal memory functioning and, even if they were, it is possible that the side effects of such drugs would mitigate against their use.

Another method of physical-condition control that is easily achieved involves the kinds of food which people eat. People can choose to eat various foods that hypothetically facilitate memory (e.g., fish and meats). Some writers have suggested improving memory in this way (Feinaigle, 1812) but, thus far, little research has been done on the role of diet in memory (Wurtman, 1981, 1982) and no one has identified an overall diet that has an ameliorative effect on memory. Some research has attempted to improve memory of elderly subjects by having them ingest glucose (Gold, 1987; Gonder-Frederick *et al.*, 1987). It is unknown whether such practices were later adopted by the elderly in these studies, but we do know of college students who made consistent use of such knowledge in their exam preparation after being told of the findings. Finally, several studies indicate that memory performance is enhanced by consistent exercise (jogging), which improved physical condition (Blomquist & Danner, 1987; Blumenthal & Madden, 1988; Harma, Ilmarinen, Knauth, & Rutenfranz, 1988 cf. Tomporowski & Ellis, 1986).

2. Emotional State

a. Control. Memory registration and retrieval can be impaired by negative emotions (Matlin & Stang, 1978) or by very intense emotions (Freud, 1901) involving general anxiety (Dixon, Hertzog, & Hultsch, 1986) and situationally induced stress (Broadbent, Cooper, Fitzgerald, & Parkes, 1982; Hartley, Morrison, & Arnold, 1989; Reason, 1988; Reason & MyCielska, 1983). Also depression may lead to poorer memory performance (Zarit, Gallagher & Kramer, 1981), and intense, negative events may be repressed (Erdelyi & Goldberg, 1979).

b. Improved Control. Much research has attempted to improve memory performance by treatments that reduce extremes in emotionality or that increase positive affect. For instance, with anxious college students, therapeutic interventions to reduce anxiety have been known for some time to improve academic performance (Meichenbaum, 1972; Spielberger, Gonzales, & Fletcher, 1979).

Congruency between a person's moods during acquisition and retrieval leads to better recall than that obtained without congruency (Bower, 1981; Ellis, Thomas, & Rodriguez, 1984; M. H. Johnson & Magaro, 1987;

Singer & Salovey, 1988). Medications that alleviate depression will tend to improve memory performance (Wolkowitz & Weingartner, 1988). Apparently, manipulations of emotional state affect memory performance through optimization of the autonomic nervous system (Eisdorfer, Nowlin, & Wilkie, 1970).

Simple instructions to relax appear not to improve memory performance (Watts, MacLeod, & Morris, 1988). Routine practice of meditation or physical relaxation also appears not to improve memory performance (Yuille & Sereda, 1980). However, training in relaxation techniques, that can be used as stressors arise and in some memory situations, has been shown to help the memory performance of elderly subjects in several studies (Yesavage, 1984; Yesavage & Rolf, 1984; Yesavage, Rose & Spiegel, 1982; Yesavage & Sheikh, 1988; Yesavage et al., in press; Yesavage, Sheih, Tanke, & Hill, 1988).

3. Attitude

a. Control. Attitudes influence a person's disposition to perform a memory task and, once in a task, the efficiency and nature of responding. We acquire information that protects our ego (Greenwald, 1980, 1981; Neisser, 1988; Schulster, 1981a,b, 1982, 1988), and we tend to learn more readily if we believe that we are superior at a certain learning task (Rapaport, 1942; Sullivan, 1927; see also Lachman, Steinberg, & Trotter, 1987). Additionally, social factors foster prejudicial attitudes about various topics that influence a person's memory processing (Bregman & McAllister, 1982; Holtgraves, Srull, & Socall, 1989; Wyer, 1989; Wyer & Srull, 1986). Moreover, people are disinclined to perform memory tasks when social stereotypes that apply to them indicate that they cannot perform well, such as stereotypes associated with age (Hamlett, Best, & Davis, 1985) or with gender (Crawford, Herrmann, Holdsworth, Randal, & Robbins, 1989; Loftus, Banaji, Schooler, & Foster, 1987).

b. Improved Control. People can revise their attitudes about which memory tasks they like, or do not like, to perform and create incentives for themselves that will increase their inclination to perform a task (Fowles, 1988; Herrmann, 1989; Klatsky, 1984). Experiences that lead people to pay attention to how well they perform memory tasks are especially effective in changing unrealistic attitudes about one's memory skills (Herrmann, Grubs, Sigmundi, & Grueneich, 1986; Pressley, Levin, & Ghatala, 1984). However, it must be recognized that some subjects may not want to make the effort to improve their memory performance, even with incentives (Cavanaugh & Morton, 1988).

A good deal of evidence has shown that memory performance is improved by appropriate changes in a person's attitudes. Increased positive attitudes regarding a person's memory abilities result in improved performance (Rapaport, 1942; Sullivan, 1927). Increased self-esteem leads to better memory performance in normal children (Pressley, Borkowski, & Schneider, 1988) and in retarded children (Borkowski, Carr, & Rettinger, 1987). Training that corrected negative stereotypes pertaining to the elderly resulted in temporary facilitation of memory performance (Hamlett et al., 1985; see also Elliott & Lachmann, 1988). Similarly, clinical work with learning-disabled children has indicated that improvement depends critically on whether a child's attitudes favor improving (Zecker, 1988).

4. Multiple Modes

Improved Control. A few studies have taught subjects to use a variety of manipulations representing different modes. Some of these studies have used self reports to assess the effects of training on memory performance. While self reports are undoubtedly inferior to performance tests, they are moderately valid (Herrmann, 1989). Probably the most comprehensive multimodal training study reported to date was conducted by McEvoy and Moon (1988). These researchers taught elderly subjects to use a combination of manipulations of different modes for each of several memory tasks. The manipulations included those pertaining to content, external aids, and relaxation techniques. The memory tasks included remembering appointments, learning the names of people, and others. Subjects rated their memory as improved for those tasks which were the object of training but not for tasks not included in the training.

A course of training similar to that provided by McEvoy and Moon was conducted twice at Hamilton College by Herrmann and Colleagues (Steve Andrzejewski, Lisa Malaquias, Sue Petro, and Valarie Tatro). Both courses were taken by students for academic credit. One course was taken in a "winter term," lasting 3½ weeks, and the other was taken for the entire fall semester. From 5 to 7 months after completing the course, self reports rated the degree to which each mode of manipulations—as taught in the course—changed their performance relative to what was characteristic of them before taking the course. The ratings indicated that the subjects in both courses believed that they achieved improved control in all modes, with content manipulations producing the greatest improvement. While the students had a vested interest in making higher ratings, the pattern of their ratings suggests their rating judgments were based in part on their impressions of their performance.

Additionally, the final exam of the semester course asked the students to make estimates of how much time they used before the course's final exam to perform manipulations representing each mode. The estimates of the use of the different modes again indicated that the students found a multimodal approach to learning and test taking useful, although they indicated that manipulations of social interactions and the physical environment were less useful than in everyday memory situations.

Finally, the students in the semester course were required to conduct a project to improve their memory for a particular task over the latter part of the semester (i.e., an 8-week period). Students were directed to choose the memory task that was the most difficult, or at least among the most difficult tasks, for them. The program adopted by the students typically involved four to six manipulations consisting of two to four content manipulations and one or two condition manipulations. Each student's self-designed program differed somewhat from the programs of the other students. Moreover, the programs were transparently consistent with the student's self-diagnosed cause of the memory problem. For example, several students attempted to improve their ability at learning names. Some of these students attributed their difficulty to being anxious during introductions, while other students attributed their difficulty to being disinterested in learning names. All of the students prescribed for themselves the use of content manipulations but, in addition, students concerned with anxiety sought to acquire anxiety-reduction techniques while students concerned with their disinterest sought to acquire self-motivation techniques.

Attempts to experimentally compare mode effectiveness have been infrequent. One series of studies has examined the effects of training to use relaxation techniques and content manipulations (Yesavage, 1984; Yesavage et al., in press). The results indicated that for some people, relaxation techniques may enhance memory performance as much as mental manipulations. Spielberger and colleagues (1979) have shown that anxiety reduction may facilitate academic performance as much as or more than training in study skills. Hamlett et al. (1985) showed that attitude training of elderly subjects that debunked negative stereotypes of cognitive losses with aging improved memory performance as much as training in content manipulations right after training. However, after a month the attitude training no longer facilitated performance.

Caveats are in order concerning the relative effects of the different modes. The results of such comparisons must, for the time being, be interpreted as reflecting the effects of the particular manipulations used and not the mode in general, since there is no information presently available as to the similarity and differences in the effectiveness of the range of manipulations of a particular mode. Clearly much more research needs to be done in order to determine how cross-mode comparisons can be made in a sound manner.

VI. Discussion

This article showed that the new approach to memory improvement has made worthwhile contributions to current knowledge about a person's control of memory performance. First, it has been learned that people do not continue to use control processes that are too taxing to use regardless of their effectiveness for improving memory. Memory skills, already found to be specific by laboratory memory research, were found by memory-improvement research to be even more specific—addressing particular tasks and materials. Partly because of this specificity, many practitioners and researchers of memory improvement concluded that memory cannot be satisfactorily improved by content manipulations alone. While much is known about content control processes, very little was known previously about the effects of other process modes on memory performance. Previous memory-improvement texts failed to mention the influence of other modes, with the exception of some findings about external memory aids and attitudes. The article has shown that people can control their memory performance through manipulating modes other than informational content.

A. Multimodal Influences on Memory Performance

The results reviewed here graphically demonstrate that the memory system is embedded within the entire psychological and physiological system. Memory performance emanates from the influence of all psychological modes of processing. That memory is influenced by other modes has been proposed in the past (Feinaigle, 1812; Middleton, 1888). So the new approach, instead of being truly new, is simply a reexamination of the interdependence of the memory system and other modes. In the future, new or revised models of memory will be needed to address the influence of other processing modes (Bachman, 1990; Herrmann et al., 1988; Herrmann & Searleman, 1989; Perlmutter, 1988; Rabbitt, 1988). The relationship among the nonmemory modes and the memory system remains to be worked out by future research.

The effects of these modes on memory performance may either be peripheral to the memory system or they may directly affect the system itself. Some indications about these relationships are beginning to take form. In some cases, a variable may seem to be peripheral (such as in the use of conversational manipulations); in other cases, a variable (such as in the use or nonuse of good sleeping habits) may operate on attentional mechanisms, which may or may not be seen as part of the memory system. In other cases yet, the variable may operate on the physiological basis of memory (such as in the use of adverse substances or drugs). While the nature of control differs with each mode, there are certain obvious similarities in the functioning of some of the modes as they affect memory performance. Physical condition, emotional state, and attitude modes influence a person's overall condition to perform memory tasks, without manipulating content. These modes apparently affect a person's alertness and in some cases a person's motivation to perform, which in turn influence basic memory processes (encoding, maintenance, and retrieval). Conversely, content manipulations, and manipulations of physical and social environments, do not influence a person's inclination to perform tasks. These modes influence when and how a person pays attention selectively to the content of a memory task, both overall and its parts.

Although it is difficult to conceive of how content control processes could affect a person's condition, it is clear that variations in condition (e.g., fatigue, health, emotionality) will affect a person's potential to implement content processes (such as the use of rehearsal, external aids, or conversational control ploys). Thus, memory performance is a function of both basic processing and different kinds of control processing (with their differential effects on the two kinds of attention: general and selective; Broadbent, 1971; Cowan, 1988; Eysenck, 1982, 1984; Jennings, 1986a, 1986b; Posner, 1984; Weingartner & Parker, 1984).

B. New Conception of Control Processes

Memory theory also needs to further develop the construct of control processes. As noted above, the evidence reviewed here demonstrates that people can control memory performance in ways typically not addressed by memory research. Basic memory researchers have been aware, and have investigated, control of memory performance through manipulations of the physical environment. However, the use of external memory aids has yet to be incorporated in a complete memory model, nor have the other modes of memory control (social, physical condition, emotional state, and attitudes).

Although memory theory does not yet incorporate multiple modes of control, the new approach to memory improvement serves to impart to people, or increase their usage of, control of the modes most suitable for a memory task/situation. One goal of such improvement is to lead people to use the appropriate control processes both intentionally and incidentally. Another less ambitious goal is to improve performance in intentional tasks only.

The evidence reviewed here also demonstrates that control can be exerted over a much wider interval than previously believed. Manipulations of memory performance through control of condition must occur before task performance, in contrast to context manipulations which typically occur during or just before task performance (people typically rehearse, or search memory, when the task demand is immediate). Condition-mode control may anticipate a memory task by as much as hours (control of what one eats) or even days (establishing a series of nights with sound sleep). Condition control processes require forethought in order to be carried out minutes (relaxation techniques), hours (eating properly), or even days before an upcoming memory task (obtaining adequate rest). There are exceptions to this rule (some antianxiety manipulations like deep breathing can be carried out during a task), but it is generally true that condition control processes are executed well before a task.

C. Tasks versus Situations

The research reviewed in this article indicated, first, that environmental and social variables, not normally considered part of the "memory task," affect memory performance. Second, the research indicated that many condition variables which precede a memory task also affect memory performance. The fact that memory may be affected by certain modes of control not addressed by current memory theory suggests that the "memory task" has led research to view memory through too narrow a window. The memory task has been an immensely useful construct in elucidating stimulus and task variables which affect basic processes or interact with content manipulations in memory performance. However, because this construct precludes consideration of relevant variables of other modes, it seems appropriate to propose that the object of memory research be expanded to also include any relevant variables of the memory "situation," i.e., ones which precede, attend, or are part of a task (Baddeley, 1982; Bruce, 1985; Cohen, 1989; Greeno, 1989; Lave, 1988; Neisser, 1985; Perlmutter, 1988; Rabbitt, 1988; Revelle, Anderson, & Humphreys, 1987; C. Schooler, 1988; Solomon, Goethals, Kelley, & Stephens, 1989).

D. What Is Not Known about Multimodal Control

There are likely many variables representing all the modes discussed here that have yet to be investigated. Even content manipulations, for which a great deal is known, deserve much more research. As noted earlier, the range of impact of multimodal control on memory performance is not yet known, if only because many condition and conceptual variables exist which affect performance but have not yet been studied. In order to better understand multimodal influences on memory, subjects in memory research will have to be assessed more fully, both for content manipulations (Buschke, 1987; Grafman, 1984) and for other modes (Poon, *et al.,* 1986). Two aspects of mode influence deserve special study, their applicability and durability.

Manipulations vary in how applicable they are for different memory tasks and different situations. It has already been shown that content manipulations vary in how readily they may be applied to memory tasks (Herrmann, 1987; Intons-Peterson & Fournier, 1986). The same point has been made about external memory aids, which constitute manipulations of the physical environment (Herrmann & Petro, in press; Intons-Peterson & Fournier, 1986). Applicability has not been worked out for other mode manipulations. For example, some condition manipulations may not affect various tasks differently; e.g., lost sleep may actually facilitate performance on some tasks and impair performance on others (Idzikowski, 1984).

Manipulations also vary in their durability, i.e., how long people tend to use them after training. Training or experience may impact skills that are retained only temporarily or relatively indefinitely. Present research custom has been to investigate the influence on a manipulation for a single attempt (trial or session). Infrequently, usage of a manipulation has been investigated 24 hr later; very infrequently usage of a manipulation has been investigated from 1 week to a month later. Thus, we have very little information on the durability of content manipulations and essentially no such information for the other modes.

Durability has often been regarded as an applied issue but it is just as relevant to theory development as it is to application. Processes that are not maintained after training are no longer used for a reason. Sometimes the disuse of manipulation occurs because it was not adequately learned in the first place. It has been suggested that truly superior memory skills take months or even years to develop (Chase & Ericsson, 1982; Hunt & Love, 1972). Other times, the manipulation has been well learned but its use is psychologically costly (fatiguing, distracting attention from other concurrent tasks); the classical manipulations appear to be given up because they are psychologically costly. In order to determine the relative theoretical importance of different mode manipulations, it will not be informative to examine the effects of mode control on a single session. A full understanding of mode importance will require a determination of whether control may be established temporarily or permanently.

Acknowledgments

We thank Ivan Bendiksen, Miriam Bendiksen, Tom Cunningham, Jordan Grafman, Earl Hunt, Cathy McEvoy, Zita Givens, David Payne, Carmi Schooler, Jonathan Schooler, Herb Weingartner, and Ted Zahn for valuable advice on various aspects of this article.

References

Anderson, J. R. (1982). Acquisition of a cognitive skill. *Psychological Review*, **89**, 396–406.
Atkinson, R. C. (1975). Mnemotechnics in second-language learning. *American Psychologist*, **30**, 821–828.
Atkinson, R. C., & Shiffrin, R. M. (1968). Human memory: A proposed system and its control processes. In K. W. Spence & J. T. Spence (Eds.), *The psychology of learning and motivation* (Vol. 2). New York: Academic Press.
Bachman, L. (1990). Varieties of memory compensation of older adults in episodic remembering. In L. Poon, D. Rubin, & B. Wilson (Eds.), *Everyday cognition in adult and late life*. New York: Cambridge University Press.
Baddeley, A. D. (1982). Domains of recollection. *Psychological Review*, **89**, 708–729.
Baddeley, A. D. (1986). *Working memory*. New York: Basic Books.
Baltes, P. B., & Kliegel, R. (1986). On the dynamics between growth and decline in the aging of intelligence and memory. In K. Poeck (Ed.), *Proceedings of the Thirteenth World Conference on Neurology*, Heidelberg: Springer-Verlag.
Bellezza, F. S. (1981). Mnemonic devices: Classification, characteristics, and criteria. *Review of Educational Research*, **51**, 247–275.
Bellezza, F. S. (1982). *Improve your memory skills*. Englewood Cliffs, NJ: Prentice-Hall.
Bellezza, F. S. (1983). Menemonic-device instruction with adults. In M. Pressley & J. R. Levin (Eds.), *Cognitive strategy research*. New York: Springer Verlag.
Bellezza, F. S. (1986). Mental cues and verbal reports in learning. In G. H. Bower (Ed.), *The psychology of learning and motivation* (Vol. 20). Orlando, FL: Academic Press.
Belmont, J. M. (1989). Cognitive strategies and strategic learning: The socio-instructional approach. *American Psychologist*, **44**, 1442–148.
Belmont, J. M., & Butterfield, E. C. (1971). Learning strategies as determinants of memory deficiencies. *Cognitive Psychology*, **2**, 411–420.
Birnbaum, I., & Parker, E. (Eds.). (1977). *Alcohol and human memory*. Hillsdale, NJ: Erbaum.
Bjork, R. A., & Richardson-Klavehn, A. (1989). On the puzzling relationship between environmental context and human memory. In C. Izawa (Ed.), *Current issues in cognitive processes*. Hillsdale, NJ: Erlbaum.
Blick, K. A., & Waite, C. J. (1971). A survey of mnemonic techniques used by college students in free recall learning. *Psychological Reports*, **29**, 76–78.
Block, R. I., & Wittenborn. J. R. (1984). Marijuana effects on semantic memory: Verification of common and uncommon category members. *Psychological Reports*, **55**, 503–512.
Blomquist, K. B., & Danner, F. (1987). Effects of physical conditioning on information-processing efficiency. *Perceptual and Motor Skills*, **65**, 175–186.
Blumenthal, J. A., & Madden, D. J. (1988). Effects of aerobic exercise training, age, and physical fitness on memory-search performance. *Psychology and Aging*, **3**, 280–285.

Boltwood, C. E., & Blick, K. A. (1970). The delineation and application of three mnemonic techniques. *Psychonomic Science,* **20,** 339–341.

Borkowski, J. G., Carr, M., & Rettinger, E. (1987). Self-regulated cognition: Interdependence of metacognition, attributions, and self-esteem. In B. Jones (Ed.), *Dimensions of therapy.* Hillsdale, NJ: Erlbaum.

Bower, G. H. (1970). Analysis of a mnemonic device. *American Scientist* **58,** 498–510.

Bower, G. H. (1981). Mood and memory. *American Psychologist,* **36,** 129–148.

Bowyer, P. A., Humphrey, M. S., & Revelle, W. (1983). Arousal and recognition memory: The effects of impulsivity, caffeine and time on task. *Personality and Individual Differences,* **4,** 41–49.

Bregman, N. J., & McAllister, H. A. (1982). Eyewitness testimony: The role of commitment in increasing reliability. *Social Psychology Quarterly,* **45,** 181–184.

Broadbent, D. E. (1971). *Decision and stress.* London: Academic Press.

Broadbent, D. E., Cooper, P. F., Fitzgerald, P., & Parkes, K. R. (1982). The cognitive Failures Questionnaire (CFQ) and its correlates. *British Journal of Psychology,* **21,** 1–16.

Brown, A. L., Bransford, J. D., Ferrara, R. A., & Campione, J. C. (1983). Learning, remembering, and understanding. In J. H. Flavell & E. Markman (Eds.), Handbook of child psychology (Vol. 1). New York: Wiley.

Bruce, D. (1985). The how and why of ecological memory. *Journal of Experimental Psychology: General,* **114,** 78–90.

Buschke, H. (1987). Criteria for the identification of memory deficits: Implications for the design of memory tests. In D. Gorfein & R. Hoffman (Eds.), *Memory and learning.* Hillsdale, NJ: Erlbaum.

Caplan, L. J., & Schooler, C. (1990). Problem-solving by reference to rules or previous episodes: The effects of organized training, analogical models, and subsequent complexity of experience. *Memory & Cognition,* **18,** 215–227.

Cavanaugh, J. C., Grady, J. G., & Perlmutter, M. (1983). Forgetting and use of memory aids in 20- to 70-year olds' everyday life. *International Journal of Aging and Human Development,* **17,** 113–122.

Cavanaugh, J., & Morton, K. R. (1988). Older adults attributions about everyday memory. In M. M. Gruneberg, P. E. Morris, & R. N. Sykes (Eds.), *Practical aspects of memory.* Chichester: Wiley.

Chase, W. G., & Ericsson, K. A. (1982). Skill and working memory. In G. H. Bower (Ed.), *The psychology of learning and motivation* (Vol. 16). New York: Academic Press.

Cheng, P. W. (1985). Restructuring versus automaticity: Alternative accounts of skill acquisition. *Psychological Review,* **92,** 414–423.

Cohen, G. (1989). *Memory in the real world.* Hillsdale, NJ: Erlbaum.

Cowan, N. (1988). Evolving conceptions of memory storage, selective attention, and their mutual constraints within the human information-processing system. *Psychological Bulletin,* **104,** 163–191.

Craik, F. I. M., & Lockhart, R. S. (1973). Levels of processing: A framework for memory research. *Journal of Verbal Learning and Verbal Behavior,* **11,** 671–684.

Crawford, M., Herrmann, D. J., Holdsworth, M., Randal, E., & Robbins, D. (1989). Gender differences in the perception of memory abilities in others. *British Journal of Psychology,* **80,** 391–401.

Curran, H. V., Sakulsriprong, M., & Lader, M. (1988). Antidepressants and human memory: An investigation of four drugs with different sedative and anticholinergic profiles. *Psychopharmacology,* **95,** 520–527.

Cutler, S. J., & Grams, A. E. (1988). Correlates of self-reported everyday memory problems. *Journal of Gerontology,* **43,** 582–590.

Darley, C. F., Tinklenberg, J. R., Hollister, T. E., & Atkinson, R. C. (1973). Marihuana and retrieval from short-term memory. *Psychopharmacologia, 29*, 231–238.

Davies, G. M. (1982). Composite systems for "recalling faces—helping the police with their enquiries?" In A. Trankell (Ed.), *Reconstructing the past; The role of the psychologist in criminal trials*. Stockholm: Norstedts.

Day, R. S. (1988). Alternative representations. In G. H. Bower (Ed.), *The psychology of learning and motivation* (Vol. 22). San Diego, CA: Academic Press.

Dixon, R. A., Hertzog, C., & Hultsch, D. F. (1986). The multiple relationships among metamemory in adulthood (MIA) scales and cognitive abilities in adulthood. *Human Learning, 5*, 165–178.

Druckman, D., & Swets, J. A. (1988). *Enhancing human performance*. Washington, DC: National Academy Press.

Ebbinghaus, H. (1964). *Memory*. A. Ruger & C. E. Bussenius (Trans.). New York: Dover. (Original work published 1885)

Eisdorfer, C., Nowlin, J., & Wilkie, F. (1970). Improvement of learning in the aged by modification of autonomic nervous system activity. *Science, 170*, 1327–1329.

Elliott, E., & Lachman, M. E. (1988). Enhancing memory by modifying control beliefs, attributions, and performance goals in the elderly. In P. S. Fry (Ed.), *Advances in psychology: Helplessness and control in the aged*. Amsterdam: North-Holland.

Ellis, H. C., Thomas, R. L., & Rodriguez, I. A. (1984). Emotional mood states and memory: Elaborative encoding, semantic processing, and cognitive effort. *Journal of Experimental Psychology: Learning, Memory, and Cognition, 10*, 470–482.

Erdelyi, M. H., & Goldberg, B. (1979). Let's not sweep repression under the rug: Toward a cognitive psychology of repression. In J. F. Kihlström & F. J. Evans (Eds.), *Functional disorders of memory*. Hillsdale, NJ: Erlbaum.

Ericsson, K. A. (1985). Memory skill. *Canadian Journal of Psychology, 39*, 188–231.

Ericcson, K. A., & Oliver, W. A. (1989). A methodology for assessing the detailed structure of memory skills. In A. M. Colley & J. R. Beach (Eds.), *Acquisition and performance of cognitive skills*. Chichester: Wiley.

Erikson, G. C., Hager, L. B., Houseworth, C., Dugan, J., Petros, T., & Beckwith, B. E. (1985). The effects of caffeine on memory for word lists. *Physiology & Behavior, 35*, 47–51.

Eysenck, M. W. (1982). *Attention and arousal: Cognition and performance*. Berlin: Springer.

Eysenck, M. W. (1984). *A handbook of cognitive psychology*. Hillsdale, NJ: Erlbaum.

Eysenck, M. W., & Folkard, S. (1980). Personality, time of day, and caffeinee: Some theoretical and conceptual problems in Revelle et al. *Journal of Experimental Psychology: General, 109*, 32–41.

Feinaigle, M. G. von (1812). *The new art of memory*. London: Sherwood, Neely, & Jones.

Flavell, J. (1977). *Cognitive development*. Englewood Cliffs, NJ: Prentice-Hall.

Folkard, S., & Monk, T. H. (1980). Circadian rhythms in human memory. *British Journal of Psychology, 71*, 295–307.

Fowles, D. C. (1988). Psychophysiology and pathology: A motivational approach. *Psychophysiology, 25*, 373–391.

Freud, S. (1901). *The psychopathology of everyday life*. Harmondsworth: Penguin.

Garfunkel, F., & Landau, G. (1981). *A memory retention course for the aged: Guide for leaders*. Washington, DC: The National Council in Aging.

Geiselman, R. E., Fisher, R. P., MacKinnon, D. P., & Holland, H. L. (1986). Enhancement of eyewitness memory with the cognitive interview. *American Journal of Psychology, 99*, 385–401.

Gentry, M., & Herrmann, D. J. (1990). Memory contrivances in everyday life. *Personality and Social Psychology Bulletin*, **18**, 241–253.
Gervasio, A. (1988). Barriers to memory improvement in clinical populations. In D. Payne & D. Herrmann, A *Symposium on the New Approach to the Improvement of Memory Performance and Memory ability*. Buffalo, NY: Eastern Psychological Association.
Goffman, E. (1961). *Encounters*. Indianapolis, IN: Bobbs-Merrill.
Gold, P. E. (1987). Sweet memories. *American Scientist*, **75**, 151–155.
Gonder-Frederick, L., Hall, J. L., Vogt, J., Cox, D. J., Green, J., & Gold, P. E. (1987). Memory enhancement in elderly humans: Effects of glucose ingestion. *Physiology & Behavior*, **41**, 503–504.
Grafman, J. (1984). Memory assessment and remediation in brain-injured patients: From theory to practice. In B. A. Edelstein & E. T. Couture (Eds.), *Behavioral assessment and Rehabilitation of the traumatically brain-damaged*. New York: Plenum.
Greeno, J. G. (1989). A perspective on thinking. *American Psychologist*, **44**, 134–141.
Greenwald, A. G. (1980). The totalitarian ego. *American Psychologist*, **35**, 603–618.
Greenwald, A. G. (1981). Self and memory. In G. H. Bower (Ed.), *The psychology of learning and motivation* (Vol. 15). New York: Academic Press.
Hamlett, K. W., Best, D. L., & Davis, S. W. (1985). *Modification of memory complaint and memory performance in elderly adults*. Unpublished manuscript, Catholic University of America, Washington, DC.
Harma, M. I., Illmarinen, J., Knauth, P., & Rutenfranz, J. (1988). Physical training intervention in female shift workers: II. The effects of intervention on the circadian rhythms of alertness, short-term memory, and body temperature. *Ergonomics*, **31**, 51–63.
Harris, J. E. (1980). We have ways of helping you to remember. *Journal of the British Association for Service to the Elderly*, **17**, 21–27.
Harris, J. E. (1984). Methods of improving memory. In B. A. Wilson & N. Moffatt (Eds.), *Clinical management of memory problems*. Beckenham: Croom Helm.
Hartley, L. R., Morrison, D., & Arnold, P. (1989). Stress and skill. In A. M. Colley & J. R. Beach (Eds.), *Acquisition and performance of cognitive skills*. Chichester: Wiley.
Hasher, L., & Zacks, R. T. (1979). Automatic and effortful processes in memory. *Journal of Experimental Psychology: General*, **108**, 356–388.
Hashtroudi, S., & Parker, E. S. (1986). Acute alcohol amnesia: What is remembered and what is forgotten. In H. D. Cappell, F. B. Glaser, Y. Israel, H. Kalant, W. Schmidt, E. Sellers, & R. C. Smart (Eds.), *Research advances in alcohol and drug problems*. New York: Plenum.
Herrmann, D. J. (1987). Task appropriateness of mnemonic techniques. *Perceptual and Motor Skills*, **64**, 171–178.
Herrmann, D. J. (1989). *Memory improvement*. Gaithersburg, MD: Cognitive Associates.
Herrmann, D. J. (in press). Self perceptions of memory performance. In. W. Schaie, C. Schooler, & J. Rodin (Eds.), *Self-directedness and efficacy: Causes and effects throughout the life course*. Hillsdale, NJ: Erlbaum.
Herrmann, D. J., Buschke, H., & Gall, M. (1987). Improving retrival. *Applied Cognitive Psychology*, **9**, 27–33.
Herrmann, D. J., Grubs, L., Sigmundi, R., & Grueneich, R. (1986). Awareness of memory ability before and after relevant memory experience. *Human Learning*, **5**, 91–108.
Herrmann, D. J., & Petro, S. (in press). Commercial memory aids. *Applied Cognitive Psychology*.
Herrmann, D. J., Rea, A., Andrzejewski, S., & Moore, C. (1989). *The effectiveness of learning strategies as a function of intelligence*. Bethesda, MD: National Institute of Mental Health. (under review for publication).

Herrmann, D. J., Rea, A., & Andrzejewski, S. (1988). The need for a new approach to memory training. In M. M. Gruneberg, Morris, P. E., & Sykes, R. N. (Eds.), *Practical aspects of memory*. Chichester: Wiley.

Herrmann, D. J., & Searleman, A. (1989). A multi-modal approach to memory. Unpublished manuscript, National Institute of Mental Health. Bethesda, MD.

Hertel, P. (1988). Monitoring external memory. In M. Gruneberg, P. Morris, & R. Sykes (Eds.), *Practical aspects of memory*. Chichester: Wiley.

Higbee, K. L. (1988). *Your memory* (2nd ed). Englewood Cliffs, NJ: Prentice-Hall.

Higbee, K. L. (in press). What do college students get from a memory improvement course. *Reading improvement..*

Holtgraves, T., Srull, T. K., & Socall, D. (1989). Conversation memory: The effect of speaker status on memory for the assertiveness of conversation remarks. *Journal of Personality and Social Psychology, 56*, 149–160.

Hunt, E., & Love, T. (1972). How good can memory be? In A. W. Melton & E. Martin (Eds.), *Coding processes in human memory*. Washington, DC: V. H. Winston & Sons.

Idzikowski, C. (1984). Sleep and memory. *British Journal of Psychology, 75*, 439–449.

Idzikowski, C. (1988). The effects of drugs on human memory. In M. M. Gruneberg, P. E. Morris, & R. N. Sykes, (Eds.), *Practical aspects of memory*. Chichester: Wiley.

Intons-Peterson, M. J., & Fournier, J. (1986). External and internal memory aids: When and how often do we use them? *Journal of Experimental Psychology: General. 115*, 267–280.

Jackson, J. L., Bogers, H., & Kerstholt, J. (1988). Do memory aids aid the elderly in their day to day remembering? In M. Gruneberg, P. Morris, & R. Sykes (Eds.), *Practical aspects of memory: Current research and issues*. New York: Wiley.

Jacoby, L. L., & Dallas, M. (1981). On the relationship between autobiographical memory and perceptual learning. *Journal of Experimental Psychology: General, 110*, 306–340.

Jennings, J. R. (1986a). Bodily changes during attending. In M. G. H. Coles, E. Donchin, & S. W. Porges (Eds.), *Psychophysiology: systems, processes, and applications*. New York: Guilford.

Jennings, J. R. (1986b). Memory, thought, and bodily response. In M. G. H. Coles, E. Donchin, & S. W. Porges (Eds.), *Psychophysiology: systems, processes, and applications*. New York: Guilford.

Johnson, M. H., & Magaro, P. A. (1987). Effects of mood and severity on memory processes in depression and mania. *Psychological Bulletin, 101*, 28–40.

Johnson, R. E. (1980). Memory-based rehearsal. In G. H. Bower (Ed.), *The psychology of learning and motivation* (Vol. 14). New York: Academic Press.

Khan, A. U. (1986). *Clinical disorders of memory*. New York: Plenum.

Klatsky, R. L. (1984). *Memory and awareness*. New York: Freeman.

Koriat, A., Ben-Zur, H., & Sheffer, D. (1988). Telling the same story twice: Output monitoring and age. *Journal of Memory and Language, 27*, 23–39.

Kosslyn, S. M. (1989). Understanding charts and graphs. *Applied Cognitive Psychology, 3*, 185–226.

Labouvie-Vief, G., & Gonda, J. N. (1976). Cognitive strategy training and intellectual competence in the elderly. *Journal of Gerontology, 31*, 327–332.

Lachman, M. E., Steinberg, E. S., & Trotter, S. D. (1987). Effects of control beliefs and attributions on memory self-assessments and performance. *Psychology and Aging, 2*, 266–271.

Landauer, T. K., & Bjork, R. A. (1978). Optimum rehearsal patterns and name learning. In M. M. Gruneberg, P. E. Morris, & R. N. Sykes (Eds.), *Practical aspects of memory*. London: Academic Press.

Landauer, T. K., & Ross, B. H. (1977), Can simple instructions to use spaced practice improve ability to remember a fact?: An experimental test using telephone numbers. *Bulletin of the Psychonomic Society,* **10**, 215–218.

Lapp, D. (1983). Commitment: Essential ingredient in memory training. *Clinical Gerontologist,* **2**, 58–60.

Larkin, J. H., & Simon, H. A. (1987). Why a diagram is (sometimes) worth ten thousand words. *Cognitive Science,* **11**, 65–99.

Lave, J. (1988). *Cognition in practice.* Cambridge: Cambridge University Press.

Lawlor, B. A., Sunderland, T., Martinez, R. A., Molchan, S. E., & Weingartner, H. (in press). Drugs and memory. In T. Yanagihara & R. C. Petersen (Eds.), *Memory disorders in clinical practice.* Rochester, MN: Mayo Foundation.

Lister, R. G., & Weingartner, H. J. (1987). Neuropharmacological strategies for understanding psychobiological determinants of cognition. *Human Neurobiology,* **6**, 119–127.

Loke, W. H. (1988). Effects of caffeine on mood and memory. *Physiology of Behavior,* **44**, 367–372.

Loftus, E. F., Banaji, M. R., Schooler, J. W., & Foster, R. A. (1987). Who shall remember?: Gender differences in memory. *Michigan Quarterly Review,* **26**, 64–85.

Logue, A. W. (1986). *The psychology of eating and drinking.* New York: Freeman.

Malpass, R. (1981). Training in face recognition. In G. Davies, H. Ellis, & J. Sherherd (Eds.), *Perceiving and remembering faces.* New York: Academic Press.

Matlin, M., & Stang, D. (1978). *The pollyanna principle.* Cambridge, MA: Schenkman.

McDaniel, M. A., & Kearny, E. M. (1984). Optimal learning strategies and their spontaneous use: The importance of task-appropriate processing. *Memory & Cognition,* **12**, 361–373.

McDaniel, M. A., & Pressley, M. (1987). *Imagery and related mnemonic processes: Theories, individual differences, and applications.* New York: Springer-Verlag.

McEvoy, C. L., & Moon, J. R. (1988). Assessment and treatment of everyday memory problems in the elderly. In M. M. Gruneberg, P. E. Morris, & R. N. Sykes (Eds.), *Practical aspects of memory: Current research and issues.* New York: Wiley.

Meerwaldt, S. (1986). *Memory and valium.* New York: American Psychological Association.

Meichenbaum, D. (1972). Cognitive modification of test anxious college students. *Journal of Consulting and Clinical Psychology,* **39**, 370–380.

Middleton, A. E. (1888). *Memory systems: New and old.* New York: G. S. Fellows.

Miller, S. S. (Ed.). (1976). *Symptoms: The complete home medical encyclopedia.* New York: Crowell-Collier.

Miyata, Y., & Norman, D. A. (1986). Psychological issues in support of multiple activities. In D. A. Norman & S. W. Draper (Eds.), *User centered system design: New perceptives on Human computer interaction.* Hillsdale, NJ: Erlbaum.

Morris, C. D., Bransford, J. D., & Franks, J. J. (1977). Levels of processing versus transfer appropriate processing. *Journal of Verbal Learning and Verbal Behavior,* **16**, 519–534.

Morris, P. E. (1977) Practical strategies for human learning and remembering. In M. Howe (Ed.), *Adult learning: Psychological research and applications.* London: Wiley.

Morris, P. E., Jones, S., & Hampson, P. (1978). An imagery mnemonic for the learning of people's names. *British Journal of Psychology,* **69**, 335–336.

National Center for Health Statistics (1989). *Questionnaire design in the cognitive research laboratory* (Publ. No. (PHS) 89-1076). Hyattsville, MD: U.S. Department of Health and Human Services.

Naugle, R., Prevey, M., Naugle, C., & Delaney, R. (1988). New digital watch as a compensatory device for memory dysfunction. *Cognitive Rehabilitation,* **6**, 22–23.

Neisser, U. (1985). The role of theory in the ecological study of memory: Comment on Bruce. *Journal of Experimental Psychology: General*, **114**, 272–276.

Neisser, U. (1988). Time present and time past. Gruneberg, P. E. Morris, & R. N. Sykes (Eds.), *Practical aspects of memory*. Chichester: Wiley.

Norman, D. A. (1981). Categorization of action slips. *Psychological Review*, **88**, 1–15.

Palmer, D. J., & Goetz, E. T. (1988). Selection and use of study strategies: The role of the studier's beliefs about self and strategies. In C. E. Weinstein, E. T. Goetz, and P. A. Alexander (Eds.), *Learning and study strategies*. San Diego; Academic Press.

Parks, D., Cavanaugh, J., & Smith, A. (1986). Metamemory2: Memory researchers' knowledge of their own memory abilities. Washington, DC: American Psychological Association.

Peeke, S. C., & Peeke, H. V. (1984). Attention, memory and cigarette smoking. *Psychopharmacology*, **84**, 205–216.

Perkins, D. (1985). Are cognitive skills general? In J. W. Segal, S. F. Chapman, & R. Glaser (Eds.), *Thinking and learning skills (Vol. 1)*. Hillsdale, NJ: Erlbaum.

Perlmutter, M. (1988). Research on memory and its development: Past, present, and future. In F. E. Weinert & M. Perlmutter (Eds.), *Memory development: Universal changes and individual differences*. Hillsdale, NJ: Erlbaum.

Petros, T., Beckwith, B. E., Erickson, G. C., Arnold, M. E., & Sternhagen, S. (1987). *The effects of caffeine on the efficience of working memory*. Presented at the annual meeting of the American Psychological Association, New York.

Poon, L. W. (1980). A systems approach for the assessment and treatment of memory problems. In J. M. Ferguson & C. B. Taylor (Eds.), *The comprehensive handbook of behavior medicine* (Vol. 1, pp. 191–212). Washington, DC: American Psychological Association.

Poon, L. W., Gurland, B. J., Eisdorfer, C., Crook, T., Thompson, L. W., Kaszniak, A. W., & Davis, K. L. (1986). Integration of experimental and clinical precepts in memory assessment: A tribute to George Talland. In L. W. Poon (Ed.), *Clinical memory assessment of older adults*. Washington, DC: American Psychological Association.

Posner, M. I. (1984). Selective attention and the storage of information. In G. Lynch, J. L. McGaugh, & N. M. Weinberger (Eds.), *Neurobiology of learning and memory*, New York: Guilford.

Pressley, M., Levin, J. R., & Ghatala, E. S. (1984). Memory strategy monitoring in adults and children. *Journal of Verbal Learning and Verbal Behavior*, **23**, 270–288.

Pressley, M., Forrest-Pressley, D. L., Elliot-Faust, D., & Miller, G. (1985). Children's use of cognitive strategies. How to teach strategies, and what to do if they can't be taught. In M. Pressley & C. J. Brainerd (Eds.), *Cognitive learning and memory in children*. New York: Springer-Verlag.

Pressley, M., Borkowski, J. G., & Schneider, W. (1987). Good strategy users coordinate metacognition, strategy use and knowledge. In R. Vasta & G. Whitehurst (Eds.), *Annals of child development*, Vol. 4. Greenwich, CT: JAI Press.

Rabbitt, P. A. (1981). Talking to the old. *New Society*, **22**, 140–141.

Rabbitt, P. (1988). Does fast last? Is speed a basic factor determining individual differences in memory? In M. M. Gruneberg, P. E. Morris, & R. N. Sykes (Eds.), *Practical aspects of memory*. Chichester: Wiley.

Rapaport, D. (1942). *Emotions and memory*. Baltimore, MD: Williams & Wilkins.

Reason, J. T. (1988). Stress and cognitive failure. In S. Fisher & J. T. Reason (Eds.), *Handbook of life stress, cognition and health*. New York: Wiley.

Reason, J. T., & MyCielska, M. (1983). *Absentmindedness*. Hillsdale, NJ: Prentice-Hall.

Revelle, W., Anderson, K. J., & Humphreys, M. S. (1987). Empirical tests and theoretical extensions of arousal-based theories of personality. In J. Strelau & H. J. Eysenck (Eds.), *Personality dimensions and arousal*. New York: Plenum.

Revelle, W., Humphreys, M. S., Simon, L., & Gilliland, K. (1980). The interactive effect of personality, time of day, and caffeine: A test of the arousal model. *Journal of Experimental Psychology: General, 109,* 1–31.

Rosenzweig, M. R. (1984). Experience, memory, and the brain. *American Psychologist, 39,* 365–376.

Royce, J. R. (1973). The present situation in theoretical psychology. In B. B. Wolman (Ed.), *Handbook of general psychology*. Englewood Cliffs, NJ: Prentice-Hall.

Rundus, D. (1971). Analysis of rehearsal processes in free recall. *Journal of Experimental Psychology, 89,* 63–77.

Ryan, E. B. (1986). Memory for goblins: A computer game for assessing and training working memory skill. *Clinical Gerontologist, 6,* 64–67.

Schacter, D. L., & Glisky, E. L. (1986). Memory remediation: Restoration alleviation, and the acquisition of domain-specific knowledge. In *Clinical neuropsychology of intervention*. New York: Martinus Nijhoff.

Schneider, W., & Shiffrin, R. M. (1977). Controlled and automatic human information processing: I. Detection, search, and attention. *Psychological Review, 84,* 1–66.

Schooler, C. (1988). Social structural effects and experimental situations: Mutual lessons of cognitive and social science. In K. W. Schaie & C. Schooler (Eds.), *Social structure and aging: Psychological processes*. Hillsdale, NJ: Erlbaum.

Schooler, J. W., & Engstler-Schooler, T. (in press). Verbal overshadowing of visual memories: Some things are better left unsaid. *Cognitive Psychology*.

Sehulster, J. R. (1981a). Phenomenological correlates of a self theory of memory. *American Journal of Psychology, 94,* 527–537.

Sehulster, J. R. (1981b). Structure and pragmatics of a self theory of memory. *Memory & Cognition, 9,* 263–276.

Sehulster, J. R. (1982). Phenomenological correlates of a self theory of memory II: Dimensions, *American Journal of Psychology, 95,* 441–454.

Sehulster, J. R. (1988). Broader perspectives on everyday memory. In M. M. Gruneberg, P. E. Morris, & R. N. Sykes (Eds.), *Practical aspects of memory: Current research and issues*. New York: Wiley.

Shiffrin, R. M., & Schneider, W. (1977). Controlled and automatic human information processing: II. Perceptual learning, automatic attending and a general theory. *Psychological Review, 84,* 127–190.

Singer, J. A., & Salovey, P. (1988). Mood and memory: evaluating the network theory of affect. *Clinical Psychology Review, 8,* 211–251.

Skillbeck, C. (1984). Computer assistance in the management of memory and cognitive impairment. In B. A. Wilson & N. Moffat (Eds.), *Clinical management of memory problems*. Rockville, MD: Aspen Systems.

Smith, A. (1988). Effects of meals on memory and attention. In M. M. Gruneberg, P. E. Morris, & R. N. Sykes (Eds.), *Practical aspects of memory*. Chichester: Wiley.

Solomon, P. R., Goethals, G. R., Kelley, C. M., & Stephens, B. R. (Eds.). (1989). *Memory: Interdisciplinary approaches*. New York: Springer-Verlag.

Spielberger, C. D., Gonzales, H. P., & Fletcher, T. (1979). Test anxiety reduction, learning strategies, and academic performance. In H. F. O'Neill, Jr. & C. D. Spielberger (Eds.), *Cognitive and affective Learning strategies,* New York: Academic Press.

Spilich, G. (1986, August). Cigarette smoking and memory: Good news and bad news. In G. J Spilich (Chair), *Symposium on Cognitive and Environmental Agents: Theoretical and Pragmatic Implications*. New York City: American Psychological Association.

Stamford, B. A., Hambacher, W., & Fallica, A. (1974). Effects of daily exercise on the psychiatric state of institutionalized geriatric mental patients. *Research Quarterly*, **45**, 35–41.

Stern, L., & Fogler, J. (1989). *Improving your memory: A guide for older adults.* Ann Arbor: University of Michigan Medical Center, Turner Geriatric Services.

Sullivan, E. B. (1927). Attitude in relation to learning. *Psychological Monographs*, **36**, 1–149, *104* 163–191.

Tilley, A., & Statham, D. (1989). The effect of prior sleep on retrieval. *Acta Psychologica*, **70**, 199–203.

Tomporowski, P. D., & Ellis, N. R. (1986). Effects of exercise on cognitive processes: A review. *Psychological Bulletin*, **99**, 338–346.

Watts, F. N., MacLeod, A. K., & Morris, L. (1988). A remedial strategy for memory and concentration problems in depressed patients. *Cognitive Therapy and Research*, **12**, 185–193.

Wegner, D. M., Giuliano, M., & Hertel, P. (1985). Cognitive interdependence in close relationships. In W. Ickes (Ed.), *Compatible and incompatible relationships.* New York: Springer Verlag.

Weingartner, H., & Parker, E. S. (1984). *Memory consolidation: Psychobiology of cognition.* Hillsdale, NJ: Erlbaum.

Weinstein, C. E., Goetz, E. T., & Alexander, P. A. (Eds.) (1988). *Learning and study strategies.* San Diego: Academic Press.

West, R. L. (1985). *Memory fitness over forty.* Gainesville, FL: Triad Publishing Company.

West, R. L. (1990). Planning practical memory training for the aged. In L. Poon, D. Rubin, & B. Wilson (Eds.), *Everyday cognition in adult and late life.* New York: Cambridge University Press.

Wilkinson, R. T. (1961). Interaction of lack of sleep with knowledge of results, repeated testing and individual differences. *Journal of Experimental Psychology*, **62**, 263–271.

Wilkinson, R. T. (1963). Interaction of noise with knowledge of results and sleep deprivation. *Journal of Experimental Psychology*, **66**, 332–337.

Willis, L., Yeo, R. A., Thomas, P., & Garry, P. J. (1988). Differential declines in cognitive function with aging: The possible role of health status. *Developmental Neuropsychology*, **4**, 23–28.

Wilson, B. (1987). *Rehabilitation of memory.* Guilford: New York.

Wilson, B., & Moffat, N. (1984). *Clinical management of memory problems.* Rockville, MD: Aspen Systems.

Winograd, E., & Soloway, R. M. (1985). Hiding things from ourselves: Objects and special places. *Journal of Experimental Psychology: General*, **115**, 366–372.

Wittenborn, J. R. (1988). Assessment of the effects of drugs on memory. *Psychopharmacology*, **6**, 67–78.

Wolkowitz, O. M., & Weingartner, H. (1988). Defining cognitive changes in depression and anxiety: A psychobiological analysis. *Psychiatry & Psychobiology*, **3**, 1–8.

Wurtman, R. J. (1981). The effects of nutritional factors on memory. *Acta Neurological Scandanavica, Supplementum*, **89**, 145–154.

Wurtman, R. J. (1982). Nutrients that modify brain function. *Scientific American*, **246**, 50–59.

Wyer, R. S. (1989). Social memory and social judgment. In P. R. Solomon, G. R. Goethals, C. M. Kelley, & B. R. Stephens (Eds.), *Memory: Interdisciplinary approaches.* New York: Springer-Verlag.

Wyer, R. S., & Srull, T. K. (1986). Human cognition in its social context. *Psychological Review*, **93**, 322–359.

Yates, F. A. (1966). *The art of memory*. London: Routledge & Kegan Paul.
Yesavage, J. A. (1984). Relaxation and memory training in 39 elderly patients. *American Journal of Psychiatry*, **141**, 778–781.
Yesavage, J. A. (1985). Nonpharmacologic treatments for memory losses with normal aging. *American Journal of Psychiatry*, **142**, 600–605.
Yesavage, J. A., & Rolf, J. (1984). Effects of relaxation and mnemonics on memory, attention, and anxiety in the elderly. *Experimental Aging Research*, **10**, 211–214.
Yesavage, J. A., Rose, T. L., & Spiegel, D. (1982). Relaxation training and memory improvement in elderly normals: Correlations of anxiety ratings and recall improvement. *Experimental Aging Research*, **8**, 195–198.
Yesavage, J. A., & Sheikh, J. I. (1988). Nonpharmacologic treatment of age-associated memory impairment. *Comprehensive Therapy*, **14**, 44–46.
Yesavage, J. A., Sheikh, J. I., & Lapp, D. (1990). Mnemonics as modified for use by the elderly. In L. Poon, D. Rubin, & B. Wilson (Eds.), *Everyday cognition in adult and late life*. New York: Cambridge University Press.
Yesavage, J. A, Sheikh, J., Tanke, E. D., & Hill, R. (1988). Response to training and individual differences in verbal intelligence and state anxiety. *American Journal of Psychiatry*, **145**, 636–639.
Young, M. N., & Gibson, W. B. (1962). *How to develop an exceptional memory*. Hollywood, CA: Wilshire Books.
Yuille, J. C., & Sereda, L. (1980). Positive effects of mediation: A limited generalization? *Journal of Applied Psychology*, **65**, 333–340.
Zarit, S. H., Gallagher, D., & Kramer, N. (1981). Memory training in the community aged: Effects on depression, memory complaint, and memory performance. *Educational Gerontology*, **6**, 11–27.
Zecker, S. (1988). The role of motivation in memory remediation of brain damaged adults. In D. Payne & D. Herrmann, A *Symposium on the New Approach to the Improvement of Memory Performance and Memory Ability*. Buffalo, NY: Eastern Psychological Association.

A TRIPHASIC APPROACH TO THE ACQUISITION OF RESPONSE-SELECTION SKILL

Robert W. Proctor
T. Gilmour Reeve
Daniel J. Weeks

I. Introduction

The shift in psychology from a stimulus–response (S–R) approach to an information-processing approach, beginning in the 1950s, led to a greater interest in the cognitive processes that intervene between stimuli and responses (Lachman, Lachman, & Butterfield, 1979). One method used to investigate these intervening processes is the chronometric method, for which measures of reaction time (RT) are the primary dependent variables. Through examining the effects of various manipulations on RT, the nature of the underlying representations and processes can be determined (e.g., Posner, 1978; Sternberg, 1969). The resulting research has converged to indicate several distinct stages of processing.

A. Stages of Information Processing

The notion of distinct processing stages has historical precedence stemming from the work of de Jaager (1865/1970) and Donders (1868/1969). In that tradition, contemporary behavioral scientists have found it useful to distinguish among at least three stages of information processing in choice-reaction tasks. These stages, which are illustrated in Fig. 1, are assigned various labels by different authors. Despite the various labeling

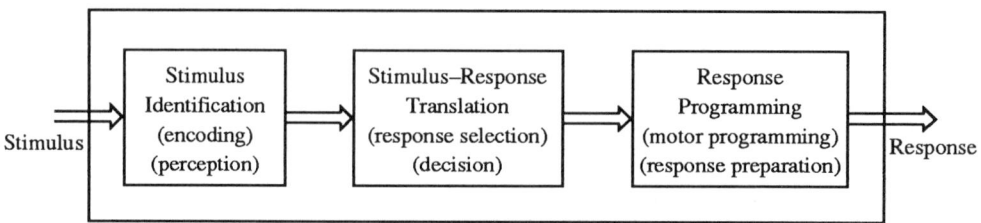

Fig. 1. The three-stage model of human information processing in choice-reaction tasks.

schemes, the distinction is among stimulus identification, stimulus–response translation, and response-programming stages.

The stimulus-identification stage involves detection, encoding, and classification of environmental information (e.g., Sternberg, 1969). Within the identification stage, this information is transformed into neurologically relevant stimulus codes. These stimulus codes then are passed to the next stage, in which they are translated to an appropriate response code from a set of alternative responses (e.g., Teichner & Krebs, 1974). Following identification and translation, an overt response is compiled and initiated in the response-programming stage (e.g., Henry & Rogers, 1960).

The three-stage model continues to provide a useful heuristic for investigating and organizing factors involved in the performance of choice-reaction tasks (e.g., Schmidt, 1982). The model is of value in delineating whether various manipulations in such tasks have their primary influences on perceptual, cognitive, or motor processes. Once the locus of an effect has been determined, its underlying nature can be pursued.

Although all three stages of information processing have been investigated, the stage that is of particular importance for cognitive psychology is stimulus–response translation. This stage is deemed important because it represents the central, cognitive processes that mediate between environmental events and behavioral actions. Consequently, the research described in this article has focused on the translation stage.

B. THE TRANSLATION STAGE

Because the translation stage reflects the processes involved in the interface between stimuli and responses, one phenomenon that has received considerable research interest is that of S–R compatibility (e.g., Schmidt, 1982; Teichner & Krebs, 1974; Welford, 1976). Compatibility refers to the effects that different assignments or mappings of stimuli to responses have on performance. Much of the recent research on S–R compatibility has used a two-choice task, with left and right stimulus locations mapped to left and right response locations. Responding is faster when the mapping is direct (i.e., left stimulus to left response and right stimulus to right response) than when the mapping is reversed (i.e., left stimulus to right response and right stimulus to left response). This difference in RTs typically is attributed to additional S–R translation that is required for the reversed mapping (e.g., Umiltá & Nicoletti, 1990).

The translation stage also has been implicated as the basis for findings obtained in more complex response-precuing tasks. In such tasks, subjects are provided advance information regarding one or more features of a limb movement (e.g., arm, direction, or extent) that is signaled subsequently (see Rosenbaum, 1983, for a discussion of this procedure). A common finding from response-precuing studies is that RTs are dependent on the advance information that is provided, thus producing differential precuing benefits for the respective features (Larish & Frekany, 1985; Rosenbaum, 1980). Although the response-precuing procedure was intended initially to investigate aspects of the response-programming stage, converging evidence has indicated that the differential precuing benefits are a function of the S–R translation stage (Dornier & Reeve, 1990; Goodman & Kelso, 1980; Larish, 1986; Zelaznik, 1978).

A variation of the response-precuing task uses discrete finger responses rather than limb movements (e.g., Miller, 1982). For this variation, a response is made with either the index or middle finger from the left or right hand. The response features that can be precued are the hand (left or right) and/or the finger (index or middle). As with limb movements, a pattern of differential precuing benefits is obtained (Miller, 1982; Reeve & Proctor, 1984). However, considerable evidence again indicates that these differential benefits are a function of the S–R translation stage (Proctor & Reeve, 1986b; Reeve & Proctor, 1984, 1985). Taken together, the research using two-choice tasks and more complex precuing tasks thus shows a major role for the translation stage in diverse situations.

C. Phases of Skill Acquisition

When particular phenomena are attributable to a specific processing stage, the roles of various operations within that stage must be articulated. A conceptual framework is needed to distinguish these roles. Because the nature and contribution of the translation stage is assumed to change with practice (e.g., Teichner & Krebs, 1974), the most suitable framework for this stage is one that reflects these changes.

Historically, the changes that occur in the processes that translate environmental information into action have been characterized as proceeding in a series of phases (Adams, 1971; Anderson, 1982, 1983, 1987; Fitts, 1964; Fitts & Posner, 1967; Welford, 1976). The most influential taxonomy has been one proposed by Paul Fitts (Fitts, 1964; Fitts & Posner, 1967). This taxonomy distinguishes three phases of skill acquisition: (1) a cognitive phase, (2) an associative phase, and (3) an autonomous phase. More recently, Anderson has made a similar distinction between phases, referring to them as (1) the declarative phase, (2) the associative phase, and (3) the procedural phase. In both taxonomies, the first phase of skill acquisition is one in which declarative, cognitive coding is used, sometimes in the form of verbal mediation. The second phase involves a shift from a reliance on declarative codings and cognitive mediation to procedures that are specific to the task or domain. The third phase involves continued tuning of the task-specific procedures at a more abstract, schematic level. The triphasic model of skill acquisition serves to organize our recent work on spatial- and symbolic-cuing tasks.

II. Cognitive Phase

The initial phase of skill acquisition involves forming a representation of the task. At least two major factors contribute to the representation that is formed: (1) the knowledge that the subject brings to the task, and (2) his or her cognitive coding of the task situation. From the standpoint of understanding the nature of the cognitive phase, the latter of these factors is of primary concern. As stated by Fitts (1964) over 25 years ago, "Central to all information-processing is the general concept of *coding*. . . . One goal of an informational analysis of behavior is to specify the codes involved in human behavior" (p. 248). Although the concept of skill has broadened considerably since Fitts made this statement (e.g., Schmidt, 1982), the specification of coding operations remains a central goal of cognitive psychology (e.g., Posner, Peterson, Fox, & Raichle, 1988).

Even for relatively easy situations, such as two-choice reaction tasks, subjects must form representations that include codings of the stimulus and response sets and their relations. The manner in which the sets are coded determines how rapidly and efficiently stimulus information can be translated into a response. Thus, it is important to understand the codes that are used in the cognitive phase to perform a novel task and the factors that influence them. As documented in the next section, the codes often are spatial in nature.

A. SPATIAL CODING

Evidence for spatial coding has been obtained in choice-reaction tasks that have examined S–R compatibility phenomena. In two-choice reaction tasks for which spatially located stimuli are assigned to key-press responses, compatibility is manipulated by comparing direct and reversed assignments of left and right stimulus locations to left and right response locations. When only a single placement of effectors is used, the locations of the responses are confounded with the particular effectors at those locations (e.g., with a normal hand placement, the left and right hands are confounded with the left and right locations). This confound can be resolved by manipulating the assignment of effectors to response locations (e.g., by crossing the limbs). Such manipulations typically show that the assignment of stimulus locations to response locations is crucial, rather than the assignment of stimulus locations to effectors (Anzola, Bertoloni, Buchtel, & Rizzolatti, 1977; Brebner, 1973; Brebner, Shephard, & Cairney, 1972; Umiltá & Nicoletti, 1990).

Evidence for spatial coding has been obtained for compatibility effects that occur when target location is relevant (e.g., Anzola et al., 1977), when target location is irrelevant (Wallace, 1971), when stimulus- and response-effector locations are dissociated (Nicoletti, Anzola, Luppino, Rizzolatti, & Umiltá, 1982), when response locations and response effectors are dissociated (Riggio, Gawryszewski, & Umiltá, 1986), when S–R sets are on orthogonal spatial axes (Nicoletti, Umiltá, Tressoldi, & Marzi, 1988), when responses are unimanual as well as bimanual (Heister, Schroeder-Heister, & Ehrenstein, 1990), and when the stimulus modality is either auditory or visual (Simon, 1990). Thus, the findings of numerous studies indicate that spatial coding predominates in a variety of two-choice reaction tasks. The pervasiveness of the evidence for spatial coding in these tasks makes it one of the most robust findings in cognitive psychology.

Spatial coding also has been implicated in our research with relatively more complex four-choice spatial-precuing and symbolic-cuing tasks. In an initial study, four spatially located stimuli were assigned to the index and middle fingers of the two hands (Reeve & Proctor, 1984).[1] The stimulus display that was used is shown in Table I. On each trial, a row of four plus signs appeared as a warning signal. Following a brief, fixed interval,

[1] In our earlier work, the precue conditions were labeled according to the anatomical distinctions of hand and finger. However, because the evidence has implicated spatial coding as the predominant factor in these tasks, we have relabeled the conditions according to spatial locations in the present article.

TABLE I

Stimulus Displays for Each Precue Condition When the Target Indicates the Left–Outer Response

Condition and stimulus	Locations[a]			
	LO	LI	RI	RO
Uncued				
Warning	+	+	+	+
Precue	+	+	+	+
Target	+			
Left–right				
Warning	+	+	+	+
Precue	+	+		
Target	+			
Inner–outer				
Warning	+	+	+	+
Precue	+			+
Target	+			
Alternate				
Warning	+	+	+	+
Precue	+		+	
Target	+			

[a]L, left; R, right; O, outer; I, inner.

a precue row appeared immediately below the warning row. On some trials, the precue consisted of plus signs in all four locations and, thus, was not informative regarding the imperative stimulus and response. However, on most trials, the precue consisted of plus signs in only two of the four possible locations. On these trials, the precue provided valid information regarding the imperative stimulus, which occurred subsequently in one of the two cued locations.

The precuing effect that occurs in this situation is as follows. Responses are fastest when either the two leftmost or two rightmost locations are cued, intermediate when either the two inner or two outer locations are cued, and slowest when either pair of alternate locations is cued (Miller, 1982; Reeve & Proctor, 1984). However, similar to the two-choice tasks, a confound exists in the assignment of effectors to response locations when only a normal adjacent-hand placement is used. That confound was removed by having subjects perform with an overlapped-hand placement, for which the fingers from the two hands are alternated. By

TABLE II

MEAN REACTION TIMES (MSEC) FOR THE CUING CONDITIONS AS A FUNCTION OF HAND PLACEMENT[a]

Cuing condition	Hand placement	
	Adjacent	Overlapped
Uncued	551	771
Left–right	502	721
Inner–outer	516	746
Alternate	547	765

[a]From Reeve and Proctor (1984).

dissociating the specific effectors from the response locations, we were able to show that the pattern of differential precuing benefits remained with the spatial locations (see Table II) and, thus, is not attributable to the specific effectors (Reeve & Proctor, 1984).

To accrue additional evidence for a spatial-coding interpretation of the pattern of differential precuing benefits, we developed another version of the spatial-precuing task (Proctor & Reeve, 1986b). This version arose from a concern with the coding interpretation of the results obtained when horizontal stimulus and response sets were used (Miller, 1985). With those sets, responses are approximately 200 msec slower overall for the overlapped-hand placement than for the adjacent-hand placement. A difference of this magnitude could reflect a qualitative change in the nature of the response set and thus invalidate a comparison of the two hand placements (Miller, 1985). Our intention with the new version of the task was to manipulate hand placement without affecting the overall levels of RTs.

For the new version of the spatial-precuing task, the stimulus set was oriented vertically rather than horizontally. The four response locations extended at a 90° angle along the midsagittal plane, with respect to the subject. With this "vertical" response set, subjects were required to turn their hands inward to place their fingers on the response keys (see Fig. 2). For the adjacent placement, the fingers from each hand are situated on adjacent response locations. For the overlapped placement, the fingers from each hand are placed on alternate response locations, without the hands being overlapped physically. With this version of the spatial-precuing task, the overall RTs did not differ significantly between the two hand placements (see Fig. 3). However, the pattern of differential precuing

ADJACENT HANDS

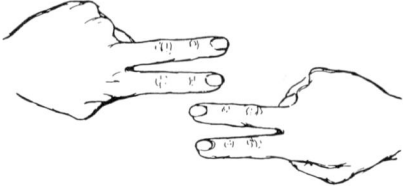

OVERLAPPED HANDS

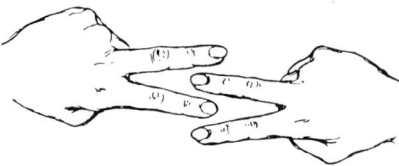

Fig. 2. Examples of the adjacent and overlapped hand placements used with the vertical stimulus and response arrangements. From Proctor & Reeve (1986b).

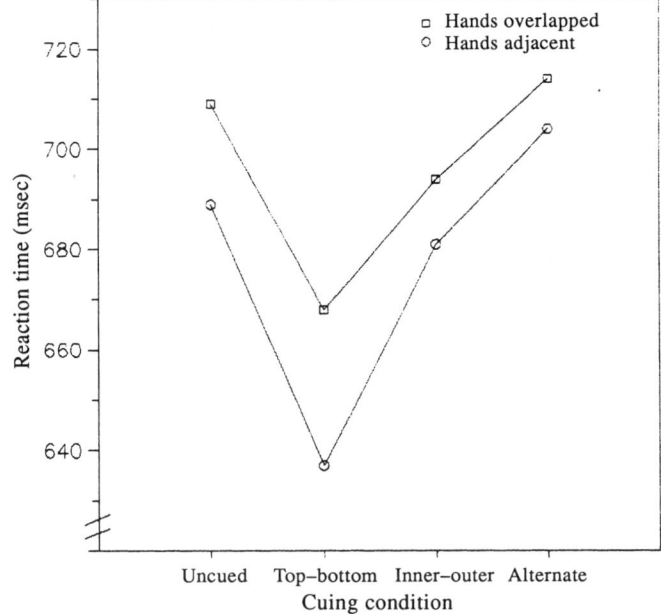

Fig. 3. Mean reaction times as a function of hand placement and cuing condition. From Proctor & Reeve (1986b).

benefits still was a function of the spatial locations, thus confirming our previous conclusion that the pattern reflects spatial coding used to translate between stimuli and responses.

To emphasize further the role of cognitive coding in spatial-precuing tasks, we reinterpreted the results from another study that used "diamond-shaped" arrangements of stimuli and responses, with the hands placed in adjacent or separated positions (Miller, 1985). For the adjacent placement, the fingers were on the four center keys (G, Y, B, H) of a computer keyboard, whereas for the separated placement, the fingers of each hand were placed at extreme diagonals of the keyboard (e.g., A, Z and P,;). With this version of the task, an advantage was obtained for precuing two fingers from the same hand.

On the surface, this same-hand advantage suggests that response preparation is more efficient for fingers on the same hand (Miller, 1985). Yet, when the data were replotted as a function of hand position, it was clear that the advantage occurred only when the hands were in the separated position (Reeve & Proctor, 1985). When the fingers from both hands were placed in a spatially neutral, distinct diamond-shaped arrangement (i.e., the adjacent position), all pairs of fingers showed equal precuing benefits. However, when the hands were separated, and the diamond shape of the response arrangement was eliminated, RTs increased for precued fingers on different hands but not for those on the same hand. In other words, only when the interhand distances between finger responses were substantially greater than the intrahand distances did a "hand" advantage arise. Thus, as expected on the basis of spatial coding, the correspondence of the spatial locations was crucial and not the anatomical status of the responding effector.

To summarize, the coding that is used in the cognitive phase of two-choice reaction tasks and four-choice precuing tasks is predominantly spatial. When first presented with these tasks, subjects form representations based on the environmental locations of the stimuli and responses. These representations, and the correspondence between them, determine the efficiency of S–R translation.

B. HAND CODING

Although spatial coding is implicated in the two-choice and four-choice tasks, other sources of coding are apparent. For example, in the version of the spatial-precuing task that used a vertical stimulus set, with the hands turned inward to engage a vertical response set, evidence for coding in terms of the hand distinction was apparent (Proctor & Reeve, 1986b). Although, in that task, the pattern of differential precuing benefits was a function of the spatial locations, the magnitude of the difference in RTs between the two extreme precuing conditions was enhanced for the adjacent-hand placement relative to the overlapped placement (see Fig. 3). Moreover, the difference also was greater than that found for the equivalent conditions in the original, horizontal version of the spatial-precuing task.

The increased difference in precuing benefits for the adjacent-hand placement with the vertical stimulus and response arrangements apparently reflects the addition of hand coding. This additional coding of the hand distinction arises from turning the hands inward (see Fig. 2). Evidence to support the hand-coding interpretation comes from several situations. For one situation, the vertical version of the spatial-precuing task was used, but subjects responded with the four fingers from a single hand (Proctor & Reeve, 1986b). With the single-hand placement, the enhanced precuing benefit previously obtained for the adjacent placement was not apparent. There was a similar failure to find the enhancement using an adjacent-hand placement, for which both hands were placed to the right side of the body and aligned with respect to the vertical stimulus display. Thus, the additional precuing benefit due to hand coding occurs only when the hands are turned inward and the hand distinction is congruent with the salient top–bottom spatial feature of the stimulus and response sets.

Further evidence supporting the importance of congruence with a salient feature is apparent in the previously described diamond-shaped version of the spatial-precuing task (Miller, 1985; Reeve & Proctor, 1985). For this version of the task, when the fingers were placed on adjacent response positions, no precuing enhancement attributable to the hand distinction was obtained, even though the hands were turned toward each other. This lack of an enhancement when the hands are turned toward each other has been replicated with another spatially neutral version of the precuing task in which the stimulus and response sets formed square-shaped patterns (Reeve, Proctor, Weeks, & Dornier, 1990b). Thus, although the hand distinction can be coded as a feature when the hands are turned inward, such coding is not evident with spatially neutral arrangements. Consequently, in the spatial-precuing task, congruence with a salient spatial feature seems to be necessary for the hand distinction to be used.

To summarize, under certain circumstances the hand distinction can be coded as a feature of the response set (see also Klapp, Greim, Mendicino, & Koenig, 1979; Ladavas & Moscovitch, 1984). The important implication is that the environmental locations of the stimuli and responses are not the sole determinants of the codings that are used in the cognitive phase. Based on this finding, it should be possible to show that salient nonspatial aspects of stimulus sets also can be coded as features for relating these sets to response sets.

C. SYMBOLIC CODING

For situations in which stimuli differ in terms of nonspatial features and are presented at a single location, it is unlikely that they would be coded spatially. Such a situation was examined with tasks for which two-dimensional symbolic stimuli were assigned to the four key-press responses (Proctor & Reeve, 1985). One of the two stimulus dimensions was more salient than the other. The crucial manipulation involved the assignment of stimuli to responses. By manipulating assignments, the salient feature of the stimulus set could correspond with different features of the response set.

For two experiments, the stimuli o, O, z, and Z were used. For this stimulus set, letter identity is salient relative to size (Proctor & Reeve, 1985). That is, subjects can distinguish letter identity faster than size. Two assignments of stimuli to response locations were used. For one assignment, letter identity corresponded with the left–right feature of the response set (e.g., a left-to-right assignment of O, o, z, Z—the OozZ assignment), whereas for another assignment, identity corresponded with the least salient alternate-location feature (e.g., a left-to-right assignment of O, z, o, Z—the OzoZ assignment). When subjects performed with the adjacent-hand placement, responses were faster with the OozZ assignment than with the OzoZ assignment (see Fig. 4, left panel). Moreover, similar results were obtained with a single-hand response set, thus indicating that the relation of the letter-identity feature to spatial locations is crucial.

As with the spatial-precuing task, evidence for hand coding also was apparent with the symbolic-cuing task. When the overlapped-hand placement was used, no difference in RT occurred between the assignments for which letter identity corresponded with the left–right feature (the OozZ assignment) of the response set and those for which it did not (the OzoZ assignment; see Fig. 4, right panel). Moreover, compared to other experiments, this lack of a difference in RTs was due to the OzoZ assignment being relatively fast. The important factor is that when the OzoZ assignment is used with the overlapped-hand placement, the salient letter-identity feature corresponds to the distinction between the hands. Thus, when there is no correspondence between the salient stimulus feature and the left–right spatial distinction of the response set, coding occurs on the basis of the hand distinction.

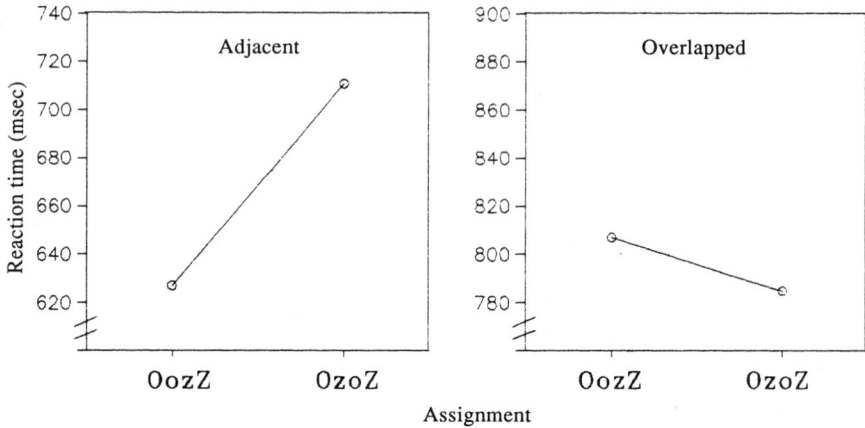

Fig. 4. Mean reaction times for the OozZ and OzoZ assignments, as a function of adjacent (left) and overlapping (right) hand placement. From Proctor & Reeve (1985).

The evidence for hand coding in the symbolic-cuing task was found with the overlapped-hand placement, which had shown no evidence for hand coding in the spatial-precuing task. The important difference is that in the symbolic-cuing task, the overlapped-hand placement brings about a congruence between the salient stimulus feature and the hand distinction. Just as turning the hands inward for the vertical version of the spatial-precuing task creates a congruence that allows the hand to be coded, a similar congruence induces hand coding in the symbolic-cuing task. Thus, the hand placement *per se* does not determine whether the hand distinction will be coded. Rather, it is the congruence with a salient symbolic or spatial feature that determines whether hand coding is used.

In a related set of experiments (Proctor & Reeve, 1985), consonant–vowel stimuli composed from the letters B, M, E, and O were used. For the resulting stimulus set of BE, BO, ME, and MO, the consonant feature is more salient than the vowel feature (Miller, 1982). The unique aspect of this symbolic set is that a precuing procedure can be used, because it is possible to present either the consonant or the vowel first. Thus, the procedure can approximate more closely that of the spatial-precuing task.

When the assignment of the letters was one in which the salient consonant feature distinguished the two leftmost and two rightmost response locations, a precuing advantage was obtained similar to the advantage that is apparent in the spatial-precuing task. That is, responses were faster when the consonant served as the precue, rather than the vowel, and this consonant-precuing advantage occurred both with the hands adjacent and with them overlapped. Moreover, faster responses were associated with the assignments in which the salient consonant feature corresponded with the left–right spatial distinction (e.g., BE, BO, ME, and MO assigned in a left-to-right manner to response locations) than for the assignments in which that distinction corresponded with the nonsalient vowel feature (e.g., BE, ME, BO, and MO). Thus, once again, we were able to demonstrate that performance in the cognitive phase of skill acquisition is best when a correspondence exists between the salient features of the stimulus and response sets.

D. CODING OF SALIENT FEATURES

The crucial point that emerges from the results obtained with the spatial- and symbolic-cuing tasks is that the efficient translation of stimulus information to a response is not a function of any particular dimensional characteristic of the respective sets. Rather, efficient translation is a function of the salient features of the stimulus and response sets and their correspondence. This fact is captured by what we refer to as the *salient-features coding principle:* "Stimulus and response sets are coded in terms of the salient features of each, with response determination occurring most rapidly when the salient features of the respective sets correspond" (Proctor & Reeve, 1986b, p. 278).

The salient-features coding principle has provided an effective means for theoretical integration of the existing literature and has introduced a host of empirical issues that must be reconciled for the full range of coding operations in the cognitive phase to be understood. One empirical issue that arises from the principle is the relative manipulability of saliency, and thus the extent to which stimulus and response coding can be altered.

We have addressed the issue of the manipulability of salient features in a series of experiments based on the Gestalt organizational principles of similarity and spatial proximity (e.g., Koffka, 1935/1963; Pomerantz & Kubovy, 1986). In these experiments, organizational factors were introduced into the stimulus and response sets of the four-choice spatial-precuing task (Reeve *et al.*, 1990b).

In the first experiment, the four spatial locations were designated by two instances of each of the characters "+" and "o". An ungrouped control display was included in which the same character was used for all four locations. Thus, the experiment evaluated whether pairs of locations that share a similar character are grouped in a manner that influences the coding of the stimulus and response sets. These similarity groupings could correspond to the left–right, inner–outer, or alternate-location distinctions of the spatial arrays (see Table III).

TABLE III

Example Displays for Similarity Grouping

Stimuli	Display grouping			
	Ungrouped	Left–right	Inner–outer	Alternate
Version 1				
Warning	+ + + +	+ + o o	+ o o +	+ o + o
Precue	+ +	+ +	+ o	+ o
Target	+	+	+	+
Version 2				
Warning	o o o o	o o + +	o + + o	o + o +
Precue	o o	o o	o +	o +
Target	o	o	o	o

Relative to the ungrouped arrays, the similarity grouping had no effect when it was congruent with the alternate-location distinction. However, the similarity grouping was beneficial when it was congruent with either the left–right or the inner–outer distinctions. For these latter situations, RTs were reduced for all precuing conditions as well as for the uncued condition. Moreover, with the inner–outer similarity grouping, RTs for the inner–outer and alternate-location precue conditions were reduced to the level for the left–right precue condition.

In another experiment, square arrangements were used to create stimulus and response sets that are spatially neutral. The similarity manipulation had no effect on RTs when it distinguished either the two left and two right locations or the two top and two bottom locations. Moreover, no effects of hand placement on either the left and right sides or the top and bottom sides were apparent. Thus, the similarity grouping is used in coding only when it is congruent with a spatial feature of either high (i.e., the left–right distinction) or intermediate (i.e., the inner–outer distinction) salience.

Grouping of the stimulus and response sets by spatial proximity also was used as a means for manipulating relative saliency. These experiments employed the horizontal stimulus and response sets but varied the absolute separations between the locations. One experiment included a factorial manipulation of the spatial separation between the two leftmost and two rightmost stimulus and response locations. For the stimulus and response sets, either the locations were equally spaced (+ + + +) or they were separated by a large, central gap (+ +   + +). The only effect of separating the response set was to increase RTs overall when the stimulus

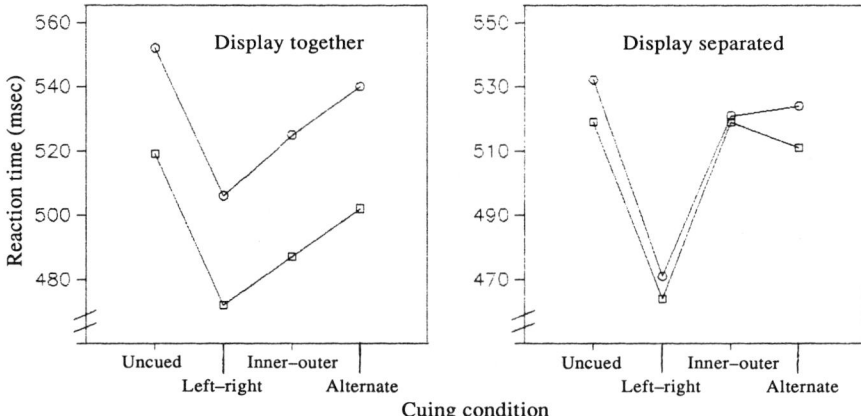

Fig. 5. Mean reaction times as a function of cuing condition and hand placement for the display-together and display-separated conditions. (Squares denote the response-together condition and circles denote the response-separated condition.)

set was not also separated (see Fig. 5, left panel). However, separating the stimulus set elevated RTs for the precue conditions involving the inner–outer and alternate locations, relative to the conditions involving the left–right locations, regardless of whether the response set was separated (see Fig. 5, right panel). Thus, the two conditions for which precued locations occurred on both halves of the display were hindered by the separation of the halves.

Another experiment included a display in which gaps were inserted into the stimulus set such that they partitioned the two inner locations from the two outer locations (+ ++ +). In this experiment, subjects responded only with the hands together. With the partitioned display, the benefits were greatest for the precuing condition that utilized the distinction between the inner and outer locations (see Fig. 6). Thus, the RTs were fastest for the pairs of locations made most salient by the proximity grouping of the display.

The experiments involving similarity and proximity grouping show that such manipulations affect performance. These performance changes are consistent with the view that the correspondence between salient stimulus and response features promotes efficient translation. To date, the manipulations of grouping for the response set have not been shown to be an effective means for influencing the efficiency of translation. However, it is possible that other response-grouping manipulations may be found to be effective.

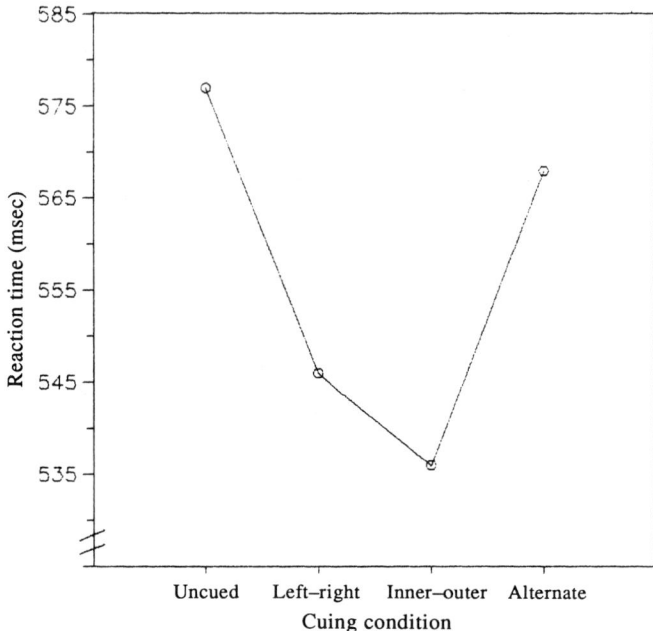

Fig. 6. Mean reaction times as a function of cuing condition for the partitioned display.

E. Coding of Orthogonal Dimensions

In the preceding sections, numerous factors other than spatial characteristics of the environment have been shown to contribute to the coding of the stimulus and response sets. However, for all versions of the spatial-precuing task, the stimulus and response sets have been presented along the same physical dimension (either both horizontal or both vertical), and a direct mapping of the relative locations has been maintained.

An implication of the salient-features coding principle is that evidence for such coding also should be apparent when subjects are required to translate from stimuli that vary in one spatial dimension to a response set that varies in another. Thus, the next series of experiments examined situations for which the orientation of the stimulus set was orthogonal to that of the response set.

In one spatial-precuing experiment, different groups of subjects performed with the factorial combinations of the horizontal and vertical stimulus sets and the horizontal and vertical response sets (Reeve, Proctor, Weeks, & Dornier, 1990a). For the situations in which the orientations of

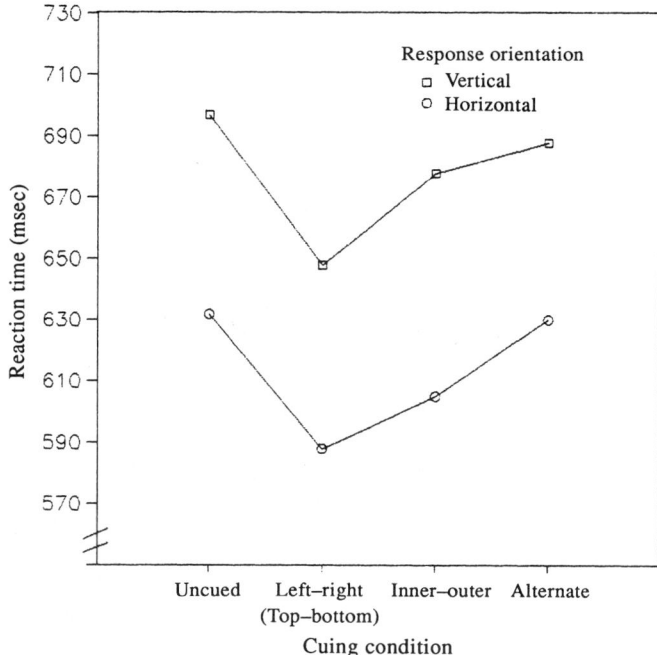

Fig. 7. Mean reaction times as a function of response orientation and cuing condition.

the sets were orthogonal, the left-to-right ordering of horizontal locations was mapped to the bottom-to-top ordering of vertical locations. Responses were faster with the horizontal response set than with the vertical response set (see Fig. 7) and when the orientations of the stimulus and response sets were the same than when they were different. A similar pattern of differential precuing benefits was obtained for the two response orientations, regardless of whether the orientations were parallel or orthogonal. Thus, differential precuing benefits on the basis of spatial location were apparent even when the S–R translation processes required a transformation between dimensions. Although this transformation takes time, it does not affect the coding based on the relative locations of the stimuli and responses.

The finding that spatial-compatibility effects occur with orthogonal stimulus and response sets in the spatial-precuing task raises the question of whether such effects occur for an orthogonal version of the standard two-choice task. We have conducted several experiments to examine the nature of coding in such tasks. One experiment used an up–down stimulus set and a left–right response set (Weeks & Proctor, in press). Both up (stimulus)–right (response)/down–left and up–left/down–right mappings of stimulus locations to response locations were used. Within each of these mapping conditions, subjects responded in separate blocks of trials with their limbs in either an uncrossed or a crossed placement (e.g., Anzola *et al.*, 1977). An S–R compatibility effect was evident. Specifically, RTs were faster for the up–right/down–left spatial mapping than for the reserve mapping. Moreover, this preference was apparent for both limb placements.

Another experiment obtained evidence for a similar mapping preference using either up–down or left–right spatial stimulus sets paired with symbolic response sets. These response sets were comprised of vocal responses that implied either the parallel or the orthogonal spatial dimension relative to the stimulus set. When the spatial dimension depicted by the stimulus set and the dimension implied by the response set were parallel, responding was faster if the dimensional labels matched (e.g., left–"left"/right–"right") than if they did not (e.g., left–"right"/right–"right"). More interesting is the pattern of results when the depicted stimulus dimension and the implied response dimension were orthogonal. For this situation, there was a clear preference for mappings that paired *up* with *right* and *left* with *down,* regardless of which dimension was depicted by the stimulus set or implied by the response set. Thus, for a situation in which the response set was not comprised of effectors assigned to environmental locations, a compatibility effect consistent with the previous two-choice experiment nevertheless was obtained.

Finally, an additional two-choice experiment was conducted in which both the stimulus and the response sets were symbolic in nature. The stimuli were centrally positioned, left- or right-facing arrows. The responses were vocal utterances that implied either the parallel or the orthogonal spatial dimension relative to the arrow stimuli. The results showed that if the stimulus and response sets designated parallel dimensions, responding was faster when the spatial labels were consistent relative to when they were not. For the orthogonal situation, there again was a clear preference for the left- and right-facing arrow stimuli to be mapped to the "below" and "above" responses, respectively.

Thus, across these two-choice experiments, a rather clear picture emerges. For orthogonal stimulus and response dimensions, regardless of whether they are depicted spatially or implied symbolically, a mapping preference exists: The characteristics of *right* go with *up* and *left* with *down.* Because this result is obtained for situations in which the absolute and relative relations across the sets are arbitrary, we interpret these findings as reflecting a fundamental property of the way in which subjects represent spatial dimensions that have no inherent organizing feature. Studies indicate that *right* is more salient than *left* and *up* is more salient than *down* (Clark, 1973; Sholl & Egeth, 1981). Thus, the most compatible assignment is one for which the more salient features of the respective sets correspond.

F. SUMMARY

The research reported in this section has shown that the coding used in the cognitive phase to translate between stimuli and responses is complex and dynamic. This coding is influenced by the salient features of the stimulus and response sets, with the efficiency of the translation processes being a function of the correspondence among the features. Thus, response tendencies have been shown to be influenced by manipulations of the relative salience within stimulus sets, the correspondence of stimulus-set features to response-set features, and fundamental spatial-representational factors. In short, the coding of the task environment is of primary importance in determining performance in the initial, cognitive phase of skill acquisition.

III. Associative Phase

Although cognitive coding operations of the type described in the previous section are important initially for translating between stimuli and responses, their role diminishes with practice (Fitts, 1964; Teichner & Krebs, 1974; Welford, 1976). With sufficient practice, direct stimulus–response associations are established, for which the translation is "built in" and unitized (Welford, 1976). These associations often are referred to as procedures or productions (e.g., Anderson, 1983) that are task specific. Thus, issues of concern regarding the associative phase of skill acquisition involve the development of the task-specific procedures, their retention, and their basic nature as revealed by transfer tasks.

A. PRACTICE AND RETENTION

One finding of many of the previously described experiments is that the pattern of differential precuing benefits largely is eliminated by a long precuing interval of 3 sec (e.g., Reeve & Proctor, 1984, 1988). In other words, given sufficient time, processes associated with translating the precue information can be completed. The implication of this finding is that the pattern of differential precuing benefits occurs because shorter precuing intervals impose a time constraint on the translation processes.

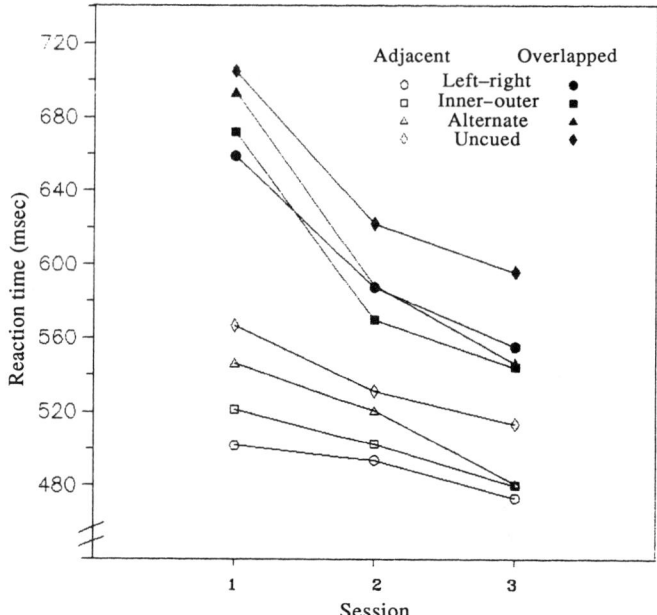

Fig. 8. Mean reaction times, as a function of cuing condition, hand placement, and session. From Proctor & Reeve (1988).

Consequently, if these processes can be made more efficient through practice, the pattern of differential precuing benefits should disappear for the shorter intervals.

The experiments used to investigate the cognitive phase of skill acquisition typically included only a single session of 300 trials. Consequently, an initial experiment was conducted to determine whether the predicted effect of practice would be found for the basic four-choice spatial-precuing task if additional sessions were included (Proctor & Reeve, 1988). Testing was increased to three sessions. For both the adjacent- and overlapped-hand placements, the pattern of differential precuing benefits evident in the first session was eliminated by the third session (see Fig. 8). Recently, we have shown that the effects of practice are essentially the same for the symbolic-cuing task (Proctor, Reeve, Weeks, Dornier, & Van Zandt, 1990). The important point is that the role of the translation stage becomes minimized as task-specific procedures develop with practice.

The next question is whether the task-specific procedures that have developed reflect the acquisition of more durable representations. To answer this question, 1-week retention tests were used in conjunction with the spatial-precuing and symbolic-cuing tasks. For each task, subjects who had practiced for three sessions showed evidence of having retained the procedures for at least a week. Specifically, when tested a week after the third practice session, the initial differences in RT were not reinstated. Thus, the task-specific procedures that characterize the associative phase of skill acquisition are relatively durable.

B. Transfer

The practice and retention data suggest that procedures in the associative phase specify relations between the stimuli and responses used for the task. These relations would be stipulated most directly if the particular effector that executes the response associated with a given stimulus was specified by the procedure. The implication, then, is that the effects of practice should be specific to a particular response set.

To test this implication, a series of experiments using transfer designs was conducted (Proctor & Reeve, 1988). In these experiments, subjects practiced with the spatial-precuing task for three sessions, using either the adjacent- or overlapped-hand placement. In the fourth session, half of the subjects in each group were transferred to the opposite hand placement. Regardless of whether transfer was from the overlapped to the adjacent placement or vice versa, the pattern of differential precuing benefits reappeared in the transfer session. This reappearance indicates that subjects reverted to cognitive coding operations in the transfer sessions.

Reinstatement of the pattern of differential precuing benefits also has been shown in another transfer experiment (Reeve et al., 1990a). In this experiment, the arrangement of the stimulus and response sets in the practice sessions was (1) vertical–vertical (with hands turned inward), (2) vertical–vertical side (with both hands placed to right side of the body), or (3) horizontal–horizontal. In the transfer session, all subjects performed with the vertical–vertical side arrangement. The pattern of differential precuing benefits was absent in the transfer session only for those subjects who had practiced with the vertical–vertical side arrangement. The pattern was reinstated fully for those subjects who practiced with either the vertical–vertical or the horizontal–horizontal arrangements.

A question that arises is whether changes in stimulus orientation lead to a similar reinstatement of the precuing pattern. In an additional experiment, subjects practiced with either the horizontal stimulus set and horizontal response set or with the vertical stimulus set and horizontal response set. In the transfer session, only the horizontal–horizontal situation was used. Unlike the cases for which the hand placement was changed, the pattern of differential precuing benefits did not reappear when only the orientation of the stimulus set was changed. Thus, the procedures acquired with practice relate relative locations within the stimulus set to the specific finger responses. These procedures are not sensitive to the orientation of the stimulus set.

The general point thus far is that the procedures that develop with practice are specific to the assignments of stimuli to response effectors and do not transfer to different response sets. Thus, when transferred to new response sets, subjects revert to coding operations characteristic of those used initially in the cognitive phase. Although the acquired procedural knowledge is not transferable to the new task situation, the subjects are not entirely naive. That is, they bring with them to the new task their experience with a highly related and relevant task. Thus, they should possess more complete declarative knowledge regarding the new task situation, which in turn should affect their performance relative to that of naive subjects. Consequently, the cognitive coding operations used to translate the new stimulus–response situation will not necessarily be veridical to those used by naive subjects.

Two findings lend some credence to the notion that pertinent declarative knowledge is modified by practice on a related task. First, when subjects practice with the adjacent-hand placement and transfer to the overlapped placement, the pattern of differential precuing benefits is of reduced magnitude in the transfer session compared to the magnitude obtained in an initial session (Proctor & Reeve, 1988). The crucial factor seems to be that when practicing with the adjacent placement, the hand distinction is paired with the salient left-right spatial distinction. The relation of the hand distinction to certain precued locations likely becomes more obvious as a consequence of the practice. When transferred to the overlapped placement, the hand distinction then may be used in the coding to benefit the alternate-location precue condition.

Results from subjects who were transferred to a situation for which the hands were crossed completely (i.e., the left-to-right ordering of fingers was right index, right middle, left middle, and left index), after practicing with the adjacent-hand placement, lend support to this account (Proctor & Reeve, 1988). With the crossed-hands placement, the hand distinction remains congruent with the left–right spatial distinction. Thus, hand coding would not be able to benefit the alternate-location precue condition. When transferred to the crossed-hands placement, the pattern of differential precuing benefits was of the magnitude typically obtained in the first session.

In another experiment, subjects practiced for a single session with the spatial-precuing task (Proctor *et al.,* 1990). This practice involved presentation of either only the left–right precue condition or only the alternate-location precue condition. Subjects then were transferred to the symbolic-cuing task, with assignments being either of the OozZ type or the OzoZ type. For subjects who practiced with the left–right distinction, the typical RT advantage of the former assignment over the latter was observed. In contrast, for subjects who practiced with the alternate-location distinction, no difference between the assignments was obtained. This lack of a difference apparently was a function of the alternate locations being made more salient with practice. Thus, practice with the spatial-precuing task influenced the way that subjects subsequently coded the symbolic stimulus set to the response set.

C. Summary

The associative phase of skill acquisition is characterized by the development of task-specific procedures that relate stimuli directly to response effectors. In addition, the phase allows for the modification of declarative representations that can be used during a reinstated cognitive phase with task variations for which the task-specific procedures are not applicable.

IV. Autonomous Phase

A number of models propose that a third, autonomous phase of skill acquisition exists. However, the factors that influence the shift to this phase have not been the focus of much investigation, primarily because such studies require several weeks, if not months, of practice. As a consequence, there is little consensus regarding the specific processes that might operate in the autonomous phase. Schmidt (1982) notes that, "As a result, . . . we must assume that the methods and principles that apply to the associative phase are the same ones that apply in the autonomous phase" (p. 567). However, given the paucity of research, Schmidt recognizes that "this assumption could easily be incorrect" (p. 567).

A. Extended Practice

Evidence that quantitative and qualitative changes in skilled performance continue over long acquisition periods is apparent from a number of sources. It has been known for some time that quantitative changes in practice are fit best by a power law (Newell & Rosenbloom, 1981; Snoddy, 1926). For example, Crossman (1959) examined the time required for people to make cigars on a hand-operated machine. Operators were tested whose experience ranged up to 6 yr. Speed of performance increased as a power function up to 4 yr, at which point the minimum machine-cycle time limited performance from improving further.

In addition to quantitative changes, evidence for qualitative changes has existed since one of the earliest documented studies of long-term practice. In a study of the acquisition of telegraphic language, Bryan and Harter (1899) noted that virtually years of practice were necessary for performance to reach asymptote. More importantly, they characterized acquisition as occurring in a hierarchical progression that proceeded from basic stimulus elements to more complex, abstract units of language.

Our own work has provided results consistent with the hypothesis that there exists a distinct, third phase of skill acquisition. These results come from two studies that used more extended practice than did our earlier studies (Proctor & Reeve, 1989). In one experiment, subjects practiced for 12 sessions with the spatial-precuing task, using the overlapped-hand placement. They then were transferred to the adjacent placement for four additional sessions. There was only a nonsignificant tendency for the pattern of differential precuing benefits to reappear in the first transfer session. This result is in contrast to the complete reinstatement of the pattern that occurs when transfer is after just three sessions of practice (Proctor & Reeve, 1988). One interpretation of the extended-practice results is that response-selection comes to be mediated by schematic representations that are more abstract than are the task-specific procedures characteristic of the associative phase of skill acquisition.

Supporting evidence for this interpretation was obtained in another experiment for which subjects received eight sessions of practice with the letter-identity and size version of the symbolic-cuing task (Proctor *et al.*, 1990). Each subject performed with either an assignment of the OozZ type or one of the OzoZ type, for all of the practice sessions. In a ninth session, all subjects completed the spatial-precuing task. Performance in this transfer session did not depend on the particular type of assignment with which the subject had practiced. Regardless of the assignment, the pattern of differential precuing benefits was apparent, but at a reduced magnitude from a typical first session. These results again suggest that an abstract response-selection schema may have been acquired with practice.

Additional evidence that response selection may be mediated by an abstract representation is reported by Gopher (1984). He describes work conducted by A. Schelach in which subjects engaged in 20 hr of training on a letter-shape typing task. Subjects were required to learn to enter each letter by pressing two successive chords of one, two, or three fingers. The upper and lower halves of the corresponding letter shape were entered by the first and second chords, respectively. For the training sessions, the subjects used three fingers from the dominant hand. Following the training sessions, subjects were required to perform the task with their nondominant hand. Substantial positive transfer occurred, indicating that a primary component of the skill is generalizable across the limbs. The implication is that this component is an abstract spatial representation.

B. SKILLED PERFORMERS

Given the difficulties inherent in obtaining systematic laboratory data pertinent to the autonomous phase of skill acquisition, an alternative source of evidence is to consider people who are highly skilled in a particular domain. Studies of such individuals have proved to be useful in specifying components of pattern recognition and memory that could not be studied in standard laboratory situations (e.g., Chase & Simon, 1973). The understanding of human pattern recognition and memory gained from such studies has enabled characterization of the abstract, schematic knowledge that accompanies skill.

Although less widely investigated, the systematic study of skilled performers may be of similar value for broadening our understanding of abstract representations in response selection. For example, Castiello and Umiltá (1987) showed that the translation processes that underlie spatial compatibility effects are influenced by the nature of experience. They compared performance on a two-choice spatial-compatibility task for athletes skilled at either volleyball or soccer. Compatibility effects were much stronger for the volleyball experts than for the soccer experts. Castiello and Umiltá interpreted this difference in terms of the unique requirements of the two sports (i.e., the asymmetric and symmetric limb control that is required for skill at volleyball and soccer, respectively). Thus, the unique requirements, and the considerable experience required to become skilled in these sports, promote the acquisition of abstract, spatial response-selection schemata with distinct characteristics.

Similarly, in an examination of various levels of skill at typewriting, West and Sabban (1982) provided evidence consistent with a hierarchy of skill levels. Cognitive mediation was characteristic of the performance of slow typists. Individuals with higher typing speeds showed proficiency at associative letter-by-letter habits and also letter-sequence habits confined to short, high-frequency words and to portions of words. However, only the very fastest typists showed more general word-level unitization, which the authors interpreted as being characteristic of a shift into the autonomous phase of typing skill.

From a series of experiments and simulations of typing skill, Rumelhart and Norman (1982) have developed a simulation model of an expert typist. The central tenet of the model is that typing performance is a function of hierarchical schemata that direct the patterns of responding. The schematic representations emphasize the spatial properties of the movement and the environmental coordinates necessary for response selection. The order for emitting the keystrokes is determined by patterns of activation and inhibition among the abstract schemata.

C. Summary

Although the evidence is not conclusive, several findings suggest that a qualitatively distinct third phase of skill may emerge as a result of extended practice with a task. Further research with extended practice is needed to establish more clearly the existence and properties of this phase. Also, whereas investigations of skilled performers generally have been limited to tasks that are regarded as involving high-level cognition (e.g., chess), investigations of such individuals also may prove to be useful in uncovering the nature of abstract representations that determine skilled response selection.

V. Conclusions

The three-stage model of information processing in choice-reaction tasks distinguishes processes that operate as a function of stimulus characteristics, stimulus–response relations, and response characteristics. Of the three stages, the one that is most purely cognitive is the second, which often is referred to as stimulus–response translation or response selection. The cognitive nature of this stage is illustrated by the fact that mental codes form the basis for the translation processes.

The notion of cognitive coding has considerable precedence in the psychology of human performance (Fitts, 1964; Fitts & Posner, 1967; Fitts & Seeger, 1953). The general concept of coding is consistent with the contemporary view of humans as information processors. Moreover, codes and coding processes also comprise the fundamental elements of psychobiological investigations regarding the human organism (Uttal, 1973).

Our research program has been concerned primarily with determining the coding factors that pertain to the effective translation between stimulus information and response information. We have examined numerous choice-reaction tasks in which the relations between stimulus and response sets have been manipulated. Because the translation stage is the one that is most influenced by practice (Welford, 1976), the results of our studies can be organized around a triphasic model of skill acquisition.

A. Cognitive Phase

In the initial cognitive phase, the subject's pretask knowledge and coding of the experimental environment determine his/her cognitive representation of the task. The coding of the environment includes both the stimulus set and the response set. In most of our studies, subjects enter the experiment at the cognitive phase of acquisition, because they are naive to the task and are performing in an initial session. The evidence from these studies indicates that spatial coding predominates in the translation between stimuli and responses. When spatial location cannot be used to code the stimulus set (i.e., when all stimuli are presented at a single, central location), the set can be coded on the basis of salient symbolic features. In such situations, performance is a function of the correspondence between the salient symbolic features and features of the response set. Coding of the response set in terms of the anatomical distinction between the two hands also is evident in certain situations.

Taken together, the results from the spatial-precuing and symbolic-cuing tasks implicate coding based on a hierarchy of features. The hierarchy is structured around the relative saliency of the features that comprise the stimulus and response sets. Translation is most efficient when the salient features of the sets correspond.

One implication of a hierarchy of salience is that it should be possible to increase or decrease the relative salience of specific features. When organization is introduced into the stimulus and response sets by similarity and proximity grouping, performance is affected systematically. The relative efficiency of translation from precue stimuli to responses is enhanced for those subsets that are consistent with the induced stimulus groupings. Thus, manipulations of stimulus organization influence the hierarchy of saliency and, consequently, the coding that is used to translate between the stimuli and the responses. In contrast, the influence of response grouping seems to be minimal.

In the spatial-precuing task, the hierarchy of spatial coding does not depend on the stimulus and response sets having the same orientations. When the orientation of the response set is orthogonal to that of the stimulus set, the pattern of performance is similar to that found with parallel orientations.

Within spatial dimensions themselves, another hierarchy exists. This hierarchy is based on the relative locations of the elements. In two-choice tasks, the mapping up–right/down–left consistently is preferred regardless of whether the stimulus dimension is vertical and the response dimension horizontal, or vice versa, and of whether the dimensions are physical or implied symbolically. Because other studies show that up and right are more salient than down and left, the up–right/down–left mapping preference again indicates that translation is most efficient when the salient features of the stimulus and response sets correspond.

B. ASSOCIATIVE PHASE

Through practice, performance progresses to the associative phase, which is characterized by the acquisition of unitized procedural knowledge that is specific to the particular S–R relations in the task. In this phase, the coding operations characteristic of the cognitive phase diminish in importance. For the spatial-precuing task, this diminished importance is evident in the finding that all precue conditions produce approximately equivalent benefits by the third session. Similarly, in the symbolic-cuing task, the difference between assignments decreases across the first three sessions.

The practice effects seem to reflect the development of task-specific procedures that directly specify the responses signaled by particular stimuli. Support for this point comes from transfer studies in which subjects switch to a new hand placement after three sessions of practice. In the transfer session, subjects revert to the coding that is characteristic of the cognitive phase of skill acquisition. Moreover, our retention studies indicated that the task-specific procedures of the associative phase are quite durable.

The task-specific procedures are based on the relative locations within the stimulus set. Transfer studies indicate that performance is maintained across changes in orientations of the stimulus set. However, performance is not maintained when the orientation or placement of the response set is changed in the transfer session. Thus, the task-specific procedures are less dependent on the particular stimulus set than they are on the response set.

C. AUTONOMOUS PHASE

Models of skill acquisition suggest that, given sufficient practice, an individual can develop abstract, schematic representations of a task. The task representations of this autonomous phase are more independent from the specific practice conditions and, thus, enable broader transferability. Evidence regarding the autonomous phase of skill acquisition is limited, primarily because many sessions of practice on a task are required.

We have generated preliminary evidence with the spatial- and symbolic-cuing tasks that is consistent with the proposed third stage of skill acquisition. Extended practice with the spatial-precuing task, followed by transfer to a new hand placement, results in only a tendency toward reappearance of the initial differences in precuing benefits. This result is in contrast to the complete reappearance of the differences that occurs when a lesser amount of practice precedes the transfer session. Additionally, transfer between the symbolic- and spatial-cuing tasks after extended practice indicates that the pattern of differential precuing benefits is of reduced magnitude. Thus, the data from these studies suggest that the third stage of skill acquisition in choice-reaction tasks may be characterized by an abstract response-selection schema.

D. Issues and Implications

The research described in this article illustrates the pivotal role of the S-R translation stage in human information processing. To study translation processes effectively, an approach to research is required in which properties of the stimuli and properties of the responses are covaried. The relative success of our research program is attributable in part to taking such an approach.

The importance of considering stimulus and response properties in choice-reaction tasks is analogous to the importance of considering input and output properties in tasks designed to assess human memory. A number of memory researchers have argued that manipulation of input conditions alone provides an incomplete means for inferring the basic characteristics of learning and memory (e.g., Lee, 1988; Morris, Bransford, & Franks, 1977; Tulving, 1984). That is, without manipulating output conditions, the inferred structure of memory could be a function of the particular output condition that is used. Thus, only through the consideration of interactions between input and output factors can an accurate understanding of the cognitive processes that mediate memory performance be gained. The general point that emerges is that regardless of one's specific interests regarding cognition, a research strategy that is sensitive to both stimulus and response factors likely will be more successful than one that is not.

Even for the relatively basic choice-reaction tasks examined in this article, the translation processes that characterize the cognitive phase of skill acquisition constitute the primary determinants of initial performance. Translation processes are dynamic and flexible, with the particular codings that are used being dependent on relatively subtle factors. The subtle nature of these factors is illustrated by the pattern of differential precuing benefits obtained in spatial-precuing tasks. All of the variations of this task described in this article used a direct assignment of stimulus locations to response locations. Such an assignment typically is assumed to be highly compatible, with the translation stage making only a minimal contribution to performance (e.g., Larish & Frekany, 1985). Yet, we have demonstrated an influence of translation processes for tasks involving discrete finger responses and tasks involving limb movements. Given the major influence of translation processes in the relatively simple tasks that we have examined, the likelihood is great that such processes are the predominant determinants of performance in more complex tasks (e.g., Proctor & Reeve, 1986a).

Researchers who have been most sensitive to the role of translation processes in human performance have been those who study S–R compatibility (Proctor & Reeve, 1990). Research on S–R compatibility effects constitutes one of the largest, most systematic bodies of literature in psychology. Moreover, researchers from various areas are rediscovering that the implications of compatibility extend beyond the simple mappings of stimuli to responses often studied in laboratory tasks (e.g., Kantowitz, Triggs & Barnes, 1990; Rosenbloom & Newell, 1987). These implications extend to Gibsonian theories of perception and action (Michaels, 1988, 1989), speech perception and production (Gordon, 1990), cognitive neuropsychology (Bashore, 1990; Verfaellie, Bowers, & Heilman, 1990), complex decision making (Tversky, Sattath, & Slovic, 1988), and engineering models of human performance (Eberts & Posey, 1990; John & Newell, 1990). Yet, despite the rich literature and crucial implications of research on S–R compatibility, the topic rarely is discussed at all, much less at any length, in cognitive psychology texts. Until the importance of the translation between the perception of stimuli and the subsequent execution of actions is appreciated fully, a complete understanding of human cognition cannot emerge.

ACKNOWLEDGMENTS

Much of the research reported in this article was supported by Grant #88-0002 from the Cognition Program of the Air Force Office of Scientific Research, Alfred R. Fregly, Program Manager, and John Jonides, Consultant to the Program. We would like to thank Lanie Dornier for assisting with some of the studies reported in this article, Trish Van Zandt for preparing the figures, and Julie Smith for typing the manuscript.

REFERENCES

Adams, J. A. (1971). A closed-loop theory of motor learning. *Journal of Motor Behavior*, **3**, 111–149.

Anderson, J. R. (1982). Acquisition of cognitive skill. *Psychological Review*, **89**, 369–406.

Anderson, J. R. (1983). *The architecture of cognition*. Cambridge, MA: Harvard University Press.
Anderson, J. R. (1987). Skill acquisition: Compilation of weak-method problem solutions. *Psychological Review*, **94**, 192–210.
Anzola, G. P., Bertoloni, G., Buchtel, H. A., & Rizzolatti, G. (1977). Spatial compatibility and anatomical factors in simple and choice reaction time. *Neuropsychologia*, **15**, 295–302.
Bashore, T. R. (1990). Stimulus-response compatibility viewed from a cognitive psychophysiological perspective. In R. W. Proctor & T. G. Reeve (Eds.), *Stimulus-response compatibility: An integrated perspective* (pp. 183–223). Amsterdam: North-Holland.
Brebner, J. (1973). S-R compatibility and changes in RT with practice. *Acta Psychologica*, **37**, 93–106.
Brebner, J., Shephard, M., & Cairney, P. (1972). Spatial relationships and S-R compatibility. *Acta Psychologica*, **36**, 1–15.
Bryan, W. L., & Harter, N. (1899). Studies on the telegraphic language. The acquisition of a hierarchy of habits. *Psychological Review*, **6**, 345–375.
Castiello, U., & Umiltá, C. (1987). Spatial compatibility effects in different sports. *International Journal of Sport Psychology*, **18**, 276–285.
Chase, W. G., & Simon, H. A. (1973). Perception in chess. *Cognitive Psychology*, **4**, 55–81.
Clark, H. H. (1973). Space, time, semantics, and the child. In T. E. Moore (Ed.), *Cognitive development and the acquisition of language* (pp. 27–63). New York: Academic Press.
Crossman, E. R. F. W. (1959). A theory of the acquisition of speed-skill. *Ergonomics*, **2**, 153–156.
de Jaager, J. J. (1970). Reaction time and mental processes. In J. Brozek & M. S. Sibinga (Eds. & Trans.), *Origins of psychometry*. Nieuwkoop: B. de Graaf. (Original work published 1865)
Donders, F. C. (1969). On the speed of mental processes. In W. G. Koster (Ed. & Trans.), *Attention and performance II* (pp. 412–431). Amsterdam: North-Holland. (Original work published 1868)
Dornier, L., & Reeve, T. G. (1990). Evaluation of compatibility effects in the precuing of arm and direction parameters. *Research Quarterly for Exercise and Sport*, **61**, 37–49.
Eberts, R. E., & Posey, J. W. (1990). The mental model in stimulus-response compatibility. In R. W. Proctor & T. G. Reeve (Eds.), *Stimulus-response compatibility: An integrated perspective* (pp. 389–425). Amsterdam: North-Holland.
Fitts, P. M. (1964). Perceptual-motor skill learning. In A. W. Melton (Ed.), *Categories of human learning* (pp. 243–285). New York: Academic Press.
Fitts, P. M., & Posner, M. I. (1967). *Human performance*. Belmont, CA: Brooks/Cole.
Fitts, P. M., & Seeger, C. M. (1953). S-R compatibility: Spatial characteristics of stimulus and response codes. *Journal of Experimental Psychology*, **46**, 199–210.
Goodman, D., & Kelso, J. A. S. (1980). Are movements prepared in parts? Not under compatible (naturalized) conditions. *Journal of Experimental Psychology: General*, **109**, 475–495.
Gopher, D. (1984). The contribution of vision-based imagery to the acquisition and operation of a transcription skill. In W. Prinz & A. F. Sanders (Eds.), *Cognition and motor processes* (pp. 195–208). New York: Springer-Verlag.
Gordon, P. C. (1990). Perceptual-motor processing in speech. In R. W. Proctor & T. G. Reeve (Eds.), *Stimulus-response compatibility: An integrated perspective* (pp. 343–362). Amsterdam: North Holland.
Heister, G., Schroeder-Heister, P., & Ehrenstein, W. H. (1990). Spatial coding and spatial-

anatomical mapping: Evidence for a hierarchical model of spatial stimulus-response compatibility. In R. W. Proctor & T. G. Reeve (Eds.), *Stimulus-response compatibility: An integrated perspective* (pp. 117–143). Amsterdam: North-Holland.

Henry, F. M., & Rogers, D. E. (1960). Increased response latency for complicated movements and a "memory drum" theory of neuromotor reaction. *Research Quarterly,* **31,** 448–458.

John, B. E., & Newell, A. (1990). Toward an engineering model of stimulus-response compatibility. In R. W. Proctor & T. G. Reeve (Eds.), *Stimulus-response compatibility: An integrated perspective* (pp. 427–479). Amsterdam: North-Holland.

Kantowitz, B. H., Triggs, T. J., & Barnes, V. E. (1990). Stimulus-response compatibility and human factors. In R. W. Proctor & T. G. Reeve (Eds.), *Stimulus-response compatibility: An integrated perspective* (pp. 365–388). Amsterdam: North-Holland.

Klapp, S. T., Greim, D. M., Mendicino, C. M., & Koenig, R. S. (1979). Anatomic and environmental dimensions of stimulus-response compatibility: Implications for theories of memory coding. *Acta Psychologica,* **43,** 367–379.

Koffka, K. (1963). *Principles of gestalt psychology.* New York: Harcourt, Brace, & World. (Original work published 1935)

Lachman, R., Lachman, J. L., & Butterfield, E. C. (1979). *Cognitive psychology and information processing: An introduction.* Hillsdale, NJ: Erlbaum.

Ladavas, E., & Moscovitch, M. (1984). Must egocentric and environmental frames of reference be aligned to produce spatial S-R compatibility effects? *Journal of Experimental Psychology: Human Perception and Performance,* **10,** 205–215.

Larish, D. D. (1986). Influence of stimulus-response translation on response programming: Examining the relationship of arm, direction, and extent of movement. *Acta Psychologica,* **61,** 53–70.

Larish, D. D., & Frekany, G. A. (1985). Planning and preparing expected and unexpected movements: Reexamining the relationship of arm, direction, and extent of movement. *Journal of Motor Behavior,* **17,** 168–189.

Lee, T. D. (1988). Transfer-appropriate processing: A framework for conceptualizing practice effects in motor learning. In D. G. Meijer & K. Roth (Eds.), *Complex movement behaviour: The motor-action controversy* (pp. 201–215). Amsterdam: North-Holland.

Michaels, C. F. (1988). S-R compatibility between response position and destination of apparent motion: Evidence of the detection of affordances. *Journal of Experimental Psychology: Human Perception and Performance,* **14,** 231–240.

Michaels, C. F. (1989). S-R compatibilities depend on eccentricity of responding hand. *Quarterly Journal of Experimental Psychology,* **41A,** 263–272.

Miller, J. (1982). Discrete versus continuous models of human information processing: In search of partial output. *Journal of Experimental Psychology: Human Perception and Performance,* **8,** 273–296.

Miller, J. (1985). A hand advantage in preparation of simple keypress responses: Reply to Reeve and Proctor (1984). *Journal of Experimental Psychology: Human Perception and Performance,* **11,** 221–233.

Morris, C. D., Bransford, J. D., & Franks, J. J. (1977). Levels of processing versus transfer appropriate processing. *Journal of Verbal Learning and Verbal Behavior,* **16,** 519–533.

Newell, A., & Rosenbloom, P. (1981). Mechanisms of skill acquisition and the law of practice. In J. R. Anderson (Ed.), *Cognitive skills and their acquisition* (pp. 1–56). Hillsdale, NJ: Erlbaum.

Nicoletti, R., Anzola, G. P., Luppino, G., Rizzolatti, G., & Umiltá, C. (1982). Spatial compatibility effects on the same side of the body midline. *Journal of Experimental Psychology: Human Perception and Performance,* **8,** 664–673.

Nicoletti, R., Umiltá, C., Tressoldi, E. P., & Marzi, C. A. (1988). Why are left-right spatial codes easier to form than above-below ones? *Perception & Psychophysics, 43,* 287–292.

Pomerantz, J. R., & Kubovy, M. (1986). Theoretical approaches to perceptual organization: Simplicity and likelihood principles. In K. R. Boff, L. Kaufman, & J. P. Thomas (Eds.), *Handbook of perception and human performance: Vol. II. Cognitive processes and performance* (pp. 36-1–36-46). New York: Wiley.

Posner, M. I. (1978). *Chronometric explorations of mind.* Hillsdale, NJ: Erlbaum.

Posner, M. I., Peterson, S. E., Fox, P. T., & Raichle, M. E. (1988). Localization of cognitive operations in the human brain. *Science, 240,* 1627–1631.

Proctor, R. W., & Reeve, T. G. (1985). Compatibility effects in the assignment of symbolic stimuli to discrete finger responses. *Journal of Experimental Psychology: Human Perception and Performance, 11,* 623–639.

Proctor, R. W., & Reeve, T. G. (1986a). A caution regarding use of the hint procedure to determine whether partial stimulus information activates responses. *Perception & Psychophysics, 40,* 110–118.

Proctor, R. W., & Reeve, T. G. (1986b). Salient-feature coding operations in spatial precuing tasks. *Journal of Experimental Psychology: Human Perception and Performance, 12,* 277–285.

Proctor, R. W., & Reeve, T. G. (1988). The acquisition of task-specific productions and modification of declarative representations in spatial-precuing tasks. *Journal of Experimental Psychology: General, 117,* 182–196.

Proctor, R. W., & Reeve, T. G. (1989). Stimulus–response compatibility in spatial precuing and symbolic identification: Effects of coding, practice, retention, and transfer. *Final Rep. No. AFOSR-88-0002.* Washington, D.C.: Air Force Office of Scientific Research.

Proctor, R. W., & Reeve, T. G. (Eds.), (1990). *Stimulus-response compatibility: An integrated perspective.* Amsterdam: North-Holland.

Proctor, R. W., Reeve, T. G., & Weeks, D. J., Dornier, L., & Van Zandt, T. (1990). A skill-acquisition perspective on performance in spatial-precuing and symbolic-cuing tasks. Manuscript submitted for publication.

Reeve, T. G., & Proctor, R. W. (1984). On the advance preparation of discrete finger responses. *Journal of Experimental Psychology: Human Perception and Performance, 10,* 541–553.

Reeve, T. G., & Proctor, R. W. (1985). Nonmotoric translation processes in the preparation of discrete finger responses: A rebuttal of Miller's (1985) analysis. *Journal of Experimental Psychology: Human Perception and Performance, 11,* 234–240.

Reeve, T. G., & Proctor, R. W. (1988). Determinants of two-choice reaction-time patterns for same-hand and different-hand finger pairings. *Journal of Motor Behavior, 20,* 317–340.

Reeve, T. G., Proctor, R. W., Weeks, D. J., & Dornier, L. (1990a). *Correspondence between stimulus- and response-set orientations in spatial-precuing tasks.* Manuscript submitted for publication.

Reeve, T. G., Proctor, R. W., Weeks, D. J., & Dornier, L. (1990b). *Manipulating the saliency of stimulus and response features in spatial-precuing tasks.* Manuscript submitted for publication.

Riggio, L., Gawryszewski, L. de G., & Umiltá, C. (1986). What is crossed in crossed-hand effects? *Acta Psychologica, 62,* 89–100.

Rosenbaum, D. A. (1980). Human movement initiation: Specification of arm, direction, and extent. *Journal of Experimental Psychology: General, 109,* 444–474.

Rosenbaum, D. A. (1983). The movement precuing technique: Assumptions, applications and extensions. In R. A. Magill (Ed.), *Memory and control of action* (pp. 231–274). Amsterdam: North-Holland.

Rosenbloom, P. S., & Newell, A. (1987). An integrated computational model of stimulus-response compatibility and practice. In G. H. Bower (Ed.), *The psychology of learning and motivation* (Vol. 21, pp. 1–52). San Diego, CA: Academic Press.

Rumelhart, D. E., & Norman, D. A. (1982). Simulating a skilled typist: A study of cognitive motor performance. *Cognitive Science, 6,* 1–36.

Schmidt, R. A. (1982). *Motor control and learning: A behavioral emphasis.* Champaign, IL: Human Kinetics.

Sholl, M. J., & Egeth, H. E. (1981). Right-left confusion in the adult: A verbal labeling effect. *Memory & Cognition, 9,* 339–350.

Simon, J. R. (1990). The effects of an irrelevant directional cue on human information processing. In R. W. Proctor & T. G. Reeve (Eds.), *Stimulus-response compatibility: An integrated perspective* (pp. 31–86). Amsterdam: North-Holland.

Snoddy, G. S. (1926). Learning and stability. *Journal of Applied Psychology, 10,* 1–36.

Sternberg, S. (1969). The discovery of processing stages: Extensions of Donders' method. In W. G. Koster (Ed.), *Attention and performance II* (pp. 276–315). Amsterdam: North-Holland.

Teichner, W. H., & Krebs, M. J. (1974). Laws of visual choice reaction time. *Psychological Review, 81,* 75–98.

Tulving, E. (1984). *Elements of episodic memory.* New York: Oxford University Press.

Tversky, A., Sattath, S., & Slovic, P. (1988). Contingent weighting in judgment and choice. *Psychological Review, 95,* 371–384.

Umiltá, C., & Nicoletti, R. (1990). Spatial stimulus-response compatibility. In R. W. Proctor & T. G. Reeve (Eds.), *Stimulus-response compatibility: An integrated perspective.* Amsterdam: North-Holland.

Uttal, W. R. (1973). *The psychobiology of sensory coding.* New York: Harper & Row.

Verfaellie, M., Bowers, D., & Heilman, K. M. (1990). Attentional processes in spatial stimulus-response compatibility. In R. W. Proctor & T. G. Reeve (Eds.), *Stimulus-response compatibility: An integrated perspective* (pp. 261–275). Amsterdam: North-Holland.

Wallace, R. J. (1971). S-R compatibility and the idea of a response code. *Journal of Experimental Psychology, 93,* 163–168.

Weeks, D. J., & Proctor, R. W. (in press). Salient-features coding in the translation between orthogonal stimulus and response dimensions. *Journal of Experimental Psychology: General.*

Welford, A. T. (1976). *Skilled performance: Perceptual and motor skills.* Glenview, IL: Scott, Foresman.

West, L. J., & Sabban, Y. (1982). Hierarchy of stroking habits at the typewriter. *Journal of Applied Psychology, 67,* 370–376.

Zelaznik, H. N. (1978). Precuing response factors in choice reaction time: A word of caution. *Journal of Motor Behavior, 10,* 77–79.

THE STRUCTURE AND FORMATION OF NATURAL CATEGORIES

Douglas Fisher
Pat Langley

I. Introduction

Cognitive simulation fits computational mechanisms to the constraints of psychological data, but there has been long-term debate over the appropriate starting point for this process. Newell and Simon (1972) recommend an initial task analysis, in which one identifies alternative approaches to a given task (e.g., cryptarithmetic). Anderson (in press) suggests a more formal rational analysis, in which one associates a general category of behaviors (e.g., concept formation) with a performance function to be optimized. In both views, the guiding assumption is that natural organisms are rational but resource-bounded decision makers (Simon, 1969). A similar but less formal view is implicit in speculative analyses (Hall & Kibler, 1985), which posit high-level computational principles that constrain human processing (e.g., Kolodner, 1983).

This article focuses on COBWEB (Fisher, 1987a, 1987b), a cognitive simulation of concept formation and recognition. In particular, we trace the origins of the system to rational and speculative analyses of this task. Concept formation is a process of organizing observations into categories based on internalized measures of category "quality," without the aid of an external tutor. Moreover, this process of category formation should be guided by two principles. First, learning should be incremental, in that observations should be efficiently incorporated into memory as they are encountered. Second, learning should benefit performance on some task, in this case predictions about unknown properties of novel observations.

To realize these objectives, the COBWEB model borrows a measure of concept quality developed by Gluck and Corter (1985) in their work on *basic-level effects* in humans (also see Corter & Gluck, 1985). In hierarchical classification schemes, humans tend to prefer one level of abstraction (the "basic" level) over others. Gluck and Corter's measure, *category utility,* came from a rational analysis which postulated that basic concepts are preferred because they optimize inference ability. COBWEB also incorporates ideas from Kolodner's (1983) CYRUS and Lebowitz's (1982) UNIMEM, which provide general strategies of efficient classification and concept formation. This union yields a system that meets the computational objectives of efficient retrieval and accurate prediction. In addition, the model accounts for certain *typicality* effects (Rosch & Mervis, 1975) and *fan* effects (Anderson, 1976). Thus, it provides a unified account for a number of memory phenomena in a single, parameter-free model of concept representation and concept formation.

In the following section, we introduce some computational and psychological principles of concept learning and representation. Notably, we view concept formation and related tasks in terms of *search* through a state space. After this, Section III reviews psychological findings that constrain the representation, access, and acquisition of concepts. In Section IV we describe COBWEB, a model of concept formation that incorporates these constraints. Section V then evaluates the model in terms of its ability to explain a variety of psychological effects and the relation among them. In the final section, we speculate on other applications of the model, including the transition from novice to expert problem-solving skills. Implicitly, our discussion will endorse Anderson's rational view of cognitive simulation as a profitable methodology to pursue issues at the boundary of cognitive psychology and artificial intelligence.

II. Concept Learning

Concept learning has been widely studied in both artificial intelligence (AI) and psychology. However, both fields have traditionally emphasized learning tasks in which a tutor provides class information. We begin this section by discussing methods for such supervised learning, since they provide important background for our later discussion of concept formation. In particular, we introduce the view of concept learning as a search process, in which learning mechanisms may vary along two dimensions:

search control and search direction. We then extend the search framework to clustering and concept formation, types of unsupervised learning in which there is no external tutor to provide class information.

A. SUPERVISED LEARNING

Many psychological studies of learning have focused on concept acquisition or identification (Bruner, Goodnow, & Austin, 1956; Hunt, Marin, & Stone, 1966; Medin & Schaffer, 1978; Reed, 1972), in which a subject must learn to identify novel members of categories, given training observations that are classified by the experimenter. In many experimental settings, the subject is shown a sequence of observations; after viewing each observation, the subject must predict the category membership of that observation and is then told the correct category. Thus, the experimental setting usually requires continuous and active participation by the subject. Psychological investigations have focused on characterizing the number of observations that subjects require to consistently predict correct category membership and on the number of classification errors made before they attain criterial accuracy.

Because it involves external feedback, concept acquisition is sometimes referred to as supervised learning. In artificial intelligence, this task is more commonly called learning from examples (Dietterich & Michalski, 1983; Mitchell, 1982; Quinlan, 1979; Winston, 1975), since a tutor supplies preclassified examples from which the learning system must discover an appropriate concept (intensional) description. Many machine learning systems assume that the target concept to be learning is conjunctive; thus the learner acquires concept(s) that capture shared conditions over all of the observations.

The notion of *search* plays a traditional role in characterizing AI systems, and one can apply this idea to systems that learn concepts (Mitchell, 1982; Simon & Lea, 1974). One important aspect is the direction of the search process. Many AI concept-learning systems begin by comparing two observations and extracting the commonalities between them (F. Hayes-Roth & McDermott, 1978; Vere, 1980). They then compare these common features to a third observation, again extracting the collective commonality. This process continues until they have exhausted all the observations, thus yielding the common structure that summarizes the entire set. This strategy follows a specific-to-general direction, since the set of common features is initialized as a specific instance and gradually becomes more general as more observations are seen. In contrast, other systems follow a general-to-specific strategy (Langley, 1987; Schlimmer & Fisher, 1986). These systems begin with very general concept descriptions, making them more specific as errors suggest the need for more constrained conditions. Further errors lead to even more specific concepts, until they achieve a description that summarizes all the training instances. Still other systems (Anderson & Kline, 1979; Mitchell, 1982; Schlimmer & Granger, 1986) combine these two strategies, carrying out bidirectional search through the space of concept descriptions.

Concept learning systems also vary in terms of their search control strategy. In general, there will be many concept descriptions that cover the training observations, and one must somehow deal with these alternatives. For example, suppose the learner sees two card hands, one with three Jacks and two Kings, and a second with two Jacks and three Kings. One hypothesis that summarizes these observations is that the hands contain at least two Jacks and at least two Kings, but an alternative summary is that they contain two cards of one face and three of another (i.e., a full house). Such alternatives are the cause of search in concept learning, and researchers have used a variety of strategies to control this search. These methods range from exhaustive techniques like breadth-first search, which retain all concepts that are consistent with the known observations (e.g., Mitchell, 1982), to heuristic methods like beam search (Michalski, 1983), which retains only the "best" hypotheses that are consistent with the observations.

Unlike experimental human subjects in psychology, many AI learning systems are not required to actively predict class membership for each incoming observation. Rather, they process all available observations en masse to produce a set of concept descriptions that are consistent with the observations. This is not to say that many systems could not be adapted to actively predict membership, but they were not designed with this performance task in mind. For instance, Quinlan's (1979, 1986) ID3 algorithm uses a heuristic that requires examination of all observations, thus complicating any strategy for generating intermediate predictions. However, one can modify the basic method to construct descriptions incrementally (Schlimmer & Fisher, 1986; Utgoff, 1988), giving it the ability to make predictions after each training instance.

Although nonincremental approaches have predominated in the literature on machine learning, a growing number of researchers have examined incremental methods for concept learning. Examples include a system by Winston (1975) and Schlimmer and Granger's (1986) STAGGER system, which generate predictions for each incoming observation. One can view such systems as conducting a form of constrained search called hill climbing, which maintains a single "active" concept description that may be modified after each training instance.[1] These systems keep no explicit memory of previous hypotheses, though they may simulate backtracking (return to an earlier hypothesis) by application of their learning mechanisms.

Limiting search to one change per observation characterizes hill-climbing learners: A single alternative is kept in memory and intermediate predictions are made efficiently. Of course, placing limits on memory and backtracking ability means that the order of training instances can have an important effect, sometimes leading the learning system astray. However, such order effects have also been observed in human learners. (e.g., Kline, 1983), making them desirable characteristics of a computational model. We will return to the notion of incremental hill climbing when we discuss the task of concept formation.

B. UNSUPERVISED LEARNING

Despite the attractiveness of supervised learning tasks, there are many scenarios in which a learner cannot rely on external feedback. In such cases, the learner must invoke internalized heuristics to organize its observations. For example, many machine learning systems incorporate a notion of "similarity." Such a bias also occurs in work on numerical taxonomy (Everitt, 1980; Gennari, 1989), in which algorithms use a similarity measure (e.g., the inverse of Euclidean distance) to group similar observations into the same category.

To clarify this point, let us consider some algorithms from the numerical taxonomy literature. For instance, "nearest-neighbor" methods place an observation in the category that has the most similar current member. Other methods compute a theoretical observation that represents the central tendency (i.e., the centroid) of each category; they then place the new observation with the category having the most similar centroid. These methods have the emergent effect of placing great emphasis on maximizing the intracategory (i.e, within-category) similarity of observations.

Although this approach has intuitive appeal, it presents difficulties if one wishes to break the observations into a number of contrasting categories. In reference to psychological models, Medin (1983) points out that

---

[1] Not all incremental learning systems should be viewed as hill climbers. For instance, some methods (Anderson & Kline, 1979; Langley, 1987) retain a large set of competing descriptions, using the competitor with the highest "strength" to make a prediction. In addition, Winston's system is not a strict hill climber in that it retains some true backtracking ability, but nonetheless it has many of the characteristics that we deem important for incremental learning.

the set of singleton categories optimizes intracategory similarity, since each observation is maximally similar to itself. Thus, attention on intracategory similarity alone does not provide a sufficient basis for deciding upon the appropriate number of clusters. As a result, clustering methods often require that the user specify the number of categories to be formed. Alternatively, they build a tree called a dendogram, in which each node specifies a cluster of lower-level nodes, terminating in individual observations. Following the clustering process, the user severs the tree at various points to obtain the desired number of clusters.

Some techniques of numerical taxonomy explicitly seek to optimize a function of contrasting categories. However, just as intracategory similarity favors singleton classes, intercategory dissimilarity favors a single all-inclusive category, since there are no contrasting categories to share properties with it (Medin, 1983). Thus, a reliance on both these measures might reduce the need for user intervention. To this end, some methods incorporate a trade-off between intragroup and intergroup similarities, favoring categories whose members have much in common with each other and little in common with members of contrasting categories. In Section III we examine one such trade-off function.

Recently, machine learning researchers have developed methods for conceptual clustering. For example, Michalski and Stepp's (1983) CLUSTER attempts to form categories that have "good" concept descriptions, which can be stated as conjunctive expressions of features that are common to all or most category members. One criterion, simplicity, dictates that the conjunctive expression should be short for the sake of comprehensibility. A second criterion, fit, prefers detailed (specific) conjunctive descriptions. These criteria (and others) trade off against one another in much the same way as intracategory and intercategory similarity. The ability to form very simple discriminating concepts for contrasting categories implies very little overlap between members of different categories, whereas forming specific categories implies that there is considerable intracategory similarity.[2]

Other nonincremental clustering systems include Hanson and Bauer's (1989) WITT and Cheeseman *et al.*'s (1988) AUTOCLASS. The former computes correlations between feature pairs, forming clusters so as to maximize the intracategory pairwise correlations across all features and to minimize the average intercategory pairwise correlations across all fea-

---

[2]Studies by Medin, Wattenmaker, and Michalski (1986) qualify the extent to which fit and simplicity trade against each other in human sorting tasks in which subjects have simultaneous access to all observations. Their experimental task corresponds to nonincremental, unsupervised learning.

tures and all contrasting categories. AUTOCLASS represents another probabilistic approach to clustering, using a Bayesian method to calculate the "most probable" categories present in the observations. Intuitively, the most probable clusters are those whose feature distributions vary most from a presumed prior distribution. As with WITT, AUTOCLASS is sensitive to intracategory and intercategory similarities, and thus need not be told the number of clusters to form. The systems are also similar in their lack of any method for making intermediate predictions.[3] We now turn to methods for unsupervised learning that support continuous interaction with the environment.

C. Concept Formation

The unsupervised systems that we have described so far are nonincremental, requiring all training instances at the outset. However, in many cases human learners appear to assimilate instances as they become available. We will refer to this process—the incremental unsupervised acquisition of categories and their intensional descriptions—as *concept formation*. As with learning from examples, concept formation can be described in terms of search, and two general approaches have been explored in psychology and machine learning.

The first scheme employs a specific-to-general search, incrementally comparing each new observation to existing categories and adding it to one or more of the best-matching categories. In Kolodner's (1983) CYRUS and Lebowitz's (1982) UNIMEM, matching is a function of the number of features shared by the new observation and a given concept description. These systems generalize a concept if the match with the new observation is sufficiently good. If an observation does not match any concept to a prespecified degree then the new observation is used to create a singleton category that may be generalized with future observations. In this process, UNIMEM and CYRUS form an abstraction hierarchy of concepts that they use to classify future cases, filtering each observation through levels of the hierarchy by recursive application of the matching procedure. Both systems can be viewed as advanced versions of Feigenbaum's (1963) EPAM, which formed discrimination networks (actually trees) with tests that were restricted to single features.

One can also employ a general-to-specific strategy for concept formation, as shown by Martin's (1989) CORA system. Like its precursor

---

[3]Hanson and Bauer note that their system can be run in incremental mode, but it was not designed with prediction in mind. In contrast, AUTOCLASS is strongly motivated by the need for accurate prediction, but it is nonincremental.

STAGGER (Schlimmer & Granger, 1986), the model incrementally conjoins features, but it relies on correlations between features to trigger this chunking process rather than monitoring correct and incorrect predictions of category membership. CORA's reliance on feature correlations is similar to that used in WITT, but it descends most directly from Chalnick and Billman's (1988) work. However, whereas CORA uses observed correlations to conjoin features, its ancestor uses observed correlations to slowly generalize initially saved instances. Neither CORA nor the earlier system forms an abstraction hierarchy; they simply create concepts that are conjunctions of features and that describe (possibly nondisjoint) categories.

Although approaches to concept formation may differ in search direction, they seem to universally share the hill-climbing organization of their incremental counterparts for supervised learning. As such, they may suffer from ordering effects, in that they may discover different categories depending on the order in which they process observations. The design of concept-formation methods differs from that of nonincremental clustering systems in that it is largely motivated by the realization that many real-world domains require continuous interaction with the environment. Mechanisms for concept formation are designed to be rational but resource-bounded learners (Simon, 1969). Each observation triggers small changes to the current categorical structure, although simulated forms of backtracking may be used to ensure that major changes can occur over time. For example, UNIMEM deletes a node and its associated subtree if the node's corresponding concept becomes poor by a criterion similar to CLUSTER/2's fit measure. This allows a new subtree to be grown to reflect the characteristics of future data. Section IV elaborates on some of these issues in the context of our COBWEB system.

III. Psychological Constraints on Concept Formation

The previous section touched upon psychological considerations in concept learning, but its main focus was on search as a generic framework in which to view this task. This section considers psychological findings in greater detail, notably typicality and basic-level effects, along with their implications for the representation and formation of concepts.

A. Typicality Effects and Probabilistic Concepts

Smith and Medin (1981) refer to conjunctive descriptions, discussed earlier, as classical representations of conceptual structure. One implication of such classical representations is that all concept members are treated equally during classification, since an observation either has the requisite conjunction of features or it does not. However, experiments have repeatedly shown that human subjects do not treat concept instances equally, but regard certain members as more typical than others. For example, in a target-recognition task, subjects must determine if a test instance is a member of a target category (e.g., "Is a *robin* a *bird?*"). Several studies (Rips, Shoben, & Smith 1973: Rosch & Mervis, 1975) indicate that subjects consistently respond affirmatively more quickly to certain positive instances than to others. For example, they may more quickly affirm that a robin is a bird than they will affirm that a chicken is a bird. The relative ranking of positive test items corresponds to a typicality ranking of category members, and this conclusion is bolstered by results in a variety of other experimental tasks (Mervis & Rosch 1981; Smith & Medin, 1981).

1. *Probabilistic Concepts: Independent Cue Models*

Classical representations do not easily account for typicality effects, and in response, researchers have proposed a number of alternative concept representations. Rosch and Mervis (1975) made an early attempt to discover the structural determinants of typicality, finding that category members sharing features with many other members of the same category tend to be judged more typical. In addition, when a disjoint, contrasting category is involved, members that share few features with members of the contrasting category tend to be judged more typical. This sensitivity to intracategory and intercategory overlap of features is captured by the notion of *family resemblance* (Rosch & Mervis, 1975).

The apparent relation between family resemblance and typicality indicates the importance of feature distributions in human classification. Although classical representations cannot capture such distributional information, probabilistic concept representations (Smith & Medin, 1981) manage this by associating a probability, weight, or some other confidence number with each feature of a concept definition. A straightforward implementation is to store the conditional probability, $P(f|C_k)$, of each feature f's presence with respect to each category C_k; this is more commonly called the *category validity* (Medin, 1983) of the feature. Recognition or classification using probabilistic concepts usually involves summing the weights of features that are present in a new observation (Collins & Loftus, 1975; Smith & Medin, 1981; Smith, Shoben, & Rips, 1974). Classification may be based on whether this sum passes a specified threshold (Smith & Medin, 1981), as in neuronlike processing units (Hinton, 1989; Nilsson,

1965), or one may assign an observation to the category that maximizes the sum, as in Bayesian classifiers (Duda & Hart, 1973).

The probabilistic account offers an explanation of typicality effects in that typical instances will have features shared by many other members of the same category, giving them higher category validities. If one assumes that recognition time is inversely proportional to these sums, then observations with high intracategory similarity will be recognized more quickly and thus be regarded as more typical. On its own, this scheme does not explain the impact of intercategory similarity on typicality, but one can easily imagine extensions that include cue validities (the conditional probability of a category given a feature).

A more important limitation of this model stems from the fact that the recognition procedure is based on individual, presumably independent, category validities. For this reason, it has been called the *independent-cue* model of concepts. A number of authors (Hanson & Bauer, 1989; Medin, 1983; Smith & Medin, 1981) point out that independent-cue models are representationally incomplete, since summation of individual weights limits recognition to linearly separable categories (Nilsson, 1965). More generally, independent-cue models do not capture the feature correlations that are necessary for completeness and to which humans seem naturally attuned (Medin, 1983; Mervis & Rosch, 1981).

2. *Alternatives to Independent Cue Models*

The apparent inability of independent-cue models to capture bundles of correlated features has led to a number of alternative models. One way to keep track of feature correlations is simply to remember instances of a concept, since each instance can be viewed as a maximally specific conjunction of features. This is the approach taken in exemplar representations (Smith and Medin, 1981). An example of this approach is Reed's (1972) proximity model, which retains an extensional listing of a concept's known members, classifying a new object as a member of a category, C_k, if it matches another member of C_k more closely than a member of a contrasting category.

A disadvantage of the proximity model is that retaining an extensional listing of known category instances becomes expensive as the number of observations grows. In response, some systems (Aha & Kibler, 1989) selectively retain only certain useful observations. A simple strategy is to retain only observations that resulted in a misclassification during learning.[4]

---

[4]All of the exemplar models that we have reviewed assume a supervised learning scenario, but similar best-match procedures for classification are used in the single-linkage clustering methods that we discussed in Section II, B (Everitt, 1980).

Computational experiments demonstrate this strategy's advantage in terms of storage, but they also show accuracy benefits, presumably because idiosyncratic observations are ignored and thus are not used in classification.

In contrast to selective retention, Medin and Schaffer's (1978) context model supports a form of abstraction through selective attention. In particular, the model allows that a subject may not attend to a feature, effectively dropping the feature from an observation. Classification assumes that a new instance matches in parallel against the stored exemplars of each contrasting category, causing sufficiently matching exemplars to be retrieved; an assumption is that an exemplar is retrieved with a probability proportional to the degree that it matches the observation. An observation is classified with the first concept for which a specified number of exemplars is retrieved. Presumably, the context model would account for typicality effects, since new typical instances would more closely match the typical observations currently stored; thus, a criterial number of retrieved exemplars would tend to be reached more quickly for typical instances.

Nosofsky's (1987) generalized context model extends ideas of selective attention by allowing features to be weighted. Aha and McNulty (1989) demonstrate how these weights can be learned in a supervised task. Feature weights serve to divert attention away from uninformative features—those distributed across members of many categories—and to focus attention on informative features in classification. This variable treatment of features can capture the importance of intracategory and intercategory overlap, and adaptations should model a variety of typicality effects.[5]

Another alternative class of models assumes a *relational-cue* representation, which generalizes on the independent-cue approach. Like their precursors, relational-cue models maintain probabilities (weights, confidence values) for individual features in concept descriptions, but they also permit joint probabilities of larger features configurations, such as $p(\text{Color} = \text{red} \land \text{Size} = \text{large} \land \text{Shape} = \text{sphere} | C_k)$. Syntactically, these models are also generalizations of exemplar models, since an instance can be viewed as a conjunction of features. However, the representational power of exemplar and relational-cue models is theoretically equivalent, since one can use stored exemplars, as needed, to compute all the information used in relational-cue models.

One example of a relational-cue model is B. Hayes-Roth and Hayes-

---

[5]Feature weighting appears to serve a purpose that is similar to reasons for feature weights in independent-cue models, but exemplar models do not force a category to be represented by a single summary description as do single independent-cue concepts.

Roth's (1977) property-set model, which supposes that a feature conjunction is stored with a count of the observations in which it occurred. A new observation is classified with the concept that contains the most "diagnostic" conjunction of features (i.e., the combination with the highest cue validity). The feature conjunction for which $P(C_k|\langle\text{conjunction}\rangle)$ is maximized (over all C_k) dictates that an observation that satisfies the conjunction should be classified as a member of C_k. The property-set model stores the frequencies needed to compute cue validities (rather than category validities) for all single features and conjunctions of features.

In many cases, a feature combination may be useless for classification; trivially, if small objects are equally split between two classes, then smallness alone will give no help in classification. Thus, a reasonable storage strategy would throw out feature conjunctions that do not aid classification (e.g., those with cue validities that are roughly equal for all categories). This strategy has been used for supervised learning by Anderson and Kline's (1979) ACT and by Schlimmer and Granger's (1986) STAGGER, whereas Chalnick and Billman (1988) have used relational-cue representations for concept formation. The latter system removes features that do not add to the informativeness of a composite feature. Martin (1989) takes the opposite approach, adding features to a conjunction only if they add to the informativeness of the conjunction.

3. Probabilistic Concept Hierarchies

Exemplar and relational-cue models both address a purported weakness of independent cue models—their inability to explicitly capture correlations between features. However, as we will show, this limitation does not apply to networks of independent-cue representations. A combination of such concepts has the same representational power as exemplar and relational-cue models. Similar completeness arguments occur in the literature on neural computing (Nilsson, 1965), where networks of simple classifiers (e.g., linear threshold units) can achieve representational completeness even though their components are severely limited.

As we have noted, concepts that are represented using independent cues are individually limited to the recognition of linearly separable categories. Medin (1983) suggests that if independent-cue models are the basis of human conceptual structure, then linearly separable categories should be easier to learn than nonlinearly separable ones. An investigation into this question required that subjects learn, under supervision, one of the two category pairs displayed in Table 1. Observations were characterized in terms of four binary-valued attributes, A_1 through A_4. Subjects judged the linearly separable set more difficult to learn, and this set also resulted

TABLE I
Linearly Separable and Nonlinearly Separable Categories[a]

	Category C_1					Category C_2			
	V_1	V_2	V_3	V_4		V_1	V_2	V_3	V_4
				Linearly separable objects					
1)	1	1	1	0	5)	1	0	1	0
2)	1	0	1	1	6)	0	1	1	0
3)	1	1	0	1	7)	0	0	0	1
4)	0	1	1	1	8)	1	1	0	0
				Nonlinearly separable objects					
9)	1	0	0	0	13)	0	0	0	1
10)	1	0	1	0	14)	0	1	0	0
11)	1	1	1	1	15)	1	0	1	1
12)	0	1	1	1	16)	0	0	0	0

[a]From Medin (1983).

in more recognition errors. Gluck, Bower, and Hee (1989) have accounted for similar data with a relational-cue model in which pairwise composite cues are used to convert the nonlinearly separable categories to linearly separable categories. This transformation makes the concept easier to learn in composite-cue space than the original linearly separable categories.

An alternative account of these data exploits the notion of probabilistic concept hierarchies. Consider the concept trees of Fig. 1, which discriminate the category pairs of Medin's experiments.[6] An independent-cue

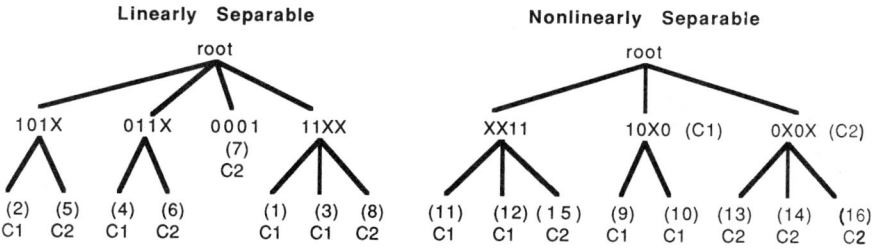

Fig. 1. Concept trees over nonlinearly and linearly separable categories.

[6]For simplicity, the concepts for the nodes in Fig. 1 are abbreviated by a pattern (e.g., 101X) that is common to all category (node) members; X denotes an attribute in which no single value is common to all members (i.e., a "don't care" condition).

model insists that each node divides the total set of observations into linearly separable categories. However, this division need not correspond to the sets that were taught, C_1 and C_2. Rather, like a decision tree (Quinlan, 1986) or discrimination network (Feigenbaum, 1963; Feigenbaum & Simon, 1984; Kolodner, 1983), members of a given class may reside in distinct portions of the hierarchy.

One can think of tree construction as being guided by the simple heuristic of grouping objects having the most features in common. The actual method used to form the hierarchies in the figure is more complicated (as described in Section III, B), but the simplification is consistent with this technique and with intuitions about independent-cue representations. The trees reveal that several atypical members of C_1 in the linear separable set share many properties with C_2 and vice versa. Thus, these similar items are reasonably placed within the same middle-level nodes of the hierarchy. Observation 7 is quite unlike any other instance, placing it in a separate category. On the other hand, there are fairly specific patterns that perfectly discriminate many members of contrasting categories in the nonlinear domain. Medin's finding can be explained in terms of the average depth to which observations must be classified before one can perfectly distinguish members of C_1 from C_2. The linearly separable set requires an average depth of 1.87 before reaching a node that contains only members of one category; in contrast, the nonlinearly separable set has 1.37 as its average depth.

Our demonstration is simplified, but it nonetheless illustrates that hierarchies or other networks of independent-cue concepts have the same representational power as exemplar and relational-cue models. Linearly separable representations direct classification to deeper levels of the tree until a perfect discrimination can be made. In addition to their representational strength, hierarchies offer efficiency advantages. A tree structure allows recognition to occur in logarithmic time as a function of stored observations, rather than in linear or exponential time, as it does for some alternatives. We now turn our attention to heuristics for guiding the formation of such concept hierarchies, focusing on the evidence for preferred concepts in human memory.

B. Basic-Level Effects and Concept Quality

Psychological studies have shown that, within hierarchical classification schemes, there appears to be a basic level preferred by human subjects. For example, in a hierarchy containing {animal, vertebrate, mammal, dog, collie}, subject behavior may indicate that "dog" lies at the basic level. Rosch, Mervis, Gray, Johnson, and Boyes-Braem (1976) used a target-recognition task to show that subjects are quicker to confirm that a test item is a member of such a basic category than they are for a superordinate or subordinate category. In a forced naming task (Jolicour, Gluck, & Kosslyn, 1984; Rosch et al., 1976), a subject is shown a picture of a particular item and asked to respond with its identity.

1. Early Measures for Predicting the Basic Level

The identification of preferred concepts in humans must constrain any model of human classification, and it may also provide a basis for principled measures of concept quality for use in concept formation by human and machine. In fact, researchers have proposed a number of measures designed to predict the basic level. An early proposal (Rosch et al., 1976) postulated that a basic-level category maximizes the total cue validity of a category over features that are shared by all or most members of the category (i.e., only features with high category validity). This can be stated formally as

$$\Sigma_j P(C_k|V_j) \quad \text{for features } V_j, \text{ such that } P(V_j|C_k) \approx 1.0.$$

Rosch did not specify how close to unity a category validity must come before it is included in the calculation of total cue validity.

Jones (1983) has proposed another measure, called *collocation*, that directly incorporates category validity into the prediction of basic level. This function can be stated as

$$\text{collocation}(V_j, C_k) = P(C_k|V_j)P(V_j|C_k).$$

He argued that a basic-level node (e.g., *bird*) has more collocation-maximizing values among its ancestral-related nodes (e.g., *animal, robin*) than concepts at other levels. Neither Rosch nor Jones compared their measures' predictions against experimental results, but both suggest that the basic level maximizes a trade-off between cue and category validities over descriptive features.

2. Category Utility

The notion of a trade-off is also important to a third measure that has been proposed to predict basic-level categories (Corter & Gluck, 1985; Gluck & Corter, 1985). This function, called *category utility*, can be developed from a weighted variation on the collocation measure,

$$\sum_j P(V_j)P(C_k|V_j)P(V_j|C_k), \qquad (1)$$

where $P(V_j)$ weights the contribution of individual feature collocations by the base rate of the respective feature. In essence, this measure reflects the importance of increasing cue and category validities for more frequently occurring features.

However, Corter and Gluck did not express category utility as an extension to collocation. Rather, they devised it with the idea that basic-level categories are preferred because they best facilitate predictions about observations in the environment. In their view, category utility is a function of a category's prediction potential, or

$$P(C_k)E(\text{number of correctly predicted } V_j|C_k),$$

which is a trade-off between the expected number of features that can be correctly predicted about a member of a category C_k and the proportion of the environment $P(C_k)$ to which those predictions apply.

Assuming a probability-matching strategy for prediction (Bruner *et al.*, 1956), the expectation can be further formalized by noting that one can predict a feature with probability $P(V_j|C_k)$, and that this prediction will be correct with the same probability:

$$P(C_k)\sum_j P(V_j|C_k)^2. \qquad (2)$$

Clearly, a probability-maximizing strategy (Bruner *et al.*, 1956) has advantages in actually generating predictions. However, it is important to realize that it is not superior in terms of heuristically ordering categories in terms of prediction potential, which is the intent behind category utility. In fact, there are important advantages to assuming a probability-matching strategy when forming categories, as detailed by Fisher (1987a).

Simple algebraic manipulations show the equivalence of functions (1) and (2). Thus, category utility can be viewed as a trade-off between cue and category validity, as well as a function that measures a category's prediction potential. More intuitively, these views can be unified by noting that the $P(V_j|C_k)$ term reflects the importance of categories with predictable features (Kolodner, 1983; Lebowitz, 1982; Tversky, 1977), but that features must also be predictive or discriminating of a category (Kolodner, 1983; Lebowitz, 1982; Tversky, 1977) so that one can classify an instance and access predictable features. Finally, Corter and Gluck (1985) define category utility as the increase in the expected number of features that can be correctly predicted, given knowledge of a category, over the expected number of correct predictions without such knowledge. The expression

$$CU(C_k) = P(C_k)[\sum_j P(V_j|C_k)^2 - \sum_j P(V_j)^2] \qquad (3)$$

provides a formal statement of their complete definition of the category utility CU.

3. Properties of Category Utility

There are several properties of category utility that are worth mentioning at this point. First, the measure has the desirable property that it will be zero if all feature distributions are independent of membership in a category. That is, if

$$P(V_j|C_k) = P(V_j),$$

then

$$P(V_j|C_k)^2 - P(V_j)^2 = 0,$$

and V_j will be "irrelevant" to a category's score and presumably to an observation's membership in C_k. If all such features are independent, then $CU(C_k) = 0.0$.

Second, category utility is not a function of feature correlations, but categories that capture feature correlations will tend to have higher scores for this measure. If category C_k captures a correlation between N features, then the sum of the individual category validities will be higher than if the correlation is captured only in part or not at all. This property has important implications for the process of concept formation in that it lets one capture feature intercorrelations without their "direct" computation. Rather than computing $P(V_1 \wedge V_2 \wedge \ldots \wedge V_n)$ explicitly, concept formation can introduce a category C_k that converts the task of computing $P(V_1 \wedge V_2 \wedge \ldots \wedge V_n)$ to one of computing $P(C_k) \prod_{i=1}^{n} P(V_i|C_k)$. In words, C_k is an auxiliary variable that may lead to conditional independence among some features (Pearl, 1985).

To see this point, consider the hierarchies of Fig. 1, which were formed using category utility as a decision heuristic. Note that the term $P(V_i|C_k)$ equals 1.0 for those features shown within each middle-level category. Trivially, the distributions of these features are conditionally independent of other features within the same class. Nodes in the tree tend to capture distinct sets of correlated features; the probability of each conjunction of features shown at a node is simply the probability of the category, $P(C_k)$, since $\Pi_{i=1}^{n} P(V_i|C_k) = \Pi_{i=1}^{n} 1.0 = 1.0$. These computations may not be so clean in other domains, but one can nonetheless efficiently and effectively compute such feature correlations through the interaction of mechanisms for concept formation and an independent cue heuristic.

C. Summary

To summarize, psychological findings indicate that there are important constraints on the representation and access of concepts. In particular, typicality effects suggest that classical concept representations are untenable in many situations, since some category members receive preferential treatment. We have advanced probabilistic concept hierarchies as a representation scheme that supports these preferences, in which features vary in their contribution to family resemblance and classification. Furthermore, tree-structured probabilistic concepts are representationally complete; they do not suffer from the limitations of independent-cue concepts in isolation, such as a restriction to linearly separable categories.

In addition to intracategory preferences implied by typicality rankings, basic-level effects suggest that humans also give preferential treatment to certain categories over others. These preferences can be predicted in static memory structures by measures like category utility. However, these same human preferences undoubtedly play a significant role in concept learning as well as retrieval. This supposition is supported by studies (Rosch et al., 1976) which indicate that basic-level categories are learned before either subordinate or superordinate categories. We now describe the manner in which predictors of human categorization preferences can be adapted to the task of concept learning and classification.

IV. A Model of Concept Retrieval and Learning

In this section we describe COBWEB (Fisher, 1987a, 1987b), a concept-formation system that adapts category utility to the task of concept learning and recognition. Our initial motivation for using category utility was that it rewards categories that improve prediction, a characteristic made evident by Gluck and Corter's analysis. Thus, this section's perspective is primarily computational, but rational (Anderson, in press) and speculative (Hall & Kibler, 1985) analyses posit that computational and psychological concerns are not independent. In Section V, we expand our discussion to selected psychological findings.

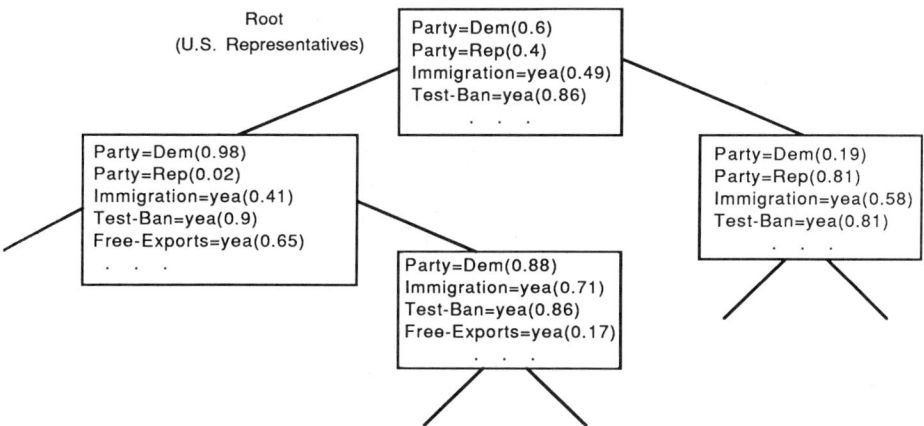

Fig. 2. A sample probabilistic concept tree over congressional voting records.

We will describe COBWEB in terms of the search framework that we presented earlier. Conveniently, one can easily transform category utility from a characteristic function of static concept hierarchies to a heuristic guide for concept learning. In particular, one can partition a known set of observations into contrasting categories, C_k, so as to maximize the average utility of categories in the partition, or

$$\frac{\sum_{k=1}^{n} CU(C_k)}{n},$$

where n is the number of categories in the partition. Because category utility requires only information about individual feature distributions within each C_k, one can effectively represent a category with an independent-cue representation, where each feature, V_j, is weighted by $P(V_j|C_k)$.

Figure 2 illustrates that contrasting categories can be organized under a root node whose features are weighted by applicable base-rate probabilities, $P(V_j|\text{root}) = P(V_j)$. In this case, observations correspond to the voting records of U.S. congresspersons on key issues with values of "yea" or "nea" (Lebowitz, 1987).[7] In addition, we assume that each category is weighted by the proportion of observations, $P(C_k)$, classified under it. By definition $P(\text{root}) = 1.0$. Collectively, $P(C_k)$'s, $P(V_j)$'s, and

---

[7]We only list "yea" values on selected votes, but all features with nonzero probability at a node are stored at the node.

$P(V_j|C_k)$'s supply the requisite information for calculating category utility.

Conceptually, the easiest way to find an optimal set of contrasting categories is to exhaustively search the possible partitions of the known observations. This can proceed in a manner similar to the specific-to-general search that we described earlier: Given a partition over m observations, consideration of the $m + 1$st observation generates m new partitions, each the result of placing the observation into one of the existing categories. In addition, there is an $m + 1$st partition that results from creating a new singleton category that contains only the new observation. The search for the best partition ceases when one encounters the last observation; one can then identify the partition with the best average category utility from among the alternatives. At this point, one can simply return the best partition or one may further decompose each category of the best partition by recursively applying the exhaustive search procedure over the subset of observations that are classified by the category. This recursive procedure results in a tree of probabilistic concepts.

This exhaustive approach is clearly impractical, since the procedure requires that one examine alternative partitions that grow exponentially with the number of observations. Search is reduced significantly in systems like CLUSTER/2 by maintaining a fixed number of alternatives after each observation. The hill-climbing approach described in Section II, C restricts the number of alternative partitions that are maintained to one. In particular, Fisher's (1987a, 1987b) COBWEB assimilates an $m + 1$st observation by evaluating the partitions that result by adding the observation to each existing category and the partition that results from creating a new singleton category. It then evaluates each of these alternatives using category utility and retains the best choice. If the instance is incorporated into an existing category, then the observation is assimilated into the respective subtree by the same procedure.[8] Anderson (in press) has recently described a similar approach, in which is Bayesian measure guides the incremental assimilation of new observations.

As with assimilation, COBWEB also uses category utility to guide object recognition: An observation is sorted down a path of "best-matching" categories to a leaf, at which point the new observation may be recognized as matching the leaf. For example, consider the congressional voting records classified by the tree of Fig. 2. A new voting record of unknown political party may be recognized (perhaps incorrectly) as an

---

[8]COBWEB only handles nominally valued attributes, but Gennari, Langley, and Fisher (1989) describe CLASSIT, a descendant of COBWEB that assumes continuously valued attributes.

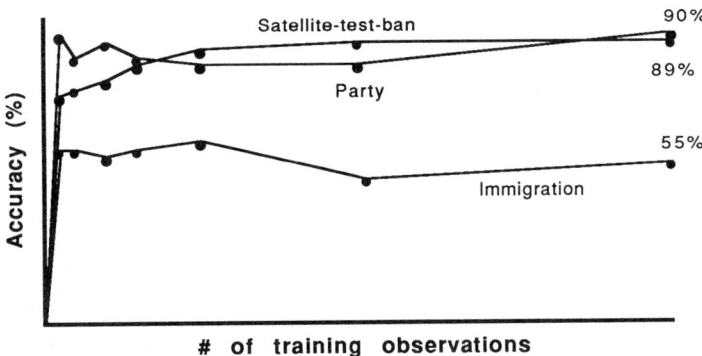

Fig. 3. Learning curves for three attributes in the congressional domain.

instance of the political party of the best-matching leaf. As we discussed in relation to linearly separable categories, this strategy lets category members be distributed throughout the tree and not restricted to one node of the tree.

Recognition need not be limited to any particular category label (e.g., party), so that one can predict any unknown feature in this manner. This capability can be tested systematically by measuring predictive accuracy at intermittent points in the evolution of a probabilistic tree. The system is presented each "test" item with one or more attributes removed, it sorts the incomplete observation to the best-matching leaf of the concept hierarchy, and it predicts the missing attributes based on those in the leaf. This occurs for all attributes of all test items, thus yielding an accuracy level for each attribute. The graph in Fig. 3 shows sample learning curves for the attributes political party, immigration vote, and satellite-test-ban.

In general, prediction accuracy for an attribute is closely related with the attribute's intercorrelation with other attributes of the domain. Political party is highly correlated with other attributes, whereas a congressman's vote on an immigration bill is relatively uncorrelated with other features. These data support earlier claims that category utility captures correlations in the data when coupled with appropriate learning mechanisms. Similar findings hold for other natural domains and for artificial domains in which one can systematically vary the amount of intercorrelation (Fisher, 1987a, 1987b; Gennari *et al.*, 1989). Not surprisingly, in domains with very little intercorrelation, the learning rate and the asymptotic accuracy suffer greatly. For some features, the system's predictive ability may even be worse than chance.

The reason for COBWEB's poor behavior with respect to some features is that classification to a leaf often simulates a *probability-matching* strategy (Bruner *et al.*, 1956). Viewed in statistical terms, sorting to a leaf may overfit the data. Recall from Section III, B that category utility has the desirable property that features which are independent of category membership will not influence classification at deeper levels, since $P(V_j|C_k)^2 - P(V_j)^2 = 0$. Inversely, an attribute's independence should also signal that deeper classification will not aid prediction of the attribute. Thus, one should follow a probability-maximizing strategy at an appropriate point in classification. Several heuristics for identifying points of approximate feature independence and points of optimal prediction (Fisher, 1989; Quinlan, 1986) have produced significant advantages in terms of prediction accuracy.

Our summary of COBWEB has been brief, in part because the precise nature of the learning operators is of limited relevance to the forthcoming discussion. Rather, the important assumptions are that memory is organized into probabilistic concept hierarchies, and in a manner that is guided by category utility. This section has illustrated that one can perform the process incrementally and in a manner that seems consistent with many aspects of human learning (Anderson, in press; Langley, Gennari, & Iba, 1987; Simon, 1969). However, as described here, COBWEB's hill-climbing learning method exhibits ordering effects that we have detailed elsewhere, along with simulated backtracking mechanisms that mitigate the effect (Fisher, 1987a, 1987b; Gennari *et al.*, 1989). Finally, our evaluation of COBWEB has been in terms of prediction accuracy of features and category labels. This is an important evaluation criterion in machine learning, but one that is intimately related to the psychological literature on recognition (e.g., Feigenbaum, 1963). We will now investigate the psychological plausibility of our methods for recognition, classification, and prediction.

V. An Analysis of Memory Phenomena

In this section we extend our analysis of COBWEB and category utility to a number of psychological phenomena. Our discussion is very much in line with Anderson's (in press) rational analysis of cognition. In effect, Gluck and Corter's derivation of category utility stemmed from the prescription that categories facilitate accurate prediction. We open the section by introducing some conventions that are important in our analysis of the basic-level, typicality, and fan-effect data that follow.

A. CATEGORY MATCH

A common thread in each of the psychological studies that we examine is the use of subject response time to queries about experimental stimuli. For example, subjects might be required to verify that a stimulus is a member of a previously learned category. This section illustrates that response time in each of these studies is well predicted by a simple variation of category utility that is only a function of the features occurring in the observation (stimulus) being classified:

$$P(C_k)\sum_j[P(V_j|C_k)^2 - P(V_j)^2]$$

for V_j present in the observation. We will call this *category match* because it intuitively corresponds to the degree that an observation matches a category and the extent to which that category is activated during recognition. The measure also fits Tversky's (1977) model of category–object resemblance in that it is a function of category size ($P(C_k)$) and sums over the features that "agree" and "conflict".[9] If the amount of conflict between features outweighs the amount of agreement, then category match may be negative; trivially, if an observation has a feature that is not present in any category member, then $P(V|C) = 0.0$ and $P(V|C)^2 - P(V)^2 < 0$.

Intuitively, category match corresponds to activation strength, which we might assume to be inversely related to response time (Collins & Loftus, 1975). However, this section will concentrate primarily on the predictive (or descriptive) links between category match and human response time. That category match turns out to be a good predictor of response time is not strongly tied to particular "implementation" details (e.g., the precise nature of the classification procedure), but relies only on general assumptions about memory organization: that probabilistic concepts are hierarchically organized in a manner that is guided by category utility.[10] There will be exceptions to this section's exclusion of im-

---

[9] Most often there will not be perfect agreement or conflict between an observation's and a category's feature distributions. Rather, the amount of agreement and conflict is weighted. Hadzikadic and Yun (1989) use a measure of similar intent in their INC system, but relevance is only computed over features shared by the observation and class. Computer experiments by D. H. Fisher (1987a) indicate that classification and learning behavior using category match closely approximate the behavior of the full category utility measure, with differences only occurring very early in training.

[10] In fact, this is a desirable characteristic that is enforced by methodologies for system development that segregate stages of *specification, design,* and *implementation*. Within cognitive science, these stages are roughly analogous to Marr's (1982) three levels of description for information-processing systems.

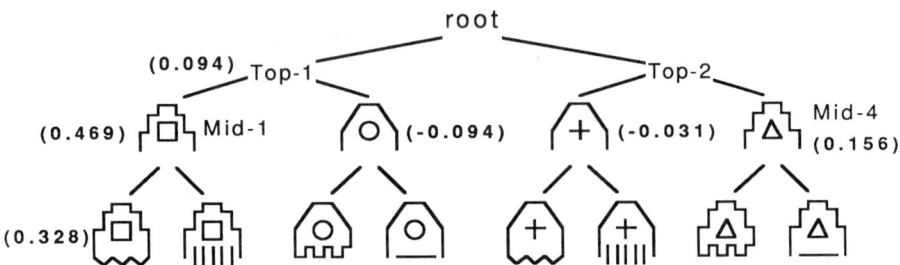

Fig. 4. Approximation of a tree from Hoffman and Ziessler basic-level studies.

plementation detail, but only on occasions when it seems most productive to explain counterintuitive findings. We will more thoroughly discuss how the predictions of category match can be implemented by the classification mechanisms of a COBWEB-like system in Section VI, but for now we turn our attention to the predictive merits of category match with respect to basic-level, typicality, and fan-effect phenomena.

B. BASIC-LEVEL EFFECTS

Gluck and Corter (1985) verified that category utility predicted the basic level in two experimental studies (Hoffman & Ziessler, 1984; Murphy & Smith, 1982): A basic-level category maximizes category utility among its ancestors and descendants. In a study by Hoffman and Ziessler, subjects learned a classification tree over "nonsense" objects like the one shown in Fig. 4. Each category (node) had a nonsense name that subjects used to identify category membership in recognition tasks. Objects were defined in terms of three attributes: the shape of the inside subcomponent with values *square, triangle, star,* or *circle* (encoded as 0, 1, 2, and 3, respectively); the outer shape, with (encoded) values of 0 and 1; and the shape of the bottom, with values 0, 1, 2, and 3. Table II shows the encoding of the Hoffman and Ziessler data that was assumed by Corter and Gluck. For the tree of Fig. 4, subjects consistently 'preferred' level 2 (where the root is at level 0).

To account for the order in which subjects verify category membership, we use the category match measure. Figure 4 shows the match scores of several categories (nodes) obtained for the observation, {outer = 0, bottom = 0, inside = 0}. The appropriate basic-level category is the most highly rated, with category match indicating a negative score for some categories for which the observation is not a member. Intuitively, a negative score indicates that an observation and a category's feature distributions conflict more than they agree. This simulation assumes that classifi-

TABLE II

Encoded Hoffman and Ziessler (1983) Tree

Classification tree			Attribute values		
Superordinate	Basic	Subordinate	Outer	Inside	Bottom
Top-1	Middle-1	Leaf-1	0	0	0
		Leaf-2	0	0	1
	Middle-2	Leaf-3	1	2	2
		Leaf-4	1	2	3
Top-2	Middle-3	Leaf-5	1	3	0
		Leaf-6	1	3	1
	Middle-4	Leaf-7	0	4	2
		Leaf-8	0	4	3

cation occurs with respect to the tree that subjects are explicitly taught, and that a verbal indication of the target category activates a corresponding node in the tree. When classification via the perceptual cues of a pictured observation reach the verbally signified node, the observation is identified as a member of the target.

Hoffman and Ziessler also explored two other trees over the same objects in Fig. 4. One variant resulted by placing nodes Middle-1 and Middle-4 under the same top-level node and Middle-2 and Middle-3 under the same top node. In this variant subjects treated the top nodes as basic, but category match predicts a tie between the top and middle nodes in this tree—middle and top nodes each match their respective observations with a score of 0.469. This is similar to the predictions found by Gluck and Corter with the full category utility measure. In Section VI we speculate on a resolution to this tie that involves selectively "masking" uninformative features in the category match computation. A third tree was also used by Hoffman and Ziessler in which subjects regarded the bottommost level of leaves to be basic. As with the tree in Fig. 4, the basic level is unambiguously identified by category match.

Gluck and Corter also evaluated category utility in light of experiments by Murphy and Smith (1982). Once again, in this study subjects were trained to recognize instances of categories arranged hierarchically. In these experiments objects were abstract "tools" that varied along four perceptual dimensions (tool size and the types of handle, shaft, and head). Our encoding of these objects is shown in Table III. Categories were assigned nonsense names of equal length, and target-recognition studies behaviorally identified one level as basic. In addition, Murphy and Smith also looked at "false" cases, in which an observation was not a member

TABLE III
OUR ENCODING OF THE MURPHY AND SMITH (1982) TREE

Classification tree			Attribute values			
Superordinate	Basic	Subordinate	Handle	Shaft	Head	Size
Top-1	Middle-1	Sub-1	2	2	0	0,1
		Sub-2	2	2	1	0,1
	Middle-2	Sub-3	0	3	3	0,1
		Sub-4	1	3	3	0,1
Top-2	Middle-3	Sub-5	3	4	4	0,1
		Sub-6	3	4	5	0,1
	Middle-4	Sub-7	4	0	6	0,1
		Sub-8	4	1	6	0,1

TABLE IV
AVERAGE RESPONSE TIMES AND MATCH RANKINGS

	True cases		False cases	
	Response time[a] (msec)	Category match	Response time (msec)	Category match
Superordinate	879	0.21	882	−0.070
Basic	678	0.53	714	−0.035
Subordinate	723	0.36	691	−0.018

[a]Response times from Murphy and Smith (1982).

of the given target. In each of the false cases, a test item from a different superordinate than the target concept was selected. Data from the true cases support previous findings on basic-level preference, but they found that subjects showed some tendency, although not statistically significant, to more quickly reject the false cases as members of subordinate target categories than basic targets.

Table IV summarizes the average subject response times and category match scores in the true and false cases. In the true cases we report category match of an observation with each category to which it belongs. In the false case, the match between an observation and unrelated superordinate, basic, and subordinate targets are reported. In both the true and false cases, category match correctly predicts response-time orders: As category match increases response time decreases. In the false cases all category-match scores are negative because there is *no* feature overlap

TABLE V

Average Response Times and Category-Match Rankings on False Data with Varying Degrees of Relatedness

Relatedness	Response time[a] (msec)	Category match
Distinct superordinate (unrelated)	691	−0.018
Same superordinate	687	−0.018
Same basic	902	+0.232

[a]Response times from Murphy and Smith (1982).

between a test observation and target concept. In fact, the difference, $P(V|C)^2 - P(V)^2$, is equal for all categories in the false case; the difference in false category-match scores is due solely to the $P(C)$ term of category match which magnifies the negative difference for higher-level categories. We have no strong hypothesis regarding these data other than to suggest that when no featural connections exist between an observation and a category, as is the case here, it is reasonable to assume that any search of the category membership proceeds in time proportional to the category's size as reflected in $P(C)$.

Murphy and Smith performed a second experiment intended to expand their findings about subordinate recognition in the false case. In particular, they reported response times for cases in which the observation was not a member of the subordinate target, but (1) was a member of the same basic category, (2) was a member of the same superordinate category, but not the same basic category, and (3) was not a member of the same superordinate category. These cases vary the relatedness of the target and the observation, with (1) being the most related of the false cases and (3) being totally unrelated. Table V shows the response times, which indicate that items of the same basic category require greater time to reject than the other two cases.

To explain their findings, Murphy and Smith propose a preparation model of classification and category structure. In this model, a verbal cue activates the target category and its "conceptual" definition. Recognition occurs by summing the number of concept features that match an observation as well as the number of conflicting features. An observation is accepted or rejected as a category member when a concept-specific threshold is reached. Separate thresholds are presumed for acceptance and rejection. Like the preparation model, our application of category match is effectively a summing procedure. However, our category-match data and our earlier discussion of classification in systems such as COBWEB suggest a different view of true and false recognition.

To motivate our processing assumptions consider the category-match scores in Table V. The negative category-match scores accurately predict no difference between the unrelated and same-superordinate case, but a positive score is shown for the same-basic condition. This violates our assumption that category match and response time are inversely related, since subordinate rejection required the longest response time. To maintain consistency we must assume that match scores on opposite sides of zero are inverted in their relation to response time. In addition, we posit that a category match of zero (or less) may be regarded as a category-independent cause for rejecting an observation. Intuitively this is desirable because a negative score suggests greater mismatch than match of features.

Conversely, we are also concerned with criteria for successful classification. Systems like COBWEB assume that an observation is classified with the category that maximizes activation. We assumed in discussing the Hoffman and Ziessler studies that successful target recognition occurred when activation that was triggered by perceptual cues reached a verbally activated target node; this suggests that recognition is not simply a process of direct comparison between target definition and observation, as the preparation model suggests, but is mediated by other memory elements. Our views of success and failure in recognition are unifiable when one considers that categories along the path to a target may induce conditional independence with respect to features that are common to all or many subordinates. Category match's subtraction of base-rate probabilities ensures that such features have no impact on classification, but an observation's remaining features may conflict with a concept and result in a negative match at that level of classification. Thus, our view is that the best-matching node in memory defines a variable threshold that cannot be achieved by any contrasting category. Competing categories are removed as candidates when their conditional matches drop below a category-independent threshold of zero. Our analysis predicts that the subordinate category of Table V is rejected more slowly because its positive score requires that it "compete" with contrasting categories for some period of time.

In summary, a qualitative characterization that captures all of the false response times (i.e., Tables IV and V) is that they vary proportionally to the absolute value of category match. In contrast, response times for true cases vary inversely with category match. More generally, we suggest that category-specific thresholds are not required in the false or true cases. Instead, positive and maximizing activation strength may be the sole determinant of categorization.

	Letter String	Intra-Category Overlap	*Typicality*		Letter String	Inter-Category Overlap	*Typicality*
	JXPHM	low	*low*		HPNWD	low	*high*
	QBLFS	"	"		HPC6B	"	"
A	XPHMQ	medium	*medium*	A	HPNSJ	medium	*medium*
	MQBLF	"	"		4KC6D	"	"
	PHMQB	high	*high*		GKNTJ	high	*low*
	HMQBL	"	"		4KCTG	"	"
	CTRVG				8SJKT		
	TRVGZ				8SJ3G		
B	RVGZK			B	9UJCG		
	VGZKD				4UZC9		
	GZKDW				4UZRT		
	ZKDWN				MSZR5		

Fig. 5. Nonsense strings used to test typicality differences.

C. TYPICALITY EFFECTS

Our discussion has replicated Gluck and Corter's analysis of basic-level effects with category match and extended it to Murphy and Smith's "false" data. In this section we extend their rational analysis of category structure further by using category match to predict typicality effects in probabilistic trees. To review briefly, typicality studies indicate that, in addition to the between-category preferences suggested by basic-level effects, humans also exhibit preferences within categories.

1. Typicality and Intracategory Similarity

To demonstrate consistency with typicality effects, we will focus on studies by Rosch and Mervis (1975). Their experiments demonstrate that typicality increases with the number of features shared with other objects of the same category and varies inversely with the number of features shared with members of contrasting classes. In their study of intracategory influences, Rosch and Mervis used the 'nonsense' strings in Fig. 5 (left). Members of category A varied in the extent to which they overlap with other members of the same class. For example, the symbols of "QBLFS" appeared in an average of 2.0 other strings of category A, whereas the symbols of "HMQBL" were shared by 3.2 other members of category A. The *interclass* overlap between members of A and B was held constant (i.e., there was no overlap). After subjects learned to distinguish categories A and B, the average time to classify letter strings as members of A or B was determined. Response time decreased as the amount of intracategory overlap increased, supporting the hypothesis that typical instances shared more properties with other members of the same class.

To analyze the Rosch and Mervis data it is important to distinguish the task performed by subjects in typicality experiments from the basic-level studies presented earlier. In the target-recognition tasks it appears that category match applied to the target concept is a good predictor of response-time ranking, but unlike the basic-level studies, Rosch and Mervis did not give subjects a target category for which membership had to be verified or rejected; they required that subjects predict the membership of an observation. Thus, assumptions about the portions of memory that may be examined during classification are less clear. For this reason our analysis will focus on two strategies of representation that might reasonably be used to encode the typicality stimuli by human subjects; by considering two alternative encodings we hope to better illustrate the robustness of category match as a predictor of response time.

The first strategy, which we term *local,* assumes that each category is associated with a distinct independent-cue concept; this is similar to our assumptions in the basic-level studies. An observation is classified with the category that maximizes category match in time that is inversely proportional to the match score. A second strategy is inspired by a general processing assumption discussed in relation to the Murphy and Smith data: Recognition effects are mediated by concepts in memory other than the target or, in this case, the possible targets. A *distributed* strategy assumes that category members may be distributed throughout memory. This was an important assumption behind our discussion of linearly separable categories in Section III and prediction accuracy in Section IV. In a distributed representation, externally defined categories need not correspond to nodes in memory, but external-category "features" or labels can be used to predict the membership of an observation. In modeling this strategy, we use COBWEB to organize the strings of the Rosch and Mervis studies, thereby simulating a subject's training phase. A test item's external-category membership is predicted at the concept tree node that maximizes category match and at which a prediction of external-category membership can be made with certainty (i.e., an external category label has a probability of 1.0 at the node). Time is assumed to be inversely proportional to the category-match score of this node.[11]

---

[11]We also could have given a distributed account of basic-level data, in which superordinate, basic, and subordinate category labels may be distributed throughout a probabilistic concept hierarchy. In general, basic-level findings from a distributed account are consistent with human data. However, an unexplained implication of this account is that a superordinate label can be predicted with certainty at any node at which a basic label can be predicted, apparently leading to equal response times. Discussion in Section VI relates to a resolution of this issue.

TABLE VI

Average Response Times and Category-Match Rankings for Rosch and Mervis (1975) Data

	Response time (msec)	Category match (local)	Category match (COBWEB)
Intraoverlap (a)			
High	560	0.948	0.910
Medium	617	0.823	0.832
Low	692	0.594	0.736
Interoverlap (b)			
Low	909	0.306	0.488
Medium	986	0.196	0.461
High	1125	0.120	0.396

Table VI (a) shows response times for category A test items and category match scores for local and distributed representations. Because COBWEB is sensitive to input order, the distributed representation scores are averaged over 20 trees constructed from random orderings of the data strings. A representative tree for these data is shown in Fig. 6. Since there is no overlap between classes A and B, COBWEB's approach of grouping similar objects almost always results in the same categories (at the top level) as those based solely on the external label[12]; recall that these topmost nodes are also the two concepts considered in the local representation. In addition, the topmost node generally maximizes the

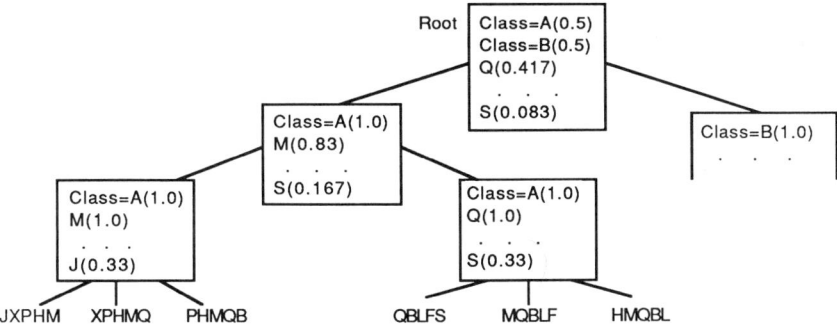

Fig. 6. A tree over the intracategory overlap data.

[12]At times atypical members of A (or B) may be placed in distinct categories.

category-match scores of the high and medium intraoverlap data, thus explaining the similarity of category-match scores for these data using the local and distributed representations. In contrast, low intraoverlap items exhibit markedly higher category-match scores using a distributed representation. This reflects the fact that low intraoverlap observations in this experiment more often match a subordinate node in the tree better than they match the top-level node. Our assumption is that classification will be more rapid with respect to the subordinate.

Regardless of whether one assumes a local or distributed representation, category-match scores are inversely related to response time. Intuitively, features that are relatively unique among category A members will cause a decrease in category match for their respective observations because they have smaller $P(V|C)$ values for these features. Conversely, the $P(V|C)$ values for unique features will be higher at subordinate nodes, thus increasing category match at lower nodes, even to the point of offsetting the reduced $P(C)$ values.

2. Typicality and Intercategory Similarity

In addition to varying intracategory overlap, Rosch and Mervis explored the impact of intercategory (between-category) similarity. Figure 5 (right) shows the stimuli for this study, in which subjects were taught to distinguish categories A and B. Intracategory overlap was held constant for category A members, but the average extent to which category A members overlapped with B varied from 0.0 (HPNWD) to 1.3 (4KCTG). As Table VII (b) indicates, category A instances that shared few symbols with strings in category B were recognized more quickly (i.e., were treated as more typical).

Once again, we used two representation strategies in testing the relationship between category-match predictions and the response-time data. For these stimuli, significant featural overlap between certain members of A and B caused COBWEB to consistently distribute class A members throughout the resultant concept hierarchy. Figure 7 shows one such tree. In this case, the most strongly indicated node may not allow a prediction of category membership to be made with certainty and alternative nodes must be examined. For example, node n_1 of the tree in Fig. 7 does not allow an unambiguous prediction of A or B membership. In this case, the category-match score of node n_2 would have to be used when classifying 4KCTG.

Table VI (b) reveals that, in the case of both local and distributed representations, category-match scores were again inversely related to Rosch and Mervis' response-time data. Scores for the distributed case are aver-

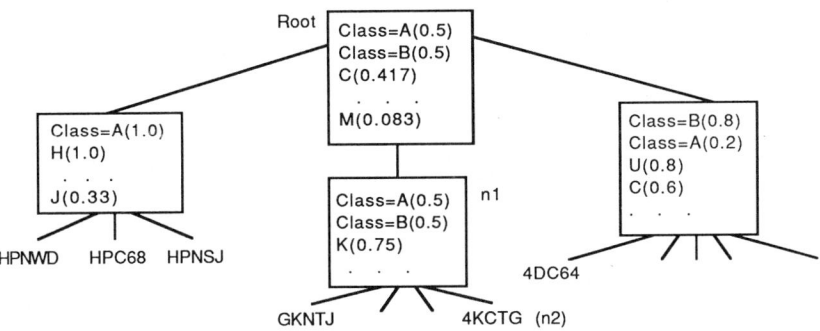

Fig. 7. Tree constructured over intercategory experimental data.

aged over 20 trials. Intuitively, intercategory (A and B) similarities tend to diffuse evidence across lateral subtrees. In cases such as "J," the feature is actually more predictive of category B than A, thus adding nothing to the category-match score of the atypical observations to which these features belong, or actually detracting from it.

3. Discussion of Typicality Results

Taken alone and collectively the data from our intracategory and intercategory studies demonstrate that category match accurately ranks test-item response time. To better illustrate this, Table VII shows the predicted response times from the local and distributed category-match

TABLE VII

HUMAN AND PREDICTED RESPONSE TIMES FOR ROSCH AND MERVIS (1975) DATA

	Response time (msec)	Predicted time (local)	Predicted time (COBWEB)
Intraoverlap (a)			
High	560	526	535
Med	617	606	615
Low	692	753	713
Interoverlap (b)			
Low	909	938	968
Med	986	1008	995
High	1125	1057	1062

scores of Table VI that were obtained from a linear regression. Category match accounts for 95.7% of the variance in response time in the local case [$F(1,4) = 88.7, p < 0.001$] and 96.6% in the distributed case [$F(1,4) = 114.1, p < 0.001$].[13] While both strategies account for most of the variance, the distributed representation compresses the category-match scores across the typicality range, possibly because it better tailors recognition to an observation. More specifically, distribution indicates that typicality rankings emerge from variation along two dimensions of categorization (Rosch, 1978). Relatively unique features to a category will tend to diffuse activation toward subordinate categories (i.e., along a vertical dimension). Features that overlap with contrasting categories diffuse activation across nodes that classify observations of more than one contrast category (i.e., a horizontal dimension). Local accounts of typicality only consider variance along this latter dimension.

A distributed model makes the vertical dimension explicit in explanations of typicality. This suggests interactions with basic-level effects, which also emerge from variation along this dimension. For example, Rosch et al. (1976) predicted and Jolicour et al. (1984) verified that the human preference for the basic level is qualified. In particular, an observation (e.g., a specific chicken) may be sufficiently atypical of its basic-level category (e.g., *bird*) that it will be first recognized as an instance of a subordinate category (e.g., *chicken*). Low intracategory overlap results in greater activation of subordinate nodes, while there is a simultaneous decrease in activation of the basic-level node for atypical objects due to less intracategory overlap and more intercategory overlap. In cases of sufficient atypicality, these tendencies may interact so that classification is initiated at a subordinate level. This is nicely illustrated by the data of Fig. 5 (left). In this simulation the category-match scores of atypical objects (nonsense strings) were higher at subordinates than at top-level nodes of a COBWEB-generated tree—presumably the basic level, since this level maximizes category utility.

D. FAN EFFECTS

To a large extent, knowledge of basic-level and typicality effects influenced our adoption of probabilistic representations and the category-match metric. However, the framework also accounts for certain fan effects (Anderson, 1976), which did not influence our representation and processing biases. Nonetheless, these phenomena are accurately predicted by application of category match to probabilistic representations.

---

[13]We considered the intracategory and intercategory data as one sample, given that our calculation of category-match scores in each case was identical. Considering the data as two separate samples yields similar accounts of variance and predicted response times.

	Trues				Falses		
	1	2	3		1	2	3
1	1111ms (1120)	1174ms (1157)	1222ms (1184)	1	1197ms (1168)	1221ms (1240)	1264ms (1306)
2	1167ms (1157)	1198ms (1195)	1222ms (1259)	2	1250ms (1240)	1356ms (1312)	1291ms (1379)
3	1153ms (1184)	1233ms (1259)	1357ms (1321)	3	1262ms (1306)	1471ms (1379)	1465ms (1444)

Fig. 8. Human and predicted (in parentheses) response times for Anderson's (1974) fan-effect data.

Fan effects indicate that observations with frequently encountered features may be more difficult to recognize than observations with relatively unique features, given that exposure across observations is relatively constant. Anderson (1974) demonstrated this principle in sentence-recognition tasks, which typically used simple sentences that consisted of a person and a location:

(1-1) The doctor is in the bank. (1-2) The fireman is in the park.
(2-1) The teacher is in the church. (2-2) The teacher is in the park.

Sentences vary in the number of features (persons, locations) that they share with other sentences. The numbers preceding each sentence indicate the number of sentences that contain the respective persons and locations. For example, sentence (2-1) indicates that *teacher* appears twice and *church* appears once in the set of four sentences.

After subjects were trained on selected sentences, they were presented with probes and asked whether they had previously observed a sentence (true) or not (false). Anderson found that recognition time increased in the true- and false-case with the frequency that a person and location was present in training sentences. Figure 8 shows matrices of nine cells each, which show the averaged human response data (Anderson, 1974) in the upper portion of each cell. Each cell corresponds to items with the number of persons and locations denoted on the horizontal and vertical dimensions, respectively. In general, response time for both true and false human data increases as one moves to the right and/or down.

Elsewhere (Silber & Fisher, 1989), we explained these effects as a special case of typicality phenomena, in which a subject was to classify test observations with respect to the singleton categories formed from the training observations. In this account, the intracategory overlap between singleton categories is identical, since each observation contains exactly two features. Response-time differences are thus explained entirely in terms of intercategory overlap. The more features that an observation shares with other observations, the greater the overlap between its corresponding singleton category and contrasting singleton categories. Observations with greater overlap should require greater response time, which is consistent with typicality findings.

In accounting for this data we will primarily be concerned with local representations, particularly in the case of true test items. The reason for this is that COBWEB may impose an organization above the singleton level, but both features of a sentence can only be predicted with certainty at the leaves. In the case of "true" test items we thus report category-match scores for the test item's corresponding singleton, since this is the strongest match. The false case is more complicated. In contrast to the Murphy and Smith experiments, subjects are not given a verbally cued target category on which to focus. Rather, we assume that all categories must be investigated and rejected. There are a number of ways that we might simulate this process, but for simplicity we report the average category-match score of an observation across all categories in memory: This is the set of singletons in the local case and singletons plus internal nodes in the distributed case. Averaging captures the intuition that larger scores indicate that more of memory must be investigated, but it makes minimal assumptions about how this might be accomplished.

In addition to the human data at the top of each cell, Fig. 8 shows predicted response times in parentheses that were generated from a linear regression. Once again, false response times are proportional to category match, and there is an inverse relation between the two in the true case. Category-match scores account for 83.8% of the variance in the true response time [$F(1,7) = 36.3, p < 0.001$] and 70.9% of the variance in false response time [$F(1,7) = 17.1, p < 0.004$].[14]

In contrast to our account of fan effects, Anderson's (1976) initial explanation suggested that items were stored in a semantic network and activation spread from the features of a test sentence until the original instance was found in memory (trues) or all links from the features had been exhausted (falses). A mathematical abstraction of Anderson's ACT processing model accounted for 83% of the variance in the true and false response times. It appears that Anderson considered the true and false cases as one sample, whereas we have modeled them separately. Overall the ACT-based model yields better predictions than our model, but it also assumes more parameters that are linked to the processing assumptions of ACT.

Recently, Anderson (in press) has provided an explanation of fan effect

---

[14]We considered the true and false data as separate samples, given differences in the calculation of category-match scores between the two cases.

based on a rational model of information retrieval systems. A key ingredient in his explanation is the cue validity of features toward a sentence. Similarly, we can see the role of cue validity in category match by reexpressing it as $\Sigma_j P(V_j)P(C|V_j)P(V_j|C) - P(V_j)P(C)P(V_j)$. Since $P(V_j|C)$'s and $P(C)$'s are constant across all singleton categories, a dominant factor in category match is the cue validities, $P(C|V_j)$. More generally, low cue validity reflects greater overlap with contrast (singleton) categories. In fact, it is the reliance on cue validity that unifies fan with typicality phenomena, notably that aspect of typicality that emerges from intercategory overlap.[15]

VI. General Discussion

In this article we presented speculative and rational analyses of basic-level, typicality, and fan effects. Our primary goal was to verify the ability of Gluck and Corter's category utility and our category-match variant to predict human response time; our precise application of category match necessarily varied with differences across the experimental studies, but collectively our various assumptions are consistent. In the case of all "true" stimuli, response time is predicted by the score of the node that maximizes category match and satisfies the conditions of the stimulus (e.g., membership in a target category; possession of both person and location features of the stimulus). In the false cases response time is predicted by a function of the match scores of nodes that must be examined in order to issue a false response with certainty (e.g., a target category if one is supplied or all categories in memory otherwise).

A benefit of exploiting Gluck and Corter's rational analysis is that it provides a specification of concept quality that has both computational and psychological merit. In particular, we coupled category utility and methods from machine learning (Kolodner, 1983; Lebowitz, 1982) in the probabilistic representations and classification strategies of COBWEB. Our ongoing research is advancing in two directions: to improve the system so that it is more fully consistent with the psychological phenomena and to expand the scope of the model to other areas of cognition, notably problem solving.

A. THE ROLE OF INDEXING

Despite the descriptive merits of our specification, we have noted that it leaves certain "implementation" issues unexplained. For example, our

---

[15]This observation was first made by Jane Silber.

analysis of the Murphy and Smith data required that false response times rise with category-match scores. However, taken alone, the assumption—that increased match implies faster access—suggests that false categories with higher match scores would be more quickly accessed, thus allowing for faster rejection. To resolve this problem, we appealed to assumptions about processing and representation which required that poorly matching categories would be more quickly rejected. We can now flesh out some general mechanisms that will realize these behavioral constraints.

Many theories of learning and memory have addressed the problem of identifying and exploiting informative features for classification. Category utility and category match suggest that a feature positively informs the categorization process if and only if $P(f|C) > P(f)$. This criterion of feature informativeness has been suggested by data in such diverse areas as stereotype theory (McCauley, Stitt, & Segal, 1980) and animal learning (Rescola, 1968), as well as other areas of AI and psychology (Schlimmer, 1986).

However, strict adherence to this criterion may still allow features of little benefit to be evaluated. For example, $P(f|C) = 1.0$ for all singleton categories, thus satisfying the criterion for most leaves. In response, Fisher (1988, 1989) and Quinlan (1986) have employed a variety of methods for determining when the $P(f|C) > P(f)$ relation is significant. Given category utility's relation to Jones' (1983) collocation measure $P(C|f) \times P(f|C)$, an attractive method would be to find nodes that maximize this product for each feature. Intuitively, these will be the most specific categories [i.e., yielding high $P(f|C)$] *for which the feature is still discriminating* [i.e., yielding high $P(C|f)$]. For example, the feature *fly* may be maximized at *birds*, but below this it does not discriminate among birds. Our heuristic assumption is that at collocation-maximizing nodes a feature's presence becomes approximately independent of membership in lower-level categories.

This heuristic creates a horizon beyond which a feature does not discriminate. We may impose this horizon through indexing (Feigenbaum & Simon, 1984; Kolodner, 1983; Lebowitz, 1982): A feature labels a link from a node to one or more of its descendants; the link is traversed only when an observation with that feature is observed. For example, in the zoological taxonomy, *fly* would index the categories *vertebrate* and *bird* from the taxonomy's root, since these nodes are within the horizon determined by collocation.[16] In many cases, a feature's collocation is maxi-

---

[16]This differs from our earlier systems (Fisher, 1988; Silber & Fisher, 1989), which directed indices *only* at collocation-maximizing nodes (e.g., *bird*, but not *vertebrate*). This strategy proved too fragile, particularly during the early stages of learning.

mized at the root and thus does not index any node. This indexing strategy may also be recursively applied so that descendents of *bird* are indexed by features that discriminate them from the *bird* node. Notice that *fly* would not index any descendant in this context, whereas *not-fly* presumably would. Conversely, *fly* would not index *mammal* from the root, but within the mammal context it would discriminate *bats*.

In the revised model, classification would be based on a category-match score that is computed only over the features of an observation that are used for indexing. All such scores will be positive, with the maximum score dictating category membership. This procedure would recurse from the maximum node until it reached a dead end, at which no indices for the observation remain. Computationally, this indexing scheme radically delimits the portions of memory that are accessed for each observation, without appealing to ad hoc thresholds.

This strategy also appears to have desirable psychological properties, but at this point we can only speculate with respect to some of the data. First, the approach breaks the basic-level tie that we reported in relation to the Hoffman and Ziessler studies; in the case of one tree, subjects treated the topmost nodes as basic, but category match predicted a tie between these nodes and their children. In this case, indexing brings all features to bear on the top-level nodes, but it removes a feature from the match computation for the middle-level nodes. Basic-level identifications are also accurately predicted in the other studies, as are typicality rankings from the Rosch and Mervis studies.

The revised model also promises to explain results with false test items. To review our earlier account of Murphy and Smith's data, the "false" target is verbally cued, which is the only cue in the case of superordinate-only relatedness and unrelatedness. Their matching score is more quickly overwhelmed by the match score of the correct category than is the false target in the basic-relatedness case. There are no concept-specific thresholds, but one can view recognition as mediated by implicit and variable thresholds that emerge from the competition among contrast categories. Membership in a category can be rejected when a dead end is reached and a competing category has a higher matching score. A similar account also applies to Anderson's data. Thus, our account of the false data suggests that low match scores in our specification translate to more dead ends in categorization.

B. Models of the Planning Process

In addition to improving our account of categorization phenomena, we are extending the model of recognition and learning to domains such as planning. This work is closely related to a growing body of research in machine learning that is focused on problem solving (e.g., Minton, 1988; Shavlik, 1989). Much of this work has focused on analytic learning methods (Mitchell, Keller, & Kedar-Cabelli, 1986) that transform knowledge from one form into another.

In contrast, we propose that learning in problem-solving domains is best modeled as concept formation, in which memory organizes problem-solving experience in a manner that facilitates efficient reuse and incrementally transforms a novice into an expert. Our approach augments a problem solver with a concept-formation component that organizes problem descriptions and solution traces (Allen & Langley, 1989; Yang & Fisher, 1989). A new problem is classified via the concept hierarchy in hopes of finding a reusable solution trace. In cases where a complete solution cannot be recovered, one may still obtain a partial solution by recovering predictable subtraces at nodes encountered during classification. Our framework is consistent with psychological (Chi, Feltovich, & Glaser, 1981) and computational (Bareiss, 1989) views that expertise involves an ability to solve problems via classification v. search.

We expect that many of the behaviors that occur in conceptual memory—such as typicality and basic-level effects—will also occur with problem-solving memory. Thus, we hope to account for many of the same types of phenomena in episodic memory that we explained for object memory. This work is also addressing some limitations of featural and probabilistic models generally and COBWEB specifically. In particular, we are extending our strategies to structural representations (Dietterich & Michalski, 1983; Smith & Medin, 1981) which allow relationships between object features or components [e.g., next-to (x,y)] and, in addition, we are using an object's function in problem solving as a guide for concept learning (Nelson, 1973; Wisniewski, 1989). More generally, we hope to develop a general-purpose cognitive architecture that is founded on the principles of human memory that we have described here (Langley, Thompson, Iba, Gennari, & Allen, 1989). Finally, we hope to illustrate that our analysis in particular, and rational/speculative analyses in general, provide generic models of intelligent behavior that cognitive scientists can exploit, regardless of the side of the psychological/computational fence on which they typically reside.

ACKNOWLEDGMENTS

We thank Dennis Kibler, Jim Corter, Mark Gluck, Richard Granger, and Jeff Schlimmer for their insights and influential discussions in the early stages of this work. In addition, we thank Jeanette Altarriba, Rogers Hall, Kevin Thompson, Jim Corter, and Mark Gluck for helpful suggestions on more recent versions of the material. Doug Fisher was supported by NASA Ames grant NCC 2-645.

REFERENCES

Aha, D., & Kibler, D. (1989). Noise-tolerant instance-based learning. In *Proceedings of the Eleventh International Joint Conference on Artificial Intelligence* (pp. 794–800). Los Altos, CA: Morgan Kaufmann.

Aha, D., & McNulty, D. (1989). Learning relative attribute weights for instance-based concept descriptions. In *Proceedings of the Eleventh Annual Conference of the Cognitive Science Society* (pp. 530–537). Hillsdale, NJ: Erlbaum.

Allen, J., & Langley, P. (1989). Using concept hierarchies to organize plan knowledge. In *Proceedings of the Sixth International Workshop on Machine Learning* (pp. 229–231). Los Altos, CA: Morgan Kaufmann.

Anderson, J. R. (1974). Retrieval of propositional information from long term memory. *Cognitive Psychology*, 6, 451–474.

Anderson, J. R. (1976). *Language, memory, and thought*. Hillsdale, NJ: Erlbaum.

Anderson, J. R. (in press). The place of cognitive architectures in a rational analysis. In K. Van Lehn (Ed.), *Architectures for Intelligence*. Hillsdale, NJ: Erlbaum.

Anderson, J. R., & Kline, P. J. (1979). A learning system and its psychological implications. In *Proceedings of the Sixth International Joint Conference on Artificial Intelligence* (pp. 16–21). Los Altos, CA: Morgan Kaufmann.

Bareiss, R. (1989). *Exemplar-based knowledge acquisition*. San Diego, CA: Academic Press.

Bruner, J., Goodnow, J., & Austin, G. (1956). *A study of thinking*. New York: Wiley.

Chalnick, A., & Billman, D. (1988). Unsupervised learning of correlational structure. In *Proceedings of the Tenth Annual Conference of the Cognitive Science Society* (pp. 510–516). Hillsdale, NJ: Erlbaum.

Cheeseman, P., Kelly, J., Self, M., Stutz, J., Taylor, W., & Freeman, D. (1988). AutoClass: A bayesian classification system. In *Proceedings of the Fifth International Machine Learning Conference* (pp. 54–64). Los Altos, CA: Morgan Kaufmann.

Chi, M., Feltovich, P., & Glaser, R. (1981). Categorization and representation of physics problems by experts and novices. *Cognitive Science*, 5, 121–152.

Collins, A., & Loftus, E. (1975). A spreading activation theory of semantic processing. *Psychological Review*, 82, 407–428.

Corter, J., & Gluck, M. (1985). Machine generalization and human categorization: An information theoretic view. In *Proceedings of the Workshop on Probability and Uncertainty in Artificial Intelligence* (pp. 201–207). Los Angeles, CA.

Dietterich, T. G., & Michalski, R. S. (1983). A comparative review of selected methods of learning from examples. In R. S. Michalski, J. G. Carbonell, & T. M. Mitchell (Eds.), *Machine learning: An artificial intelligence approach*. Los Altos, CA: Morgan Kaufmann.

Duda, R. O., & Hart, P. E. (1973). *Pattern classification and scene analysis*. New York: Wiley.

Everitt, B. (1980). *Cluster analysis*. London: Heinemann.

Feigenbaum, E. (1963). The simulation of verbal learning behavior. In E. A. Feigenbaum & J. Feldman (Eds.), *Computers and thought*. Los Altos, CA: Morgan Kaufmann.

Feigenbaum, E., & Simon, H. (1984). EPAM-like models of recognition and learning. *Cognitive Science*, **8**, 305–336.

Fisher, D. H. (1987a). *Knowledge acquisition via incremental conceptual clustering*. Doctoral dissertation. University of California Department of Information and Computer Science, Irvine.

Fisher, D. H. (1987b). Knowledge acquisition via incremental conceptual clustering. *Machine Learning*, **2**, 139–172.

Fisher, D. H. (1988). A computational account of basic level and typicality effects. In *Proceedings of the Seventh National Conference on Artificial Intelligence* (pp. 233–238). Los Altos, CA: Morgan Kaufmann.

Fisher, D. H. (1989). Noise-tolerant conceptual clustering. In *Proceedings of the Eleventh International Joint Conference on Artificial Intelligence* (pp. 825–830). Los Altos, CA: Morgan Kaufmann.

Gennari, J. (1989). *A survey of clustering methods* (Tech. Rep. 89–38). Irvine: University of California, Department of Computer Science.

Gennari, J., Langley, P., & Fisher, D. (1989). Models of incremental concept formation. *Artificial Intelligence*, **40**, 11–62.

Gluck, M. A., Bower, G., & Hee, M. (1989). A configural-cue network model of animal and human associative learning. In *Proceedings of the Eleventh Annual Conference of the Cognitive Science Society* (pp. 323–332). Hillsdale, NJ: Erlbaum.

Gluck, M. A., & Corter, J. E. (1985). Information, uncertainty, and the utility of categories. In *Proceedings of the Seventh Annual Conference of the Cognitive Science Society* (pp. 283–287). Hillsdale, NJ: Erlbaum.

Hadzikadic, M., & Yun, D. (1989). Concept formation by incremental conceptual clustering. In *Proceedings of the Eleventh International Joint Conference on Artificial Intelligence* (pp. 831–836). Los Altos, CA: Morgan Kaufmann.

Hall, R., & Kibler, D. (1985). Differing methodological perspectives in artificial intelligence. *AI Magazine*, **6**, 166–179.

Hanson, S. J., & Bauer, M. (1989). Conceptual clustering, categorization, and polymorphy. *Machine Learning*, **3**, 343–372.

Hayes-Roth, B., & Hayes-Roth, F. (1977). Concept learning and the recognition and classification of exemplars. *Journal of Verbal Learning and Verbal Behavior*, **16**, 321–338.

Hayes-Roth, F., & McDermott, J. (1978). An interference matching technique for inducing abstractions. *Communications of the ACM*, **21**, 401–410.

Hinton, G. E (1989). Connectionist learning procedures. *Artificial Intelligence*, **40**, 185–234.

Hoffman, J., & Ziessler, C. (1983). Objectidentifikation in kunstlichen begriffshierarchien. *Zeitscrift fuer Psychologie*, **16**, 43–275.

Hunt, E. B., Marin, J., & Stone, P. J. (1966). *Experiments in induction*. New York: Academic Press.

Jolicoeur, P., Gluck, M., & Kosslyn, S. (1984). Pictures and names: Making the connection. *Cognitive Psychology*, **16**, 243–275.

Jones, G. (1983). Identifying basic categories. *Psychological Bulletin*, **94**, 423–428.

Kline, P. J. (1983). *Computing the similarity of structured objects by means of heuristic search for correspondences*. Doctoral dissertation University of Michigan, Ann Arbor.

Kolodner, J. L. (1983). Reconstructive memory: A computer model. *Cognitive Science*, **7**, 281–328.

Langley, P. W. (1987). A general theory of discrimination learning. In D. Klahr, P. Langley, & D. Neches (Eds.), *Production system models of learning and development*. Cambridge, MA: MIT Press.

Langley, P. W., Gennari, J., & Iba, W. (1987). Hill-climbing theories of learning. In *Pro-

ceedings of the Fourth International Workshop on Machine Learning (pp. 312–323). Los Altos, CA: Morgan Kaufmann.

Langley, P. W., Thompson, K., Iba, W., Gennari, J., & Allen, J. (1989). *An integrated cognitive architecture for autonomous agents* (Tech. Rep). Irvine: University of California, Department of Computer Science.

Lebowitz, M. (1982). Correcting erroneous generalizations. *Cognition and Brain Theory,* **5,** 367–381.

Lebowitz, M. (1987). Experiments with incremental concept formation: UNIMEM. *Machine Learning,* **2,** 103–138.

Marr, D. (1982). *Vision.* San Francisco, CA: Freeman.

Martin, J. D. (1989). Reducing redundant learning. In *Proceedings of the Sixth International Workshop on Machine Learning* (pp. 396–399). Los Altos, CA: Morgan Kaufmann.

McCauley, C., Stitt, C., & Segal, M. (1980). Stereotyping: From prejudice to prediction. *Psychological Bulletin,* **87,** 195–208.

Medin, D. L. (1983). Structural principles of categorization. In T. Tighe & B. Shepp (Eds.), *Perception, cognition, and development.* Hillsdale, NJ: Erlbaum.

Medin, D. L., & Schaffer, M. (1978). A context theory of classification learning. *Psychological Review,* **85,** 207–238.

Medin, D. L., Wattenmaker, W. D., & Michalski, R. S. (1986). *Constraints and preferences in inductive learning* (Tech. Rep). Urbana-Champaign: University of Illinois, Department of Computer Science.

Mervis, C., & Rosch, E. (1981). Categorization of natural objects. *Annual Review of Psychology,* **32,** 89–115.

Michalski, R. S. (1983). A theory and methodology of inductive learning. In R. S. Michalski, J. G. Carbonell, & T. M. Mitchell (Eds.), *Machine learning: An artificial intelligence approach.* Los Altos, CA: Morgan Kaufmann.

Michalski, R. S., & Stepp, R. (1983). Learning from observation: Conceptual clustering. In R. S. Michalski, J. G. Carbonell, & T. M. Mitchell (Eds.), *Machine learning: An artificial intelligence approach.* Los Altos, CA: Morgan Kaufmann.

Minton, S. (1988). Qualitative results concerning the utility of explanation-based learning. In *Proceedings of the Seventh National Conference on Artificial Intelligence* (pp. 564–569). Los Altos, CA: Morgan Kaufmann.

Mitchell, T. M. (1982). Generalization as search. *Artificial Intelligence,* **18,** 203–226.

Mitchell, T. M., Keller, R., & Kedar-Cabelli, S. (1986). Explanation-based learning: A unifying view. *Machine Learning,* **1,** 47–80.

Murphy, G., & Smith, E. (1982). Basic level superiority in picture categorization. *Journal of Verbal Learning and Verbal Behavior,* **21,** 1–20.

Nelson, K. (1973). Some evidence for the cognitive primacy of categorization and its functional basis. *Merrill-Palmer Quarterly of Behavior and Development,* **19,** 21–39.

Newell, A., & Simon, H. (1972). *Human problem solving.* Englewood Cliffs, NJ: Prentice-Hall.

Nilsson, N. (1965). *Learning machines.* New York: McGraw-Hill.

Nosofsky, R. M. (1987). Attention and learning processes in the identification and categorization of integral stimuli. *Journal of Experimental Psychology: Learning, Memory, and Cognition,* **13,** 87–108.

Pearl, J. (1985). Learning hidden causes from empirical data. In *Proceedings of the Ninth International Joint Conference on Artificial Intelligence* (pp. 567–572). Los Altos, CA: Morgan Kaufmann.

Quinlan, J. R. (1979). Discovering rules by induction from large collections of examples. In

D. Michie (Ed.), *Expert systems in the micro electronic age*. Edinburgh: Edinburgh University Press.

Quinlan, J. R. (1986). Induction of decision trees. *Machine Learning, 1*, 81–106.

Reed, S. (1972). Pattern recognition and categorization. *Cognitive Psychology, 3*, 382–407.

Rescola, R. A. (1968). Probability of shock in the presence of CS in fear conditioning. *Journal of Comparative and Psysiological Psychology, 66*, 1–5.

Rips, L., Shoben, E., & Smith, E. (1973). Semantic distance and the verification of semantic relations. *Journal of Verbal Learning and Verbal Behavior, 12*, 1–20.

Rosch, E. (1978). Principles of categorization. In E. Rosch & B. Lloyd, (Eds.), *Cognition and categorization*. Hillsdale, NJ: Erlbaum.

Rosch, E., & Mervis, C. (1975). Family resemblances: Studies in the internal structure of categories. *Cognitive Psychology, 7*, 573–605.

Rosch, E., Mervis, C., Gray, W., Johnson, D., & Boyes-Braem, P. (1976). Basic objects in natural categories. *Cognitive Psychology, 18*, 382–439.

Schlimmer, J. C. (1986). *A note on correlational measures* (Tech. Rep.). Irvine: University of California, Department of Computer Science.

Schlimmer, J. C., & Fisher, D. (1986). A case study of incremental concept induction. In *Proceedings of the Fifth National Conference on Artificial Intelligence* (pp. 496–501). Los Altos, CA: Morgan Kaufmann.

Schlimmer, J. C., & Granger, R. H., Jr. (1986). Incremental learning from noisy data. *Machine Learning, 1*, 317–334.

Shavlik, J. (1989). Acquiring recursive concepts with explanation-based learning. In *Proceedings of the Eleventh International Joint Conference on Artificial Intelligence* (pp. 688–693). Los Altos, CA: Morgan Kaufmann.

Silber, J., & Fisher, D. H. (1989). A model of natural category structure and its behavioral implications. In *Proceedings of the Eleventh Annual Conference of the Cognitive Science Society* (pp. 884–891). Hillsdale, NJ: Erlbaum.

Simon, H. A. (1969). *The sciences of the artificial*. Cambridge, MA: MIT Press.

Simon, H. A., & Lea, G. (1974). Problem solving and rule induction: A unified view. In L. W. Gregg (Ed.), *Knowledge and cognition*. Hillsdale, NJ: Erlbaum.

Smith, E. E., & Medin, D. L. (1981). *Categories and concepts*. Cambridge, MA: Harvard University Press.

Smith, E. E., Shoben, E., & Rips, L. (1974). Structure and processes in semantic memory: A featural model for semantic decisions. *Psychological Review, 81*, 214–241.

Tversky, A. (1977). Features of similarity. *Psychological Review, 84*, 327–352.

Utgoff, P. E. (1988). ID5: An incremental ID3. In *Proceedings of the Fifth International Conference on Machine Learning* (pp. 107–120). Los Altos, CA: Morgan Kaufmann.

Vere, S. (1980). Multilevel counterfactuals for generalization of relational concepts and productions. *Artificial Intelligence, 14*, 139–164.

Winston, P. H. (1975). Learning structural descriptions from examples. In P. H. Winston (Ed.), *The psychology of computer vision*. New York: McGraw-Hill.

Wisniewski, E. (1989). Learning from examples: The effect of different conceptual roles. In *Proceedings of the Eleventh Annual Conference of the Cognitive Science Society* (pp. 980–986). Hillsdale, NJ: Erlbaum.

Yang, H., & Fisher, D. (1989). Conceptual clustering of means-ends plans. In *Proceedings of the Sixth International Workshop on Machine Learning* (pp. 232–234). Los Altos, CA: Morgan Kaufmann.

INDEX

A

Abstract knowledge, response–selection skill and, 231
Abstraction hierarchy, natural categories and, 247, 248
Accuracy
  metamemory and
    feeling-of-knowing, 149, 153, 154, 159, 160
    methodology, 143, 146, 147
    priveleged access, 151–153
    retrieval, 165
  natural categories and, 251
  nonverbal priming and, 90–93, 97, 105
  response–outcome relations and, 40, 42, 63, 65
  spatial memory and, 21
    characteristics, 6–12
    noncaching tests, 15, 16, 19
    seed recovery, 5, 6
Acquisition
  memory improvement and, 180, 182, 185, 188
  metamemory and
    methodology, 146–148, 160–162
    theoretical framework, 129–135
ACT, natural categories and, 252, 276
Activation, natural categories and, 263
  basic-level effects, 265, 267, 268, 274
  fan effects, 276
Adaptation
  response–outcome relations and, 30
  spatial memory and, 12, 20
Affect, nonverbal priming and, 103, 104

Age
  memory improvement and, 189
  nonverbal priming and, 89, 90
Agreement
  natural categories and, 263, 264
  response–outcome relations and, 29
Alcohol
  memory improvement and, 187
  metamemory and, 138, 139, 168
Allocation of study time, metamemory and
  acquisition, 160–162
  theoretical framework, 131, 132, 134, 135
Alternative-forced-choice test, metamemory and, 146, 152, 156, 158, 159
Amnesia
  memory improvement and, 186
  nonverbal priming and, 83
    explicit memory, 110, 111
    familiar objects, 86, 88–90, 92
    novel objects, 103, 104
    theoretical accounts, 115
Anomalies, nonverbal priming and, 88
Anxiety, memory improvement and, 188, 191
Artificial intelligence, natural categories and, 242–244, 278
Association, response–outcome relations and, 30–32, 41, 78
Associative phase, response–selection skill and, 210, 225, 229, 234
  autonomous phase, 230
  practice, 225–227
  transfer, 227–229
Associative priming, 102, 116, 117

Index

Attention
  memory improvement and, 181, 184, 193, 195
  natural categories and, 251
Attitudes, memory improvement and, 177, 184, 189, 190, 193
Attributes, natural categories and, 261, 262, 264–266
AUTOCLASS, natural categories and, 246, 247
Automaticity
  memory improvement and, 177
  response–outcome relations and, 30, 31
Autonomous phase, response–selection skill and, 210, 229, 232, 234, 235
  extended practice, 229–231
  skilled performance, 231, 232
Autoshaping, spatial memory and, 2, 21
Aversion, response–outcome relations and, 71
Avoidance
  response–outcome relations and, 31
  spatial memory and, 17

B

Backtracking, natural categories and, 245, 248, 262
Basic-level effects, natural categories and, 242, 277, 279, 280
  memory, 262, 264–270, 274
  psychological constraints, 248, 254–258
Behavior
  response–outcome relations and, 70, 74–77, 79
  spatial memory and, 21
Bias, response–outcome relations and, 42, 46, 47, 54, 78
Bidirectional rating scale, response–outcome relations and
  contingency, 56, 57
  sensitivity, 41–46
Bidirectional search, natural categories and, 244
Biology
  response–outcome relations and, 46, 79
  spatial memory and, 1, 2, 21
Birds, spatial memory in, *see* Spatial memory in corvids

Brain damage, nonverbal priming and, 85, 86
Breeding, spatial memory and, 3, 4

C

Caching corvids, spatial memory in, *see* Spatial memory in corvids
Categories
  memory improvement and, 180
  nonverbal priming and, 100
Categories, natural, 241, 242, 277
  concept learning, 242, 243
    concept formation, 247, 248
    supervised learning, 243–245
    unsupervised learning, 245–247
  concept retrieval, 258–262
  indexing, 277–279
  memory, 262
    basic-level effects, 264–268
    category match, 263, 264
    fan effects, 274–277
    typiclaity effects, 269–274
  planning process, 279, 280
  psychological constraints, 248, 258
    basic-level effects, 254–258
    typicality effects, 248–254
Category match, 263–279
Category utility, 242, 277, 278
  concept retrieval, 258, 259
  memory, 262–264
  psychological constraints, 255–258
Category validity, 249, 250, 255
Causal perception, *see* Response–outcome relations
Chunking, natural categories and, 248
Clarification, nonverbal priming and, 93, 95, 96
Classification, natural categories and, 242, 277–280
  concept learning, 247, 248
  concept retrieval, 260, 262
  memory, 263–268, 270, 272, 274
  psychological constraints, 249–252, 255, 258
CLUSTER, natural categories and, 246, 260
Clustering, natural categories and, 246–248
Coarsening, metamemory and, 140

COBWEB, natural categories and, 241, 242, 277, 280
  concept learning, 248
  concept retrieval, 258–262
  memory, 262, 264, 268, 270–274, 276
Coding, response–selection skill and, 208, 210, 225, 232, 235
  associative phase, 227, 234, 238
  hand coding, 215–217
  orthogonal dimensions, 222–225
  saliency, 219–222
  spatial coding, 211–215
  symbolic coding, 217–219
Cognitive processes
  memory improvement and, 191
  metamemory and, 125, 142, 160
  natural categories and, 241, 242, 262, 277, 280
  nonverbal priming and, 83, 103, 104
  response–outcome relations and, 28, 53–74, 78
  response–selection skill and, 207, 208, 210, 225, 232–235
    associative phase, 226–229
    autonomous phase, 231, 232
    hand coding, 215–217
    orthogonal dimensions, 222–225
    saliency, 219–222
    spatial coding, 211–215
    symbolic coding, 217–219
  spatial memory and, 1, 19, 20, 22, 23
Collocation, natural categories and, 255, 256, 262, 278
Commonality, natural categories and, 243
Comparative psychology, response–outcome relations and, 31, 32
Compatibility, response–selection skill and, 231, 236
Compensation
  memory improvement and, 178
  metamemory and, 161
Competition, spatial memory and, 4, 5
Complementary conditions, nonverbal priming and, 98
Comprehensibility, natural categories and, 246
Concept formation, natural categories and
  basic-level effects, 254–258
  learning, 242, 243, 247, 248
  memory, 241, 242, 280
  typicality effects, 248–254
Concept learning, natural categories and, 242, 280
  concept formation, 247, 248
  supervised learning, 243–245
  unsupervised learning, 245–247
Condition-process modes, memory improvement and, 183, 184, 187–192, 194
Conditioning
  nonverbal priming and, 83
  response–outcome relations and, 32–34, 65, 70
Confidence
  metamemory and
    methodology, 143
    retrieval, 165–168
    theoretical framework, 137–139
  response–outcome relations and, 64
Conflict, natural categories and, 263, 264
Conjunction
  natural categories and, 243, 246, 248–252
  response–outcome relations and, 29, 30, 33, 75
Consistency, response–outcome relations and, 33, 34
Consistent conjunction, response–outcome relations and, 29, 30, 75
Constraints
  natural categories and, 241, 242, 278
    basic-level effects, 254–258
    concept learning, 244
    typicality effects, 248–254
  response–outcome relations and, 42
Content, memory improvement and, 175, 177
  condition-process modes, 191
  control of other modes, 183
  control processes, 178–180
  manipulations, 180–183
  multimodal influences, 192, 193, 195
Content-process modes, memory improvement and, 183–187
Context
  memory improvement and, 184, 186, 194
  natural categories and, 251, 279
  nonverbal priming and, 117
  spatial memory and, 19
Contiguity, response–outcome relations and, 29

Contiguity, response-outcome relations and (*continued*)
  sensitivity, 66, 67, 69, 72
  theoretical analysis, 75–78
Contingency, response–outcome relations and, 33, 34
  cognitive processes, 53–74
  sensitivity, 35–53
  theoretical analysis, 75, 77
Control
  memory improvement and, 175, 177–180, 193–195
    condition-process modes, 187–192
    content manipulations, 180
    content-process modes, 185–187
    other modes, 183, 184
  metamemory and, 169
    acquisition, 160–162
    retrieval, 162–168
    theoretical framework, 127–129, 131
Conversational skills, memory improvement and, 186, 187
CORA, natural categories and, 247
Corvids, spatial memory in, *see* Spatial memory in corvids
Cues
  memory improvement and, 180, 181, 183, 185
  metamemory and, 135
  natural categories and, 279
    concept retrieval, 259
    memory, 265, 267, 268, 277
    psychological constraints, 249–256, 258
  nonverbal priming and
    explicit memory, 111
    familiar objects, 93, 95, 102
    theoretical accounts, 115
  response–selection skill and, 210
    associative phase, 226–229, 234
    autonomous phase, 230, 234, 235
    cognitive phase, 211–214, 217–219
  spatial memory and, 4, 5
CYRUS, natural categories and, 247

D

Decay, nonverbal priming and, 115
Declarative knowledge, response–selection skill and, 228, 229

Declarative phase, response–selection skill and, 210
Defense, spatial memory and, 1, 21
Degree of learning, metamemory and, 146, 148
Delay
  nonverbal priming and, 85
    faces, 108
    familiar objects, 86, 88, 92, 97
    novel objects, 104
  response–outcome relations and, 70–72, 76–78
Depression
  memory improvement and, 188, 189
  response–outcome relations and, 53
Deprivation, seed-caching corvids and, 11
Development, nonverbal priming and, 90, 94
Diet, memory improvement and, 188
Difference, response–outcome relations and, 29
Differential memory, seed-caching corvids and, 15, 17, 18
Discrimination
  metamemory and, 147, 148
  nonverbal priming and, 88
  response–outcome relations and, 40, 54
Displacement, spatial memory and, 5
Dissimilarity, natural categories and, 246
Dissociation, nonverbal priming and
  explicit memory, 111, 112
  facilitation of naming, 113
  familiar objects, 90, 92, 94, 97, 100
  novel objects, 103, 104
  perceptual representation, 116
  theoretical accounts, 115
Distribution, natural categories and, 270
Drugs
  memory improvement and, 187, 188
  metamemory and, 138
Duration, spatial memory and, 5
  characteristics, 10
  implications, 22
  noncaching tests, 15, 17, 18

E

Ease-of-learning, metamemory and
  acquisition, 160–162

methodology, 148
theoretical framework, 130, 131, 134, 139
Ecology, spatial memory and, 1–4, 22, 23
noncaching tests, 17, 20
species differences, 14
Elaborative encoding, nonverbal priming and, 106
Elderly, memory improvement and, 183, 185, 188–190
Emotion, memory improvement and, 177, 184, 188, 189, 193
Encoding
memory improvement and, 178, 179, 184, 186
natural categories and, 266, 270
nonverbal priming and
explicit memory, 111
familiar objects, 93, 95, 102
theoretical accounts, 115
response–selection skill and, 208
Environment
memory improvement and, 184–187, 194, 195
response–outcome relations and, 79
contingency, 65, 70, 72
Hume's theory of causation, 30
theoretical analysis, 74
spatial memory and, 2, 3, 21
EPAM, natural categories and, 247
Episodic memory
natural categories and, 280
nonverbal priming and, 106, 117
Errors
metamemory and, 137–139, 165–168
natural categories and, 244, 253
Evolution
nonverbal priming and, 84
response–outcome relations and, 32, 78
spatial memory and, 21–23
Explicit memory, nonverbal priming and, 83
explicit memory, 110–112
faces, 109
facilitation of naming, 113
familiar objects, 86–96, 98, 99, 101, 102
novel objects, 103, 104, 106, 107
perceptual representation systems, 117
theoretical accounts, 114, 115

Exposure, nonverbal priming and
faces, 108, 109
facilitation of naming, 113
novel objects, 103, 105

F

Faces, nonverbal priming and, 108–110
Facilitation
memory improvement and, 175, 195
condition-process modes, 187, 188, 190, 191
content-process modes, 185–187
natural categories and, 262, 280
nonverbal priming and, 84
faces, 108
facilitation of naming, 112–114
familiar objects, 88, 89, 91, 92, 97, 100
FACTRETRIEVAL, metamemory and, 168
feeling-of-knowing, 158
methodology, 144
priveleged access, 150–152
retrieval, 163, 166
Familiar faces, nonverbal priming and, 108–110
Familiar objects, nonverbal priming and, 84–86, 105
facilitation of naming, 112
neuropsychology, 86–91
normal young adults, 91–99
picture/word transfer, 99–102
theoretical accounts, 114
Family resemblance, natural categories and, 249, 258
Fan effects, natural categories and, 242, 262, 264, 274–277
Feedback
metamemory and, 158, 159
natural categories and, 243
Feeling-of-knowing judgments, metamemory and, 169
acquisition, 160–162
methodology, 140, 143–150
priveleged access, 151, 153
retrieval, 162–166
theoretical framework, 130, 132, 135–137, 139
underlying factors, 153–160
Flash, metamemory and, 149, 150

Forced-choice tests, nonverbal priming and, 103
Forgetting, metamemory and, 135
Fragmented pictures, nonverbal priming and
  explicit memory, 110
  facilitation of naming, 112
  familiar objects, 86–89, 91–95, 101
Free recall
  memory improvement and, 178
  nonverbal priming and
    familiar objects, 86, 93, 95
    picture/word transfer, 99, 101, 102
Functional knowledge, nonverbal priming and, 116, 117

G

Generalization
  natural categories and, 248, 251
  response–selection skill and, 231
Goals, metamemory and, 129, 130

H

Habitat, spatial memory and, 2, 3, 20
Habituation, spatial memory and, 7, 11
Hand coding, response–selection skill and, 215–217
Hand placement, response–selection skill and
  associative phase, 227, 228, 234
  autonomous phase, 230, 231, 235
  cognitive phase, 211–216, 218
Heuristic methods, natural categories and, 278
  concept learning, 244, 245
  concept retrieval, 262
  psychological constraints, 254–258
Hierarchy, natural categories and, 242, 280
  concept learning, 247, 248
  concept retrieval, 259, 261
  memory, 263, 265, 272
  psychological constraints, 252–254, 257, 258
Hippocampus, spatial memory and, 21
Hume's theory of causation, response–outcome relations and, 28–32, 78
  causal perception in humans, 44
  contingency, 61, 65

I

Identification, nonverbal priming and
  explicit memory, 110
  facilitation of naming, 112–114
  familiar objects, 87–89
    normal young adults, 92, 93, 95–98
    picture/word transfer, 99–102
  novel objects, 104
  theoretical accounts, 115
Idiosyncratic memory, 150–152
Imagery, memory improvement and, 182
Implementation, natural categories and, 277
Implicit memory, nonverbal priming and, 83–85, 110–112
  faces, 109
  facilitation of naming, 113, 114
  familiar objects, 86, 90, 92
  perceptual representation, 117
  theoretical accounts, 114
Incentive
  memory improvement and, 189
  response–outcome relations and, 47
Increments, natural categories and, 247, 248, 280
Indepedent cues, natural categories and
  concept retrieval, 259
  memory, 270
  psychological constraints, 249–252, 258
Indexing, natural categories and, 277–279
Inference
  metamemory and, 130
  natural categories and, 242
Information processing, response–selection skill and, 207, 210, 232, 235
Inhibition
  nonverbal priming and, 97
  response–selection skill and, 232
Intelligence, response–outcome relations and, 31, 66
Interference, spatial memory and, 16
Intermodal priming, 101, 102
Intramodal priming, 101, 102
Introspection, metamemory and, 127, 128

J

Judgment, response–outcome relations and, 53–74, 78
Judgments of learning, metamemory and
 methodology, 148, 154, 160
 theoretical framework, 130, 132, 134, 135, 139

K

Korsakoff's syndrome
 metamemory and, 165, 168
 nonverbal priming and, 86, 87

L

Labels
 natural categories and, 270, 271, 278
 nonverbal priming and, 96, 112–114
Language, response–selection skill and, 230
Latency
 metamemory and
  methodology, 140
  retrieval, 161–168
  theoretical framework, 136, 137
 nonverbal priming and
  faces, 109
  familiar objects, 90–92, 94, 99, 100
  novel objects, 107
Launching effect, response–outcome relations and, 33
Lexical priming, 84
 faces, 109
 familiar objects, 94, 100
 novel objects, 104
Logic, response–outcome relations and, 30
Logogen, nonverbal priming and, 114
Long-term memory
 metamemory and, 131, 134, 145–150
 nonverbal priming and, 102, 103

M

Machine learning, natural categories and, 246, 247, 277, 280
Maintenance, metamemory and, 135
Mapping, response–selection skill and, 208, 209, 236
 cognitive phase, 222, 224, 233, 234
Marijuana
 memory improvement and, 187
 metamemory and, 138, 139
Masking, natural categories and, 265
Matching, natural categories and
 concept learning, 247
 concept retrieval, 260, 261
 memory, 263–266
 psychological constraints, 251, 256
Matching law, response–outcome relations and, 77
Maximization, response–outcome relations and, 49
McGill Anomalies Test, nonverbal priming and, 88
Mechanistic laws, response–outcome relations and, 28, 30, 31, 61
Memory, see also specific memory
 natural categories and, 262, 278–280
  basic-level effects, 264–268
  category match, 263, 264
  concept learning, 245
  concept retrieval, 262
  fan effects, 274–277
  psychological constraints, 254, 258
  typicality effects, 269–274
 response–selection skill and, 231, 235
Memory improvement
 condition-process modes
  attitude, 189, 190
  emotional state, 188, 189
  multiple modes, 190–192
  physical condition, 187, 188
 content manipulations
  control-process practice, 180
  representational tendency, 180–183
 content-process modes
  physical environment, 184–186
  social environment, 186, 187
 control of other modes, 183, 184
 control processes, 177, 178
  content-general manipulations, 179, 180
  content-specific manipulations, 178, 179
 new conception, 193, 194
 multimodal influences, 192–195
 tasks, 194

Metacognition, 169
  acquisition, 160, 161
  feeling-of-knowing, 150, 154
  methodology, 142-148
  monitoring, 131, 132, 135, 136
  retrieval, 162-168
  theoretical framework, 125-128
Metamemory, 125, 168, 169
  methodology, 140-142
    acquisition, 160-162
    application, 168
    data analysis, 142, 143
    data collection, 143, 144
    FACTRETRIEVAL, 144
    feeling-of-knowing, 148-150, 153-160
    long-term memory, 145-148
    new findings, 144, 145
    priveleged access, 150-153
    retrieval, 162-168
  theoretical framework
    abstract principles, 125-128
    monitoring, 129-140
Mnemonics, memory improvement and, 178, 179, 181
Monitoring, metamemory and, 169
  acquisition, 160-162
  feeling-of-knowing, 150, 158
  methodology, 140, 142, 145-148
  retrieval, 162-168
  theoretical framework, 127-131, 135
Morphology, spatial memory and, 12, 13
Motivation
  memory improvement and, 185, 191, 193
  metamemory and, 135
  spatial memory and, 19

N

Naming
  natural categories and, 255
  nonverbal priming and
    explicit memory, 110
    faces, 108, 109
    facilitation, 112-114
    familiar objects, 90-92, 94, 95, 98-100
Natural categories, *see* Categories, natural
Natural selection
  nonverbal priming and, 84
  spatial memory and, 22

Neuropsychology
  metamemory and, 165, 168
  nonverbal priming and, 83, 85
    familiar objects, 86-91, 94
    perceptual representation, 116
    response-selection skill and, 236
No-Magic hypothesis, metamemory and, 158, 169
Nonverbal priming, 83-85
  explicit memory, 110-112
  faces, 108-110
  facilitation of naming, 112-114
  familiar objects, 85, 86
    neuropsychology, 86-91
    normal young adults, 91-99
    picture/word transfer, 99-102
  novel objects, 102-107
  perceptual representation systems, 115-117
  theoretical accounts, 114, 115
Norm of study, metamemory and, 129, 130, 132, 134
Novelty
  natural categories and, 243
  nonverbal priming and, 85, 87
    naming, 113
    objects, 102-107
  response-selection skill and, 210
Nutcracker, spatial memory in, *see* Spatial memory in corvids

O

Object memory, natural categories and, 280
Odor, spatial memory and, 4, 5
Ongoing learning, metamemory and, 131-135
Operationalization, metamemory and, 131
Optimal foraging, spatial memory and, 2
Optimization, natural categories and, 241, 242, 246
Order effects, spatial memory and, 7-9
Orientation, nonverbal priming and, 99, 113
Orthogonal dimensions, response-selection skill and, 222-225, 233, 234
Outcome advance, response-outcome relations and, 71, 78
Overlearning, metamemory and, 147, 148, 154-158, 160

P

Paired associates
  metamemory and, 144, 146, 154–156
  nonverbal priming and, 84
Paired comparisons, metamemory and, 143, 145, 146
Pattern recognition, response–selection skill and, 231
Perception
  causal, *see* Response–outcome relations
  natural categories and, 265, 268
  response–selection skill and, 236
Perceptual representation, nonverbal priming and, 115–117
Performance
  nonverbal priming and, 84
    explicit memory, 110
    facilitation of naming, 112
    familiar objects, 97, 101
    novel objects, 106
  response–outcome relations and, 53, 72
  spatial memory and, 11, 12, 19, 20
Physical condition, memory improvement and, 187, 188, 193
Physical environment, memory improvement and, 193, 195
  condition-process modes, 191
  content-process modes, 184–186
Pictogen, nonverbal priming and, 114, 115
Picture/word transfer, nonverbal priming and, 86, 99–102, 114
Pigeons, spatial memory and, 17, 18
Pinyon jays, spatial memory and, 6, 7, 12–14, 17
Practice
  memory improvement and, 180
  nonverbal priming and, 99
  response–selection skill and, 209, 233
    associative phase, 225–228, 234
    autonomous phase, 229–231, 234, 235
Precuing, response–selection skill and, 209
  associative phase, 225–229, 231
  autonomous phase, 230, 235
  cognitive phase, 209, 211–213, 215–223
Prediction
  metamemory and, 151–153, 157, 158, 160
  natural categories and, 277
    concept learning, 244, 245, 247, 248
    concept retrieval, 258, 261, 262
    fan effects, 274, 276
    memory, 262, 264, 268
    psychological constraints, 255–257
    typicality effects, 270, 272, 273
Preference
  natural categories and, 269
  nonverbal priming and, 103, 104, 114
  spatial memory and, 4–7, 13
Primacy
  memory improvement and, 178
  spatial memory and, 7
Priming, nonverbal, *see* Nonverbal priming
Priveleged access, metamemory and, 150–153
Proactive interference, spatial memory and, 16
Probabilistic contingency, response–outcome relations and, 75, 77
Probability matching, natural categories and, 262
Procedural phase, response–selection skill and, 210
Prompted recall, nonverbal priming and, 86, 87
Property-set model, natural categories and, 252
Proximity, natural categories and, 250
Proximity grouping, response–selection skill and, 221, 233
Pseudowords, nonverbal priming and, 84
Psychological constraints, natural categories and
  basic-level effects, 254–258
  typicality effects, 248–254
Punishment, response–outcome relations and, 71, 75

R

Radial-arm maze, spatial memory and, 15–17
Ranking, natural categories and, 249
Reaction time, response–selection skill and, 207, 209
  associative phase, 227, 229
  cognitive phase, 213, 215, 216, 220, 221, 224
Recall, *see also* Free recall
  memory improvement and, 179

Recall (*continued*)
  condition-process modes, 188
  content manipulations, 180–182
  content-process modes, 185
  metamemory and
    acquisition, 161, 162
    feeling-of-knowing, 149, 150, 154, 157, 158
    methodology, 140, 144, 146–148
    priveleged access, 151–153
    retrieval, 165–168
    theoretical framework, 130, 132, 134, 136, 137, 139
  natural categories and, 272
  nonverbal priming and, 83, 86–88, 102, 115
Recency, spatial memory and, 7
Recognition
  metamemory and, 168
    feeling-of-knowing, 149, 154–159
    methodology, 140, 144, 145, 147
    priveleged access, 151
    retrieval, 163
    theoretical framework, 137–139
  natural categories and, 241, 279
    concept retrieval, 258, 260–262
    memory, 264, 265, 268, 270, 272, 275
    psychological constraints, 249, 250, 252–255
  nonverbal priming and, 83
    explicit memory, 110
    faces, 109, 110
    facilitation of naming, 113
    familiar objects, 87, 88, 90
    normal young adults, 91, 92, 94, 95, 97
    novel objects, 103–107
    perceptual representation, 116
    picture/word transfer, 100, 102
    theoretical accounts, 115
Recollection, nonverbal priming and, 85, 88, 103, 110
Refinement, metamemory and, 140
Registration, memory improvement and, 188
Rehearsal
  memory improvement and, 175, 178, 193
  metamemory and, 131
Reinforcement
  response–outcome relations and
    contingency, 65–67, 69–72, 74

    sensitivity, 46, 49, 50
    theoretical analysis, 75–78
  spatial memory and, 18
Relatedness, natural categories and, 267
Relational cues, natural categories and, 251–253
Relaxation, memory improvement and, 189–191
Relearning, metamemory and, 135
Reminiscence, metamemory and, 139
Repetition, nonverbal priming and, 84
  faces, 109
  familiar objects, 102
  novel objects, 107
  theoretical accounts, 114
Response, natural categories and, 263, 266–273, 275–278
Response–outcome relations, 27, 28, 78, 79
  causal perception in humans, 33, 34
  contemporary animal learning theory, 32, 33
  Hume's theory of causation, 28, 29
    comparative psychology, 31, 32
    conditions, 29
    mechanistic model, 30, 31
    research, 34, 35
  contingency, 53–74
  sensitivity, 35–53
Response–selection skill acquisition, 207, 232, 233, 235, 236
  associative phase, 225, 229, 234
    practice, 225–227
    transfer, 227–229
  autonomous phase, 229, 232, 234, 235
    extended practice, 229–231
    skilled performers, 231, 232
  cognitive phase, 210, 225, 233, 234
    hand coding, 215–217
    orthogonal dimesnsions, 222–225
    saliency, 219–222
    spatial coding, 211–215
    symbolic coding, 217–219
  information processing, 207, 208
  phases, 209, 210
  translation stage, 208, 209
Retention
  metamemory and
    feeling-of-knowing, 154, 156
    methodology, 146–148
    theoretical framework, 130, 131, 135

natural categories and, 251
nonverbal priming and, 86, 87, 89–93, 104
response–selection skill and, 225, 227, 234
Retrieval
  memory improvement and, 178
    condition-process modes, 188
    content manipulations, 180, 181
    content-process modes, 185, 186
    control of other modes, 184
  metamemory and
    feeling-of-knowing, 158
    methodology, 144, 162–168
    theoretical framework, 131, 135–139
  natural categories and, 242
    memory, 277
    model, 258–262
    psychological constraints, 251, 258
  nonverbal priming and, 83
    explicit memory, 111
    facilitation of naming, 112
    familiar objects, 88, 92, 96, 97, 101
    perceptual representation, 118
Retrieval intentionality criterion, nonverbal priming and, 111, 113
Rhymes, memory improvement and, 180, 181

S

Saliency, response–selection skill and
  associative phase, 229
  cognitive phase, 219–222, 225, 233, 234
Same-name condition, nonverbal priming and, 97, 98
Satiation, spatial memory and, 11, 12
Schematic knowledge, response–selection skill and, 231, 232, 234
Scrub jay, spatial memory and
  implications, 20, 21
  noncaching tests, 15–19
  species differences, 12–14
Search
  metamemory and, 168
    methodology, 140
    retrieval, 162–168
    theoretical framework, 137, 138
  natural categories and, 280
    concept learning, 242, 243, 247, 248
    concept retrieval, 260

Seed-caching corvids, spatial memory in, see Spatial memory in corvids
Selective attention, natural categories and, 251
Selective retention, natural categories and, 251
Self-esteem, memory improvement and, 190
Self-paced study, metamemory and, 131, 134, 161
Semantic knowledge, nonverbal priming and, 106
Semantic network, natural categories and, 276
Semantic orienting task, nonverbal priming and, 92, 93, 97
Semantic priming
  explicit memory, 110
  faces, 109
  facilitation of naming, 113, 114
  familiar objects, 102
  perceptual representation, 116, 117
  theoretical accounts, 114, 115
Semantics, memory improvement and, 181
Sensitivity, response–outcome relations and
  contingency, 58, 61
  research, 35–53
  theoretical analysis, 75
Sentence recognition, natural categories and, 275–277
Serial learning, memory improvement and, 181
Shock, response–outcome relations and, 70
Short-term memory, 131, 134, 146, 150
Similarity, natural categories and
  concept learning, 245–247
  memory, 269–273
  psychological constraints, 250
Similarity grouping, response–selection skill and, 220, 233
Site preference, spatial memory and, 4, 5
Skill acquisition, response–selection, see Response–selection skill acquisition
Skilled performance, response–selection skill and, 229, 231, 232
Social behavior, memory improvement and, 177
Social environment, memory improvement and, 184, 193

Spatial coding, response–selection skill and
   autonomous phase, 231
   cognitive phase, 210–225, 233
Spatial cuing, response–selection skill and, 210
   associative phase, 226–229
   autonomous phase, 234, 235
Spatial location, memory improvement and, 176, 178, 181
Spatial memory in corvids, 1, 2, 22, 23
   characteristics
      decline in accuracy, 8–10
      duration, 10
      order effect, 7, 8
      performance, 11, 12
      preferences, 6, 7
   ecological problem, 2–4
   implications, 19
      comparative research, 19–21
      generality, 21, 22
      memory system, 22
   noncaching tests, 15
      nonmatching to sample, 17–19
      radial-arm maze, 15–17
   seed recovery, 4–6
   species differences, 12–14
Specificity
   memory improvement and, 181, 183, 192
   metamemory and, 140
   nonverbal priming and
      facilitation of naming, 113
      familiar objects, 94–96, 98
      theoretical accounts, 115
Speed, response–outcome relations and, 30, 53
STAGGER, natural categories and, 244, 248, 252
Stereotypes
   memory improvement and, 189, 191
   natural categories and, 278
Stimulus
   memory improvement and, 177, 179, 194
      content manipulations, 180
      content-process modes, 185
      control of other modes, 183, 184
   metamemory and, 142
   natural categories and, 263, 270, 272, 277
   nonverbal priming and, 86, 102, 103, 109
   response–outcome relations and, 32
   response–selection skill and, 207–209, 232, 235
      associative phase, 225, 227, 228, 234
      autonomous phase, 230
      cognitive phase, 211–213, 215–225, 233, 234
   spatial memory and, 19
Storage, natural categories and, 251
Stress, memory improvement and, 188
Structural description, nonverbal priming and, 106, 117
Structural orienting task, nonverbal priming and, 92, 93, 97, 98
Supervised learning, natural categories and, 242–245, 248, 251
Survival
   response–outcome relations and, 30, 31
   spatial memory and, 3
Symbolic cuing, response–selection skill and, 210
   associative phase, 226, 227, 229
   autonomous phase, 230, 234, 235
   cognitive phase, 211, 218, 219, 224, 233, 234
Symbols, natural categories and, 272

T

Target category
   memory, 265–267, 270
   psychological constraints, 249, 255
Tasks, memory improvement and, 177, 178, 193, 194
   condition-process modes, 190, 191
   content manipulations, 180–183
   content-process modes, 186
Temporal contingency, response–outcome relations and, 75, 77
Transfer
   nonverbal priming and
      familiar objects, 86, 99–102
      perceptual representation, 117
      theoretical accounts, 114, 115
   response–selection skill and
      associative phase, 227–229, 234
      autonomous phase, 230, 231, 234, 235

Translation, response–selection skill and, 208, 209, 232, 235, 236
  associative phase, 225, 226, 228
  autonomous phase, 231
  cognitive phase, 215, 219, 221–223, 225, 233, 234
Tutors, natural categories and, 242, 243
Typicality effects, natural categories and, 242, 277, 280
  memory, 262, 264, 269–277
  psychological constraints, 249–251, 258

U

Unidirectional rating scale, response–outcome relations and
  contingency, 56, 57
  sensitivity, 41, 42, 44–46
UNIMEM, natural categories and, 247, 248

Unsupervised learning, natural categories and, 243, 245–248

V

Verbal cues, natural categories and, 267, 279

W

WITT, natural categories and, 246–248
Words, nonverbal priming and
  faces, 109
  facilitation of naming, 112
  familiar objects, 86, 92, 99–102
  perceptual representation, 116
  theoretical accounts, 114, 115
Working memory, metamemory and, 131, 134

CONTENTS OF RECENT VOLUMES

Volume 16

Skill and Working Memory
    William G. Chase and K. Anders Ericsson
The Impact of a Schema on Comprehension and Memory
    Arthur C. Graesser and
    Glenn V. Nakamura
Construction and Representation of Orderings in Memory
    Kirk H. Smith and Barbee T. Mynatt
A Perspective on Rehearsal
    Michael J. Watkins and
    Zehra F. Peynircioğlu
Short-Term Memory for Order Information
    Alice F. Healy
Retrospective and Prospective Processing in Animal Working Memory
    Werner K. Honig and
    Roger K. R. Thompson
Index

Volume 17

The Structure of Human Memory
    William F. Brewer and John R. Pani
A Simulation Model for the Comprehension of Technical Prose
    David Kieras
A Multiple-Entry, Modular Memory System
    Marcia K. Johnson
The Cognitive Map of a City—50 Years of Learning and Memory
    Harry P. Bahrick

Problem Solving Skill in the Social Sciences
    James F. Voss, Terry R. Greene, Timothy A. Post, and Barbara C. Penner
Biological Constraints on Instrumental and Classical Conditioning: Implications for General Process Theory
    Michael Domjan
Index

Volume 18

Nonanalytic Cognition: Memory, Perception, and Concept Learning
    Larry L. Jacoby and Lee R. Brooks
On the Nature of Categories
    Donald Homa
The Recovery of Unconscious (Inaccessible) Memories: Laboratory Studies of Hypermnesia
    Matthew Erdelyi
Origins of Behavior of Pavlovian Conditioning
    Peter C. Holland
Directed Forgetting in Context
    Mark Rilling, Donald F. Kendrick, and Thomas B. Stonebraker
Effects of Isolation Rearing on Learning by Mammals
    Robert Holson and Gene P. Sackett
Aristotle's Logic
    Marilyn Jager Adams
Some Empirical Justification for a Theory of Natural Propositional Logic
    Martin D. S. Braine, Brian J. Reiser, and Barbara Rumain
Index

Volume 19

Memory for Experience
　Janet Kolodner
The Pragmatics of Analogical Transfer
　Keith J. Holyoak
Learning in Complex Domains: A Cognitive Analysis of Computer Programming
　Richard E. Mayer
Posthypnotic Amnesia and the Dissociation of Memory
　John F. Kihlstrom
Unit Formation in Perception and Memory
　John Ceraso
How Infants Form Categories
　Barbara A. Younger and Leslie B. Cohen
Index

Volume 20

Recognition by Components: A Theory of Visual Pattern Recognition
　Irving Biederman
Associative Structures in Instrumental Learning
　Ruth M. Colwill and Robert A. Rescorla
The Structure of Subjective Time: How Time Flies
　John Gibson
The Computation of Contingency in Classical Conditioning
　Richard H. Granger, Jr., and Jeffrey C. Schlimmer
Baseball: An Example of Knowledge-Directed Machine Learning
　Elliot Soloway
Mental Cues and Verbal Reports in Learning
　Francis S. Bellezza
Memory Mechanisms in Text Comprehension
　Murray Glanzer and Suzanne Donnenwerth Nolan
Index

Volume 21

An Integrated Computation Model of Stimulus-Response Compatibility and Practice
　Paul S. Rosenbloom and Allen Newell

A Connectionist/Control Architecture for Working Memory
　Walter Schneider and Mark Detweiler
The Intelligent Hand
　Roberta L. Klatzky and Susan J. Lederman
Successive Approximations to a Model of Human Motor Programming
　David A. Rosenbaum
Modular Analysis of Timing in Motor Skill
　Steven W. Keele and Richard I. Ivry
Associative Accounts of Causality Judgment
　David R. Shanks and Anthony Dickinson
Anxiety and the Amygdala: Pharmacological and Anatomical Analysis of the Fear-Potentiated Startle Paradigm
　Michael Davis, Janice M. Hitchcock, and Jeffrey B. Rosen
Index

Volume 22

Foraging as Operant Behavior and Operant Behavior as Foraging: What Have We Learned?
　Sara J. Shettleworth
The Comparator Hypothesis: A Response Rule for the Expression of Associations
　Ralph R. Miller and Louis D. Matzel
The Experimental Synthesis of Behavior: Reinforcement, Behavioral Stereotypy, and Problem Solving
　Barry Schwartz
Extraction of Information from Complex Visual Stimuli: Memory Performance and Phenomenological Appearance
　Geoffrey R. Loftus and John Hogden
Working Memory, Comprehension, and Aging: A Review and a New View
　Lynn Hasher and Rose T. Zacks
Strategic Control of Retrieval Strategies
　Lynn M. Reder
Alternative Representations
　Ruth S. Day
Evidence for Relational Selectivity in the Interpretation of Analogy and Metaphor
　Dedre Gentner and Catherine Clement
Index

Volume 23

Quantitative Modeling of Synaptic Plasticity
   David C. Tam and Donald H. Perkel
Computational Capabilities of Single Neurons: Relationship to Simple Forms of Associative and Nonassociative Learning in *Aplysia*
   John H. Byrne, Kevin J. Gingrich, and Douglas A. Baxter
A Biologically Based Computational Model for Several Simple Forms of Learning
   Robert D. Hawkins
Integrating Behavioral and Biological Models of Classical Conditioning
   Nelson H. Donegan, Mark A. Gluck, and Richard F. Thompson
Some Relationships between a Computational Model (SOP) and a Neural Circuit for Pavlovian (Rabbit Eyeblink)
Conditioning
   Allan R. Wagner and Nelson H. Donegan
Simulation and Analysis of a Simple Cortical Network
   Gary Lynch and Richard Granger
A Computational Approach to Hippocampal Function
   William B Levy
Index

Volume 24

Dimensional Mnemonics
   David S. Olton
Memory Processing by Pigeons, Monkeys, and People
   Anthony A. Wright
Short-Term Memory for Associations
   Bennet B. Murdock and William E. Hockley
Catastrophic Interference in Connectionist Networks: The Sequential Learning Problem
   Michael McCloskey and Neal J. Cohen
Fear, Stimulus Feedback, and Stressor Controllability
   Donald A. Warren, Robert A. Rosellini, and Steven F. Maier
Semantic Context Effects on Visual Word Processing: A Hybrid Prospective–Retrospective Processing Theory
   James H. Neely and Dennis E. Keefe
Network Structures in Proximity Data
   Roger W. Schvaneveldt, Francis T. Durso, and Donald W. Dearholt
Individual Differences in Attention
   Earl Hunt, James W. Pellegrino, and Penny L. Yee
Type A Behavior: A Social Cognition Motivational Perspective
   Nicholas A. Kuiper and Rod A. Martin
Index

Volume 25

Inferences about Word Meanings
   Richard C. Anderson
Inference Generation during Auditory Language Comprehension
   David A. Swinney and Lee Osterhout
Bridging Inferences and Enthymemes
   Murray Singer, Russell Revlin, and Michael Halldorson
The Impact of Inferences on Instructional Text
   Bruce K. Britton, Lani Van Dusen, Shawn M. Glynn, and Darold Hemphill
Integration and Buffering of New Information
   Karl Haberlandt and Arthur C. Graesser
Goal, Event, and State Inferences: An Investigation of Inference Generation during Story Comprehension
   Debra L. Long, Jonathan M. Golding, Arthur C. Graesser, and Leslie F. Clark
Content-Based Inferences in Text
   Colleen M. Seifert
Situation-Based Inferences during Narrative Comprehension
   Daniel G. Morrow, Gordon H. Bower, and Steven L. Greenspan
Expectations, Mental Representations, and Spatial Inferences
   Monika Wagener-Wender and Karl F. Wender
Causal Inferences and Text Memory
   Jerome L. Myers and Susan A. Duffy
Causal Inferences and the Comprehension of Narrative Texts
   Paul van den Broek

The Influence of Knowledge-Based Inferences
on the Reading Time of Expository Text
    Keith K. Millis, David Morgan, and
    Arthur C. Graesser
Independent Access to World Knowledge and
Newly Learned Facts
    George R. Potts, Sharyl B. Peterson,
    Mark F. St. John, and Donald Kirson
The Role of Partial Matches in Comprehension:
The Moses Illusion Revisited
    Lynne M. Reder and
    Axel Cleeremans
The Influence of Domain Knowledge on
Inferencing in Low-Aptitude Individuals
    Frank R. Yekovich, Carol H. Walker,
    Laurence T. Ogle, and
    Michele A. Thompson
Toward a Contexualist View of Elaborative
Inferences
    Paul Whitney and Diana Williams-Whitney
Methodological Issues in Evaluating the
Occurrence of Inferences
    Janice M. Keenan, Jonathan M. Golding,
    George R. Potts, Tracy M. Jennings, and
    Christine J. Aman
Dimensions of Inference
    Gail McKoon and Roger Ratcliff
Index